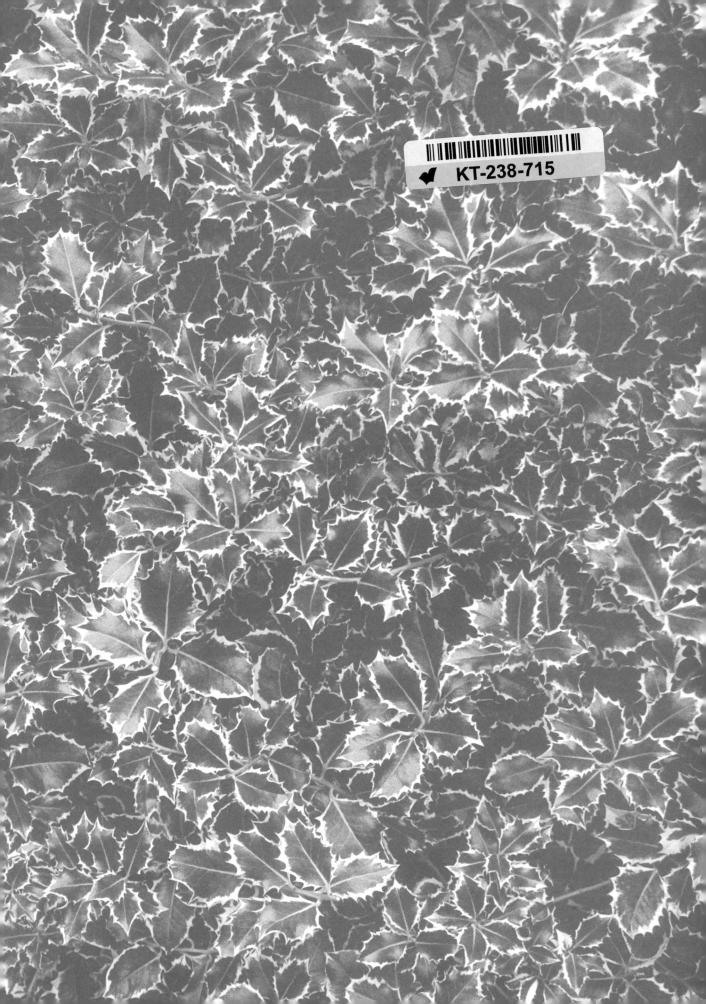

What Plant Where

What Plant Where

ROY LANCASTER

DORLING KINDERSLEY
LONDON • NEW YORK • SYDNEY • MOSCOW

A DORLING KINDERSLEY BOOK
www.dk.com

All woody plants listed, with the exception of conifers, are deciduous
unless specified evergreen. Conifers are deciduous only where specified.
Perennials are herbaceous unless described as evergreen.

PROJECT EDITOR Lesley Malkin
PROJECT ART EDITOR Colin Walton
MANAGING EDITOR Mary-Clare Jerram
MANAGING ART EDITOR Amanda Lunn
PRODUCTION MANAGER Meryl Silbert
ARTWORK RESEARCH AND COMMISSION Mustafa Sami

First published in Great Britain in 1995
by Dorling Kindersley Limited
9 Henrietta Street, London WC2 8PS

Copyright © 1995 Dorling Kindersley Limited, London
Text copyright © 1995 Roy Lancaster

8 10 9

A CIP catalogue record for this book is available from the British Library
ISBN 0–7513–0210–4

Computer page make-up by Colin Walton

Text film output by The Right Type, Great Britain
Reproduced by grb EDITRICE, Italy
Printed and bound in China by L.Rex Printing Co., Ltd.

CONTENTS

Plant Finder • 6

INTRODUCTION • 8

How This Book Works • 10

Soil Guide • 12

Aspect Guide • 13

PERENNIALS • 14

CLIMBERS • 92

SHRUBS • 108

CONIFERS • 172

TREES • 194

Index • 230

Acknowledgments • 256

Plant Finder

I F YOU HAVE a specific site, condition, or decorative effect in mind, refer to the condensed index below. The page numbers alongside each entry take you to visual lists of plants that thrive there, or the author recommends to achieve the desired effect. The colour-coded bands match the section markers.

	PERENNIALS	CLIMBERS	SHRUBS	CONIFERS	TREES
SOIL					
Alkaline soils	36		126		206
Clay soils	32		122	182	202
Lime-free soils	34		124		204
Sandy soils			128		
ASPECT					
Shady sites	30, 41	96	132		
continued	42, 44	100			
Sunny sites	28, 38	94, 98	130	184	208
continued	40				
POSITION					
Air polluted sites	48		136		212
Coastal exposure	50		138		214
Containers	62, 64		144		
Crevices and between paving	54				
Damp sites, watersides	44, 46		134		210
Fences, walls, and other vertical supports	106	102, 107			
Ground cover	28, 30		118, 121	190	
Hedge bottoms	52				
Paving and crevices	54				
Polluted (air) sites	48		136		212
Raised beds, rock gardens, and screes	56, 58		142	188	
Rock gardens, raised beds, and screes	56, 58		142	188	
Screes, rock gardens, and raised beds	56, 58		142	188	
Trees and shrubs, training into		102			
Walls, fences, and other vertical supports	106	102, 107			
Watersides, damp sites	44, 46		134		210
Wild areas	60				

	PERENNIALS	CLIMBERS	SHRUBS	CONIFERS	TREES
SIZE AND SHAPE					
Bold form, foliage	18		111		217
Columnar or tall	16			178	229
Large-sized	22		110, 112	174	196
Medium-sized	20, 22		114	180	198
Small-sized	24, 26		116, 120	188	200
Tall or columnar	16			178	229
Weeping Trees					211
Wide-spreading				176	
SEASONAL FEATURES					
Autumn interest	82		156		222, 224
Evergreen	66	104	146		216
Spring interest	78				
Summer interest	80				
Winter interest	84, 85		166, 168		224, 226
COLOUR					
Blue-grey or silver leaves	72		152	193	220
Bronze, purple, or red leaves	74		154		221
Golden or yellow leaves	70		150	192	219
Purple, red or bronze leaves	74		154		221
Silver or blue-grey leaves	72		152	193	220
Variegated leaves	68		148	191	218
OTHER PLANT FEATURES					
Berries for birds			161, 162		224
Butterflies, flowers attractive to			164		
Fragrance	76	105	158, 160		
Hedging and screening			140	186	215
Herbs	86, 88				
Multi-purpose					228
Ornamental fruits			161,162		224
Rabbit-proof	90		170		
Screening and hedging			140	186	215
Self-clinging climbers		107			
Specimen plants	18		110, 112		196
Thorns			169		

INTRODUCTION

THE DIVERSITY OF PLANTS available to gardeners today is such that we need never again suffer the disappointment of watching a recently acquired plant struggling and even dying because it was planted in the wrong place, or it was not a good plant for the job.

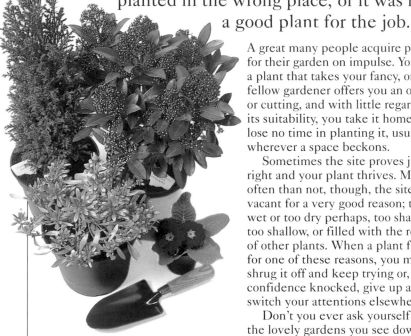

△ GARDEN CENTRE TEMPTATIONS
It is tempting to buy a plant for the initial impact of its flowers, fruit, or foliage, instead of its suitability for your garden.

A great many people acquire plants for their garden on impulse. You see a plant that takes your fancy, or a fellow gardener offers you an offset or cutting, and with little regard for its suitability, you take it home and lose no time in planting it, usually wherever a space beckons.

Sometimes the site proves just right and your plant thrives. More often than not, though, the site is vacant for a very good reason; too wet or too dry perhaps, too shady, too shallow, or filled with the roots of other plants. When a plant fails for one of these reasons, you may shrug it off and keep trying or, your confidence knocked, give up and switch your attentions elsewhere.

Don't you ever ask yourself how the lovely gardens you see down your street, on television, and in magazines are achieved? Of course you do, and although it is easy to dismiss them as the gardens of experts, you suspect that if you had the time and means to check out plants before acquiring them, you too could enjoy the same success.

GARDENERS' QUESTIONS

I worked for a major British nursery for many years, advising customers on the choice of plants for their gardens. I dealt with a variety of people; some were professionals, or gardening enthusiasts, who already had a good idea of the plants likely to grow in their gardens, but who were seeking something new or special. Most people, however, were first-time gardeners, with little knowledge or experience of plants and their uses, but who were eager to learn and anxious to make the best choice for their money.

On the whole, my enquirers belonged to one of two categories: those who had seen a plant they liked and wanted to know if it would grow in their garden; or those who had no specific idea of what they wanted but knew what purpose they wanted it for. This confirmed my belief that most people seeking help simply want to know either what plants will grow in a given situation, taking factors such as soil, aspect, and exposure into account; or what plants will create a desired effect, such as seasonal features, colour, fragrance, and ultimate size or shape.

△ AUTHOR'S GARDEN *My own garden, in Hampshire, England, is filled with plants of all kinds for year-round effect, and the walls of the house are densely planted with both climbers and shrubs.*

◁ ORIGIN OF A SPECIAL PLANT
I am particularly proud of Hypericum lancasteri, *which flowers its heart out in late summer, and was raised from a seed I collected in the hills above Kunming, City of Eternal Spring, in China.*

GARDENERS' ANSWERS

Many years of visiting gardens and interviewing people for television programmes about gardening have convinced me that poor or adverse conditions can often be improved. If this is not practical, some choice usually exists for most sites and situations as they stand, thanks to the wealth of garden plants that is currently available.

What Plant Where is a guide to selecting the best plants for given conditions and ornamental effects. It will assist beginners in finding plants suited to their gardens, and hopefully remind more seasoned gardeners of excellent contenders they may have overlooked. Never before have so many ornamental plants been available to gardeners. Among those in this book are a host of tried and tested representatives. Success with these should inspire you to try more challenging plants. Let *What Plant Where* be your guide.

LILY, WILD AND IN THE GARDEN △ ▷
An experience I cherish was first seeing Lilium regale *growing wild on a sun-drenched, rocky mountainside in China. It is one of the easiest, loveliest, and most satisfying lilies for the garden, and is delightfully fragrant, too.*

▽ THE POWER OF FOLIAGE
Conifers, ferns, bergenias, irises, and shrubs surround this small pool; their diverse foliage combines to create an effect that is dramatic, yet easy on the eye.

How This Book Works

IN THIS BOOK, my aim is to help you choose the most suitable plants for a given garden situation, taking account of the local growing conditions, different plant characteristics, and any special ornamental effects. The book is divided into five sections by plant type: Perennials, Climbers, Shrubs, Conifers, and Trees. Within each section, I suggest possible plants suitable for different types of site and decorative effects. All woody plants listed, with the exception of conifers, are deciduous unless specified evergreen. Conifers are deciduous only where specified. Perennials are herbaceous unless described as evergreen.

PLANT NAMES

Currently accepted botanical names are used throughout. Well-known synonyms appear in the index and are cross-referenced. Common names in general use are given, and where none exists, the generic name is repeated, or else an English name common to the whole genus is given. In the case of specialist groups such as roses, the category is specified.

KEY TO pH ACIDITY SYMBOL

The majority of plants will grow in most soils. Those that require lime-free soil are highlighted with this symbol *(see p.12)*.

PH ▼	*Requires lime-free soil*

KEY TO HARDINESS SYMBOLS

Hardiness is a measure of a plant's ability to withstand winter cold. It can vary depending on available shelter, favourable localized conditions, and natural variations in a plant's cold-tolerance. Frost-hardiness indicates a plant's ability to withstand winter frost. Many more plants are susceptible to late spring frosts once new growth has begun. The symbols are given as a guide to a plant's cold-tolerance and err on the side of caution.

✳✳✳	*Fully hardy – will survive winter outside in temperate climates.*
✳✳	*Semi-hardy – may require winter protection outside in temperate climates.*
✳	*Tender – may require winter protection outside, even in mild areas. Suitable for growing under glass.*

BOTANICAL AND COMMON PLANT NAMES •
Below each plant's botanical name is the common name or, if none exists, the generic name.

SYMBOLS FOR • LIGHT LEVEL, HARDINESS, AND ACIDITY
Light level and hardiness are given for all plants. The pH symbol appears only if a plant requires lime-free soil (see boxes).

Shrubs Tolerant of Shade

YOU MAY BE SURPRISED at the range of shrubs suitable for growing in shade. Many are woodlanders in the wild, preferring to grow where they are not directly exposed to the sun's rays. This does not mean they can survive without any light – all green-leaved plants need light to photosynthesize. Some, however, are more tolerant of lower light levels than others, and it is these that are most successful when planted in the shade of deciduous trees, or that cast by buildings.

Euonymus fortunei 'Sarcoxie'
EVERGREEN EUONYMUS
☼ ☀ ✳✳✳ ‡ 1.5m (5ft) ↔ 1.5m (5ft)

Strong-growing and bushy, this upright evergreen shrub has leathery, dark green, glossy-topped leaves. In autumn, creamy white capsules encase orange seeds.

Euonymus fortunei 'Vegetus'
EVERGREEN EUONYMUS
☼ ☀ ✳✳✳ ‡ 30cm (12in) ↔ 2m (6ft)

The presence of both creeping and erect stems enable this tough, bushy evergreen to form extensive patches. Its green leaves and pinkish seed capsules are numerous.

Crinodendron hookerianum
LANTERN TREE
☼ ☀ ✳✳✳ ‡ 3m (10ft) ↔ 2m (6ft)

From late spring through to early summer, the branches of this handsome evergreen are strung with beautiful red flowers that resemble lanterns. Dislikes dry soils. ♀

OTHER DECIDUOUS SHRUBS TOLERANT OF SHADE
Cornus canadensis, see p.118
Euonymus obovatus
Hydrangea macrophylla 'Generale Vicontessa de Vibraye'
Hypericum androsaemum
Kerria japonica
Rhodotypos scandens, see p.135
Rubus odoratus
Rubus spectabilis 'Olympic Double'
Symphoricarpos × chenaultii 'Hancock'

Daphne laureola var. *philippi*
SPURGE LAUREL
☼ ☀ ✳✳✳ ‡ 30cm (12in) ↔ 60cm (2ft)

A dwarf variety of a woodland evergreen, this is just as effective when grown in full sun. Crowded light green flower clusters emerge in late winter and early spring.

Hydrangea macrophylla 'Veitchii'
LACE-CAP HYDRANGEA
☼ ☀ ✳✳✳ ‡ 1.5m (5ft) ↔ 2.5m (8ft)

Broader than it is high, this bold-foliaged bush carries heads of tiny flowers, each surrounded by a ring of larger florets, from mid- to late summer. Dislikes dry soils. ♀

132

SHRUBS

KEY TO LIGHT LEVEL SYMBOLS

Light preferences are given with symbols. More than one symbol indicates plant's preferred range.

☼	*Full sun – prefers, or even requires, as much sun as is available.*
☀	*Partial-shade – tolerant of (some even prefer) limited or indirect sunlight.*
☀	*Shade – will grow in a site receiving low light, such as under a tree canopy.*

• PLANT DESCRIPTION
Gives features of interest such as flowering time(s), distinctive traits, preferred site(s) or condition(s), and specifies when plant is evergreen.

PLANT DIMENSIONS

Plant dimensions vary depending on growing conditions. Sizes are a guide to mature size in average conditions. The height includes flowering stems in perennials.

‡   *Average height*

↔   *Average spread*

‡↔   *Average height and spread*

PLANTS WITH A SEAL OF APPROVAL

The Royal Horticultural Society gives an Award of Garden Merit to plants whose decorative effect, good constitution, and availability is excellent. It identifies the best species and cultivars available. The AGM symbol is displayed on plants in garden centres.

♇   *Award of Garden Merit*

WHAT IS A PERENNIAL?

I have defined perennials in this book as non-woody plants that live for upwards of three years. Most are herbaceous, dying down below ground level usually in winter; some are evergreen, retaining their foliage throughout the winter months. A minority, bamboos for example, do have woody stems and evergreen leaves.

WHAT IS A CLIMBER?

Plants grown to climb in a variety of ways – into or over trees and shrubs, or trained to cover walls, fences, and other structures – are considered climbers here. The most commonly grown climbers are woody stemmed perennials or shrubs that are trained. Climbers may be evergreen, deciduous, or even herbaceous.

WHAT IS A SHRUB?

Shrubs are woody plants, often with a bushy habit, that usually produce more than one main stem. Several are capable of reaching heights and spreads in excess of 3m (10ft). They may be evergreen or deciduous, depending on the species. Subshrubs have a woody base, and their top growth is often cut back by frost in cold areas.

WHAT IS A CONIFER?

Conifers are a botanically distinct group of primitive, woody plants. Most are trees, typically with a single upright stem or main leader, but myriad smaller, shrubby kinds include dwarf and slow-growing selections. A minority – always stated in the text – are deciduous; the majority are evergreen with needle-like or scale-like leaves.

WHAT IS A TREE?

A tree is a woody plant that has a single main stem supporting an elevated crown of branches. Most trees grow in this way naturally, but others may produce several main stems, and they will consequently develop a bushy habit, which can be changed if preferred by careful pruning and training in early life. Trees may be deciduous or evergreen.

SHRUBS TOLERANT OF SHADE

Hydrangea serrata 'Bluebird'
LACE-CAP HYDRANGEA
☀ ✿ ✿   ‡1.2m (4ft) ↔1.5m (5ft)
The pointed leaves of this dense, bushy shrub often colour well in autumn. Violet-blue, lace-cap flowers in summer have pale marginal florets. Dislikes dry soils. ♇

Pachysandra terminalis
JAPANESE SPURGE
☀ ✿ ✿   ‡10cm (4in) ↔20cm (8in)
This evergreen, suckering shrublet likes moist soils, and makes a superb ground cover for shade. Its dark green leaves back little white flower spikes in spring. ♇

Skimmia japonica 'Fructu-albo'
SKIMMIA
☀ ✿ ✿   ‡75cm (30in) ↔75cm (30in)
If you plant a male variety of this dense, low evergreen nearby to effect pollination, this spring-flowering skimmia cultivar will produce an abundance of white berries.

• **HEIGHT AND SPREAD**
Gives the average ultimate size of the plant, in metric and imperial.

SHRUBS

Lonicera pileata
SHRUBBY HONEYSUCKLE
☀ ✿ ✿ ✿   ‡60cm (24in) ↔2m (6ft)
Its low and wide-spreading habit makes this an excellent evergreen ground cover. Tiny, inconspicuous late spring flowers are occasionally followed by violet berries.

• **THUMB MARKER**
Identifies each of the five sections in the book (see right).

Prunus laurocerasus 'Otto Luyken'
CHERRY LAUREL
☀ ✿ ✿ ✿   ‡75cm (30in) ↔1.2m (4ft)
The branches of this low evergreen shrub are clothed with narrow, glossy, leathery leaves. Erect spikes of white flowers in late spring are followed by black fruits. ♇

OTHER EVERGREEN SHRUBS TOLERANT OF SHADE
Aucuba japonica 'Rozannie', see p.146
Buxus sempervirens 'Latifolia Maculata'
Daphne pontica
x *Fatshedera lizei*, see p.144
Fatsia japonica, see p.111
Osmanthus heterophyllus
Rubus tricolor
Ruscus hypoglossum
Sarcococca confusa
Viburnum davidii, see p.119

Vinca major 'Variegata'
VARIEGATED LARGE PERIWINKLE
☀ ✿ ✿ ✿   ‡30cm (12in) ↔1.5m (5ft)
Striking, variegated leaves are margined creamy white, and form a superb ground cover that is rampant if unchecked. Blue flowers last from spring to autumn. ♇

133

Mahonia nervosa
CASCADES MAHONIA
☀ ✿ ✿ ✿   ‡60cm (24in) ↔1m (3ft)
This evergreen, suckering shrub produces short, erect stems with handsome leaves that turn red or purplish in winter. Spikes of yellow flowers appear in early summer.

• **AGM** ♇
Shows the plant has achieved the RHS Award of Garden Merit.

OTHER PLANTS •
Lists more plants suitable for the site or effect, with page references given for those illustrated elsewhere in other parts of the book.

HOW THE TREES CHAPTER WORKS.

Prunus serotina
RUM, OR BLACK, CHERRY
☀ ✿ ✿ ✿   Moderate growth   ‡15m (50ft) ↔13m (43ft)
A free-growing tree with an oval crown of pendulous or arching branches, its deep green, glossy leaves are deciduous, becoming yellow or red in autumn. Small white spring flowers are carried in drooping tassels, and give way to shining black fruits. ♇

215

TREES

• **TREE ARTWORK**
Shows typical shape of mature tree; bare branches indicate tree is deciduous, full leaf that it is evergreen.

• **GROWTH RATE**
This is given as either vigorous, moderate, or slow.

PERENNIALS   CLIMBERS   SHRUBS   CONIFERS   TREES

11

Soil Guide

THE SIZE and proportion of clay, sand, or silt particles present in your garden soil influence its chemical and physical nature. They make it either heavy (wet and poorly drained), or light (dry and free-draining), and thus determine what plants will thrive on it. Its chemical nature, or pH value, is measured on a scale of 1 to 14. Below neutral (7), soils are progressively acid (or lime-free); above neutral they are progressively alkaline (limy). You can establish what type of soil you have by looking at the colour, feeling the texture, and observing what kind of plants will grow on it or, if you prefer, by doing a soil test.

AVERAGE ideal for *Forsythia*
Different cultivation requirements and variable local conditions make average soil hard to define. Usually, it is moist but well-drained, with a reasonable humus content, neutral to slightly acid pH, and suits the widest range of plants.

HEAVY CLAY ideal for *Berberis*
Minute clay particles stick together, making clay soils slow-draining after rain, sticky, and likely to bake hard in dry sun. Often highly fertile, they can be improved by draining, or by adding grit or coarse organic matter.

SANDY ideal for *Potentilla*
Sand particles are much larger than clay particles, making sandy soils light, free-draining, and quick to warm up in spring. Some plants may need frequent irrigation and feeding, though fertility can be improved by adding organic matter.

LIME-FREE ideal for *Rhododendron*
Peaty or lime-free soils are generally dark, and rich in organic matter. Acid in nature and moisture-retentive, they are favoured by plants intolerant of alkaline soils. Can be made more free-draining by adding coarse sand.

ALKALINE ideal for *Kolkwitzia*
Limy or alkaline soils, including chalk, are usually pale, shallow, and stony. Free-draining, they warm up quickly in spring, and are moderately fertile. Like sandy soils, they benefit from the addition of organic matter.

Aspect Guide

Plants need sunlight, either directly or indirectly, to photosynthesize, so aspect is crucial to plant growth and health. Many are flexible in their light needs, preferring one aspect, but tolerating another. Most thrive as long as they are in a position open to the sky.

• THE SUN'S POSITION
The position of the sun varies during the year. In midwinter, the sun is lower and the shadows much larger. In the height of summer, the sun is high and the shadows are small.

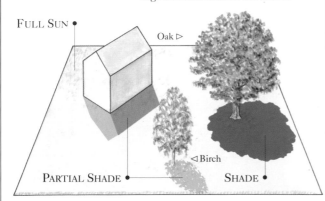

FULL SUN •

Oak ▷

◁ Birch

PARTIAL SHADE

SHADE •

☼ FULL SUN

Open to the sun for the greater part of the day, full sun sites are not subject to shade cast by trees or buildings. Numerous garden plants grown for their flowering display, including many perennials, annuals, and shrubs *(see above)*, prefer sunny sites – sun and warmth ripens woody growth, so encouraging flowering and fruiting. Many plants at their best in full sun will also tolerate a degree of shade, like that found near buildings (at certain times of day) and on the edge of woodland.

☀ PARTIAL SHADE

Sites in partial shade are subject to reduced light. They are found near buildings that block direct sunlight, but do not hide the sky above. Partial shade is also found in the lee of, if not directly beneath, trees such as birch *(Betula)*, which cast a light, dappled shade. If the soil is moist, these conditions suit many plants, some of which may also be tolerant of full sun or even heavier shade. Numerous foliage perennials, and those found naturally in woodland sites *(see above)* thrive best here.

☀ SHADE

This defines sites subject to permanent shade, or shade during the main growing season (summer). Such sites may be closely surrounded by tall buildings or, more usually, beneath or in the lee of dense-canopied trees. Even here, the degree of shade varies. If combined with dry or compacted soil, such as that often found beneath large conifers or similar evergreen trees, the choice of suitable underplanting is limited to the few shade-tolerant plants growing in such sites in the wild.

PERENNIALS

IF TREES AND SHRUBS form the bones of a garden, then perennials provide its flesh, forming the bulk of border plants and ground cover. No other plant group offers such great variety of form, flower, and foliage, from tiny rock plants through to large bamboos. This section includes bulbs (with tubers and corms), and annual or biennial plants.

△ SUN LOVING *The bold flowerheads of a superb spurge,* Euphorbia characias *subsp.* wulfenii, *enjoy a place in the sun.*

△ *Oenothera speciosa* 'Rosea'

THE BEAUTY OF PERENNIALS

- Provide massed effects in borders.
- Bold single specimens or groups can create special effects in lawns.
- Ideal for carpeting rock gardens and screes, or draping retaining walls.
- Provide mass impact as spring bulbs.
- Ideal as ground cover beneath trees.
- Perfect for planting in containers for terraces, patios, or courtyards.
- Annuals or biennials give fast results.
- Offer striking waterside or bog plants.

Some perennials have evergreen foliage, which gives year-round effect, but most are herbaceous, and die to below ground level, usually in winter. Unless otherwise stated, all plants in this section are herbaceous. The pleasurable anticipation associated with their annual re-emergence is something of which we never tire, and makes them all the more exciting and valuable in the garden.

PLANTS FOR EFFECT

For many gardeners, no finer sight exists than that of a perennial bed at its best in summer. Whether we are inspired by Gertrude Jekyll's plant associations, or prefer a more haphazard mix of colour, perennials to suit every taste abound. When

planting borders, foliage effect is just as important as floral display, and it is worth remembering the beautiful, nostalgic effects that are possible in winter when certain dead seed heads are spared.

PLANTS FOR ALL PLACES

Warm, sunny sites in the garden are ideal for growing those perennials that enjoy hot, dry conditions in the wild. The abundance of plants thriving in such situations are best planted in raised beds or beneath sunny walls in cooler areas. To take advantage of shady places, consider plants native of woodland. Ferns, spring-flowering perennials, and bulbous plants such as trilliums and miniature cyclamen tolerate shade and form attractive ground cover.

△ SHADE CARPET *Miniature cyclamen* (Cyclamen repandum) *form a lovely spring carpet in a beech tree's shade.*

◁ WINTER BEAUTY *The elegance of dead seed heads and leaves in winter is further enhanced when they are coated with frost.*

▷ EARLY SUMMER SPECTACLE *This cottage garden border boasts a glorious mix of perennials, annuals, and biennials.*

Tall Perennials for the Backs of Borders

TALL PERENNIALS lend a feeling of permanence to a bed, while their size alone guarantees attention. Even the smallest bed or border is enhanced by at least one. With few exceptions, clump-formers should be supported to prevent the stems becoming splayed in blustery weather. It is best to do this staking well before the stems are fully developed.

Eremurus himalaicus
FOXTAIL LILY
☼ ❄❄❄   ↕ 2.2m (7ft) ↔ 1m (3ft)

Clumps of strap-shaped leaves fade early in summer as dense spires of starry white flowers develop. A spectacular plant that thrives best in well-drained soils.

Aruncus dioicus
GOAT'S BEARD
☼ ☼ ❄❄❄   ↕ 2m (6ft) ↔ 1.2m (4ft)

Goat's Beard is worth growing for its bold mounds of leaves. These, however, are topped by equally striking plumes of tiny, creamy white flowers in midsummer. 🏆

Delphinium 'Fanfare'
DELPHINIUM
☼ ❄❄❄   ↕ 2m (6ft) ↔ 75cm (30in)

One of many cultivars differing in colour, this bears tall, imposing spikes of semi-double flowers in summer. It thrives in rich, deep soils, and must be staked. 🏆

Campanula lactiflora
'Prichard's Variety'
☼ ☼ ❄❄❄   ↕ 1.4m (4½ft) ↔ 75cm (30in)

Clumps of upright, leafy stems sport heads crowded with bell-shaped, violet-blue flowers from summer into early autumn. Will naturalize, even in rough grass. 🏆

Echinops sphaerocephalus
GLOBE THISTLE
☼ ❄❄❄   ↕ 1.8m (6ft) ↔ 1.1m (3½ft)

The deeply cut, prickle-toothed leaves are green on the top and grey beneath. Popular with bees and butterflies, Globe Thistle supports globular flowerheads in summer.

Eupatorium purpureum
JOE PYE WEED
☼ ❄❄❄   ↕ 2.2m (7ft) ↔ 1m (3ft)

Erect, leafy stems are crowned with dense, flattened heads of small, pinkish purple flowers in late summer and autumn. These are appreciated by bees and butterflies.

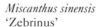

Helianthus x multiflorus
PERENNIAL SUNFLOWER
☼ ✳✳✳   ↕ 1.7m (5½ft) ↔ 1m (3ft)

This erect, leafy plant produces branched heads of large, rich yellow, daisy-like flowers in late summer and early autumn. It will spread to form large patches in time.

OTHER TALL GRASSES
Arundo donax
Calamagrostis epigejos 'Hortorum'
Chionochloa conspicua
Cortaderia fulvida
Cortaderia richardii
Cortaderia selloana 'Carnea'
Cortaderia selloana 'Rendatleri'
Miscanthus sinensis 'Grosse Fontäne'
Miscanthus sinensis 'Morning Light'
Miscanthus sinensis 'Silberfeder'
Stipa gigantea, see p.19

Lavatera cachemiriana
LAVATERA
☼ ✳✳✳   ↕ 1.7m (5½ft) ↔ 1.4m (4½ft)

A loosely branched perennial with slender stems and downy, semi-evergreen leaves. Its large pink mallow flowers are carried continuously throughout summer.

Miscanthus sinensis
'Zebrinus'
☼ ✳✳✳   ↕ 1.5m (5ft) ↔ 1.5m (5ft)

This bold, clump-forming grass requires plenty of space to show off its elegant, arching, cream-banded green leaves. Fan-shaped flower spikes develop in autumn.

OTHER TALL PERENNIALS
Cimicifuga racemosa
Cimicifuga simplex, see p.32
Crambe cordifolia, see p.18
Cynara cardunculus, see p.18
Delphinium 'Loch Leven'
Eryngium eburneum
Filipendula rubra
Inula magnifica, see p.19
Leucanthemella serotina
Rudbeckia 'Herbstsonne'
Verbascum olympicum, see p.73

Helianthus x multiflorus 'Loddon Gold'
PERENNIAL SUNFLOWER
☼ ✳✳✳   ↕ 1.5m (5ft) ↔ 75cm (30in)

Numerous double flowers, of a rich golden yellow, are produced in loosely branched heads from late summer and into early autumn. Will form patches in time.   ♔

Macleaya microcarpa
'Kelway's Coral Plume'
☼ ✳✳✳   ↕ 2.2m (7ft) ↔ 1.2m (4ft)

Spectacular clumps of boldly lobed leaves, grey-green above and whitish beneath, are topped in summer by plumes of pinkish buff flowers. These are darker in bud.   ♔

Rudbeckia laciniata 'Goldquelle'
RUDBECKIA
☼ ✳✳✳   ↕ 2m (6ft) ↔ 75cm (30in)

This erect perennial is strong-growing. Bright yellow double flowers, with green centres, appear among leafy green foliage from late summer and into autumn.   ♔

Bold Perennials for Specimen Planting

SOME PERENNIALS are so striking in flower or foliage, or both, that it is worth planting them as a special feature. A small bed surrounded by paving or gravel will show off a single specimen, but where space and scale permit, a group will create an even more spectacular display. Choose evergreens if year-round effect is desired.

Cortaderia selloana 'Sunningdale Silver'
PAMPAS GRASS
☼ ❄❄   ↕ 2.5m (8ft) ↔ 1.5m (5ft)

A most popular ornamental grass, with tall, silky plumes of creamy white spikelets from late summer. The evergreen razor-edged leaves require careful handling. ♛

Acanthus spinosus
BEAR'S BREECHES
☼ ❄❄❄   ↕ 1.2m (4ft) ↔ 1.1m (3½ft)

Lush clumps of dark green, spine-toothed leaves are topped in summer with prickly spires of mauve and white hooded flowers. It will spread freely in some soils. ♛

Beschorneria yuccoides
BESCHORNERIA
☼ ❄   ↕ 2m (6ft) ↔ 3m (10ft)

This succulent evergreen, perfect in warm sites, forms huge, yucca-like clumps of spine-tipped leaves. Its tubular summer flowers are held on stout red stems. ♛

Crambe cordifolia
CRAMBE
☼ ❄❄❄   ↕ 2m (6ft) ↔ 1.5m (5ft)

Attractive mounds of wavy-edged leaves are almost eclipsed when the clouds of small, fragrant white flowers appear in summer. Good drainage is desirable. ♛

OTHER SPECIMEN PERENNIALS

Aralia cachemirica
Arundo donax
Cortaderia richardii
Cortaderia selloana 'Rendatleri'
Cynara scolymus 'Glauca'
Dierama pulcherrimum, see p.81
Eryngium decaisneanum
Eryngium eburneum
Euphorbia characias 'Lambrook Gold'
Ferula tingitana
Filipendula kamtschatica
Filipendula purpurea, see p.46
Kniphofia 'Prince Igor'
Kniphofia rooperi
Osmunda regalis
Phormium tenax 'Purpureum'
Rodgersia pinnata 'Superba'
Yucca gloriosa, see p.67
Yucca recurvifolia

Chusquea culeou
CHILEAN BAMBOO
☼ ☼ ☀ ❄❄❄   ↕ 5m (15ft) ↔ 2.5m (8ft)

A bold, distinctive bamboo with shining evergreen leaves. Huge clumps of green canes with pale sheaths create a striking banded effect. It forms colonies in time. ♛

Cynara cardunculus
CARDOON
☼ ❄❄❄   ↕ 2m (6ft) ↔ 1.4m (4½ft)

This perennial, with attractive silver-grey leaves, is as spectacular as its relative, the Globe Artichoke. The thistle-like summer flowers have wickedly spiny bracts. ♛

Gunnera manicata
GUNNERA
☼ ❄❄   ↕ 2.2m (7ft) ↔ 2.2m (7ft)

This striking perennial is excellent for
watersides as it enjoys moist, fertile soils.
Its huge leaves rise above furry crowns,
which need protection in cold winters. ♔

Hedychium densiflorum
GINGER LILY
☼ ❄❄   ↕ 1.5m (5ft) ↔ 75cm (30in)

A member of the ginger family, this plant,
with exotic, lance-shaped leaves, produces
fragrant flower spikes in late summer. It is
ideal for moist, well-drained soils.

Inula magnifica
INULA
☼ ❄❄❄   ↕ 2m (6ft) ↔ 1.1m (3½ft)

This stout perennial, which has upright,
hairy stems and bold leaves, may need
some support. The large, daisy-like yellow
flowerheads occur in late summer.

OTHER SPECIMEN BAMBOOS
Fargesia nitida
Fargesia spathacea
Phyllostachys nigra
Semiarundinaria fastuosa
Thamnocalamus tessellatus

Rheum palmatum 'Atrosanguineum'
ORNAMENTAL RHUBARB
☼ ❄❄❄   ↕ 2m (6ft) ↔ 2m (6ft)

The large, boldly lobed leaves of this
perennial are its main ornamental feature.
In early summer they are dwarfed by
impressive heads of crimson flowers.

Rodgersia aesculifolia
RODGERSIA
☼ ☼ ❄❄❄   ↕ 1.2m (4ft) ↔ 1m (3ft)

Excellent for planting near watersides,
the rough-stalked leaves are divided into
leaflets, bronze at first, later green. It has
plumes of fragrant midsummer flowers. ♔

Stipa gigantea
GIANT, OR GOLDEN, OAT
☼ ❄❄❄   ↕ 1.7m (5½ft) ↔ 1.4m (4½ft)

A lovely ornamental grass with clumps of
narrow leaves, and pretty golden spikelets
with awns in summer. The sun-bleached
seed-husks are an additional attraction. ♔

Medium-height Perennials

SOME OF THE MOST ATTRACTIVE and most popular
perennials are found in the height range of 60–120cm
(2–4ft). These plants can be used to excellent
effect as companions for taller perennials or shrubs
in mixed plantings, or as groups or drifts in their
own right. Some are so spectacular in foliage
that they are well worth planting as specimens.
Many of the plants in this range are sturdy
and self-supporting, but those
with slender stems carrying
large or heavy heads of
flowers may require some
staking to prevent them
splaying out in the wind.

Galega orientalis
GALEGA
☼ ❄❄❄   ↕ 1.2m (4ft) ↔ 75cm (30in)

A compact, bushy perennial, with erect
stems and attractive, rich green leaves.
Spikes of violet pea-flowers occur in early
summer. It spreads in suitable conditions.

Aconitum x *cammarum* 'Bicolor'
MONKSHOOD
☼ ◐ ❄❄❄   ↕ 1.2m (4ft) ↔ 50cm (20in)

Although poisonous, monkshoods have
long been valued in the garden. This
handsome hybrid bears striking heads of
violet-blue and white summer flowers. ♆

Chrysanthemum 'Clara Curtis'
KOREAN CHRYSANTHEMUM
☼ ❄❄❄   ↕ 75cm (30in) ↔ 45cm (18in)

This bushy perennial flowers all through
summer and autumn. It has aromatic
leaves, and masses of beautiful, daisy-like
flowers. Divide every few years. ♆

Baptisia australis
FALSE INDIGO
☼ ❄❄❄   ↕ 1.2m (4ft) ↔ 60cm (24in)

Pretty blue-green foliage in early summer
turns grey, then green later. Spikes of
summer pea-flowers are replaced by seed
pods, ideal dried for winter decoration. ♆

> PERENNIALS GROWN FOR BOTH
> FLOWERS AND FOLIAGE
>
> *Acanthus hungaricus*
> *Astilbe* 'Ostrich Plume', see p.90
> *Berkheya macrocephala*
> *Euphorbia griffithii* 'Dixter'
> *Gentiana lutea*, see p.87
> *Hosta* 'Tall Boy'
> *Persicaria campanulata*
> *Phlomis russeliana*
> *Phlox paniculata* 'Harlequin'
> *Rodgersia pinnata* 'Superba'

Geranium psilostemon
BLACK-EYED SUZY
☼ ❄❄❄   ↕ 1.2m (4ft) ↔ 1.2m (4ft)

Magenta flowers with black eyes create a
spectacular effect in midsummer. Long-
stalked, deeply cut leaves often colour
richly in autumn. Needs support. ♆

Heliopsis 'Light of Loddon'
HELIOPSIS
☼ ❄❄❄   ↕1.4m (4½ft) ↔75cm (30in)

This erect perennial has branched heads
of rich orange dahlia-like flowers that last
for weeks during late summer and early
autumn. Its toothed leaves are dark green.

Lupinus 'Inverewe Red'
LUPIN
☼ ❄❄❄   ↕1.1m (3½ft) ↔60cm (24in)

Bold perennial with beautifully fingered
leaves and erect, cylindrical spikes of red
pea-flowers in early summer. There are
many other cultivars of varying colours.

Penstemon 'Garnet'
PENSTEMON
☼ ❄❄❄   ↕65cm (26in) ↔60cm (24in)

One of the hardiest and most reliable of a
colourful genus. It bears narrow, semi-
evergreen leaves and spires of red flowers
from midsummer to early autumn. ♈

Hemerocallis 'Golden Chimes'
DAY LILY
☼ ❄❄❄   ↕75cm (30in) ↔60cm (24in)

From early to midsummer, thin branched
heads of golden yellow trumpet-flowers
are carried above bold clumps of grass-like
leaves. Each flower lasts for one day. ♈

Lythrum virgatum 'The Rocket'
LYTHRUM
☼ ❄❄❄   ↕1m (3ft) ↔45cm (18in)

Erect clumps of slender, leafy stems bear
long spikes of rich rose-red flowers in
summer. This plant thrives best in rich,
moist soils, making it ideal for watersides.

Sidalcea 'William Smith'
GREEK MALLOW
☼ ❄❄❄   ↕1.2m (4ft) ↔1m (3ft)

Justifiably a most popular perennial, this
has handsome clumps of deeply cut leaves
and erect stems bearing warm salmon-
pink mallow flowers in summer. ♈

Kniphofia 'Percy's Pride'
TORCH FLOWER
☼ ❄❄❄   ↕1m (3ft) ↔60cm (24in)

Dense, poker-like spikes of canary yellow
flowers rise above clumps of strap-shaped
leaves in late summer. A striking plant to
brighten a border late in the season.

Paeonia 'Bowl of Beauty'
PEONY
☼ ❄❄❄   ↕1m (3ft) ↔1m (3ft)

Above lush clumps of leaves, huge pink
summer flowers with cream petaloids are
borne. The leaves of this superb peony
colour well in autumn. Needs support. ♈

**OTHER MEDIUM-HEIGHT
PERENNIALS**

Aster cordifolius 'Silver Spray'
Centaurea pulcherrima
Echinacea purpurea 'Robert Bloom'
Gillenia trifoliata
Knautia macedonica
Linaria purpurea 'Canon J. Went'
Phlox maculata 'Omega', see p.77
Salvia nemorosa 'May Night'
Veronica spicata 'Romiley Purple',
   see p.49

Medium to Large Annuals and Biennials

HOWEVER THOROUGHLY you plant a bed or border, you can guarantee that gaps will occur. Plants may fail, or grow more slowly than expected, and you are left with unwanted spaces. An ideal solution is to fill these gaps with a temporary display of annuals or biennials to tide you over until the permanent planting makes good, or dead plants are replaced.

Consolida ambigua
LARKSPUR
☼ ✳✳✳ ↕ 1.2m (4ft) ↔ 30cm (12in)

Larkspur is a robust, free-growing annual with finely divided, feathery foliage, and erect spikes of spurred summer flowers, in white or shades of pink and blue.

Alcea rosea
HOLLYHOCK
☼ ✳✳✳ ↕ 2m (6ft) ↔ 60cm (24in)

This biennial herb is a long-standing cottage garden favourite. Its spikes of large, saucer-shaped flowers tower above bold foliage in summer and early autumn.

Amaranthus caudatus
LOVE-LIES-BLEEDING
☼ ✳✳ ↕ 1.2m (4ft) ↔ 45cm (18in)

Striking tassels crowded with tiny red flowers drape the branches of this robust, bushy annual from summer into autumn. The large leaves are a pale green colour.

Digitalis purpurea 'Sutton's Apricot'
FOXGLOVE
☼ ✳✳✳ ↕ 1.5m (5ft) ↔ 45cm (18in)

Tall spikes of nodding, bell-shaped flowers rise from bold rosettes of crinkly leaves in summer. 'Sutton's Apricot' is a lovely selection of a popular biennial. ♔

OTHER LARGE ANNUALS

Agrostemma githago 'Milas', see p.26
Amaranthus caudatus 'Green Cascade'
Amaranthus hybridus
Atriplex hortensis var. *rubra*, see p.88
Centaurea cyanus
Chenopodium quinoa Andean
  Hybrids Mixed
Consolida ambigua Imperial Series
Coreopsis grandiflora 'Mayfield Giant'
Cosmos 'Sensation'
Helianthus annuus 'Taiyo'
Hibiscus manihot 'Cream Cup'
Impatiens balsamina
Leonurus sibiricus
Malope trifida
Scabiosa atropurpurea Cockade Series
Schizanthus pinnatus
Tithonia rotundifolia 'Torch'
Zea mays 'Gracillima Variegata'

Cleome hassleriana 'Colour Fountain'
SPIDER FLOWER
☼ ✳ ↕ 1.2m (4ft) ↔ 60cm (24in)

This bushy annual has elegant, fingered leaves held on long stalks. In summer, each stem is crowned by a single, loose, spidery head of narrow-petalled flowers.

Papaver somniferum
OPIUM POPPY
☼ ✳✳✳　‡75cm (30in) ↔ 30cm (12in)

Both the stems and foliage of this lush,
leafy, fast-growing annual have a greyish
tint. Its large summer flowers are available
in pink, red, purple, or white.

Papaver somniferum
Peony-flowered Series
☼ ✳✳✳　‡75cm (30in) ↔ 30cm (12in)

A spectacular selection of this popular
annual, in which the large, rounded
flowers, in a range of colours, resemble
peonies and have frilled, crowded petals.

OTHER LARGE BIENNIALS
Alcea rosea 'Chater's Double'
Calomeria amaranthoides
Campanula pyramidalis
Digitalis Excelsior Hybrids
Digitalis purpurea 'Heywoodii'
Lunaria annua var. *alba*
Matthiola 'Giant Excelsior'
Onopordum acanthium
Onopordum arabicum
Silybum marianum, see p.89
Smyrnium perfoliatum

Lunaria annua 'Variegata'
VARIEGATED HONESTY
☼ ☼ ✳✳✳　‡75cm (30in) ↔ 60cm (24in)

This vigorous biennial is worth growing
for its leaves alone. Its purplish flowers in
spring and early summer are followed by
attractive, disc-like seed capsules.

Eryngium giganteum 'Silver Ghost'
MISS WILLMOTT'S GHOST
☼ ✳✳✳　‡1.2m (4ft) ↔ 75cm (30in)

This striking upright biennial has heart-
shaped basal leaves, and stiff, silvery stems
with prickly leaves. These support domed
summer flowerheads on a ruff of bracts.

Nicotiana langsdorfii
ORNAMENTAL TOBACCO
☼ ✳✳　‡1.5m (5ft) ↔ 60cm (24in)

Leafy at its base, this ornamental tobacco
plant is an elegant biennial that bears many
small, drooping, pale green, bell-shaped
flowers from summer into autumn.

Salvia sclarea var. *turkestanica*
CLARY
☼ ✳✳✳　‡75cm (30in) ↔ 60cm (24in)

This fast-growing biennial produces bold
rosettes of downy, aromatic leaves, above
which branching stems bear clusters of
small lavender-purple flowers in summer.

Small Perennials for Front of Border and Small Beds

SOME OF THE MOST GORGEOUS and reliable perennials fall in the small-size range, with flowering stems in the region of 60cm (24in) or less. They are ideally suited for planting in groups or alone where space is limited, as it is in smaller beds, but they can be equally valuable for fronting taller perennials, or even shrubs in large beds and borders. All the following are relatively easy to cultivate, and many have both attractive flowers and foliage.

Digitalis x *mertonensis*
FOXGLOVE
☼ ☼ ❄❄❄ ↕ 75cm (30in) ↔ 30cm (12in)

This unusual but desirable foxglove forms clumps of softly hairy evergreen leaves and upright, downy stems that carry full spikes of nodding summer flowers. ♔

Astilbe simplicifolia 'Sprite'
ASTILBE
☼ ❄❄❄ ↕ 50cm (20in) ↔ 60cm (24in)

Low clumps of divided, glossy leaves are topped by feathery plumes of tiny, star-shaped summer flowers. Thrives in soils that do not dry out in summer. ♔

Coreopsis verticillata
COREOPSIS
☼ ❄❄❄ ↕ 50cm (20in) ↔ 30cm (12in)

The erect stems of this cheerful, highly reliable perennial are clothed with finely divided, feathery leaves. Its bright yellow flowers appear throughout summer. ♔

Buphthalmum salicifolium
YELLOW OX-EYE
☼ ❄❄❄ ↕ 60cm (24in) ↔ 1m (3ft)

Bright yellow, daisy-like flowers top loose clumps of hairy stems with narrow leaves throughout summer. Yellow Ox-eye may require support, especially in a windy site.

OTHER SMALL FLOWERING PERENNIALS

Aster lateriflorus 'Horizontalis'
Aster thomsonii 'Nanus'
Astrantia maxima
Bergenia 'Silberlicht'
Campanula 'Burghaltii'
Epimedium x *versicolor* 'Sulphureum'
Eryngium bourgatii, see p.36
Helleborus argutifolius
x *Heucherella alba* 'Bridget Bloom'
Incarvillea delavayi
Lathyrus vernus
Liatris spicata 'Kobold'
Penstemon 'Apple Blossom'
Platycodon grandiflorus, see p.37
Ranunculus aconitifolius
Sedum spectabile 'Brilliant'
Tradescantia x *andersoniana*
  'Zwanenburg Blue'

Erysimum 'Bowles Mauve'
PERENNIAL WALLFLOWER
☼ ❄❄ ↕ 60cm (24in) ↔ 1m (3ft)

One of the best little evergreen perennials for sunny sites, this produces long flower spikes over an extended period from early spring, above blue-grey foliage. ♔

Euphorbia polychroma
EUPHORBIA
☼ ❄❄❄   ↕50cm (20in) ↔50cm (20in)

A reliable, justifiably popular perennial,
this forms low mounds of leafy stems, and
star-shaped yellow flowerheads, lasting for
several weeks in spring.   ♈

Omphalodes cappadocica
'Cherry Ingram'
☼ ❄❄❄   ↕20cm (8in) ↔30cm (12in)

Loose sprays of rich blue, forget-me-not
flowers appear among low tufts of neat,
oval leaves from spring into early summer.
Prefers soils that are moist in summer.   ♈

Geranium 'Johnson's Blue'
CRANESBILL
☼ ❄❄❄   ↕30cm (12in) ↔60cm (24in)

This cranesbill is superb, forming clumps
of long-stalked, deeply and prettily
divided leaves. Its branched lavender-
blue flowerheads are held in summer.   ♈

**OTHER SMALL FOLIAGE
PERENNIALS**

Alchemilla mollis
Brunnera macrophylla 'Dawson's
   White', see p.68
Festuca glauca 'Blaufuchs'
Hakonechloa macra 'Alboaurea'
Heuchera micrantha 'Palace Purple'
Hosta lancifolia
Persicaria virginiana 'Painter's Palette'
Pulmonaria saccharata 'Argentea'
Stachys byzantina 'Silver Carpet'

Schizostylis coccinea 'Sunrise'
KAFFIR LILY
☼ ❄❄❄   ↕60cm (24in) ↔30cm (12in)

This relative of the gladiolus has upright
stems rising from clumps of grassy leaves.
They carry spikes of star-flowers through
autumn, sometimes into early winter.   ♈

Helichrysum 'Schweffellicht'
HELICHRYSUM
☼ ❄❄❄   ↕50cm (20in) ↔30cm (12in)

In summer, the softly downy stems bear
terminal clusters of fluffy, everlasting
sulphur-yellow flowerheads above mats
of similarly coated silver-grey leaves.   ♈

Prunella grandiflora
SELF HEAL
☼ ❄❄❄   ↕15cm (6in) ↔30cm (12in)

The low, semi-evergreen mats of foliage
provide a pleasant foil for the short, erect
spikes of two-lipped, funnel-shaped
purple flowers, borne in summer.   ♈

Stachys macrantha 'Superba'
STACHYS
☼ ❄❄❄   ↕45cm (18in) ↔60cm (24in)

In summer, eye-catching spires crowded
with hooded purple-violet flowers top low
clumps of large, heart-shaped, prominently
veined, and crinkly leaves.   ♈

Small Annuals and Biennials

A RICH VARIETY of small annual and biennial plants is suitable and widely available for the garden. Many are colourful and attractive, and are especially useful for filling temporary seasonal gaps in perennial plantings. The following selection contains less familiar examples as well as some old favourites. Most are hardy and easy to grow from seed.

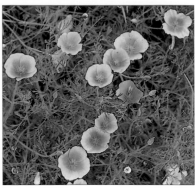

Eschscholzia californica (mixed)
CALIFORNIA POPPY
☼ ❄❄❄ ↕ 30cm (12in) ↔ 15cm (6in)

This popular, fast-growing annual has blue-green, feathery leaves and cup-shaped flowers in shades of yellow, cream, orange, and red in summer and early autumn.

Brachyscome iberidifolia
SWAN RIVER DAISY
☼ ❄❄❄ ↕ 45cm (18in) ↔ 45cm (18in)

Masses of small, fragrant blue, mauve, pink, or white flowers cover this bushy, slender-stemmed annual with finely cut leaves in summer and early autumn.

Gypsophila elegans
GYPSOPHILA
☼ ❄❄❄ ↕ 60cm (24in) ↔ 30cm (12in)

A bushy annual, this has erect, slender stems and grey-green, paired leaves. Many tiny, white, star-like flowers form branched heads from summer into early autumn.

Agrostemma githago 'Milas'
CORN COCKLE
☼ ❄❄❄ ↕ 75cm (30in) ↔ 30cm (12in)

Slender and fast-growing, this annual has erect stems and narrow, paired leaves, and freely produces its purplish-pink flowers with darker lines in summer.

Cheiranthus cheiri 'Fire King'
WALLFLOWER
☼ ☼ ❄❄❄ ↕ 38cm (15in) ↔ 30cm (12in)

An evergreen perennial, this old-fashioned favourite is commonly grown as a biennial. Its fragrant flowers come in many different colours, and open in the spring.

Iberis amara
CANDYTUFT
☼ ❄❄❄ ↕ 30cm (12in) ↔ 15cm (6in)

Candytuft has long been an old favourite annual; it is bushy with erect stems and narrow leaves, and has flattened heads of sweet-scented white flowers in summer.

Nemophila maculata
FIVE-SPOT
☼ ❄❄❄   ↕ 15cm (6in) ↔ 20cm (8in)

Five-spot is a charming, spreading annual with deeply lobed leaves and a summer-long succession of striking flowers. Each petal is purple-veined with a violet tip.

Nigella damascena 'Persian Jewels'
LOVE-IN-A-MIST
☼ ❄❄❄   ↕ 45cm (18in) ↔ 20cm (8in)

This slender, upright annual has feathery leaves and showy summer flowers in blue, pink, and white. Its attractive green seed pods, suitable for drying, follow.

Reseda odorata
SWEET MIGNONETTE
☼ ❄❄❄   ↕ 50cm (20in) ↔ 30cm (12in)

From summer into autumn, this upright, branching, leafy annual produces dense, conical heads of small, starry white flowers with orange-brown stamens. Very fragrant.

Tropaeolum majus 'Alaska'
NASTURTIUM
☼ ☼ ❄❄❄   ↕ 30cm (12in) ↔ 30cm (12in)

Fast-growing and bushy, this annual has fleshy stems and long-stalked, variegated leaves. Spurred red and yellow flowers last all through summer and into autumn.

OTHER SMALL ANNUALS AND BIENNIALS

Collinsia grandiflora
Euphorbia marginata
Omphalodes linifolia
Platystemon californicus

Papaver rhoeas Shirley Series
SHIRLEY POPPY
☼ ❄❄❄   ↕ 60cm (24in) ↔ 30cm (12in)

Nodding buds in summer reveal delicate single flowers in many colours. Erect and slender-stemmed with pale green leaves, there is also a double strain of this annual.

Xeranthemum annuum (double)
IMMORTELLE
☼ ❄   ↕ 60cm (24in) ↔ 45cm (18in)

Heads of daisy-like summer flowers, in shades of pink, mauve, purple, or white, are excellent for drying. This is an erect annual with narrow silvery leaves.

Perennials for Ground Cover in Sun

THERE IS NO REASON why soil in the garden should remain bare given the number of plants with low spreading or carpeting growth. Many of these grow well on problematic banks and most have ornamental foliage or flowers. Some spring- or early summer-flowering plants can be trimmed after flowering to encourage a second display later in the season.

Geranium endressii 'Wargrave Pink'
CRANESBILL
☼ ❋❋❋   ↕ 50cm (20in) ↔ 60cm (24in)

Of dense, leafy habit, this evergreen is free flowering. Attractively lobed leaves form a carpet above which the warm salmon-pink flowers bloom throughout summer. ♈

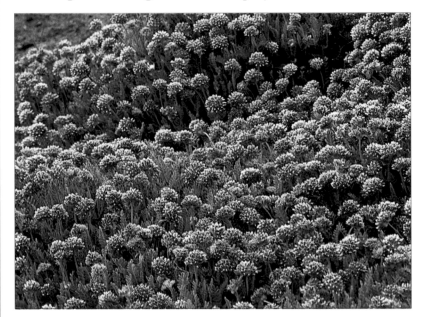

Anthyllis montanta
ANTHYLLIS
☼ ❋❋   ↕ 20cm (8in) ↔ 30cm (12in)

Prettily divided leaves create downy mats, and rounded heads of pale pink and red flowers appear in late spring and early summer. Does best in well-drained soils.

Geranium sanguineum var. *striatum*
CRANESBILL
☼ ❋❋❋   ↕ 13cm (5in) ↔ 30cm (12in)

Better known as var. *lancastriense*, this low, mound-forming perennial has small, attractively fingered leaves and pale pink flowers over many months in summer. ♈

Asarina procumbens
ASARINA
☼ ☼ ❋❋   ↕ 5cm (2in) ↔ 30cm (12in)

This softly hairy semi-evergreen has trailing stems, rounded leaves, and pale snapdragon flowers through summer into early autumn. It dislikes winter wet. ♈

Cerastium tomentosum
SNOW-IN-SUMMER
☼ ❋❋❋   ↕ 8cm (3in) ↔ indefinite

A reliable ground cover favourite that has carpets of silver-grey leaves and stems. Star-shaped flowers occur from late spring into summer. Prolific if conditions suit.

OTHER PERENNIALS FOR GROUND COVER IN SUN

Acaena 'Blue Haze'
Achillea clavennae
Anthemis punctata subsp. *cupaniana*,
   see p.50
Arabis caucasica 'Rosabella', see p.54
Aubrieta 'Joy', see p.54
Euphorbia cyparissias
Euphorbia myrsinites, see p.36
Globularia cordifolia
Gypsophila repens
Hippocrepis comosa
Othonopsis cherifolia
Persicaria vacciniifolia, see p.55
Phlox douglasii 'Boothman's Variety',
   see p.57
Potentilla alba
Prunella grandiflora, see p.25
Silene schafta

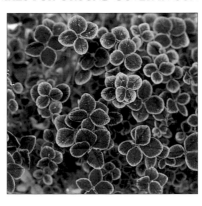

Glechoma hederacea 'Variegata'
VARIEGATED GROUND IVY
☀ ✽✽✽ ↕15cm (6in) ↔indefinite

The slender, trailing stems of this ground
ivy form extensive carpets of heart-shaped,
toothed evergreen leaves. The flowers are
small and generally hidden from view.

Persicaria affinis 'Donald Lowndes'
PERSICARIA
☀ ✽✽✽ ↕11cm (4½in) ↔45cm (18in)

Dense flower spikes occur in summer and
early autumn; the pink flowers darken with
age. The mats of evergreen leaves will
colour attractively in winter when old. ♔

Trifolium repens 'Purpurascens'
PURPLE-LEAVED CLOVER
☀ ✽✽✽ ↕10cm (4in) ↔45cm (18in)

An easy and attractive form of clover worth
growing for its carpets of pretty bronze or
purple leaves with a bright green edge.
White flowerheads are borne in summer.

Helianthemum 'Wisley Pink'
ROCK ROSE
☀ ✽✽✽ ↕30cm (12in) ↔45cm (18in)

Dense evergreen carpets of grey-green
leafy stems bear saucer-shaped flowers
in early summer. Other cultivars with a
range of flower colours are just as good. ♔

Phuopsis stylosa
CAUCASIAN CROSSWORT
☀ ✽✽✽ ↕30cm (12in) ↔60cm (24in)

The stems and foliage of this plant form
low mounds and have a pungent aroma.
Its small summer flowers, however, have a
sweet scent. Vigorous once established.

Saponaria ocymoides
TUMBLING TED
☀ ✽✽✽ ↕5cm (2in) ↔45cm (18in)

A long-established favourite in the garden,
reliable for its low mounds of trailing leaf
stems covered in pale to dark pink flowers
in summer. There is also a white form. ♔

STONECROPS AND HOUSELEEKS

Sedum acre 'Aureum'
Sedum album 'Coral Carpet'
Sedum kamtschaticum
Sedum obtusatum
Sedum spathulifolium 'Purpureum'
Sedum spurium 'Schorbuser Blut'
Sempervivum arachniodeum
Sempervivum ciliosum
Sempervivum 'Commander Hay'
Sempervivum 'Othello'
Sempervivum tectorum

Veronica peduncularis 'Georgia Blue'
CAUCASIAN SPEEDWELL
☀ ☼ ✽✽✽ ↕13cm (5in) ↔45cm (18in)

A fast-creeping perennial with wiry stems
and tiny evergreen leaves, bronze-purple
when young. Flowers plaster the growth
in spring, and often again later in the year.

Perennials for Ground Cover in Shade

A SHADY SITE will support a wide selection of perennials, including many that make ideal ground cover, providing that it is not in the dry shade of an evergreen canopy, nor filled by tree roots. Results are achieved more quickly by planting in large numbers, even for creeping perennials. All these plants need some moisture in the soil during summer.

Galium odoratum
SWEET WOODRUFF
☼ ☀ ❄❄❄   ↕ 15cm (6in) ↔ indefinite

The stems of this strong-growing, aromatic perennial are clothed in whorls of narrow leaves. Clusters of tiny star-flowers open in summer. Thrives in alkaline soils.

Acanthus mollis
BEAR'S BREECHES
☼ ☼ ☀ ❄❄❄   ↕ 1.2m (4ft) ↔ 1m (3ft)

One of the boldest ground covers, this has semi-evergreen leaves and its mauve-pink flowers appear in summer. The leaves of *A. mollis* 'Latifolius' are more attractive.

Anemone nemorosa 'Robinsoniana'
WOOD ANEMONE
☼ ☀ ❄❄❄❄   ↕ 15cm (6in) ↔ 20cm (8in)

A beautiful form of a charming perennial, this forms carpets of ferny leaves and star-shaped lavender-blue flowers in spring. Dies down by midsummer.   ♔

> **OTHER EVERGREEN PERENNIALS FOR GROUND COVER IN SHADE**
>
> *Asarum caudatum*
> *Cardamine trifolia*
> *Euphorbia amygdaloides*
>   subsp. *robbiae*, see p.53
> *Lamium maculatum* 'Beacon Silver'
> *Luzula sylvatica* 'Marginata'
> *Saxifraga* x *geum*
> *Saxifraga* x *urbium*
> *Vinca minor* 'Azurea Flore Pleno'
> *Vinca minor* 'Gertrude Jekyll'

Aegopodium podagraria 'Variegatum'
VARIEGATED GROUND ELDER
☼ ☀ ❄❄❄   ↕ 10cm (4in) ↔ indefinite

No one would dream of planting invasive Ground Elder, but this less vigorous form makes an attractive ground cover with its boldly variegated, creamy white leaves.

Asarum europaeum
ASARABACCA
☼ ☀ ❄❄❄❄   ↕ 12.5cm (5in) ↔ indefinite

Evergreen mats of kidney-shaped, glossy, dark green leaves conceal small, brownish purple, bell-shaped flowers, each with three lobes, in spring. Easy and reliable.

Hosta 'Shade Fanfare'
PLANTAIN LILY
☼ ☀ ❄❄❄❄   ↕ 75cm (30in) ↔ 1m (3ft)

This clump-forming perennial bears large, heart-shaped, light green leaves, each with a bold creamy margin. Erect stems carry nodding lavender flowers in summer.   ♔

Lamium galeobdolon 'Florentinum'
VARIEGATED ARCHANGEL
☀ ☀ ❋❋❋   ↕ 25cm (10in) ↔ indefinite

This scrambling evergreen quickly forms
a dense carpet of nettle-shaped, silver-
striped leaves, borne in pairs. Its whorls of
two-lipped yellow flowers open in summer.

Tiarella cordifolia
FOAM FLOWER
☀ ☀ ❋❋❋   ↕ 20cm (8in) ↔ indefinite

Delicate, fluffy spires of tiny white flowers
rise above the evergreen carpets of lobed,
heart-shaped, bright green leaves from
late spring into early summer.   ♛

Waldsteinia ternata
WALDSTEINIA
☀ ☀ ❋❋❋   ↕ 10cm (4in) ↔ indefinite

Three-parted, toothed, strawberry-like
leaves form mats and are semi-evergreen.
Potentilla-like yellow flowers are borne in
late spring and early summer.

Saxifraga spathularis
SAINT PATRICK'S CABBAGE
☀ ☀ ❋❋❋   ↕ 25cm (10in) ↔ indefinite

Evergreen rosettes of dark-green, toothed
leaves form low carpets. Tiny, starry white
flowers are held in airy, branched clusters
in summer. Dislikes dry soils.

Symphytum grandiflorum
DWARF COMFREY
☀ ☀ ❋❋❋   ↕ 25cm (10in) ↔ indefinite

Cream-coloured tubular flowers, reddish
when in bud, are carried in clusters above
the rich green leaves in spring. The foliage
quickly forms low clumps and patches.

Tolmiea menziesii 'Taff's Gold'
PICK-A-BACK PLANT
☀ ☀ ❋❋❋   ↕ 60cm (24in) ↔ 45cm (18in)

Clumps of long-stalked, yellow-speckled,
hairy leaves are either evergreen or semi-
evergreen. Tall spikes carrying tiny green
and brown flowers are borne in spring.

> **OTHER HERBACEOUS PERENNIALS
> FOR GROUND COVER IN SHADE**
>
> *Eomecon chionantha*
> *Geranium macrorrhizum* 'Ingwersen'
> *Symphytum* 'Hidcote Pink'
> *Trachystemon orientalis*

Perennials for Heavy Clay Soils

EVERYONE WHO GARDENS on heavy clay soils knows they are usually wet and sticky in winter, and hard and dry in summer. They are at least fertile, and if their structure is improved, they can support a wide range of ornamental plants. Many perennials will grow anyway, provided there is enough moisture in summer and the soil is not waterlogged in winter.

Astrantia major
MASTERWORT
☼ ☀ ✳✳✳ ↕60cm (24in) ↔45cm (18in)

The leaves of this tough and reliable clump-forming plant are long-stalked. Its flowers are greenish white or pink-tinted, and appear from summer into autumn.

Aster novae-angliae 'Alma Pötschke'
MICHAELMAS DAISY
☼ ✳✳✳ ↕75cm (30in) ↔60cm (24in)

Erect clumps of leafy stems produce large, branching heads of daisy-like flowers, with yellow centres, in autumn. Provides a most striking colour for late in the season. ♟

Cimicifuga simplex
BUGBANE
☼ ☀ ✳✳✳ ↕1.7m (5½ft) ↔60cm (24in)

Erect plant, with glossy, divided leaves that may colour attractively before they wither. Tiny, slightly fragrant flowers are carried on tall, slender spikes in autumn.

Aster novi-belgii 'Carnival'
MICHAELMAS DAISY
☼ ✳✳✳ ↕75cm (30in) ↔45cm (18in)

Like most michaelmas daisies, this one is ideal for clay soils. It has an upright habit and brilliantly coloured autumn flowers. Susceptible to mildew in dry conditions.

Astilbe 'Montgomery'
ASTILBE
☼ ☀ ✳✳✳ ↕75cm (30in) ↔35cm (14in)

Tapering plumes of deep red flowers rise above clumps of delicate, glossy, fern-like leaves in summer. There are many other cultivars with red, pink, or white flowers.

CREEPING PERENNIALS THAT COLONIZE HEAVY CLAY SOILS

Circium rivulare var. *atropurpureum*
Epimedium x *perralchicum*, see p.42
Geranium macrorrhizum
  'Ingwersen's Variety'
Houttuynia cordata 'Flore Pleno'
Mentha x *gentilis* 'Variegata'
Mentha longifolia
Peltiphyllum peltatum 'Nanum'
Persicaria bistorta 'Superba', see p.47
Saponaria officinalis

Helenium 'Moerheim Beauty'
HELENIUM

☼ ✳✳✳ ↕ 1m (3ft) ↔ 60cm (24in)

This is an old and reliable border plant.
Upright and close-packed, clumps of leafy
stems bear rich bronzy red flowerheads
with a brownish centre in late summer.

Monarda 'Cambridge Scarlet'
BERGAMOT

☼ ✳✳✳ ↕ 1m (3ft) ↔ 75cm (30in)

A popular and handsome bergamot with
dense clusters of rich red, tubular flowers
throughout summer. Its leaves are aromatic
when bruised. It thrives in moist soils. ♚

Rudbeckia fulgida
'Goldsturm'

☼ ✳✳✳ ↕ 75cm (30in) ↔ 45cm (18in)

Black-eyed Susan is one of the most
reliable and attractive of all perennials,
flowering in late summer and autumn.
The leaves will wilt in dry conditions. ♚

Heliopsis 'Ballet Dancer'
HELIOPSIS

☼ ✳✳✳ ↕ 1.1m (3½ft) ↔ 75cm (30in)

This perennial is of upright habit and has
bold foliage. In late summer it carries a
profusion of large, daisy-like flowerheads,
with frilled, rich yellow petals.

Polemonium reptans
'Lambrook Mauve'

☼ ☀ ✳✳✳ ↕ 45cm (18in) ↔ 30cm (12in)

A low, mound-forming relative of Jacob's
Ladder, this has similarly much-divided
leaves and loose lilac-blue flowerheads in
late spring and early summer. ♚

Solidago 'Goldenmosa'
GOLDEN ROD

☼ ✳✳✳ ↕ 1m (3ft) ↔ 60cm (24in)

A smaller and superior version of the old-
fashioned tall Golden Rod. Sturdy clumps
of leafy stems bear handsome plumes of
yellow flowers in late summer. ♚

Kirengeshoma palmata
KIRENGESHOMA

☼ ✳✳✳ ᴾᴴ ↕ 1m (3ft) ↔ 75cm (30in)

A handsome perennial, both in flower and
leaf. The sprays of waxy flowers occur
from late summer into autumn. Thrives
best in a moist, but well-drained soil. ♚

Pulmonaria saccharata
JERUSALEM SAGE

☼ ☀ ✳✳✳ ↕ 30cm (12in) ↔ 60cm (24in)

Low mounds and hummocks of pointed
leaves are covered with whitish spots and
speckles. Spring flowers, borne in clusters,
open pink, and turn blue as they age.

**OTHER PERENNIALS FOR
HEAVY CLAY SOILS**

Aconitum 'Bressingham Spire'
Anemone x *hybrida* 'Honorine Jobert',
  see p.52
Brunnera macrophylla
Crocosmia 'Lucifer'
Eupatorium maculatum 'Atropurpureum'
Inula hookeri, see p.77
Ligularia stenocephala 'The Rocket'
Prunella grandiflora 'Loveliness'
Rodgersia podophylla, see p.47

Perennials for Lime-free Soils

R ELATIVELY FEW garden perennials prefer or thrive best in soils devoid of lime; those that do are natives of woodland or mountain areas, especially in Asia and North America. Of the following, many are suited to raised beds, rock or peat gardens, and most need a constant supply of moisture in summer, although not boggy conditions.

Iris innominata
Pacific Coast Hybrids
☼ ❈❈❈ ♇ ‖ ↕ 21cm (8in) ↔ 45cm (18in)

These evergreen iris are superb for the edge of beds or as ground cover in well-drained soils. Delicately veined flowers of various colours occur from late spring.

Adiantum pedatum
NORTHERN MAIDENHAIR FERN
☼ ❈❈❈ ♇ ↕ 45cm (18in) ↔ 45cm (18in)

In time, this lovely fern forms small colonies of fingered fronds on erect, wiry stalks. It thrives in moist, shady soils, especially in peat or woodland gardens. ♈

Celmisia walkeri
NEW ZEALAND DAISY
☼ ❈❈❈ ♇ ↕ 23cm (9in) ↔ 1m (3ft)

Dense rosettes of shiny evergreen leaves form low mounds. Above these, slender stems each bear a daisy-like flower in summer. Needs moist, well-drained soils.

Lewisia Cotyledon Hybrids
LEWISIA
☼ ❈❈❈ ♇ ↕ 25cm (10in) ↔ 15cm (6in)

This evergreen, with attractive rosettes of strap-shaped leaves, is suitable for cracks in rocks or stone walls. Erect heads of pink to purple flowers appear in early summer.

OTHER PERENNIALS FOR LIME-FREE SOILS

Blechnum spicant
Celmisia coriacea, see p.66
Celmisia spectabilis
Cryptogramma crispa
Epigaea gaultherioides
Galax urceolata
Gentiana x *macaulayi* 'Edinburgh'
Gentiana sino-ornata
Kirengeshoma koreana
Kirengeshoma palmata, see p.33
Linnaea borealis
Lithodora diffusa 'Grace Ward'
Maianthemum canadense
Phlox adsurgens 'Red Buttes'
Phlox x *procumbens* 'Millstream'
Phlox stolonifera 'Blue Ridge'
Shortia galacifolia
Viola pedata

Gentiana x *macaulayi* 'Well's Variety'
GENTIAN
☼ ❈❈❈ ♇ ↕ 5cm (2in) ↔ 20cm (8in)

A striking gentian, forming mats of narrow evergreen leaves. Gorgeous, upturned blue trumpet flowers appear in late summer. Needs moist soils in a rock or peat garden.

Lithodora diffusa 'Heavenly Blue'
LITHODORA
☼ ❈❈❈ ♇ ↕ 15cm (6in) ↔ 60cm (24in)

An evergreen carpeting perennial, with small, hairy grey-green leaves, prized for its small, star-shaped early summer flowers. It is ideal for banks or wall tops. ♈

Luzula nivea
SNOWY WOODRUSH
☼ ❄❄❄❄ PH ↕ 60cm (24in) ↔ 50cm (20in)

Evergreen clumps of narrow, whiskery-edged, grass-like leaves surround erect, slender stems bearing loose clusters of glistening white spikelets in early summer.

Phlox stolonifera 'Ariane'
PHLOX
☼ ❄❄❄❄ PH ↕ 15cm (6in) ↔ 30cm (12in)

Low, leafy evergreen mats produce loose heads of long-tubed, saucer-shaped white flowers in early summer. This is a good companion to *P. adsurgens* 'Wagon Wheel'.

Podophyllum hexandrum
HIMALAYAN MAY APPLE
☼ ❄❄❄❄ PH ↕ 40cm (16in) ↔ 30cm (12in)

A single white or pale pink, yellow-centred flower is borne in spring, above brown and green mottled leaves. The flowers may be followed by pendent red seed pods.

Meconopsis betonicifolia
BLUE POPPY
☼ ❄❄❄❄ PH ↕ 1.2m (4ft) ↔ 45cm (18in)

A popular plant famed for its blue flowers in late spring or early summer. The leaves decrease in size up the stem from a basal rosette. Dislikes dry soils. ♈

Phlox adsurgens 'Wagon Wheel'
PHLOX
☼ ❄❄❄❄ PH ↕ 10cm (4in) ↔ 30cm (12in)

Branched heads of small, wheel-shaped pink flowers rise above mats of evergreen leafy stems in summer. Thrives in humus-rich, but well-drained, soils.

MECONOPSIS FOR LIME-FREE SOILS
Meconopsis chelidoniifolia
Meconopsis grandis
Meconopsis x *sarsonsii*
Meconopsis x *sheldonii*
Meconopsis villosa

Smilacina racemosa
FALSE SPIKENARD
☼ ❄❄❄❄ PH ↕ 85cm (34in) ↔ 45cm (18in)

This is an excellent flowering and foliage plant. Bold, arching, leafy stems end in plumes of white flowers from spring into summer. Dislikes dry soils. ♈

Perennials for Alkaline Soils

T̲HE DRY, TYPICALLY WELL-DRAINED conditions provided by alkaline soils suit a variety of perennials; if they are combined with a sunny aspect, so much the better. Many perennials are so content in these conditions that they seed around, giving even more spectacular displays, as well as seedlings for you to pass on to gardening friends.

Eryngium bourgatii
ERYNGIUM
☼ ❋❋❋   ↕60cm (24in) ↔30cm (12in)

Branched, wiry stems carry many small, thistle-like flowers from mid- to late summer. Leathery, spine-toothed leaves are marbled grey-green, with white veins.

Anthericum liliago
ST. BERNARD'S LILY
☼ ❋❋❋   ↕60cm (24in) ↔30cm (12in)

White, star-shaped flowers with light yellow stamens are carried on loose spires in early summer. These rise above clumps of long, narrow grey-green leaves. ♔

Campanula glomerata 'Superba'
CLUSTERED BELLFLOWER
☼ ❋❋❋   ↕75cm (30in) ↔1m (3ft)

Sturdy, leafy stems sport dense heads of bell-shaped purple flowers in summer. This vigorous, clump-forming perennial will seed itself in suitable sites. ♔

Euphorbia myrsinites
EUPHORBIA
☼ ❋❋   ↕8cm (3in) ↔30cm (12in)

This fleshy evergreen has trailing stems crowded with blue-grey leaves, and bears yellowish green spring flowers. Pinkish seed heads follow. ♔

Asphodeline lutea
YELLOW ASPHODEL
☼ ❋❋❋   ↕1.2m (4ft) ↔60cm (24in)

Grassy clumps of sea-green leaves appear in autumn, and these form a good base for its tall spikes of star-shaped flowers in late spring. Self-seeds in well-drained soils.

Dianthus 'Gran's Favourite'
OLD-FASHIONED PINK
☼ ❋❋❋   ↕30cm (12in) ↔60cm (24in)

Fragrant flowers, borne in summer, have white petals with raspberry-red bases and margins. The hummocks of blue-grey foliage are evergreen. ♔

Geranium pratense
'Plenum Violaceum'
☼ ❋❋❋   ↕75cm (30in) ↔60cm (24in)

Erect, branching stems carry small, deep violet, rosette-like flowers in summer. The bold clumps of finely divided leaves will often colour well in autumn. ♔

Origanum laevigatum
ORIGANUM
☼ ✳✳ ↕ 30cm (12in) ↔ 25cm (10in)

This aromatic, mat-forming plant sends
up slender, branching stems that support
numerous cerise-pink summer flowers,
popular with bees and butterflies. ⚱

Platycodon grandiflorus
BALLOON FLOWER
☼ ✳✳✳ ↕ 60cm (24in) ↔ 45cm (18in)

Loose clumps of erect stems, clothed with
fleshy, bluish green leaves, produce pale,
balloon-like buds in summer. These
expand into large blue or purple bells. ⚱

Verbascum 'Gainsborough'
MULLEIN
☼ ✳✳✳ ↕ 1.2m (4ft) ↔ 60cm (24in)

From a semi-evergreen rosette of leaves,
tall, branching spikes of small, saucer-
shaped flowers rise in summer. A short-
lived perennial, sometimes biennial. ⚱

Oxalis adenophylla
OXALIS
☼ ✳✳✳ ↕ 5cm (2in) ↔ 10cm (4in)

A beautiful carpeting perennial, this has
neat tufts of deeply divided grey-green
leaves, through which large, dark-eyed,
purplish pink flowers appear in spring. ⚱

Pulsatilla vulgaris
PASQUE FLOWER
☼ ✳✳✳ ↕ 25cm (10in) ↔ 25cm (10in)

Tufts of fine feather foliage produce hairy
stems, each with a single nodding bellflower, in spring. This flower opens wide
and later becomes a silky seed head. ⚱

Pennisetum villosum
ABYSSINIAN FEATHERTOP
☼ ✳✳ ↕ 1m (3ft) ↔ 50cm (20in)

In late summer and autumn the narrow
leaves of this pretty ornamental grass give
way to slender, downy shoots bearing
creamy spikes with long, bearded bristles.

**OTHER PERENNIALS FOR
ALKALINE SOILS**

Acanthus spinosus, see p.18
Achillea 'Coronation Gold'
Bergenia cordifolia 'Purpurea', see p.66
Campanula latifolia 'Brantwood',
  see p.52
Campanula persicifolia 'Chettle Charm'
Cortaderia selloana 'Pumila', see p.85
Crepis incana
Euphorbia nicaeensis
Gypsophila paniculata 'Rosenschleier'
Iris unguicularis
Linum narbonense
Phlomis russeliana
Salvia x *superba*
Sedum 'Vera Jameson'
Sidalcea 'Sussex Beauty'
Stipa gigantea, see p.19
Viola cornuta

Verbena bonariensis
VERBENA
☼ ✳✳ ↕ 1.5m (5ft) ↔ 50cm (20in)

Tall, wiry, branching stems carry narrow,
paired leaves and small, dense clusters of
tiny, fragrant flowers through summer into
autumn. Self-seeds in suitable sites. ⚱

Perennials for Dry, Sunny Sites

OVER-DRY SOILS IN SUN are not exclusive to the warmer, drier countries of the world. One summer drought can put many garden perennials in temperate climates under stress unless water is available. Plants grown in light or sandy soils are often the first to suffer. It pays, therefore, to choose at least some perennials that tolerate of warm, dry conditions.

Campanula persicifolia
'Telham Beauty'
☼ ❋❋❋　　　　　↕ 1m (3ft) ↔ 30cm (12in)

This lovely cultivar of the Peach-leaved Bellflower has upright, slender stems and narrow leaves. It is adorned by sprays of large, nodding bell-flowers in summer.

> **CUSHION AND HUMMOCK PLANTS FOR DRY, SUNNY SITES**
>
> *Acantholimon glumaceum*
> *Armeria juniperina*
> *Armeria maritima* 'Vindictive'
> *Artemisia schmidtiana* 'Nana', see p.56
> *Astragalus angustifolius*
> *Aubrieta* 'Elsa Lancaster'
> *Azorella trifurcata*
> *Dianthus* 'Pike's Pink'
> *Erinacea anthyllis*
> *Phlox subulata* 'Marjory'

Anthemis tinctoria 'E.C. Buxton'
GOLDEN MARGUERITE
☼ ❋❋❋　　　　　↕ 1m (3ft) ↔ 1m (3ft)

A colourful and reliable bushy perennial with aromatic, fern-like leaves. Branching stems bear a succession of daisy-like flowers from summer into autumn. ♔

> **OTHER PERENNIALS FOR DRY, SUNNY SITES**
>
> *Anthemis punctata* subsp. *cupaniana*, see p.50
> *Asphodeline lutea*, see p.36
> *Campanula persicifolia* 'George Chiswell'
> *Crepis incana*
> *Eryngium bourgatii*, see p.36
> *Linum narbonense* 'Heavenly Blue'
> *Oenothera odorata*
> *Origanum* 'Kent Beauty', see p.57

Bletilla striata
BLETILLA
☼ ❋❋　　　　　↕ 60cm (24in) ↔ 45cm (18in)

A beautiful terrestrial orchid, well worth growing just for its attractive patches of ribbed leaves. Above these, loose flower sprays occur in late spring or early summer.

Diascia rigescens
DIASCIA
☼ ❋❋❋　　　　　↕ 25cm (10in) ↔ 25cm (10in)

The stems of this trailing, leafy perennial curve upwards to bear flower spikes over a long period, from summer into autumn. A most spectacular, reliable ground cover. ♔

Eryngium alpinum
ALPINE ERYNGO
☼ ✳✳✳   ↕85cm (34in) ↔60cm (24in)

This most spectacular perennial has basal
rosettes of heart-shaped leaves, and stout,
branching stems carrying conical summer
flowerheads with softly spiny ruffs.   ♀

Hordeum jubatum
SQUIRREL-TAIL GRASS
☼ ✳✳✳   ↕45cm (18in) ↔30cm (12in)

One of the most beautiful ornamental
grasses when, from summer into autumn,
erect stems sport feathery plumes of silky
spikelets, green at first, ripening to gold.

Dictamnus albus var. *purpureus*
BURNING BUSH
☼ ✳✳✳   ↕1m (3ft) ↔60cm (24in)

A famous plant, slow to establish, but well
worth the wait once the loose spikes of
lilac to purple-pink flowers appear above
deeply divided leaves in summer.   ♀

Gypsophila paniculata 'Bristol Fairy'
GYPSOPHILA
☼ ✳✳✳   ↕70cm (28in) ↔1m (3ft)

A splendid form of the well-known Baby's
Breath that is much used by florists. Its
wiry, multi-branched stems together
produce clouds of tiny summer flowers. ♀

Linum flavum 'Compactum'
FLAX
☼ ✳✳✳   ↕15cm (6in) ↔15cm (6in)

This small, bushy perennial has narrow
green leaves, and pretty heads of funnel-
shaped, bright yellow flowers, from late
spring into summer.

Echinops ritro 'Veitch's Blue'
GLOBE THISTLE
☼ ✳✳✳   ↕1.2m (4ft) ↔75cm (30in)

Silvery stems above handsome clumps of
jagged leaves support many tight, globular
blue flowerheads. They are popular with
bees and butterflies in late summer.   ♀

Helianthemum 'Wisley Primrose'
ROCK ROSE
☼ ✳✳✳   ↕25cm (10in) ↔60cm (24in)

Low hummocks of evergreen foliage are
joined by a plentiful supply of saucer-
shaped flowers in summer. Other varieties
in different colours are available.   ♀

Oenothera speciosa 'Rosea'
EVENING PRIMROSE
☼ ✳✳✳   ↕45cm (18in) ↔30cm (12in)

The pink flowers of this lovely evening
primrose are carried above deeply cut
leaves. Nodding buds open in summer,
unusually for this genus, during the day.

Bulbs for Dry, Sunny Sites

MANY BULBS ARE FOUND in dry, often hot and arid places in the wild, or they appreciate such conditions at certain times of the year. In gardens, these bulbs will struggle if you plant them in shade or in a deep, rich soil; although they may survive for a time, many will eventually die. The following selection performs best in good drainage and as much sun and warmth as possible. A raised bed or a border at the foot of a sunny wall is usually perfect.

Lilium candidum
MADONNA LILY
☼ ❄❄❄　　　　　　↕ 1.5m (5ft)

In summer, a large, loose head of broad, funnel-shaped, fragrant white flowers, with yellow throats, crowns each erect, leafy stem. Thrives in alkaline soils. ♈

Allium christophii
ORNAMENTAL ONION
☼ ❄❄❄　　　　　　↕ 40cm (16in)

The large, globular head of star-spangled flowers in summer makes this one of the most spectacular of all alliums. Its flowerheads are also attractive dried. ♈

Eucomis comosa
PINEAPPLE FLOWER
☼ ❄❄　　　　　　↕ 70cm (28in)

Wavy-margined, strap-shaped leaves are topped in late summer by a single purple-spotted stem with a spike of pink-flushed star-flowers, and a crown of green bracts.

Triteleia laxa
TRITELEIA
☼ ❄❄　　　　　　↕ 50cm (20in)

Loose umbels of funnel-shaped flowers, pale to deep blue, or purple-blue, are borne above tufts of narrow green leaves in early summer. Seeds around if content.

Amaryllis belladonna
BELLADONNA LILY
☼ ❄❄　　　　　　↕ 60cm (24in)

This lovely autumn-flowering bulb bears scented, funnel-shaped pink flowers carried elegantly on sturdy, purplish stems. The strap-shaped leaves follow in winter.

OTHER BULBS FOR DRY SUN

Allium karataviense
Anemone blanda
Anemone pavonina
Anomatheca laxa
Anomatheca laxa var. *alba*
Arum creticum
Colchicum agrippinum, see p.58
Fritillaria imperialis, see p.79
Gladiolus communis subsp. *byzantinus*, see p.61
Hermodactylus tuberosus
Ixiolirion tataricum
Lilium x *testaceum*
Muscari armeniacum
Ornithogalum umbellatum
Scilla peruviana
Tulipa clusiana
Tulipa praestans
Tulipa sprengeri

Tulipa saxatilis
TULIP
☼ ❄❄❄　　　　　　↕ 35cm (14in)

In early spring, branched stems support up to four pink to lilac flowers, each with a yellow eye, above attractive, glossy green leaves. Forms patches in warm, dry soils.

Bulbs for Shady Sites

FAR OUTNUMBERED by the sun-lovers, an appreciable variety of bulbs enjoy shady conditions in soils that remain moist in summer. Many of these bulbs are wood-landers, originating from the temperate regions, and so are ideal for sunless situations in the garden, provided that the shade is not too heavy, and that they do not have to compete with the roots of trees growing nearby. Plant in groups to create the best effect. Many will seed around if content.

Corydalis flexuosa
CORYDALIS
☼ ☀ ❄❄❄ ↕ 15cm (6in)

The striking blue flowers of this beautiful clump-forming plant open in spring. Its fern-like leaves are sometimes bronze-tinted. Several cultivars are available.

Erythronium hendersonii
TROUT LILY
☼ ☀ ❄❄ ↕ 30cm (12in)

In spring, Trout Lily's nodding lavender-pink flowers, with gracefully swept back petals, rise above a pair of fleshy leaves, mottled green and brown. ♈

Ornithogalum nutans
ORNITHOGALUM
☼ ☀ ❄❄❄❄ ↕ 35cm (14in)

In spring, loose spikes of large, drooping, bell-shaped flowers, translucent and green-tinted, are produced among tufts of narrow leaves. Prefers well-drained soils. ♈

OTHER BULBS FOR SHADE

Allium moly
Arisaema sikokianum, see p.44
Arisaema triphyllum
Arisarum proboscideum, see p.44
Arum italicum 'Marmoratum'
Brimeura amethystina
Cyclamen repandum
Eranthis hyemalis, see p.60
Galanthus nivalis 'Flore Pleno', see p.84
Galanthus plicatus
Leucojum aestivum

Cyclamen coum
HARDY CYCLAMEN
☼ ☀ ❄❄❄ ↕ 10cm (4in)

A charming and reliable winter-flowering bulb, this has pads of small, plain green or silver-zoned, kidney-shaped leaves. These are topped by bright carmine flowers. ♈

Hyacinthoides hispanica
SPANISH BLUEBELL
☼ ☀ ❄❄❄❄ ↕ 30cm (12in)

This bold, clump-forming perennial has upright, fleshy stems and shining green leaves. Loose spikes of drooping white, blue, or pink bell-flowers appear in spring.

Trillium sessile
TOADSHADE
☼ ☀ ❄❄❄❄ ↕ 35cm (14in)

Red-brown spring flowers nestle above the leaves, which have white, pale green, or bronze markings. In time, this plant forms handsome clumps. Prefers rich soils.

Perennials for Dry Shade

THE DRY SHADE BENEATH TREES is regarded as one of the most difficult soil situations in which to grow plants. In summer, dense leaf canopies and root systems conspire to keep available moisture to a minimum. If possible, it is worth trying to improve conditions by reducing overhead shade, regularly applying ample organic mulch, and irrigating. But if all else fails, the following perennials, which mainly grow wild in woodlands, are more tolerant of dry shade than most.

Epimedium x *perralchicum*
BISHOP'S HAT
☼ ☀ ✳✳✳   ‡ 45cm (18in) ↔ 45cm (18in)

Mounds of wiry-stemmed, deeply divided leaves, with bold, glossy green leaflets, are evergreen. The spires of short-spurred yellow flowers emerge in spring.   ♈

Geranium macrorrhizum
BALKAN CRANESBILL
☼ ☀ ✳✳✳   ‡ 35cm (14in) ↔ 60cm (24in)

In most soils and situations, this carpeting semi-evergreen makes excellent ground cover. Magenta flower sprays top fragrant, deeply cut leaves in early summer.

Convallaria majalis
LILY OF THE VALLEY
☼ ☀ ✳✳✳   ‡ 15cm (6in) ↔ indefinite

This old favourite spreads by underground stems to form patches of erect shoots with attractive foliage and sprays of nodding, fragrant white bell-flowers in spring.   ♈

OTHER HERBACEOUS PERENNIALS FOR DRY SHADE

Anemone nemorosa 'Allenii'
Dicentra 'Langtrees', see p.72
Dicentra 'Luxuriant'
Geranium macrorrhizum 'Album'
Geranium x *monacense* 'Muldoon'
Geranium phaeum
Petasites fragrans
Polygonatum multiflorum
Symphytum 'Hidcote Pink'
Trachystemon orientalis

Dicentra formosa
WILD BLEEDING HEART
☼ ☀ ✳✳✳   ‡ 45cm (18in) ↔ 30cm (12in)

This clump-forming perennial has fern-like grey-green leaves and arching sprays of nodding pink or reddish, locket-shaped flowers in spring or early summer.

Geranium nodosum
CRANESBILL
☼ ☀ ✳✳✳   ‡ 45cm (18in) ↔ 45cm (18in)

Excellent in shade, this clump-former gives continuous supplies of delicate lilac-mauve flowers in spring and all through summer. Long-stalked, three-lobed leaves.

Iris foetidissima
GLADWIN, ROAST-BEEF PLANT
☼ ☀ ❋❋❋   ↕ 60cm (24in) ↔ 1m (3ft)

A clump of long, pointed evergreen leaves forms a backdrop to yellow-tinged, dull purple flowers in summer, and brilliant orange seed clusters throughout winter.

OTHER EVERGREEN PERENNIALS FOR DRY SHADE

Asplenium scolopendrium, see p.44
Epimedium perralderianum
Epimedium pinnatum subsp. *colchicum*
Epimedium pubigerum
Galax urceolata
Geranium endressii
Helleborus foetidus, see p.66
Polystichum munitum, see p.45
Reineckiea carnea
Speirantha convallarioides

Liriope muscari
LIRIOPE
☼ ☀ ❋❋❋   ↕ 30cm (12in) ↔ 45cm (18in)

Dense evergreen clumps of deep green, strap-shaped leaves are joined in autumn by narrow spikes, crowded with tiny, purplish blue, bell-shaped flowers. ♈

Pachyphragma macrophyllum
PACHYPHRAGMA
☼ ☀ ❋❋❋   ↕ 30cm (12in) ↔ indefinite

In spring, heads of white, four-petalled flowers rise above mats or carpets of heart-shaped, glossy green leaves, held on long stalks. Makes excellent ground cover.

Lunaria rediviva
PERENNIAL HONESTY
☼ ☀ ❋❋❋   ↕ 75cm (30in) ↔ 75cm (30in)

Clouds of white or lilac spring flowers are followed by flattened silvery seed pods, pointed at both ends. Clumps of much-branched stems bear toothed, oval leaves.

Tellima grandiflora
FRINGE CUPS
☼ ☀ ❋❋❋   ↕ 60cm (24in) ↔ 60cm (24in)

Erect stems support spires of whiskery mouthed, bell-shaped cream flowers in spring, above a basal mound of evergreen, purple-tinted, hairy, heart-shaped leaves.

Lamium maculatum
SPOTTED DEADNETTLE
☼ ☀ ☀ ❋❋❋   ↕ 15cm (6in) ↔ indefinite

This vigorous semi-evergreen perennial forms dense carpets of heart-shaped green leaves with a white central stripe. Clusters of hooded spring flowers are mauve-pink.

Meconopsis cambrica
WELSH POPPY
☼ ☀ ❋❋❋   ↕ 45cm (18in) ↔ 30cm (12in)

Single orange or yellow poppy flowers are held on slender stems in spring. Its foliage is light green and fern-like. Forms with double flowers are also available.

Viola labradorica 'Purpurea'
VIOLET
☼ ☀ ❋❋❋   ↕ 7.5cm (3in) ↔ 15cm (6in)

In time this reliable little perennial forms tuffets and patches of kidney-shaped, purplish green leaves. Small purple flowers continue from spring all through summer.

Perennials for Cool, Moist Soils in Shade

NUMEROUS BEAUTIFUL PERENNIALS, many native to woodland, are suitable for gardens in full or partial shade. Such plants prefer a cool, reasonably moist, if well-drained, soil, particularly during the growing season (spring to early summer). If necessary, construct a raised bed filled with soil of a high organic content. Few, if any, thrive in heavy, dry shade.

Helleborus orientalis
LENTEN ROSE
☼ ☀ ❊❊❊ ↕ 45cm (18in) ↔ 45cm (18in)

This is one of the most popular garden perennials, with its evergreen leaves and nodding winter or early spring flowers. Several colour selections are available. ♈

Arisarum proboscideum
MOUSE-TAIL PLANT
☼ ☀ ❊❊❊ ↕ 10cm (4in) ↔ 30cm (12in)

An amusing little tuberous-rooted plant, forming patches of arrow-shaped leaves in time. Beneath these, curious, long-tailed, hooded flowers hide in spring.

Jeffersonia dubia
JEFFERSONIA
☼ ☀ ❊❊❊ ↕ 15cm (6in) ↔ 23cm (9in)

Jeffersonia is a choice perennial producing tufts of kidney-shaped, boldly toothed blue-green leaves and saucer-shaped, long-stalked, poppy-like flowers in spring.

Arisaema sikokianum
ARISAEMA
☼ ☀ ❊❊ ↕ 50cm (20in) ↔ 30cm (12in)

The long-stalked leaves of this striking, tuberous-rooted perennial each have three beautifully marked leaflets. Single early-summer flowers have white interiors.

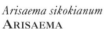

OTHER PERENNIALS FOR COOL, MOIST SHADE

Arisaema erubescens
Arisaema thungbergii
Arisaema triphyllum
Eomecon chionantha
Epimedium acuminatum
Epimedium davidii
Glaucidium palmatum
Glaucidium palmatum
  var. *leucanthum*
Haquetia epipactis
Helleborus viridis
Jeffersonia diphylla
Meconopsis chelidoniifolia
Sanguinaria canadensis
Sanguinaria canadensis 'Plena'
Trientalis borealis
Trillium ovatum
Trillium sessile, see p.41

Asplenium scolopendrium
HART'S-TONGUE FERN
☼ ☀ ❊❊❊ ↕ 75cm (30in) ↔ 60cm (24in)

This distinguished, resilient fern forms bold evergreen clumps of broad, strap-shaped fronds, banded beneath with spores. It will also grow in shady walls. ♈

Mertensia virginica
VIRGINIAN COWSLIP
☼ ☀ ❊❊❊ ↕ 50cm (20in) ↔ 30cm (12in)

A charming perennial, this has a delicate appearance; blue-green stems and leaves, and nodding clusters of tubular flowers that emerge in spring. Beware of slugs. ♈

Ourisia macrophylla
OURISIA
☼ ☀ ❄❄❄ ↕60cm (24in) ↔20cm (8in)

A vigorous perennial, this forms mats of
evergreen, heart-shaped leaves in time,
above which spring flowerheads rise.
Thrives in rich, especially moist, soils. ♈

Polystichum munitum
CHRISTMAS FERN, SWORD FERN
☼ ☀ ❄❄❄ ↕90cm (36in) ↔90cm (36in)

In time, this handsome evergreen fern
forms bold clumps of shining, ladder-like
fronds. Good alone, or planted in groups,
especially with other woodland plants. ♈

OTHER FERNS FOR MOIST SHADE

Adiantum pedatum, see p.34
Adiantum pedatum var. *aleuticum*
Arachniodes standishii
Asplenium scolopendrium 'Crispum'
Blechnum tabulare, see p.66
Cyrtomium japonicum
Dryopteris erythrosora
Hypolepsis millfolium
Polystichum acrostichoides
Polystichum setiferum 'Divisilobum',
  see p.67
Woodwardia orientalis
Woodwardia radicans

Trillium grandiflorum
WAKE-ROBIN
☼ ☀ ❄❄❄ ↕38cm (15in) ↔38cm (15in)

Few woodland perennials are more eye-
catching than this, when the large white
flowers are held above its leaves in spring.
It slowly forms substantial clumps. ♈

Scopolia carniolica
SCOPOLIA
☼ ☀ ❄❄❄ ↕50cm (20in) ↔50cm (20in)

This uncommon, clump-forming perennial
has rich green, boldly toothed leaves and
nodding bell-flowers in spring. These are
purplish brown with yellow interiors.

Tricyrtis formosana
TOAD LILY
☼ ☀ ❄❄❄ ↕75cm (30in) ↔45cm (18in)

Clumps of erect, fleshy stems, rising from
a creeping rootstock, carry boldly veined
leaves and loose heads of curious, purple-
spotted flowers in early autumn. ♈

Uvularia grandiflora
BELL-WORT, MERRY BELLS
☼ ☀ ❄❄❄ ↕60cm (24in) ↔30cm (12in)

A charming member of the lily family,
this forms clumps of erect, slender, leafy
stems with drooping clusters of long,
bell-shaped yellow flowers in spring. ♈

Perennials for Bog Gardens

SOILS THAT ARE permanently wet or squelchy have some gardeners scratching their heads as to what plants, if any, will grow in these seemingly inhospitable conditions. The bog garden is often the best, most challenging solution. Numerous interesting and ornamental perennials will not only survive, but actually thrive there. Usually associated with pond or stream-sides, bog gardens can also be planted around a natural spring, or some artificial source of water. Whatever their size, these sites can support an exciting range of perennials, which should be selected as much for their varied effect as for their tolerance of wet conditions.

Astilbe 'Bressingham Beauty'
ASTILBE
☼ ✻✻✻   ↕ 1.1m (3½ft) ↔ 1.1m (3½ft)

The bold clumps of leaves are attractive, especially in spring, but the erect plumes of tiny flowers in summer are spectacular. Dried seed heads are a bonus in winter.

Filipendula purpurea
FILIPENDULA
☼ ✻✻✻   ↕ 1.2m (4ft) ↔ 75cm (30in)

Handsome in both foliage and flower, this has big, bold clumps of large, deeply lobed leaves above which heads of little, rosy crimson flowers rise in summer.   ♔

Euphorbia palustris
EUPHORBIA
☼ ☼ ✻✻✻   ↕ 1m (3ft) ↔ 1m (3ft)

A reliable and attractive perennial with upright, leafy stems, and branched heads of green and yellow spring flowers. The leaves often colour richly in autumn.   ♔

Gentiana asclepiadea
WILLOW GENTIAN
☼ ✻✻✻   ↕ 75cm (30in) ↔ 60cm (24in)

Lush clumps of slender, leafy stems arch gracefully under the weight of numerous blue trumpet flowers in late summer and early autumn. A white form exists.   ♔

Hosta 'Frances Williams'
PLANTAIN LILY
☼ ✻✻✻   ↕ 75cm (30in) ↔ 75cm (30in)

A cultivar of the popular *H. sieboldiana*. Bold mounds of heart-shaped, bluish grey leaves have yellow margins that darken with age. It bears flowers in summer.   ♔

Mimulus luteus
BLOOD-DROP-EMLETS
☼ ✿✿✿   ↕ 30cm (12in) ↔ 30cm (12in)

Sometimes also known as Monkey Musk, and particularly suited to watersides, this low-spreading, fleshy plant produces many yellow flowers with red spots in summer.

Primula pulverulenta
CANDELABRA PRIMULA
☼ ✿✿✿   ↕ 75cm (30in) ↔ 40cm (16in)

This striking candelabra primula forms lush, leafy clumps above which rise erect stems. In early summer these support tubular, dark-eyed crimson flowers. ♔

Ligularia przewalskii
LIGULARIA
☼ ☼ ✿✿✿   ↕ 1.5m (5ft) ↔ 1.1m (3½ft)

A striking perennial with long-stalked, large, jaggedly cut leaves above which slender-stemmed spires of yellow flower-heads rise in mid- to late summer. ♔

Peltiphyllum peltatum
UMBRELLA PLANT
☼ ☼ ✿✿✿   ↕ 1.1m (3½ft) ↔ 75cm (30in)

The creeping rhizomes of this distinctive plant send up hairy stems topped with spring flowerheads. The umbrella leaves that follow colour richly in autumn. ♔

Rodgersia podophylla
RODGERSIA
☼ ☼ ✿✿✿   ↕ 1.1m (3½ft) ↔ 1m (3ft)

A bold, clump-forming perennial this is worth growing for its striking leaves, which colour richly in autumn. Creamy white flowerheads are a bonus in summer. ♔

OTHER PERENNIALS FOR BOG GARDENS

Astilboides tabularis
Gunnera manicata, see p.19
Hosta sieboldiana 'Elegans', see p.65
Iris ensata
Iris sibirica
Ligularia dentata 'Othello'
Lobelia siphilitica
Lysichiton americanum
Lysimachia clethroides, see p.91
Lythrum salicaria 'The Beacon'
Osmunda regalis
Persicaria amplexicaulis 'Firetail'
Persicaria campanulata
Primula florindae
Rheum palmatum 'Atrosanguineum', see p.19
Symphytum x uplandicum 'Variegatum', see p.69

Persicaria bistorta 'Superba'
BISTORT
☼ ✿✿✿   ↕ 70cm (28in) ↔ 60cm (24in)

This excellent bistort forms dense clumps of large pointed leaves above which, in early summer, rise slender stems bearing conical pokers of soft pink flowers. ♔

Trollius x cultorum 'Alabaster'
GLOBEFLOWER
☼ ☼ ✿✿✿   ↕ 45cm (18in) ↔ 45cm (18in)

Beautiful and unusual, this globeflower has long-stalked, deeply divided and dissected leaves. Its branching heads of creamy yellow flowers appear in spring.

Perennials Tolerant of Air Pollution

IN MANY AREAS, particularly in towns, cities, and near to industrial estates, atmospheric pollution is still a problem. Over the years, however, gardeners have come to rely upon the surprisingly large number of perennials that have proved tolerant of such conditions. Fortunately, they include some of our most popular, colourful, and reliable plants.

Anaphalis margaritacea var. *yedoensis*
PEARLY EVERLASTING
☼ ✱✱✱ ↕75cm (30in) ↔60cm (24in)

Clumps of erect stems and narrow leaves are covered in a grey, woolly down. Small white flowerheads appear in late summer, and retain their colour when dried. ♔

OTHER PERENNIALS TOLERANT
OF AIR POLLUTION

Achillea 'Coronation Gold'
Achillea ptarmica 'The Pearl'
Ajuga reptans 'Catlin's Giant'
Anaphalis triplinervis
Aster novae-angliae 'Alma Pötschke',
    see p.32
Astrantia major subsp. *involucrata*
    'Shaggy'
Bergenia x *schmidtii*
Dicentra eximea 'Spring Morning'
Echinops ritro 'Veitch's Blue', see p.39
Geranium macrorrhizum, see p.42
Lamium maculatum 'Album'
Leucanthemum x *superbum*
    'Esther Read'
Persicaria bistorta 'Superba', see p.47
Potentilla 'Gibson's Scarlet'
Rudbeckia fulgida 'Goldsturm', see p.33

Aster x *frikartii* 'Mönch'
ASTER
☼ ✱✱✱ ↕1m (3ft) ↔45cm (18in)

This is a strong-growing perennial, which may require support. Its striking daisy-flowers are produced over many weeks, from midsummer well into autumn. ♔

Astrantia major 'Hadspen Blood'
MASTERWORT
☼ ◐ ✱✱✱ ↕45cm (18in) ↔60cm (24in)

Loosely branched heads of dark ruby-red flowers rise above eye-catching clumps of attractive, rich green, toothed, and deeply lobed leaves in summer. ♔

Centaurea montana
PERENNIAL CORNFLOWER
☼ ✱✱✱ ↕50cm (20in) ↔60cm (24in)

This long-standing garden favourite forms leafy clumps and produces large heads of blue flowers in early summer. Other forms have purple, pink, or white flowers. ♔

Geranium himalayense
CRANESBILL
☼ ✱✱✱ ↕30cm (12in) ↔60cm (24in)

Easy and reliable, this clump-forming perennial has deeply cut leaves and cup-shaped lilac-blue flowers in summer. Its foliage often colours richly in autumn. ♔

Geum 'Borisii'
GEUM
☼ ✱✱✱ ↕30cm (12in) ↔30cm (12in)

Above hummocks of lush green leaves, loosely branched heads of single, rich orange flowers open in early summer. This geum is an excellent ground cover.

Liatris spicata
KANSAS GAY-FEATHER
☼ ✳✳✳   ↕ 60cm (24in) ↔ 30cm (12in)

Kansas Gay-feather forms dense tufts of grassy foliage from which the stiff stems, holding poker-like spikes of fuzzy rose-purple flowers, rise in late summer.

Malva moschata
MUSK MALLOW
☼ ✳✳✳   ↕ 1m (3ft) ↔ 60cm (24in)

The finely divided leaves of this bushy perennial are aromatic. Spikes of saucer-shaped, pale pink flowers occur in early summer. 'Alba' is a lovely white form.

Veronica spicata 'Romiley Purple'
VERONICA
☼ ✳✳✳   ↕ 1.2m (4ft) ↔ 60cm (24in)

Erect stems, supporting whorls of narrow leaves, form fine clumps. The slender, tapering spikes of tiny purple flowers are carried in summer. May require support.

Lupinus 'The Chatelaine'
RUSSELL LUPIN
☼ ✳✳✳   ↕ 1.2m (4ft) ↔ 45cm (18in)

Prominent clumps of many-fingered, long-stalked leaves are topped by tapering spikes crowded with pink and white pea-flowers in early summer. Prone to slugs. ♈

Lychnis chalcedonica
MALTESE CROSS
☼ ✳✳✳   ↕ 1.2m (4ft) ↔ 45cm (18in)

Few perennials have flowers that are a richer colour than this clump-forming campion. Dense, flattened vermilion-red flowerheads appear in early summer. ♈

Solidago 'Laurin'
GOLDEN ROD
☼ ✳✳✳   ↕ 75cm (30in) ↔ 45cm (18in)

A miniature version of the old-fashioned Golden Rod, this has sturdy, densely leafy stems, crowned by branched heads of deep yellow flowers in late summer.

JAPANESE ANEMONES TOLERANT OF AIR POLLUTION

Anemone x *hybrida* 'Bressingham Glow'
Anemone x *hybrida* 'Honorine Jobert', see p.52
Anemone x *hybrida* 'Whirlwind'

Perennials Tolerant of Coastal Exposure

FEW CONDITIONS ARE TOUGHER for plants than those found in coastal gardens, where strong winds batter them and, even in sheltered sites, salt spray may burn them. Generally, perennials are more vulnerable in spring, when new growth emerges. Fortunately, many perennials are tolerant of these conditions, some growing near the sea in their wild state.

Artemisia arborescens
ARTEMISIA
☼ ✳✳   ↕ 1m (3ft) ↔ 1m (3ft)

Well-known for its silver-grey filigree foliage, this evergreen carries clusters of small yellowish flowers from summer into early autumn. Prune hard to keep it tidy.

Centranthus ruber
RED VALERIAN
☼ ✳✳✳   ↕ 75cm (30in) ↔ 75cm (30in)

This long-flowering perennial is ideal for seaside gardens. Bushy, with fleshy grey-green leaves, it has crowded red, white, or pink flowerheads from spring to autumn.

Anthemis punctata subsp. *cupaniana*
ANTHEMIS
☼ ☼ ✳✳✳   ↕ 30cm (12in) ↔ 60cm (24in)

A reliable, adaptable plant that produces masses of long-stalked daisy-flowers in early summer, above mounds of silver-grey foliage, that becomes green in winter. ♔

Agapanthus praecox subsp. *orientalis*
AFRICAN LILY
☼ ✳   ↕ 1m (3ft) ↔ 60cm (24in)

Bold clumps of semi-evergreen, strap-shaped leaves are topped in late summer by strong-stemmed umbels of sky-blue flowers. Plant in a container in cold areas.

OTHER PERENNIALS TOLERANT
OF COASTAL EXPOSURE

Agapanthus Headbourne Hybrids
Allium christophii, see p.40
Catananche coerulea 'Major'
Centaurea cineraria 'White Diamond'
Centaurea gymnocarpa
Eryngium tripartitum
Fascicularia pitcairniifolia
Kniphofia caulescens
Oenothera odorata
Phormium cookianum

Erigeron glaucus
SEASIDE ASTER
☼ ✳✳✳   ↕ 25cm (10in) ↔ 1m (3ft)

One of the most satisfactory perennials for coastal areas, this forms dense mats of grey-green evergreen leaves, and is covered throughout summer with large daisies.

Osteospermum jucundum
AFRICAN DAISY
☼ ❄❄   ↕ 30cm (12in) ↔ 30cm (12in)

Masses of large, soft pink daisy-flowers, with dark eyes, rise on long stalks above neat, low mounds of evergreen foliage in late summer. An excellent carpeter. ♈

CARPETING PERENNIALS TOLERANT OF COASTAL EXPOSURE

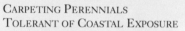

Armeria maritima 'Düsseldorfer Stolz'
Carpobrotus edulis
Erigeron glaucus 'Elstead Pink'
Eriogonum umbellatum

Kniphofia 'Royal Standard'
RED-HOT POKER
☼ ❄❄❄   ↕ 1.2m (4ft) ↔ 60cm (24in)

Clumps of narrow leaves are dominated in late summer by stout-stemmed pokers of lemon-yellow flowers, scarlet in bud. In cold areas, protect the crowns in winter. ♈

Othonna cheirifolia
OTHONNA
☼ ❄❄   ↕ 25cm (10in) ↔ 30cm (12in)

This mat-forming evergreen does best in a warm, sheltered pocket. Solitary, long-stalked daisy-flowers appear amid grey-green, paddle-shaped leaves in summer. ♈

Eryngium x *oliverianum*
ERYNGIUM
☼ ❄❄❄   ↕ 1m (3ft) ↔ 50cm (20in)

In late summer, blue-tinted stems carry dome-shaped lavender-blue flowers that nestle in prickly ruffs. These rise from a basal rosette of heart-shaped leaves. ♈

Lathyrus latifolius
PERENNIAL PEA
☼ ❄❄❄   ↕ 2m (6ft) ↔ 2m (6ft)

A strong-growing perennial, this scrambles by means of leaf tendrils. From summer to autumn it produces long-stalked spikes of small pea-flowers. Needs support.

Physostegia virginiana 'Vivid'
OBEDIENT PLANT
☼ ❄❄❄   ↕ 60cm (24in) ↔ 45cm (18in)

This is a distinguished and reliable clump-forming perennial, with erect stems that carry crowded spikes of tubular flowers in late summer and early autumn. ♈

Perennials for Growing in Hedge Bottoms

H OW OFTEN DO YOU SEE GARDENS with borders and beds filled with perennials, but the hedge bottoms choked with grass? It is a common situation, yet it can very easily be avoided. Many ornamental perennials are sufficiently robust to compete with grass and roots, giving the hedge a colourful, interesting, and attractive fringe.

Chelidonium majus 'Flore Pleno'
GREATER CELANDINE
☼ ☀ ✻✻✻   ↕ 60cm (24in) ↔ 30cm (12in)

Clumps of much-divided, pale green leaves nestle below the branched heads of small, double, bright yellow flowers from spring into summer. Will self-seed.

Anemone x *hybrida* 'Honorine Jobert'
JAPANESE ANEMONE
☼ ☀ ✻✻✻   ↕ 1.5m (5ft) ↔ 60cm (24in)

From late summer into autumn, numerous yellow-eyed, white flowers are held on branching stems. This vigorous perennial will form patches in time. ♔

Campanula latifolia 'Brantwood'
GIANT BELLFLOWER
☼ ☀ ✻✻✻   ↕ 1.2m (4ft) ↔ 60cm (24in)

A handsome and stately plant, this bold clump-former has upright, leafy stems that terminate in spikes of large, nodding violet-purple bell-flowers in summer.

Crocosmia 'Bressingham Blaze'
MONTBRETIA
☼ ✻✻✻   ↕ 75cm (30in) ↔ 30cm (12in)

In late summer, arching sprays of red flowers complement clumps of handsome, sword-shaped leaves. Montbretia grows from corms, which are easily detached.

Aquilegia vulgaris
GRANNY'S BONNET, COLUMBINE
☼ ☀ ✻✻✻   ↕ 1m (3ft) ↔ 50cm (20in)

This old-fashioned favourite forms clumps of attractive blue-green leaves. Branched stems carry showers of nodding flowers in early summer, in a variety of colours.

Campanula poscharskyana
BELLFLOWER
☼ ☀ ✻✻✻   ↕ 13cm (5in) ↔ indefinite

One of the most rampant of its kind, the leafy stems soon spread to fill any existing gaps. Attractive, star-shaped violet-blue flowers crowd these stems in summer.

OTHER PERENNIALS FOR GROWING IN HEDGE BOTTOMS

Anemone x *hybrida* 'Bressingham Glow'
Anemone x *hybrida* 'Geant des Blanches'
Bidens ferulifolia, see p.62
Brunnera macrophylla
Campanula lactiflora 'Prichard's Variety', see p.16
Campanula latifolia 'Gloaming'
Campanula latifolia var. *macrantha alba*
Campanula rapunculoides
Campanula trachelium var. *alba*
Chaerophyllum hirsutum 'Roseum'
Cicerbita plumieri
Senecio tanguticus
Symphytum orientale
Symphytum x *uplandicum*
Tanacetum vulgare
Vinca major subsp. *hirsuta*

Myrrhis odorata
SWEET CICELY, WILD ANISEED
☼ ☼ ❄❄❄ ↕ 1m (3ft) ↔ 60cm (24in)

Erect stems bear flattened heads of tiny white flowers in early summer, above mounds of finely divided, fern-like leaves. All parts smell of aniseed when bruised.

Dryopteris affinis
GOLDEN MALE FERN
☼ ☼ ☼ ❄❄❄ ↕ 1.2m (4ft) ↔ 1m (3ft)

The bright green, deeply divided semi-evergreen fronds of this distinguished fern grow on upright, golden, scaly stalks, and together they form a large shuttlecock. ▽

Euphorbia amygdaloides subsp. *robbiae*
MRS ROBB'S BONNET
☼ ☼ ☼ ❄❄❄ ↕ 60cm (24in) ↔ indefinite

This tough evergreen eventually forms a carpet of upright stems with dark green leaves, and carries loose heads of yellow-green or lime-green flowers in spring. ▽

Pentaglottis sempervirens
GREEN ALKANET
☼ ☼ ❄❄❄ ↕ 1m (3ft) ↔ 60cm (24in)

In spring, dense sprays of small, deep blue forget-me-not flowers, held on branching stems, top clumps of large, roughly hairy leaves. A reliable, early-flowering plant.

OTHER FERNS FOR GROWING IN HEDGE BOTTOMS

Athyrium filix-femina
Dryopteris dilatata
Dryopteris filix-mas
Polystichum setiferum

Lysimachia punctata
SPOTTED LOOSESTRIFE
☼ ☼ ❄❄❄ ↕ 75cm (30in) ↔ 75cm (30in)

The upper leaf axils of this easy, reliable perennial are crowded with yellow flowers in summer. It forms dense clumps of erect, leafy stems, and is best in moist soils.

Symphytum caucasicum
CAUCASIAN COMFREY
☼ ☼ ❄❄❄ ↕ 60cm (24in) ↔ 60cm (24in)

Bristly, branching stems bear loose clusters of nodding, funnel-shaped blue flowers in the spring, amid its bold clumps of large, pointed, roughly hairy leaves.

Perennials for Wall Crevices and Between Paving

MANY PERENNIALS THAT ENJOY good drainage grow in rock crevices in the wild, and find retaining walls and paved areas a home-from-home. Sunny walls soak up the sun's heat, which encourages flowering, and trailing plants in bloom are splendid tumbling down a wall. Some plants prefer the cool, slightly moist conditions usually provided by sunless walls.

Campanula cochleariifolia
FAIRY'S THIMBLES
☼ ❉❉❉   ↕ 8cm (3in) ↔ indefinite

This delightful creeping perennial forms low carpets of small, rounded leaves. Numerous charming little bell-flowers appear above the foliage in summer. ♔

Arabis caucasica 'Rosabella'
ARABIS
☼ ❉❉❉   ↕ 15cm (6in) ↔ 30cm (12in)

One of the most reliable perennials suited to walls, this forms evergreen mats of soft foliage, above which sprays of pink flowers open in spring and early summer.

Aubrieta 'Joy'
AUBRIETA
☼ ❉❉❉   ↕ 10cm (4in) ↔ 30cm (12in)

Aubrietas are among the most reliable and popular of all rock and wall plants. This cultivar is covered by pale mauve flowers in spring, above evergreen hummocks.

OTHER PERENNIALS FOR WALL CREVICES AND BETWEEN PAVING

Androsace sarmentosa
Asarina procumbens, see p.28
Ceterach officinarum
Erigeron karvinskianus
Phlox 'Emerald Cushion'
Saxifraga 'Southside Seedling'
Sedum spathulifolium 'Cape Blanco', see p.73
Sempervivum tectorum
Verbascum dumulosum

Arenaria balearica
SANDWORT
☼ ☀ ❉❉❉   ↕ 1cm (½in) ↔ indefinite

This creeping perennial makes a charming carpeter for a damp, cool place. Little flowers pepper an evergreen film of tiny leaves in late spring and early summer.

Aurinia saxatilis
GOLD DUST
☼ ❉❉❉   ↕ 23cm (9in) ↔ 30cm (12in)

Along with *Arabis* and *Aubrieta*, this genus dominates the wall plant world. Mats of evergreen grey-green leaves are hidden in spring by clouds of rich yellow flowers. ♔

Chiastophyllum oppositifolium
CHIASTOPHYLLUM
☼ ☀ ❉❉❉   ↕ 20cm (8in) ↔ 15cm (6in)

Hummocks of fleshy evergreen leaves are topped in late spring and early summer by drooping yellow flower sprays, making this plant resemble a tiny weeping willow.

Lewisia 'George Henley'
LEWISIA
☼ ❈❈❈❈ ^{PH}   ↕ 15cm (6in) ↔ 10cm (4in)

Loose sprays of dark-veined, deep pink
flowers appear from late spring and all
through summer above rosettes of narrow,
fleshy leaves. Best when grown in a wall.

Corydalis ochroleuca
CORYDALIS
☼ ☼ ❈❈❈❈   ↕ 25cm (10in) ↔ 25cm (10in)

The fleshy stems of this reliable crevice
plant carry clusters of tubular flowers
in late spring and early summer, amid
clumps of fern-like evergreen leaves.

Persicaria vacciniifolia
PERSICARIA
☼ ❈❈❈   ↕ 20cm (8in) ↔ indefinite

A free-growing, prostrate evergreen, this
forms dense carpets of small green leaves,
tinted red in autumn. Red-stalked flower
spikes rise in late summer and autumn. ♀

Dryas octopetala
MOUNTAIN AVENS
☼ ❈❈❈   ↕ 6cm (2½in) ↔ indefinite

Small, glossy green leaves form dense
evergreen carpets. White, anemone-like
flowers appear from late spring into early
summer. Pretty, silky seed heads follow. ♀

Erinus alpinus
FAIRY FOXGLOVE
☼ ❈❈❈   ↕ 8cm (3in) ↔ 8cm (3in)

This charming, short-lived perennial, best
in a wall, forms neat tuffets with delicate
purple, pink, or white flower spikes in late
spring and summer. It may self-seed.   ♀

Ramonda myconi
RAMONDA
☼ ◐ ❈❈❈   ↕ 8cm (3in) ↔ 10cm (4in)

Evergreen rosettes of strongly veined,
crinkly leaves provide a perfect foil for the
stalked flower clusters in late spring and
early summer. Best in a cool, moist wall. ♀

Perennials for Screes and Rock Gardens

Usually referred to as rock plants or alpines, a huge range of small or prostrate perennials are easily grown and best displayed in a rock garden. They generally need full sun and good drainage, although there are some exceptions. You can also grow them in scree beds, specially prepared with a good draining medium topped by a layer of gravel or chippings.

Gentiana verna
SPRING GENTIAN
☼ ✽✽✽   ↕ 5cm (2in) ↔ 5cm (2in)

A beautiful, but often short-lived, gentian with tuffets of evergreen leaves. Erect, long-tubed flowers of an intense blue, with a white throat, appear in early spring. ♛

Aethionema grandiflorum
PERSIAN STONE CRESS
☼ ✽✽✽   ↕ 30cm (12in) ↔ 25cm (10in)

This shrubby semi-evergreen perennial, with tiny, narrow blue-green leaves, has loose flower clusters in late spring and early summer. Needs good drainage. ♛

Artemisia schmidtiana 'Nana'
ARTEMISIA
☼ ✽✽   ↕ 8cm (3in) ↔ 20cm (8in)

A lovely little hummock with silvery grey, aromatic, filigree-like foliage that shines in the sun. Flowers are few and insignificant. Thrives in a well-drained situation. ♛

Geranium cinereum var. *subcaulescens*
CRANESBILL
☼ ✽✽✽   ↕ 13cm (5in) ↔ 30cm (12in)

This popular cranesbill forms low mats of small, rounded, deeply divided leaves, and loosely branched heads of saucer-shaped magenta flowers, each with a black eye. ♛

Arenaria purpurascens
SANDWORT
☼ ✽✽✽   ↕ 1cm (½in) ↔ 15cm (6in)

This mat-forming perennial, with dense evergreen rosettes of tiny, sharply pointed leaves, is covered in early spring with small clusters of pink, star-shaped flowers.

Dianthus 'La Bourboule'
ALPINE PINK
☼ ✽✽✽   ↕ 5cm (2in) ↔ 8cm (3in)

This alpine pink has low carpets of narrow evergreen leaves and abundant, small pink flowers, with good fragrance, in summer. Ideal in a well-drained, alkaline soil. ♛

Leontopodium alpinum
EDELWEISS
☼ ✽✽✽   ↕ 18cm (7in) ↔ 18cm (7in)

An ever-popular alpine, this edelweiss is short lived, but very reliable. It has silvery white, furry flowerheads in spring or early summer. Good drainage is essential. ♛

Origanum 'Kent Beauty'
ORIGANUM

☼ ❄❄ ↕ 20cm (8in) ↔ 30cm (12in)

Low mats of slender stems, clothed with smooth, aromatic leaves, terminate in hop-like clusters of pale pink flowers from rose-tinted green bracts, in late summer.

Phlox douglasii 'Boothman's Variety'
ALPINE PHLOX

☼ ❄❄❄ ↕ 5cm (2in) ↔ 20cm (8in)

Neat mats of narrow evergreen leaves are covered in early summer by lovely, pale lavender-blue flowers with a violet-blue eye. This is a reliable beginner's plant. ♔

Rhodohypoxis baurii 'Margaret Rose'
RHODOHYPOXIS

☼ ☼ ❄❄ ↕ 8cm (3in) ↔ 6cm (2½in)

The delicate pink flowers of this tuberous perennial, with narrow, hairy leaves, occur from spring into early summer. Prefers a gritty soil, and to be kept dry in winter. ♔

Tropaeolum polyphyllum
TROPAEOLUM

☼ ❄❄❄ ↕ 8cm (3in) ↔ 75cm (30in)

Both the fingered leaves and fleshy stems of this sprawling perennial are a smooth blue-green colour. Small yellow flowers crowd the ends of the stems in summer.

Veronica prostrata 'Kapitan'
VERONICA

☼ ❄❄❄ ↕ 30cm (12in) ↔ 45cm (18in)

This reliable plant forms dense clumps of slender stems, clothed in narrow, toothed leaves and carrying a profusion of rich blue flower spikes in early summer.

OTHER PERENNIALS FOR SCREES AND ROCK GARDENS

Androsace carnea subsp. *laggeri*
Campanula 'G.F. Wilson'
Corydalis solida 'George Baker'
Erodium reichardii
Geranium cinereum 'Ballerina'
Gypsophila cerastioides
Nierembergia repens
Oxalis adenophylla, see p.37
Phlox bifida
Saponaria x *olivana*
Saxifraga x *apiculata*
Tanacetum argenteum, see p.73

Viola tricolor 'Bowles' Black'
VIOLET

☼ ❄❄❄ ↕ 10cm (4in) ↔ 6cm (2½in)

A short-lived, tufted perennial with loose, leafy stems, and exquisite, small blackish violet flowers, each with a gold eye. These occur from spring through to autumn.

Bulbs for Rock Gardens, Raised Beds, and Screes

SOME OF THE MOST satisfying bulbous plants are the dwarf kinds ideal for rock gardens or raised beds, where they can be admired without being crowded by any more robust neighbours. Many hail from mountainous or dry places, so need good light and sharp drainage. They like moisture during the growing season, usually in spring or summer.

Colchicum agrippinum
AUTUMN CROCUS
☼ ✿✿✿   ↕ 12cm (5in)

Funnel-shaped flowers, chequered dark purple on a paler background, appear in early autumn. The wavy, shining green leaves develop the following spring. ♈

Allium cyathophorum var. *farreri*
ORNAMENTAL ONION
☼ ✿✿✿   ↕ 22cm (9in)

Slender stems bearing nodding clusters of bell-shaped, reddish purple flowers rise through tufts of narrow leaves in summer. Thrives in moist but well-drained soils.

Anemone blanda 'Radar'
GREEK WINDFLOWER
☼ ☼ ✿✿✿   ↕ 7cm (3in)

This is a reliable tuberous perennial that produces lobed, fern-like leaves. In spring its vibrant magenta, multi-petalled flowers, with white centres, appear. ♈

Crocus biflorus
CROCUS
☼ ✿✿✿   ↕ 9cm (3½in)

This exquisite crocus produces tussocks of narrow leaves, each with a white stripe. In early spring, white or purple flowers, striped purple on the outside, emerge.

Allium oreophilum
ORNAMENTAL ONION
☼ ✿✿✿   ↕ 10cm (4in)

An easy and reliable bulb with a pair of long, thin leaves in winter. These usually wither by the time the flowers bloom from late spring into early summer. ♈

Chionodoxa luciliae
SNOW GLORY
☼ ☼ ✿✿✿   ↕ 10cm (4in)

A beautiful spring-flowering bulb, Snow Glory has strap-shaped leaves and a loose spray of brilliant blue, star-shaped flowers. It will spread by seed or by division. ♈

Iris reticulata 'J.S. Dijt'
MINIATURE IRIS
☼ ✿✿✿   ↕ 12cm (5in)

One of a group of charming miniature bulbous iris with long, upright grey-green leaves. Its single, fragrant, rich reddish purple flowers open in early spring. ♈

Muscari aucheri
GRAPE HYACINTH
☼ ✳✳✳   ↕ 10cm (4in)

Erect stems above strap-shaped leaves
support dense spikes of bright blue spring
flowers. The top of the spike is usually
paler, giving a distinct two-tone effect. ♛

**OTHER BULBS FOR ROCK GARDENS,
RAISED BEDS, AND SCREES**

Allium karataviense
Arum creticum
Crocus 'E.A. Bowles'
Fritillaria pallidiflora, see p.79
Iris histrioides 'Major'
Leucojum autumnale, see p.83
Muscari latifolium
Narcissus bulbocodium
Ornithogalum balansae
Sternbergia lutea

Puschkinia scilloides 'Alba'
PUSCHKINIA
☼ ✳✳✳   ↕ 20cm (8in)

A lovely white form of the normally blue-
flowered spring bulb, this produces pairs
of strap-shaped leaves and loose spikes of
star-shaped flowers. Dislikes dry soils.

Narcissus cyclamineus
MINIATURE DAFFODIL
☼ ✳✳✳   ↕ 15cm (6in)

This popular miniature daffodil has a
single golden yellow flower with upswept
petals, and a slender, crinkly mouthed
trumpet in late winter or early spring. ♛

Scilla siberica 'Atrocoerulea'
SCILLA
☼ ✳✳✳   ↕ 13cm (5in)

Tufts of strap-shaped, fleshy leaves are
topped in spring by the loose sprays of
rich blue, bell-shaped flowers. A popular
and easy plant that forms colonies in time.

Tulipa tarda
TULIP
☼ ✳✳✳   ↕ 15cm (6in)

One of the most popular and satisfactory
wild tulips, this is especially good in dry
soils. Star-shaped spring flowers occur,
several to a stem, above narrow leaves. ♛

Bulbs for Wild Areas

THE STIRRING SIGHT of bulbs flowering *en masse* in the wild can be re-created in your own garden by planting them in quantity where conditions are most suitable. The bulbs will naturalize to give an impressive display year after year, by seeding around or spreading vegetatively. Bulbs that come from woodland habitats will thrive in beds or borders beneath deciduous trees or shrubs; while those that are native grassland species enjoy orchards or marginal areas of grass.

Crocus tommasinianus
CROCUS
☼ ☼ ✳✳✳   ↕ 10cm (4in)

Excellent for naturalizing in short grass, these will spread quickly if unchecked. The pale lavender to purple flowers open in late winter and early spring. ♈

Anemone blanda 'Atrocaerulea'
WINDFLOWER
☼ ☼ ✳✳✳   ↕ 7cm (3in)

Deep blue, early spring flowers carpet the ground above prettily divided leaves. Particularly well suited to alkaline soils in woodland margins, or beneath shrubs. ♈

Cyclamen hederifolium
HARDY CYCLAMEN
☼ ☼ ☀ ✳✳✳   ↕ 10cm (4in)

A charming, reliable miniature cyclamen, ideal for woodland margins and shady areas that remain moist in summer. The flowers occur in abundance in autumn. ♈

OTHER BULBS FOR WILD AREAS IN LIGHT SHADE

Arum italicum 'Marmoratum'
Colchicum 'Lilac Wonder'
Colchicum 'The Giant'
Crocus kotschyanus
Cyclamen coum, see p.41
Cyclamen coum 'Album', see p.84
Cyclamen hederifolium 'Album', see p.83
Cyclamen repandum
Erythronium oregonum
Galanthus elwesii
Galanthus nivalis
Galanthus nivalis 'Flore Pleno', see p.84
Galanthus plicatus
Hyacinthoides hispanica, see p.41
Leucojum aestivum
Lilium pyrenaicum
Narcissus pseudonarcissus
Ornithogalum nutans, see p.41

Camassia leichtlinii 'Alba'
CAMASSIA
☼ ☼ ✳✳✳   ↕ 1.2m (4ft)

This striking, summer-flowering bulb has long, narrow leaves and upright spires of star-shaped flowers. It is most suitable for moist soils or damp grassland.

Eranthis hyemalis
WINTER ACONITE
☼ ✳✳✳   ↕ 8cm (3in)

These bright flowers with leafy collars are a heartening sight in late winter and early spring. Enjoys soils rich in leaf mould in woodland or short grass beneath trees. ♈

Fritillaria meleagris
SNAKE'S-HEAD FRITILLARY
☼ ❋❋❋   ↕ 30cm (12in)

Nodding, maroon- or white-chequered bells on slender stems in spring make this a favourite for naturalizing in damp grassland that remains moist in summer. ♔

Gladiolus communis subsp. *byzantinus*
GLADIOLUS
☼ ❋❋❋   ↕ 1m (3ft)

This early summer-flowering perennial soon spreads in warm, well-drained soils. It has spikes of funnel-shaped magenta flowers and sword-shaped leaves. ♔

Narcissus pseudonarcissus
subsp. *obvallaris*
☼ ☼ ❋❋❋   ↕ 22cm (9in)

This lovely form of the Lent Lily makes a very impressive spring show when planted in short grass or on woodland edges, in soils that are moist in spring. ♔

Nectaroscordum siculum
subsp. *bulgaricum*
☼ ☼ ❋❋❋   ↕ 1m (3ft)

Clusters of bell-shaped flowers in late spring and early summer give this reliable ornamental onion a stately appearance. It will spread freely in grass or borders.

Galanthus caucasicus
SNOWDROP
☼ ❋❋❋   ↕ 25cm (10in)

A striking snowdrop of robust growth, this has broad blue-green leaves, and nodding flowers in late winter and early spring. The inner flower segments have a green tip. ♔

OTHER BULBS FOR WILD
AREAS IN SUN

Chionodoxa luciliae, see p.58
Colchicum autumnale
Crocus 'Dutch Yellow'
Crocus tommasinianus 'Ruby Giant'
Crocus vernus
Lilium hansonii
Narcissus bulbocodium
Narcissus 'Peeping Tom'
Narcissus 'Spellbinder'
Tulipa kaufmanniana

Lilium martagon
MARTAGON LILY
☼ ❋❋❋   ↕ 1.5m (5ft)

This lily is excellent for naturalizing in woodland glades, beneath deciduous trees and shrubs, and in grass. The fragrant, nodding flowers appear in summer.

Tulipa sylvestris
TULIP
☼ ❋❋❋   ↕ 45cm (18in)

Probably the most commonly naturalized tulip species, this thrives in well-drained grassland, particularly in orchards and open woodland, where it flowers in spring.

Flowering Perennials for Containers

CONTAINERS PROVIDE the opportunity to cultivate a wide range of hardy perennials in hard-surfaced or small gardens; most flowering perennials will grow well in such conditions. In cold areas, pots and tubs also give the exciting opportunity of growing tender perennials, as you can move them under glass for protection during the winter.

Argyranthemum 'Mary Wooton'
MARGUERITE, OR PARIS, DAISY
☼ ❀   ↕ 1m (3ft) ↔ 1m (3ft)

All through summer, this bushy evergreen, with its attractive, finely divided, fern-like leaves, carries large pink daisy-flowers, with anemone centres, on slender stems.

Bidens ferulifolia
BIDENS
☼ ❀   ↕ 1m (3ft) ↔ 1.2m (4ft)

An abundance of golden yellow flowers covers this slender-stemmed, sometimes scrambling, perennial with finely cut leaves, from late summer into autumn. ♈

Chrysanthemum 'Pennine Flute'
SPRAY CHRYSANTHEMUM
☼ ❀❀❀   ↕ 1.2m (4ft) ↔ 75cm (30in)

This erect, much-branched perennial has aromatic foliage and, in early autumn, a profusion of large pink daisy-like flowers, each with a yellow centre. ♈

OTHER TENDER FLOWERING PERENNIALS FOR CONTAINERS

Agapanthus inapertus var. *pendulus*
Argyranthemum 'Chelsea Girl'
Eucomis bicolor
Hedychium gardnerianum
Osteospermum 'Pink Whirls'
Osteospermum 'Silver Sparkler'
Pelargonium 'Morwenna'

Begonia sutherlandii
TUBEROUS BEGONIA
☼ ☼ ❀❀❀   ↕ 45cm (18in) ↔ 45cm (18in)

One of the hardiest of all begonias, this is a tuberous-rooted species forming clumps of bright green, toothed leaves, and loose clusters of orange summer flowers. ♈

Canna 'Assaut'
INDIAN SHOT
☼ ❀   ↕ 1.2m (4ft) ↔ 60cm (24in)

A dense head of large scarlet flowers with purple bracts is supported by an erect stem with lush foliage. Different cultivars have flowers of other colours. Dislikes dry soils.

Lotus berthelotii
CORAL GEM
☼ ❀   ↕ 15cm (6in) ↔ 60cm (24in)

Summer clusters of scarlet pea-flowers are a bonus, as Coral Gem is worth growing for its semi-evergreen, trailing silver foliage alone. Effective in hanging baskets. ♈

Osteospermum 'Buttermilk'
AFRICAN DAISY
☼ ❄   ↕ 60cm (24in) ↔ 45cm (18in)

Large, pale yellow, daisy-like flowers with dark centres are supported on erect stems, above toothed evergreen leaves that are grey-green, from summer into autumn. ♈

Pelargonium 'Bredon'
REGAL PELARGONIUM
☼ ❄   ↕ 45cm (18in) ↔ 30cm (12in)

In summer, this robust evergreen sub-shrub or perennial carries clusters of large maroon flowers above its rich green, lobed and toothed, aromatic foliage. ♈

Strelitzia reginae
BIRD-OF-PARADISE FLOWER
☼ ❄   ↕ 1m (3ft) ↔ 75cm (30in)

Exquisite orange and blue spring flowers are reminiscent of the heads of exotic cranes. The blue-green evergreen leaves are erect and form bold clumps. ♈

HARDY FLOWERING PERENNIALS FOR CONTAINERS

Agapanthus Headbourne Hybrids
Bergenia 'Silberlicht'
Dicentra spectabilis f. *alba*
Francoa sonchifolia
Lilium regale, see p.81
Liriope muscari, see p.43
Paeonia mlokosewitschii
Saxifraga fortunei 'Rubrifolia'
Veronica peduncularis 'Georgia Blue', see p.29

OTHER TRAILING FLOWERING PERENNIALS FOR CONTAINERS

Diascia 'Lilac Mist'
Persicaria affinis 'Superba'
Saponaria 'Bressingham'
Verbena 'Silver Anne'

Pelargonium 'Red Cascade'
IVY-LEAVED PELARGONIUM
☼ ❄   ↕ 45cm (18in) ↔ 45cm (18in)

This evergreen, a charming miniature of *P.* 'Ivy-leaf', has fleshy, ivy-shaped leaves and trailing stems. Clusters of red flowers open all year long in mild areas. ♈

Verbena 'Sissinghurst'
VERBENA
☼ ❄   ↕ 20cm (8in) ↔ 45cm (18in)

Low, with a wide-spreading habit, this verbena has small, aromatic, deeply cut leaves and charming heads of bright pink flowers throughout summer. ♈

Foliage Perennials for Containers

MANY PERENNIALS are worth growing in containers solely for their attractive leaves. Some have the added bonus of attractive flowers, but the selection here has been chosen mainly for foliage effect. Treating them as container plants allows greater flexibility in their placement, and also enables you to shelter more tender plants, liable to winter damage.

Aloe arborescens 'Variegata'
ALOE
☼ ❄   ↕ 2m (6ft) ↔ 2m (6ft)

Succulent, spine-toothed evergreen leaves are blue-green with cream margins and stripes. In late winter and spring, long-stalked spikes of red flowers are a bonus.

Carex flagellifera
SEDGE
☼ ☼ ❄❄❄   ↕ 60cm (24in) ↔ 50cm (20in)

This tough, little, grass-like evergreen perennial forms a dense tuffet of slender, arching leaves which are tinged red, and often darken in winter. Dislikes dry soils.

Agave americana 'Variegata'
VARIEGATED CENTURY PLANT
☼ ❄   ↕ 1.5m (5ft) ↔ 1.5m (5ft)

Spine-toothed, pointed leaves, each with a yellow margin, eventually form a large evergreen rosette. In maturity, statuesque white flower spikes appear in summer.

Aeonium 'Zwartkop'
AEONIUM
☼ ❄   ↕ 60cm (24in) ↔ 1m (3ft)

The branches of this evergreen succulent are topped with bold rosettes of polished, dark purple leaves. Its conical heads of yellow flowers appear in spring. ♔

OTHER HARDY FOLIAGE PERENNIALS FOR CONTAINERS

Acorus gramineus 'Ogon'
Athyrium nipponicum var. *pictum*
Bergenia 'Bressingham Ruby'
Gunnera tinctoria
Hosta 'Gold Standard'
Hosta 'Sum and Substance'
Hosta 'Wide Brim'
Houttuynia cordata 'Chamaeleon'
Peltiphyllum peltatum, see p.47
Rodgersia podophylla, see p.47

Dicksonia antarctica
AUSTRALIAN TREE FERN
☼ ❄   ↕ 5m (15ft) ↔ 4m (12ft)

A magnificent, tree-like fern, this has a stout, fibrous "stem" which is crowned by a huge rosette of big, beautifully dissected fronds. Dislikes exposure and dry soils. ♔

Phormium 'Sundowner'
MOUNTAIN FLAX
☼ ❄❄   ↕1.8m (6ft) ↔ 1.2m (4ft)

A vigorous evergreen plant, excellent for
a large container, this has tufts of glossy,
sword-shaped bronze-green leaves, edged
dark rose-pink and fading to cream. ♟

Hosta sieboldiana var. *elegans*
PLANTAIN LILY
☼ ☼ ❄❄❄   ↕1m (3ft) ↔ 1.5m (5ft)

The large, heart-shaped, blue-grey leaves
of this big, bold perennial are puckered
and strongly veined. Drooping, pale lilac
trumpet-flowers open in early summer. ♟

> **OTHER TENDER FOLIAGE
> PERENNIALS FOR CONTAINERS**
>
> *Arundo donax* 'Variegata'
> *Aspidistra elatior*
> *Astelia nervosa* 'Silver Spear'
> *Canna musifolia*
> *Canna* 'Striata'
> *Cyrtomium falcatum*
> *Melianthus major*
> *Musa acuminata* 'Dwarf Cavendish'
> *Musa basjoo*
> *Phormium tenax* 'Yellow Wave', see p.66

Pelargonium 'Royal Oak'
SCENTED-LEAVED PELARGONIUM
☼ ❄   ↕38cm (15in) ↔ 30cm (12in)

Bushy and spicily fragrant, this compact
evergreen has boldly lobed, slightly sticky
leaves with brown central zones. Mauve-
pink summer flowers have dark blotches.

Ricinus communis 'Impala'
CASTOR-OIL PLANT
☼ ❄❄   ↕1.5m (5in) ↔ 1m (3ft)

The leaves of this vigorous evergreen are
large, deeply lobed and a striking deep
bronze. Usually treated as an annual, it
carries autumn clusters of spiky red fruit.

Pelargonium 'Dolly Varden'
ZONAL PELARGONIUM
☼ ❄   ↕30cm (12in) ↔ 23cm (9in)

Eye-catching, aromatic evergreen foliage
is basically green with purplish brown
and crimson zoning and irregular cream
margins. Summer flowers are scarlet. ♟

Pelargonium tomentosum
PEPPERMINT GERANIUM
☼ ❄   ↕60cm (24in) ↔ 1m (3ft)

Bold, lobed evergreen leaves are covered,
as are the stems, in velvety down. Bushy
and spreading, they smell of mint when
bruised. Bears white flowers in summer.

Tradescantia pallida 'Purple Heart'
TRADESCANTIA
☼ ❄   ↕40cm (16in) ↔ 30cm (12in)

Low in habit, this distinctive evergreen
forms patches of dark glowing purple
stems and leaves, and produces small,
pink, three-petalled flowers in summer. ♟

Evergreen Perennials

FOLIAGE THAT REMAINS fresh and alive in winter is a valuable attribute in any perennial, given that so many either disappear entirely below ground, or are left with leaves that look tired, if not withered. Green foliage in winter is welcome enough, but if red, purple, or any other colours are available, this only adds to the visual variety. Evergreens also provide an excellent foil for winter- and early spring-flowering bulbs. Many make impressive specimens.

Helleborus argutifolius
CORSICAN HELLEBORE
☼ ☀ ✻✻✻   ‡60cm (24in) ↔ 45cm (18in)

This bold, stout-stemmed hellebore has large, three-parted leaves. Its impressive clusters of cup-shaped, apple-green flowers open from late winter into spring. ♛

Bergenia cordifolia 'Purpurea'
ELEPHANT'S EAR
☼ ☀ ☀ ✻✻✻   ‡↔ 50cm (20in)

The erect stems of this tough plant carry sprays of bell-shaped rose-pink flowers in late winter and early spring, above bold clumps of fleshy, heart-shaped leaves. ♛

Celmisia coriacea
NEW ZEALAND DAISY
☼ ☀ ✻✻✻ ^{PH} ‡30cm (12in) ↔ 30cm (12in)

In time, this magnificent perennial forms a striking clump of silvery, sword-shaped leaves, topped by large, single white daisy-flowers in summer. Dislikes dry soils.

Phormium tenax 'Yellow Wave'
MOUNTAIN FLAX
☼ ✻✻   ‡1.2m (4ft) ↔ 1.2m (4ft)

The sword-shaped, strongly arching, soft yellow leaves grow in bold clumps and develop chartreuse tones in autumn. Each has a bright lime-green margin. ♛

Blechnum tabulare
BLECHNUM
☼ ☀ ✻✻   ‡1m (3ft) ↔ 1m (3ft)

Ideal for a sheltered spot, the deep green, much-divided fronds, which are leathery, large, and arching, may be bronze when young, and form bold clumps. ♛

Helleborus foetidus
STINKING HELLEBORE
☼ ☀ ✻✻✻   ‡45cm (18in) ↔ 45cm (18in)

Bell-shaped flowers opening in late winter and early spring are maroon-mouthed and pale green. These, and the leathery, dark green, fingered leaves are poisonous. ♛

Phyllostachys nigra var. *henonis*
BAMBOO
☼ ☀ ✻✻✻   ‡5m (15ft) ↔ 3m (10ft)

Capable of twice the above height in warm, sheltered conditions, this lovely bamboo has narrow, shiny leaves and erect canes, maturing from green to yellow. ♛

Phyllostachys viridiglaucescens
BAMBOO

☼ ☀ ✳✳✳ ↕ 6m (20ft) ↔ indefinite

This vigorous bamboo has bold clumps of
arching green canes carrying lush, shiny
green foliage. It may grow extremely tall
in warm, sheltered conditions. ♔

OTHER EVERGREEN PERENNIALS

Aciphylla aurea
Asplenium scolopendrium 'Marginatum'
Eryngium eburneum
Eryngium pandanifolium
Euphorbia x *martinii*
Geranium palmatum
Kniphofia caulescens
Kniphofia northiae
Phlomis russelliana
Phormium cookianum 'Tricolor'
Polystichum munitum, see p.45

Sasa veitchii
BAMBOO

☼ ☀ ☀ ✳✳✳ ↕ 1.2m (4ft) ↔ indefinite

In time, this fast-creeping bamboo forms
extensive patches of upright stems, well-
clothed with eye-catching, oblong green
leaves. These develop white margins.

Polystichum setiferum 'Divisilobum'
SOFT SHIELD FERN

☼ ☀ ✳✳✳ ↕ 60cm (24in) ↔ 45cm (18in)

A lovely evergreen or, in severe winters,
semi-evergreen fern forming dense clumps
of finely divided, rich green fronds, pale
and scaly when young. Dislikes dry soils.

Shibataea kumasasa
BAMBOO

☼ ☀ ☀ ✳✳✳ ↕ 1m (3ft) ↔ 60cm (24in)

Particularly suited to small gardens, this
bamboo forms compact clumps of upright,
slender canes that are all densely crowded
with relatively broad, pointed leaves.

Yucca gloriosa
SPANISH DAGGER

☼ ✳✳✳ ↕ 2m (6ft) ↔ 1.4m (4½ft)

Rigid, spine-tipped, grey-green leaves
grow in striking clumps. A short, woody
stem eventually supports branched heads
of ivory-white bell-flowers in summer. ♔

Perennials with Variegated Leaves

CHOOSING A VARIEGATED PERENNIAL for a special planting scheme can be tricky as so many types exist. Blotches, spots, streaks, and stripes abound, but most common, and often most effective, are leaves with margins of a different colour. Whatever their pattern, variegated plants will bring both interest and contrast to the mixed border or bed.

Mentha x *suaveolens* 'Variegata'
VARIEGATED APPLE MINT
☼ ☀ ❊❊❊ ‡45cm (18in) ↔60cm (24in)

This free-growing perennial in time forms colonies. It has pale green, softly downy stems, and the leaves, splashed white and cream, are aromatic when bruised.

Astrantia major
'Sunningdale Variegated'
☼ ☀ ❊❊❊ ‡60cm (24in) ↔45cm (18in)

Long-stalked and deeply lobed leaves are striped and splashed cream and yellow. Loose, greenish white flowerheads are produced in summer and early autumn. ♛

Hosta fortunei 'Aureomarginata'
PLANTAIN LILY
☼ ☀ ❊❊❊ ‡75cm (30in) ↔1m (3ft)

Green, heart-shaped leaves with irregular, creamy yellow margins grow in clumps. Trumpet-shaped flowers in summer are violet. Thrives in moist or rich soils. ♛

Phlox paniculata 'Norah Leigh'
PERENNIAL PHLOX
☼ ❊❊❊ ‡1m (3ft) ↔60cm (24in)

Sturdy clumps of erect stems are clothed in creamy white leaves, each with an irregular green centre. Conical, pale lilac flowerheads top the foliage in summer.

Brunnera macrophylla
'Dawson's White'
☼ ❊❊❊ ‡45cm (18in) ↔60cm (24in)

This most effective variegated perennial has clumps of hairy, heart-shaped leaves with irregular cream-white margins. Sprays of forget-me-not flowers appear in spring.

Hosta undulata var. *univittata*
PLANTAIN LILY
☼ ☀ ❊❊❊ ‡60cm (24in) ↔60cm (24in)

Vigorous and clump-forming, this hosta has glossy, oval leaves, each with a central white stripe. Mauve trumpet-flowers occur in summer. Enjoys moist or rich soils. ♛

OTHER PERENNIALS WITH WHITE OR CREAM VARIEGATED FOLIAGE

Agapanthus praecox 'Variegatus'
Armoracia rusticana 'Variegata'
Cortaderia selloana 'Albolineata'
Hemerocallis fulva 'Kwanzo Variegata'
Hosta 'Shade Fanfare', see p.30
Iris pallida 'Argentea Variegata'
Miscanthus sinensis 'Variegata'
Physostegia virginiana
   subsp. *speciosa* 'Variegata'
Pulmonaria saccharata 'Leopard'

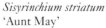

Sisyrinchium striatum 'Aunt May'
☼ ✻✻✻ ↕ 60cm (24in) ↔ 30cm (12in)

The iris-like clumps of semi-evergreen, erect grey-green leaves are striped cream. Spikes of straw-yellow, purple-streaked flowers are produced in summer.

OTHER PERENNIALS WITH YELLOW VARIEGATED FOLIAGE

Carex oshimensis 'Evergold', see p.70
Convallaria majalis 'Hardwick Hall'
Cortaderia selloana 'Aureolineata'
Hakonechloa macra 'Aureola'
Hosta 'Gold Standard'
Iris pallida 'Variegata'
Pleioblastus auricomus, see p.71
Symphytum 'Goldsmith'
Trifolium pratense 'Susan Smith'
Yucca flaccida 'Golden Sword'

Polemonium caeruleum 'Brise d'Anjou'
VARIEGATED JACOB'S LADDER
☼ ✻✻✻ ↕ 45cm (18in) ↔ 30cm (12in)

This handsome perennial has mounds of neatly "laddered" leaves with numerous cream-margined leaflets. Its small bluish flowers bloom in early summer.

Symphytum x *uplandicum* 'Variegatum'
VARIEGATED RUSSIAN COMFREY
☼ ☼ ✻✻✻ ↕ 1m (3ft) ↔ 60cm (24in)

Large, hairy leaves with bold margins form robust clumps. Nodding flower clusters, in late spring and early summer, change from pink to blue. Thrives in moist soils. ♔

Pleioblastus variegatus
DWARF WHITE-STRIPED BAMBOO
☼ ✻✻✻ ↕ 80cm (32in) ↔ indefinite

A popular dwarf bamboo, this will form evergreen clumps and, later, colonies. Its narrow green-and-white-striped leaves clothe erect, slender, woody canes. ♔

Scrophularia auriculata 'Variegata'
VARIEGATED WATER FIGWORT
☼ ☼ ✻✻✻ ↕ 1.5m (5ft) ↔ 60cm (24in)

Bold clumps of leaves that are striped and splashed cream make this an impressive perennial. Its tall stems bear tiny summer flowers. Thrives in rich or moist soils.

Yucca gloriosa 'Variegata'
VARIEGATED ADAM'S NEEDLE
☼ ✻✻ ↕ 2m (6ft) ↔ 1.2m (4ft)

Stiff, sword-shaped grey-green leaves are striped yellow and make a grand rosette. A magnificent ivory-white flower spike tops each mature plant in late summer. ♔

Perennials with Golden or Yellow Leaves

M OST GOLDEN- or yellow-leaved forms of perennial plants originated as seedlings or bud-mutations, and have been propagated vegetatively to keep them in cultivation. The strength and degree of colour varies considerably, but they can bring a welcome touch of warmth to the garden, especially when contrasted with green or reddish foliage.

Lysimachia nummularia 'Aurea'
GOLDEN MONEYWORT

☼ ✳✳✳ ↕ 5cm (2in) ↔ indefinite

The creeping stems of this moneywort form carpets of rounded and paired, pale yellow leaves. These are joined in summer by bright yellow, cup-shaped flowers. ♈

Carex oshimensis hachijoensis 'Evergold'
GOLDEN JAPANESE SEDGE GRASS

☼ ✳✳✳ ↕ 20cm (8in) ↔ 20cm (8in)

This bold, tufted sedge is evergreen. The arching, narrow, grassy leaves are glossy and each has a conspicuous, creamy yellow central stripe. It forms a low mound. ♈

OTHER HERBACEOUS PERENNIALS WITH GOLDEN LEAVES
Alopecurus pratensis 'Aureovargiegatus'
Campanula garganica 'Dickson's Gold'
Centaurea montana 'Gold Bullion'
Hakonechloa macra 'Aureola'
Hosta fortunei 'Aurea'
Hosta 'Golden Prayers'
Hosta 'Midas Touch'
Hosta 'Piedmont Gold'
Hosta sieboldiana 'Golden Sunburst'
Hosta 'Sum and Substance'
Hosta 'Sun Power'
Hosta 'Wogon Gold'
Melissa officinalis 'All Gold'
Milium effusum 'Aureum'
Symphytum 'Gold in Spring'
Symphytum ibericum 'All Gold'
Tanacetum parthenium 'Aureum'
Tanacetum vulgare 'Isla Gold'

Filipendula ulmaria 'Aurea'
GOLDEN MEADOW SWEET

☼ ☀ ✳✳✳ ↕ 60cm (24in) ↔ 30cm (12in)

Although the familiar, sweetly scented white flowers of this plant are attractive, it is the impressive golden yellow spring foliage that merits most attention.

Hosta 'Zounds'
PLANTAIN LILY

☀ ✳✳✳ ↕ 75cm (30in) ↔ 1m (3ft)

A spectacular perennial that forms a bold mound of large, rounded, and puckered yellow leaves, above which spikes of pale lavender flowers rise in early summer.

Melissa officinalis 'Aurea'
GOLDEN LEMON BALM

☼ ☀ ✳✳✳ ↕ 60cm (24in) ↔ 45cm (18in)

The golden, variegated leaves of this bushy herb smell of lemon when bruised. Trim growths after flowering to encourage a summer-long succession of colour.

PERENNIALS

Origanum vulgare 'Aureum'
GOLDEN MARJORAM
☼ ❄❄❄   ↕ 8cm (3in) ↔ indefinite

As summer advances, the dense, low pads of bright yellow, aromatic spring foliage begin to pale. At the same time, sparse clusters of tiny mauve flowers emerge. ♈

Saxifraga moschata 'Cloth of Gold'
GOLDEN MOSSY SAXIFRAGE
☼ ❄❄❄   ↕ 13cm (5in) ↔ 15cm (6in)

Neat rosettes of deeply divided golden leaves form evergreen mounds. White, star-shaped summer flowers rise on thin stalks. Prefers moist, but well-drained soil.

Stachys byzantina 'Primrose Heron'
LAMB'S TONGUE
☼ ❄❄❄   ↕ 38cm (15in) ↔ 60cm (24in)

This creeping evergreen forms mats of woolly silver-grey leaves, suffused pale yellow, especially when young. Mauve-pink flower spikes are carried in summer.

Pleioblastus auricomus
BAMBOO
☼ ❄❄❄   ↕ 1.5m (5ft) ↔ indefinite

One of the best dwarf bamboos for colour, this evergreen will form large colonies in time, but it is also good in containers. The yellow leaves are striped green. ♈

Valeriana phu 'Aurea'
VALERIAN
☼ ❄❄❄   ↕ 38cm (15in) ↔ 30cm (12in)

The young spring foliage of this tufted perennial is lemon-yellow, and completely upstages the white, clustered flowers that follow in summer. ♈

OTHER EVERGREEN PERENNIALS WITH GOLDEN LEAVES

Acanthus mollis 'Holland's Gold'
Acorus gramineus 'Ogon'
Carex elata 'Aurea'
Lamium maculatum 'Cannon's Gold'

Veronica prostrata 'Trehane'
VERONICA
☼ ❄❄❄   ↕ 15cm (6in) ↔ 30cm (12in)

A choice and reliable little perennial that forms mats of toothed yellow leaves that turn yellowish green, and carries spikes of deep violet-blue flowers in early summer.

Perennials with Silver or Blue-grey Leaves

SILVER- OR GREY-LEAVED perennials are among the most valuable in the garden, providing a gentle foil to pastel shades or to strongly coloured leaves or flowers. The greyish leaves provide a useful contrast in planting schemes that contain mainly plants of interesting foliage. Here are a few of the many that are suitable and available.

Dicentra 'Langtrees'
DICENTRA
☼ ☀ ❊❊❊   ↕ 45cm (18in) ↔ 30cm (12in)

This vigorous perennial forms patches of erect, fleshy stems with blue-grey, ferny leaves. Arching sprays of white flowers are borne in late spring and early summer. ♔

Hosta 'Hadspen Blue'
PLANTAIN LILY
☼ ☀ ❊❊❊   ↕ 45cm (18in) ↔ 45cm (18in)

The heart-shaped and attractively veined, deep blue-grey leaves make this a striking foliage perennial. Lavender flower spikes appear in summer. Dislikes dry soils.

Artemisia ludoviciana
WHITE SAGE
☼ ❊❊❊   ↕ 1.2m (4ft) ↔ 60cm (24in)

Both the dense clumps of erect stems, and the willow-like, sharply toothed, aromatic leaves that clothe them, are downy. Tiny grey-white flowerheads occur in summer.

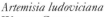

OTHER PERENNIALS WITH SILVER OR BLUE-GREY LEAVES
Acaena 'Blue Haze'
Anaphalis triplinervis
Artemisia stelleriana 'Mori's Form'
Convolvulus althaeoides
Cynara scolymus 'Glauca'
Hosta 'Blue Angel'
Iris pallida var. *dalmatica*
Lysimachia ephemerum
Macleaya cordata 'Flamingo'
Thalictrum speciosissimum

Artemisia 'Powis Castle'
ARTEMISIA
☼ ❊❊   ↕ 1m (3ft) ↔ 1.2m (4ft)

The grey branches of this evergreen sub-shrub or perennial carry aromatic, silver, filigree foliage. Its summer flowerheads are tiny and not that numerous. ♔

Lychnis flos-jovis
FLOWER OF JOVE
☼ ❊❊❊   ↕ 45cm (18in) ↔ 45cm (18in)

Like the leaves, the upright stems of this old-fashioned, favourite clump-former are clothed with a pelt of woolly grey down. Pretty summer flowers are rose-pink.

Onopordum acanthium
SCOTCH, OR COTTON, THISTLE
☼ ❋❋❋   ↕ 2.2m (7ft) ↔ 1.4m (4½ft)

Vigorous and prickly, this stately biennial
(or short-lived perennial) has downy stems
and leaves. Its purplish pink flowerheads,
borne in summer, are most impressive.

Ruta graveolens 'Jackman's Blue'
RUE
☼ ❋❋❋❋   ↕ 60cm (24in) ◄► 75cm (30in)

The evergreen, fern-like, blue-grey foliage
of this aromatic perennial or subshrub may
cause an allergic rash. Clusters of small
flowers are produced in summer.   ♈

Sedum spathulifolium 'Cape Blanco'
STONECROP
☼ ☀ ❋❋❋   ↕ 5cm (2in) ↔ indefinite

Evergreen rosettes of succulent, silvery
green leaves develop into dense pads and
mats, above which eye-catching clusters
of yellow flowers rise in summer.   ♈

Stachys byzantina
LAMB'S-TONGUE, BUNNIES' EARS
☼ ❋❋❋   ↕ 38cm (15in) ↔ 60cm (24in)

One of the most popular and satisfactory
evergreen perennials, this forms dense
carpets of soft, woolly silver-grey foliage,
with mauve-pink flower spikes in summer.

Tanacetum argenteum
TANACETUM
☼ ❋❋❋   ↕ 23cm (9in) ↔ 23cm (9in)

A small, aromatic evergreen hummock of
intensely grey stems. Charming, finely cut
silver-grey leaves back the white daisy-
flowers that are freely borne in summer.

Verbascum olympicum
MULLEIN
☼ ❋❋❋   ↕ 2m (6ft) ↔ 1m (3ft)

This distinctive semi-evergreen biennial
or short-lived perennial often branches
near the base, and has woolly stems and
leaves. Summer flower spikes are yellow.

Perennials with Purple, Red, or Bronze Leaves

PERENNIALS WITH PURPLE or similarly dark leaves are most valuable in the garden, especially when contrasted with foliage that is green or yellow. Such plants are best planted in moderation, as their effect can be a little sombre. Most of the following are at their darkest in spring, when young growth first appears, although there are some impressive exceptions.

Euphorbia dulcis 'Chameleon'
PURPLE-LEAVED SWEET SPURGE
☼ ☼ ✳✳✳ ↕ 30cm (12in) ↔ 30cm (12in)

Masses of reddish purple leaves colour richly in autumn and tiny, yellowish green flower clusters are a bonus in spring. The milky sap is caustic, so handle with care.

Ajuga reptans 'Atropurpurea'
PURPLE-LEAVED BUGLE
☼ ☼ ☀ ✳✳✳ ↕ 15cm (6in) ↔ 1m (3ft)

The shining bronze-purple leaves of this evergreen, borne in lush rosettes, form a close carpet. Short spikes of blue flowers appear in spring. Thrives in moist soil. ▽

Clematis recta 'Purpurea'
ERECT CLEMATIS
☼ ✳✳✳ ↕ 1.5m (5ft) ↔ 50cm (20in)

A profusion of fragrant white flowers rises above coppery-purple leaves in summer. The erect, much-branched stems of this clump-forming perennial need support.

Foeniculum vulgare 'Purpureum'
PURPLE-LEAVED FENNEL
☼ ✳✳✳ ↕ 2m (6ft) ↔ 45cm (18in)

Clumps of feathery young leaves in spring emerge a deep mahogany or treacly purple, and pale to bronze as they mature. Tiny flowers borne in umbels open in summer.

Anthriscus sylvestris 'Ravenswing'
PURPLE-LEAVED COW PARSLEY
☼ ☼ ☀ ✳✳✳ ↕ 1.2m (4ft) ↔ 60cm (24in)

Mounds of finely divided, fern-like leaves are a rich dark purple in spring; they pale later. Umbels of tiny white, pink-bracted flowers open in late spring.

Euphorbia amygdaloides 'Rubra'
PURPLE-LEAVED WOOD SPURGE
☼ ☼ ☀ ✳✳✳ ↕↔ 30cm (12in)

The evergreen leaves, and stems, of this bushy perennial are suffused purple-red. Small yellow flowers appear in spring. Be careful of its caustic, milky sap,

Heuchera micrantha 'Palace Purple'
PURPLE-LEAVED HEUCHERA
☼ ✳✳✳ ↕ 45cm (18in) ↔ 45cm (18in)

Clumps of long-lived, heart-shaped leaves on tall stalks are a metallic copper-purple colour. The clouds of tiny flowers appear in early summer. Will self-seed. ▽

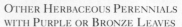

OTHER HERBACEOUS PERENNIALS
WITH PURPLE OR BRONZE LEAVES

Astilbe 'Dunkellachs'
Cimicifuga simplex 'Brunette'
Imperata cylindrica 'Rubra'
    Ligularia dentata 'Othello'
    Melica altissima 'Atropurpurea'
    Oenothera glaber
    Plantago major 'Rubrifolia'
  Primula 'Garryarde Guinevere'
Rheum palmatum 'Artopurpureum'
Saxifraga 'Wada'

Penstemon digitalis 'Husker's Red'
PENSTEMON

☼ ❄❄❄   ↕ 75cm (30in) ↔ 30cm (12in)

The young leaves and shoots of this erect
perennial are a rich purple in spring but
fade to green-tinged purple when the
tubular flowers appear in early summer.

OTHER EVERGREEN PERENNIALS
WITH PURPLE OR BRONZE LEAVES

Ajuga reptans 'Braunherz'
Bergenia 'Ballawley' in winter, see p.90
Bergenia 'Bressingham Ruby' in winter
Epimedium x *rubrum* in winter/spring,
    see p.90
Galax aphylla in winter
Phormium 'Bronze Baby'
Phormium tenax 'Purpureum'
Veronica peduncularis 'Georgia Blue'
    in spring, see p.29

Lobelia 'Queen Victoria'
LOBELIA

☼ ❄❄   ↕ 1m (3ft) ↔ 30cm (12in)

Striking red flowers are carried on spikes
from summer into early autumn. Sturdy,
erect stems and narrow leaves are a deep,
reddish purple. Requires moist soils. ▽

Sedum telephium subsp.
maximum 'Atropurpureum'

☼ ❄❄❄   ↕ 60cm (24in) ↔ 60cm (24in)

Bold clumps of succulent stems, clothed
in large, rich dark maroon leaves, produce
flattened heads of tiny, reddish white
flowers in late summer. ▽

Ophiopogon planiscapus 'Nigrescens'
OPHIOPOGON

☼ ☼ ❄❄❄❄   ↕ 23cm (9in) ↔ 30cm (12in)

This creeping evergreen forms a dense tuft
of narrow, strap-shaped, blackish purple
leaves. Slender spikes bearing tiny lilac
flowers are produced in summer. ▽

Salvia officinalis 'Purpurascens'
PURPLE SAGE

☼ ❄❄❄   ↕ 60cm (24in) ↔ 1m (3ft)

The downy, aromatic evergreen leaves of
this shrubby perennial are flushed purple
when new, and mature to greyish green.
Flower spikes are carried in summer. ▽

Tellima grandiflora 'Purpurea'
PURPLE-LEAVED FRINGE CUPS

☼ ❄❄❄   ↕ 60cm (24in) ↔ 60cm (24in)

Clumps of evergreen, boldly veined,
reddish purple leaves are heart-shaped.
Above these, spikes of nodding, pinkish
cream flowers rise in late spring.

Perennials with Fragrant Flowers

OTHER PERENNIALS WITH FRAGRANT FLOWERS

Convallaria majalis, see p.42
Crambe cordifolia, see p.18
Hosta 'Invincible'
Iris graminea
Iris unguicularis
Meehania urticifolia
Paeonia emodi
Petasites fragrans
Phlox maculata 'Alpha'
Viola odorata 'Wellsiana'

PARTICULARLY ON WARM, still summer evenings, the flowers of certain perennials give off a strong fragrance, readily enjoyed by everyone nearby, even those without a keenly developed sense of smell. Closer encounters may be needed to appreciate more subtle-scented flowers, but even fleeting fragrances wafting by are a welcome asset in any garden.

Cheiranthus cheiri 'Harpur Crewe'
PERENNIAL WALLFLOWER
☼ ✻✻✻   ↕ 30cm (12in) ↔ 30cm (12in)

From spring into midsummer, above a low, compact mound of evergreen leaves, a succession of richly scented yellow flower spikes rise. Best in poor or stony soils. ♔

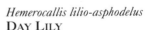
Hemerocallis lilio-asphodelus
DAY LILY
☼ ✻✻✻   ↕ 60cm (24in) ↔ 60cm (24in)

The fragrance of these lovely, lily-like flowers in late spring and early summer is unforgettable. The blooms rise above a striking clump of strap-shaped leaves. ♔

Clematis recta
HERBACEOUS CLEMATIS
☼ ✻✻✻   ↕ 1.5m (5ft) ↔ 50cm (20in)

Long stems, with deeply divided leaves, carry clouds of small, sweetly fragrant summer flowers. Train this clump-former over small shrubs, or give it some support.

Dianthus 'Doris'
MODERN PINK
☼ ✻✻✻   ↕ 30cm (12in) ↔ 30cm (12in)

All through summer, this popular pink provides a fragrant succession of pale pink flowers, each with a dark central zone. Its evergreen leaves form a silvery mound. ♔

OTHER BORDER PINKS WITH FRAGRANT FLOWERS

Dianthus 'Becky Robinson'
Dianthus 'Devon Glow'
Dianthus 'Gran's Favourite', see p.36
Dianthus 'Haytor White'
Dianthus 'Kesteven Kirkstead'
Dianthus 'Lincolnshire Poacher'
Dianthus 'Monica Wyatt'
Dianthus 'Mrs Sinkins'
Dianthus 'Musgrave's Pink'
Dianthus 'Old Mother Hubbard'

Hesperis matronalis
DAME'S VIOLET, SWEET ROCKET
☼ ❄❄❄　　　‡ 1.2m (4ft) ↔ 60cm (24in)

This fragrant, old-fashioned cottage garden
favourite has erect, leafy stems and heads
of white or violet summer flowers. Short-
lived, it grows best in poor or stony soils.

Iris 'Early Light'
BEARDED IRIS
☼ ❄❄❄　　　‡ 1m (3ft) ↔ indefinite

Swollen, creeping rhizomes produce fans
of sword-shaped grey-green leaves, and
branched stems support frilled cream and
yellow flowers in early summer.　　♈

Phlox maculata 'Omega'
PERENNIAL PHLOX
☼ ◐ ❄❄❄　　　‡ 1m (3ft) ↔ 45cm (18in)

Strong, leafy stems form an erect clump
and each is topped by loosely cylindrical
heads of fragrant, lilac-eyed flowers. Likes
moist soils.　　♈

Hosta plantaginea 'Grandiflora'
FRAGRANT PLANTAIN LILY
☼ ❄❄❄　　　‡ 60cm (24in) ↔ 1.2m (4ft)

From late summer into autumn, slender,
fragrant white trumpet-flowers, which
open in the evening, are carried above
bold mounds of glossy, pale green leaves.

Monarda 'Croftway Pink'
BERGAMOT
☼ ❄❄❄　　　‡ 1m (3ft) ↔ 60cm (24in)

The dense whorls and clusters of hooded,
soft pink summer flowers are scented, and
the leaves, on strong, upright stems, are
pleasantly aromatic. Dislikes dry soils.　♈

Primula veris
COWSLIP
☼ ❄❄❄　　　‡ 20cm (8in) ↔ 20cm (8in)

Umbels of nodding yellow spring flowers,
with a distinctive scent, crown upright
stems that rise out of small, neat rosettes
of wrinkled foliage. Dislikes dry soils.　♈

Inula hookeri
INULA
☼ ❄❄❄　　　‡ 1m (3ft) ↔ 1m (3ft)

A series of woolly buds in summer opens
into large, scented, yellow daisy-flowers.
Upright stems, forming a bold clump, are
densely clothed with downy leaves.

Nicotiana sylvestris
ORNAMENTAL TOBACCO
☼ ❄❄　　　‡ 1.5m (5ft) ↔ 75cm (30in)

Loose heads of long-tubed late summer
flowers are especially fragrant in the early
evening. A perennial in warm, sheltered
gardens, but an annual elsewhere.　　♈

Verbena rigida
VERBENA
☼ ❄❄　　　‡ 30cm (12in) ↔ 30cm (12in)

Neat and compact in habit, this popular,
tuberous-rooted perennial has branching
stems topped from midsummer onwards
with fragrant, pale violet flower spikes.　♈

Spring-flowering Bulbs

NO OTHER PLANTS signal the end of winter and the arrival of spring more convincingly than bulbs do. To eyes that are dulled by long winter nights, and short sharp days, the gradual emergence of brilliant tulips, golden daffodils, and a host of crocuses breathe new life into the garden. More than at other times of the year, you are aware of great variety, beauty, and charm. Whether in small groups or large drifts, there is no denying their impact on the garden landscape.

Crocus vernus 'Princess Juliana'
CROCUS
☼ ✳✳✳ ↕9cm (3½in)

A bold-flowered, easily grown crocus that has narrow leaves. Its purple flowers have large, frilly orange or deep yellow stigmas. Excellent for naturalizing in beds or grass.

Anemone blanda 'White Splendour'
GREEK WINDFLOWER
☼ ☼ ✳✳✳ ↕8cm (3in)

Ferny leaves rising from knobbly tubers are topped by multi-petalled, early spring flowers. Once established, this reliable variety increases to form patches. ♔

x *Chionoscilla allenii*
CHIONOSCILLA
☼ ☼ ✳✳✳ ↕13cm (5in)

A choice, easy dwarf bulb, this has sprays of deep blue, star-shaped flowers above strap-like leaves. Good in a cool pocket on a rock garden. It forms colonies in time.

BULBS FOR SPRING BEDDING
DISPLAY

Hyacinthus orientalis 'Delft Blue'
Hyacinthus orientalis 'L'Innocence'
Hyacinthus orientalis 'Pink Pearl'
Muscari armeniacum
Narcissus 'Mount Hood'
Narcissus 'Spellbinder'
Tulipa 'China Pink'
Tulipa 'Garden Party'
Tulipa 'Keizerskroon'
Tulipa 'White Dream'

Chionodoxa forbesii
SNOW GLORY
☼ ☼ ✳✳✳ ↕13cm (5in)

Popular and reliable, this dwarf bulb has sprays of star-shaped flowers. It spreads by seed once established, especially beneath deciduous trees and shrubs. ♔

Crocus dalmaticus
CROCUS
☼ ✳✳✳ ↕9cm (3½in)

A charming crocus, this is suited to the rock garden or scree. It has tufts of narrow leaves and beautiful flowers, in varying shades of purple, with yellow centres.

Erythronium dens-canis
DOG'S-TOOTH VIOLET
☼ ✳✳✳ ↕20cm (8in)

Above a pair of fleshy, mottled leaves a single flower with swept back petals rises. Easy in a rock garden or border, this species seeds to form colonies. ♔

Erythronium 'Pagoda'
ERYTHRONIUM
☼ ❊❊❊   ↕ 30cm (12in)

Above the lush, faintly mottled leaves of
this vigorous plant rise dark stems. These
support pendent flowers with pointed,
upswept petals. Soon self-seeds. ▽

Fritillaria pallidiflora
FRITILLARY
☼ ❊❊❊   ↕ 45cm (18in)

This vigorous bulb has attractive, fleshy
leaves, and several large, greenish yellow,
pendulous flowers, normally chequered
faintly inside. Needs good drainage. ▽

Narcissus 'Kingscourt'
DAFFODIL
☼ ☼ ❊❊❊   ↕ 45cm (18in)

A strong-growing daffodil, this is good for
bedding and for naturalizing. Erect stems
bear a single, flared, rich golden yellow
trumpet surrounded by paler petals. ▽

Fritillaria imperialis
CROWN IMPERIAL
☼ ❊❊❊   ↕ 1.2m (4ft)

A popular plant of robust growth, in time
forming clumps of erect, leafy stems, and
nodding umbels of bell-shaped flowers
beneath a crown of erect, leaf-like bracts.

OTHER SPRING-FLOWERING BULBS
Allium narcissiflorum
Anemone pavonina
Corydalis solida 'George Baker'
Crocus etruscus
Cyclamen repandum
Erythronium californicum   'White Beauty'
Erythronium revolutum
Fritillaria pyrenaicum
Ipheion uniflorum 'Wisley Blue'
Tulipa clusiana

Ipheion uniflorum 'Froyle Mill'
IPHEION
☼ ❊❊❊   ↕ 13cm (5in)

Slender, erect stems each carry a single
flower above clumps of narrow, onion-
scented leaves. Perfect for planting under
deciduous shrubs or in a cool border. ▽

Narcissus 'February Gold'
DAFFODIL
☼ ☼ ❊❊❊   ↕ 32cm (13in)

This is a popular daffodil for mass planting
or naturalizing. The solitary flowers have
clear yellow petals and a deeper-coloured
trumpet. A long-lasting, reliable plant. ▽

Tulipa fosteriana 'Madame Lefeber'
TULIP
☼ ❊❊❊   ↕ 40cm (16in)

This bold-flowered, vigorous selection of
a gorgeous wild tulip sports enormous,
black-eyed, brilliant red flowers above its
handsome grey-green foliage.

Tulipa praestans
'Van Tubergen's Variety'
☼ ❊❊❊   ↕ 28cm (11in)

A striking tulip with downy stems and
grey-green leaves, above which large
orange-red flowers, yellow at their bases,
are carried. Forms clumps in time. ▽

Summer-flowering Bulbs

To THE LAYMAN, bulbs are evocative of late winter and spring, but a surprising number and variety of bulbous plants are available to provide colour in the summer months. You can plant them on their own in clumps, between shrubs, or in herbaceous borders. Many make bold specimen plants. Those that originate in warm climates can, in cooler areas, be grown near a sheltering wall or in containers that can be brought indoors for decoration, winter protection, or both.

Crocosmia 'Citronella'
MONTBRETIA
☼ ✳✳ ↕ 70cm (28in)

The erect, sword-shaped grey-green leaves of this plant form clumps. Small, funnel-shaped golden flowers are produced in arching spikes. Best in well-drained soils.

Allium aflatunense
ORNAMENTAL ONION
☼ ✳✳ ↕ 75cm (30in)

This ornamental onion bears a dense head of star-shaped flowers, attractive to bees and butterflies. The basal leaves wither before it flowers. Best in well-drained soil.

Camassia leichtlinii 'Semiplena'
CAMASSIA
☼ ✳✳✳ ↕ 1.2m (4ft)

A stately plant with long, erect, narrow leaves. Each stem ends in a loose spike of double, narrow-petalled flowers. Grow in a well-drained soil. May need some support.

Crocosmia 'Jackanapes'
MONBRETIA
☼ ✳✳ ↕ 50cm (20in)

Erect, branching stems bear orange-red and yellow bicoloured flowers in spikes. The upright, sword-shaped leaves form clumps. Thrives in a well-drained site.

Alstroemeria 'Ligtu Hybrids'
ALSTROEMERIA
☼ ✳✳✳ ↕ 55cm (22in)

Slow to establish, but a magnificent plant. Erect, leafy stems are crowned with heads of flared flowers, often streaked. Thrives in a sheltered, well-drained site. ♈

Crinum x *powellii*
CAPE LILY
☼ ✳✳ ↕ 75cm (30in)

This striking plant eventually forms lush clumps of shiny, strap-shaped leaves. Stout stems with loose heads of fragrant trumpet flowers rise above the leaves.

Dahlia 'Bishop of Llandaff'
DAHLIA
☼ ✳✳ ↕ 1m (3ft)

A popular perennial with bronze-purple leaves and stems, and bearing large, multi-petalled flowers. It is impressive alone or in groups. Lift and store over winter.

Lilium 'Enchantment'
LILY
☼ ❄❄❄   ↕ 1m (3ft)

An old, reliable hybrid lily with erect, leafy stems, this bears loose heads of upward-facing, widespread orange flowers, spotted with black. In time, it will form clumps. ♈

Dierama pulcherrimum
WAND FLOWER
☼ ❄❄   ↕ 1.7m (5½ft)

Graceful clumps of semi-evergreen, grass-like leaves mix with arching stems of drooping flower clusters. Grows best in deep, rich soils, where it may self-seed.

OTHER SUMMER BULBS
Allium christophii, see p.40
Cardiocrinum giganteum, see p.85
Eucomis comosa, see p.40
Galtonia viridiflora
Gladiolus communis subsp. *byzantinus*, see p.61
Iris xiphium 'Dutch Iris'
Lilium martagon, see p.61
Pancratium illyricum
Triteleia laxa, see p.40
Tritonia rubrolucens
Watsonia beatricis
Zantedeschia aethiopica 'Crowborough'

Lilium regale
REGAL LILY
☼ ❄❄❄   ↕ 1.5m (5ft)

An old favourite, this produces erect stems with narrow leaves, crowned by a loose umbel of trumpet-shaped, deliciously fragrant, yellow-throated white flowers. ♈

Galtonia candicans
SUMMER HYACINTH
☼ ❄❄   ↕ 1.1m (3½ft)

Tufts of fleshy leaves form bold clumps. Above these, stout stems with pendulous, bell-shaped flowers rise. Thrives in deep, rich soils, but is prone to slugs.

Lilium auratum var. *platyphyllum*
GOLDEN-RAYED LILY
☼ ❄❄❄❄ ᴾᴴ   ↕ 1.1m (3½ft)

This spectacular lily has lance-shaped leaves, and upright stems that bear large, fragrant flowers. Each petal has a yellow central band and scattered red spots. ♈

Ornithogalum narbonense
ORNITHOGALUM
☼ ❄❄   ↕ 35cm (14in)

The strong, leafless stem of this bold clump-former is topped by a tapered head of star-shaped white flowers. Basal leaves are narrow. Needs well-drained soils.

Autumn-flowering Bulbs

So much publicity is afforded bulbs that flower in late winter, spring, and summer that it is easy for gardeners to neglect those that are at their prime in autumn. But the likes of the autumn crocus bring a welcome splash of colour at a time when many plants are either dying down or shedding their leaves. Although few in number by comparison, autumn bulbs, corms, and tubers do have the garden stage virtually to themselves, and are thus more noticeable and valued.

Crocus banaticus
CROCUS
☼ ✳✳✳   ↕ 10cm (4in)

This choice little crocus has slender tubes supporting pale violet flowers with orange stigmas. The shiny green leaves, each one with a pale midrib, appear in spring. ♔

x *Amarcrinum memoria-corsii*
AMARCRINUM
☼ ✳✳   ↕ 1m (3ft)

This hybrid between *Amaryllis* and *Crinum* forms an evergreen clump of strap-shaped leaves. Loose umbels of fragrant trumpet-flowers open from late summer to autumn.

Colchicum speciosum 'Album'
AUTUMN CROCUS
☼ ✳✳✳   ↕ 20cm (8in)

The large, goblet-shaped, slender-tubed, pure white flowers of this exquisite crocus are virtually weather-proof. Large, glossy basal leaves are produced in spring. ♔

Crocus pulchellus
CROCUS
☼ ✳✳✳   ↕ 10cm (4in)

Ultimately forming patches by division and seed, this charming crocus has small, goblet-shaped flowers of palest blue, with darker veins and a deep yellow throat. ♔

Colchicum byzantinum
AUTUMN CROCUS
☼ ✳✳✳✳   ↕ 20cm (8in)

In early autumn, this striking perennial produces numerous goblet-shaped, pale purple flowers that open in the sun. Large, green basal leaves unfurl in spring. ♔

Colchicum 'Waterlily'
AUTUMN CROCUS
☼ ✳✳✳✳   ↕ 15cm (6in)

This is one of the most popular and eye-catching of all the autumn crocus hybrids. Its bold bunches of large, slender-tubed, double flowers are a rich pinkish lilac hue.

Crocus speciosus 'Oxonian'
CROCUS
☼ ✳✳✳   ↕ 10cm (4in)

The slender-tubed, goblet-shaped flowers are a deep violet-blue, with darker veins and conspicuous orange stigmas. Ideal for naturalizing in grass or beneath shrubs.

Merendera montana
MERENDERA
☼ ❈❈❈   ↕5cm (2in)

The flowers of this crocus-like perennial
are funnel-shaped with narrow, spreading,
pinkish purple petals, white at the base.
Glossy leaves follow the flowers.

Cyclamen hederifolium 'Album'
HARDY CYCLAMEN
☼ ❈❈❈   ↕10cm (4in)

This delightful little clump-former bears
nodding white flowers, each with swept-
back petals and a dark, puckered mouth.
The leaves are beautifully marbled.

**OTHER HARDY AUTUMN-
FLOWERING BULBS**

Colchicum agrippinum, see p.58
Colchicum autumnale
Colchicum speciosum
Crocus kotschyanus
Crocus nudiflorus
Crocus speciosus
Crocus speciosus 'Albus'
Cyclamen hederifolium, see p.60
Galanthus reginae-olgae
Schizostylis coccinea 'Major'
Schizostylis coccinea 'Mrs Hegarty'
Schizostylis coccinea 'Sunrise', see p.25

Nerine bowdenii
NERINE
☼ ❈❈   ↕60cm (24in)

This clump-forming, bulbous perennial is
popular and reliable. Its sturdy stems carry
loose umbels of bright pink, frilly-petalled
flowers. Ideal beneath a sunny wall. ▽

Gladiolus papilio
GLADIOLUS
☼ ❈❈   ↕1m (3ft)

Upright stems carry up to ten cup-shaped
flowers that are a mixture of cream, smoky
dull purple, yellow, and green. Its sword-
shaped leaves are narrow. Forms patches.

Leucojum autumnale
AUTUMN SNOWFLAKE
☼ ❈❈   ↕15cm (6in)

The slender, erect stems of this charming
bulb each support up to four small white,
nodding bell-flowers, tinged pink at their
bases. Leaves are equally slender. ▽

**OTHER TENDER AUTUMN-
FLOWERING BULBS**

x *Amarygia parkeri* 'Alba'
Amaryllis belladonna, see p.40
Arum pictum
Crinum x *powellii*, see p.80
Cyclamen graecum
Eucomis bicolor
Nerine bowdenii 'Pink Triumph'
Scilla scilloides
Sternbergia lutea
Zephyranthes candida

Winter-flowering Bulbs

P ERENNIALS WILLING TO FLOWER out of doors during the winter months are extremely valuable, so gardeners are fortunate in that a number of bulbous plants choose this time of year to make their display. As well as familiar favourites, such as the snowdrops and winter aconites, several that are less well known are widely available and worth considering. Planted as small groups, all the following will spread in time to form patches, especially if lifted and divided.

Cyclamen coum 'Album'
HARDY CYCLAMEN
☼ ❄❄❄   ↕5cm (2in) ↔ 10cm (4in)

Where conditions suit, this attractive little tuberous perennial forms patches. Dainty white flowers, with dark mouths, appear above its tufts of kidney-shaped leaves.

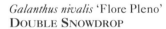

Galanthus nivalis 'Flore Pleno'
DOUBLE SNOWDROP
☼ ❄❄❄   ↕10cm (4in) ↔ 10cm (4in)

This is one of the most popular, reliable snowdrops, with its strap-shaped leaves and many-petalled white flowers with green markings. Dislikes dry soils.

Eranthis x *tubergenii*
WINTER ACONITE
☼ ❄❄❄   ↕10cm (4in) ↔ 10cm (4in)

Cheerful, cup-shaped golden flowers open above the ruffs of deeply toothed green leaves, which are bronzed when young. Tuberous, this will form carpets in time.

Galanthus 'Atkinsii'
SNOWDROP
☼ ❄❄❄   ↕25cm (10in) ↔ 10cm (4in)

Larger than the common snowdrop, this is a charming bulb, with strap-shaped grey-green leaves, and nodding white flowers on slender stems. Dislikes dry soils.

Narcissus romievxii
HOOP-PETTICOAT DAFFODIL
☼ ❄❄❄   ↕10cm (4in) ↔ 7cm (3in)

Excellent for a sheltered spot on the rock garden, this choice bulbous perennial has fragrant, skirt-like flowers and slender green leaves. Dislikes dry soils.

Decorative Seed Heads in Winter

TIDY-MINDED GARDENERS who, once autumn arrives, feel the urge to cut down and clear all spent flowering stems, lose themselves the undeniable ornamental bonus of seed heads in winter, particularly attractive when gilded by frost. Not all are worth saving, but these should certainly be spared.

Phormium tenax
NEW ZEALAND FLAX
☼ ❄❄❄   ↕ 2.5m (8ft) ↔ 2m (6ft)

This clump-forming evergreen plant has stiff, sword-shaped, dark green leaves, and in summer, tall stems bearing branched heads of red flowers. Dislikes dry soils. ♙

Achillea 'Gold Plate'
ACHILLEA
☼ ❄❄❄   ↕ 1.2m (4ft) ↔ 60cm (24in)

Sturdy-stemmed and clump-forming, this perennial has finely divided green leaves topped in summer by flattened yellow flowerheads. These pale to brown. ♙

Cortaderia selloana 'Pumila'
DWARF PAMPAS GRASS
☼ ❄❄❄   ↕ 1.5m (5ft) ↔ 1.2m (4ft)

During late summer and early autumn, the large, long-lasting plumes of creamy white spikelets appear above a mound of narrow, sharply toothed evergreen leaves. ♙

OTHER PERENNIALS WITH DECORATIVE SEED HEADS
Acanthus spinosus, see p.18
Achillea 'Coronation Gold'
Iris foetidissima, see p.43
Matteuccia struthiopteris
Phlomis russeliana
Watsonia beatricis

Cardiocrinum giganteum
GIANT HIMALAYAN LILY
☼ ❄❄   ↕ 2.5m (8ft) ↔ 60cm (24in)

Stately and impressive in winter, but also in summer, when it has a bold rosette of leaves and fragrant, creamy white trumpet flowers. Short-lived, it dislikes dry soils.

Miscanthus sinensis 'Kleine Fontane'
CHINESE SILVER GRASS
☼ ❄❄❄   ↕ 1m (3ft) ↔ 60cm (24in)

Brownish pink spikelets are produced in long-lasting, dense, finger-like sprays from summer. These top bold clumps of narrow green leaves, each with a pale midrib.

Sedum spectabile
ICE PLANT
☼ ❄❄❄   ↕ 45cm (18in) ↔ 45cm (18in)

Flattened heads of small, star-shaped pink flowers appear in late summer, and turn brown by winter. Fleshy grey-green leaves clothe its stout stems in summer. ♙

Perennial Herbs for Herbaceous Borders

SEVERAL PERENNIALS traditionally considered as herbs, and commonly cultivated as such in herb gardens have, as well as their culinary or medicinal uses, ornamental attributes that more than qualify them for the flower garden. Several are already well known, and many are useful for difficult sites or as temporary fillers, where failures have occurred.

OTHER HERBACEOUS PERENNIAL HERBS

Allium schoenoprasum 'Forescate'
Aristolochia clematitis
Artemisia absinthium 'Lambrook Silver'
Foeniculum vulgare 'Purpureum'
Inula helenium
Melissa officinalis 'All Gold'
Mentha x *suaveolens* 'Variegata', see p.68
Monarda 'Beauty of Cobham'
Myrrhis odorata, see p.53
Rumex alpinus 'Ruber'
Rumex scutatus 'Silver Shield'
Tanacetum balsamita var. *tomentosum*

Allium schoenoprasum
CHIVES
☼ ❄❄❄　　　‡ 25cm (10in) ↔ 15cm (6in)

This well-known bulbous herb makes a low clump of green, grassy, onion-scented leaves. Its pink or purple summer flowers are very popular with bees and butterflies.

OTHER EVERGREEN PERENNIAL HERBS

Asarum europaeum, see p.30
Chamaemelum nobile
Pulmonaria officinalis
Pulmonaria saccharata, see p.33
Salvia officinalis 'Purpurea'
Teucrium fruticans
Teucrium scorodonia 'Crispum'
Thymus x *citriodorus* 'Silver Queen'
Thymus vulgaris, see p.165
Viola odorata

Althaea officinalis
MARSH MALLOW
☼ ❄❄❄　　　‡ 2m (6ft) ↔ 1m (3ft)

The stems and lobed leaves of this erect, branching herb are covered in a soft pelt of grey or greyish green hairs. Pale pink flowers grow in the leaf axils in summer.

Cichorium intybus
CHICORY
☼ ❄❄❄　　　‡ 1.2m (4ft) ↔ 45cm (18in)

Branched, wiry, willowy stems rise from basal rosettes of leaves. During summer, these stems are studded with bright blue, multi-petalled, daisy-like flowers. ♈

Melittis melissophyllum
BASTARD BALM
☼ ☀ ❋❋❋   ↕ 30cm (12in) ↔ 30cm (12in)

Loose clumps of erect, hairy, four-sided
stems carry pairs of honey-scented leaves,
and pink or white, purple blotched, two-
lipped flowers early   in summer.

Foeniculum vulgare
FENNEL
☼ ❋❋❋   ↕ 2m (6ft) ↔ 45cm (18in)

Dense clumps of upright, hollow green
stems have finely divided, feathery blue-
green foliage, and these are topped in
spring with umbels of tiny yellow flowers.

Hyssopus officinalis
HYSSOP
☼ ❋❋❋   ↕ 60cm (24in) ↔ 1m (3ft)

Bees and butterflies love this low, bushy
semi-evergreen subshrub, with small,
aromatic leaves, and dense spires of blue
flowers from late summer into autumn.

Meum athamanticum
BALDMONEY,   **SPIGNEL**
☼ ❋❋❋   ↕ 30cm (12in) ↔ 15cm (6in)

Uncommon in gardens, this perennial
herb forms a low clump of finely divided,
feathery, aromatic leaves. Tiny white or
purplish white flowers occur in summer.

Gentiana lutea
YELLOW GENTIAN
☼ ❋❋❋   ↕ 1.2m (4ft) ↔ 60cm (24in)

From a basal clump of large, blue-green,
boldly veined leaves, sturdy leafy stems,
ending in dense spikes of yellow flowers,
rise in summer. A noble perennial.

Levisticum officinale
LOVAGE
☼ ☼ ❋❋❋   ↕ 2m (6ft) ↔ 1m (3ft)

This aromatic perennial forms generous
clumps of upright, hollow stems with dark
green leaves, bronze when young, and
umbels of yellow-green summer flowers.

Monarda fistulosa
WILD BERGAMOT
☼ ❋❋❋   ↕ 1.2m (4ft) ↔ 60cm (24in)

In summer, the erect stems of this free-
flowering, aromatic perennial are crowned
with dense flowerheads enjoyed by bees
and butterflies. Dislikes dry soils.

Annual and Biennial Herbs for Herbaceous Beds

NOT EVERYONE HAS SPACE in their gardens for a special herb plot, nor is one necessary. Many medicinal and culinary herbs are also ornamental, and can be attractively and easily accommodated in mixed herbaceous borders or beds. This is especially true of annual and biennial herbs, which are extremely useful as temporary fillers.

Borago officinalis
BORAGE
☼ ✳✳✳   ↕60cm (24in) ↔ 30cm (12in)

A familiar clump-forming annual, covered with pale, bristly hairs, this produces a summer-long succession of nodding, star-shaped blue flowers. Will seed around.

Anethum graveolens
DILL
☼ ✳✳   ↕60cm (24in) ↔ 30cm (12in)

One of the fennel family, this strongly aromatic annual herb produces clumps of finely divided, feathery blue-green foliage and umbels of tiny flowers in summer.

OTHER ANNUAL HERBS
Ambrosia artemisiifolia
Artemisia annua
Calendula officinalis
Calendula officinalis 'Fiesta Gitana'
Chrysanthemum coronarium
Cnicus benedictus
Nigella sativa
Ocimum basilicum 'Purple Ruffles'
Phacelia tanacetifolia
Trifolium incarnatum
Vaccaria hispanica

Atriplex hortensis var. *rubra*
RED ORACHE
☼ ✳✳   ↕1.5m (5ft) ↔ 30cm (12in)

This strong-growing annual is principally grown for its rich crimson, edible leaves and colourful stems. It contrasts well with grey-foliaged plants, and will self-seed.

OTHER BIENNIAL HERBS
Dipsacus fullonum
Eryngium maritimum
Oenothera biennis
Origanum majorana
Smyrnium olusatrum

Carthamus tinctorius
SAFFLOWER
☼ ✳✳   ↕ 1m (3ft) ↔ 30cm (12in)

The leaves of this annual are either entire or spine-toothed. Its red, orange, or yellow petals, borne on round flowerheads in late summer and early autumn, produce a dye.

Echium vulgare 'Blue Bedder'
VIPER'S BUGLOSS
☼ ✳✳✳   ↕ 30cm (12in) ↔ 20cm (8in)

This bristly biennial herb is upright, with narrow leaves. Spikes of blue, bell-shaped flowers are carried during summer. It is best grown in well-drained soils.

Isatis tinctoria
WOAD
☼ ✳✳✳   ↕ 1.2m (4ft) ↔ 45cm (18in)

Famous as a dye plant, this biennial has branching stems and large, loose heads of tiny yellow flowers in summer. These are followed by showers of dark seed capsules.

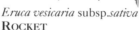

Eruca vesicaria subsp. *sativa*
ROCKET
☼ ✳✳✳   ↕ 60cm (24in) ↔ 30cm (12in)

Small, pale yellow summer flowers, held on erect spikes, have reddish veins. This annual has both deeply lobed, radish-like leaves, and smaller, toothed leaves. 🏆

Linum usitatissimum
LINSEED, COMMON FLAX
☼ ✳✳✳   ↕ 60cm (24in) ↔ 2.5cm (1in)

For centuries, this ancient herb has been grown for fibre and oil. Erect and slender-stemmed, it has narrow leaves and loose heads of summer flowers.

Coriandrum sativum
CORIANDER
☼ ✳✳✳   ↕ 50cm (20in) ↔ 30cm (12in)

The lower leaves of this popular, aromatic, annual herb are parsley-like, and its upper leaves, finely divided. Umbels of tiny, pale purple or white flowers appear in summer.

Helianthus annuus
SUNFLOWER
☼ ✳✳✳   ↕ 3m (10ft) ↔ 45cm (18in)

Popular with children, this strong-growing annual has large leaves. In summer, each plant bears a huge, golden daisy-flower with a brown centre on a stout, erect stem.

Silybum marianum
MILK THISTLE
☼ ✳✳✳   ↕ 1.3m (4½ft) ↔ 60cm (24in)

Bold, and carried in basal rosettes, the spiny green leaves of this biennial have white veins that create a marbled effect. Prickly thistle-heads appear in summer.

Rabbit-proof Perennials

E VERYONE DISAPPOINTED at finding a favourite perennial
plant damaged or eaten to the ground by rabbits will be
equally familiar with the frustration felt in attempting their
control. Those who garden in country areas, or wherever
there are large, open spaces, are particularly at risk. Where
rabbits appear to be an insoluble problem, it might be worth
growing some of the plants they find unpalatable. Many
other cultivars of the genera featured here are also suitable.

Digitalis purpurea
FOXGLOVE
☼ ✻✻✻   ↕ 1.5m (5ft) ↔ 60cm (24in)

This familiar, popular woodland plant is
usually treated as a biennial. Its rosettes of
large, downy leaves produce erect spikes
of drooping, tubular flowers in summer.

Aconitum vulparia
WOLFSBANE
☼ ✻✻✻   ↕ 1.2m (4ft) ↔ 60cm (24in)

Once used to poison wolves, all parts of
this plant are toxic. The deeply divided
leaves are dark green and slender, hooded
straw-yellow flowers open in summer.

Astilbe 'Ostrich Plume'
ASTILBE
☼ ✻✻✻   ↕ 1m (3ft) ↔ 1m (3ft)

Arching, feathery plumes of coral-pink
flowers top mounds of fern-like leaves in
summer. This, and many similar cultivars,
enjoys rich, moist soils.

DEER-PROOF PERENNIALS
Acanthus spinosus, see p.18
Aconitum carmichaelii 'Arendsii'
Dryopteris affinis, see p.53
Epimedium x *perralchicum*, see p.42
Iris sibirica
Lychnis coronaria
Paeonia 'Bowl of Beauty', see p.21
Rudbeckia fulgida 'Goldsturm', see p.33
Sisyrinchium striatum
Tellima grandiflora, see p. 43
Veratrum viride

Aster novi-belgii 'Marie Ballard'
MICHAELMAS DAISY
☼ ✻✻✻   ↕ 1m (3ft) ↔ 45cm (18in)

From late summer into autumn, branched,
leafy stems are topped by lilac daisy
flowers. Stems may need support. Other
cultivars, also rabbit-proof, are available.

Bergenia 'Ballawley'
ELEPHANT'S EAR
☼ ◐ ☀ ✻✻✻   ↕↔ 60cm (24in)

Large, rounded evergreen leaves in low
clumps turn red in winter. Its bright
crimson, bell-shaped flowers are borne in
sprays in spring. Prefers a sheltered site.

Epimedium x *rubrum*
BISHOP'S HAT
☼ ✻✻✻   ↕ 30cm (12in) ↔ 30cm (12in)

Clumps of slender-stalked, heart-shaped
leaflets are tinted brownish or reddish in
spring, when the loose clusters of small,
spurred flowers are produced.

P E R E N N I A L S

Geranium sanguineum
BLOODY CRANESBILL
☼ ✽✽✽   ↕25cm (10in) ↔30cm (12in)

Numerous deep magenta-pink flowers top
the low hummocks and mats of rounded,
deeply divided leaves in summer. Makes
excellent ground cover.

Lamium maculatum 'White Nancy'
SPOTTED DEADNETTLE
☼ ✽✽✽   ↕15cm (6in) ↔1m (3ft)

Spikes of two-lipped white flowers rise
above carpets of semi-evergreen silver-
white, heart-shaped, toothed leaves from
spring into summer. Dislikes dry soils. ▽

Nepeta x *faassenii*
CATMINT
☼ ✽✽✽   ↕45cm (18in) ↔45cm (18in)

This familiar and widely grown aromatic
perennial forms mounds of greyish green
leaves, and carries loose spikes of small
lavender-blue flowers in early summer.

Helleborus orientalis (pink form)
LENTEN ROSE
☼ ✽✽✽   ↕45cm (18in) ↔45cm (18in)

Cup-shaped flowers of a lovely dusky
pink with dark spots, emerge ahead of the
new leaves in late winter or early spring.
Its dark green, fingered leaves overwinter.

Lysimachia clethroides
LOOSESTRIFE
☼ ✽✽✽   ↕1m (3ft) ↔60cm (24in)

This fast-spreading perennial soon forms
colonies. Its leafy stems end in curved,
tapering spikes of small white flowers in
late summer. Enjoys moist soils. ▽

Tradescantia 'Purple Dome'
SPIDERWORT
☼ ✽✽✽   ↕60cm (24in) ↔45cm (18in)

Clumps of fleshy stems, clothed in lance-
shaped leaves, carry terminal clusters of
rich purple flowers in summer. Numerous
other cultivars are also suitable.

Iris 'Bold Print'
BEARDED IRIS
☼ ✽✽✽   ↕55cm (22in) ↔indefinite

Sheaves of grey-green, sword-shaped
leaves rise from a maze of thick rhizomes.
In late spring or early summer, branched
stems of purple and white flowers appear.

OTHER RABBIT-PROOF PERENNIALS

Aconitum 'Blue Sceptre'
Agapanthus Headbourne Hybrids
Anemone x *hybrida* 'Königin Charlotte'
Convallaria majalis 'Fortin's Giant'
Crocosmia 'Lucifer'
Kniphofia triangularis
Paeonia officinalis 'Rubra Plena'
Pulmonaria saccharata, see p.33
Sedum telephium subsp. *maximum*
  'Atropurpureum', see p.75
Vinca major

Trollius europaeus
GLOBE FLOWER
☼ ✽✽✽   ↕60cm (24in) ↔45cm (18in)

This reliable, clump-forming perennial
has long-stalked, deeply divided leaves,
and branching heads of beautiful spring
flowers. 'Superbus' is an excellent form.

CLIMBERS

THE MOST COMMON climbers are woody-stemmed perennials or shrubs with scrambling or otherwise long, slender stems. Self-clinging by adhesive tendril tips or aerial roots, or in need of artificial support from wire or a trellis, they may be trained into trees and shrubs, and to cover walls or other structures.

△ IVY-CLAD SHED *This bold-leaved ivy (Hedera colchica 'Dentata Variegata') is perfect for covering an unsightly wall.*

△ *Abutilon megapotamicum*

THE BEAUTY OF CLIMBERS
• Useful as cover on tree stumps or unsightly buildings.
• Offer flowers for every season.
• Versatile shrubs double as climbers.
• Provide bold or decorative foliage.
• Offer fragrant flowers.
• Give shelter or nesting sites for birds.
• Provide brilliant leaf tints in autumn.
• Offer decorative fruit or seed heads.
• Create multi-season effects if one plant is used as support for another.

All plants recommended in this section are either true climbers, or shrubs suitable for training against walls. They offer a large variety of effects, from colourful or prolific flowers to decorative or unusual fruits. Many have attractive leaves, and some deciduous climbers are also noted for their autumn tints. Once established, both wall shrubs and climbers can support further plants, creating, when planned, a continuous, multi-season feature. All the climbers recommended on the following pages are deciduous unless specified as evergreen.

CLIMBING TO THE SUN
Numerous climbers grown for their flowering qualities thrive best in a sunny site; most honeysuckles for instance, and climbing roses. Two popular favourites, clematis and wisteria, prefer to have their heads in the sun and their roots shaded (place a large stone or tile over their roots). When grown against a wall, climbers benefit from the reflected heat, which helps ripen growth and initiate flower bud formation.

WOODLAND SHADE
The cooler conditions of sunless walls, often combined with moist but well-drained soils, are a perfect home for many natural woodland climbers. Ivies are a good example, especially coloured-leaved varieties, which flourish on shady or partially shaded walls, as do those lovely South American woodlanders, *Lapageria* and *Berberidopsis*.

△ SUPPORT IN DISGUISE *Evergreen, spring-flowering ceanothus and twining honeysuckle beautifully decorate this pole.*

◁ PRETTY WINDOW *Wisteria, rose, and two clematis varieties combine to provide a delightful frame for this window.*

▷ SUMMER SENSATION *A luxuriant early summer growth of clematis, purple vine, and golden hop clothes this wall.*

Climbers for Warm, Sunny Walls and Fences

SUNNY WALLS AND FENCES are excellent for climbers. When carefully selected and matched, several can be trained to grow into one another to give continuous effect. The surface, especially of a brick or stone wall, absorbs heat, and this helps promote growth, and encourages flowering. All the climbers featured here require support from wires or netting.

Lonicera x *americana*
HONEYSUCKLE
☼ ❄❄❄   ↕ ↔ 7m (22ft)

This free-flowering climber has clusters of fragrant, long-tubed, creamy yellow flowers from summer into early autumn. Its leaves are purplish when young. ♈

Actinidia kolomikta
ACTINIDIA
☼ ❄❄❄   ↕ ↔ 4.5m (13ft)

This striking climber is slow to establish, but it is well worth the wait. It has bold, heart-shaped leaves, often splashed cream and pink, and white flowers in summer. ♈

Passiflora caerulea
BLUE PASSION FLOWER
☼ ❄❄   ↕ ↔ 10m (30ft)

Fast-growing with fingered leaves, this climber bears beautiful, unusual flowers from summer into autumn. They may be followed by attractive seed pods. ♈

Clematis 'Bill Mackenzie'
CLEMATIS
☼ ❄❄❄   ↕ ↔ 7m (22ft)

Vigorous and scrambling, this clematis has beautiful, lantern-like, nodding flowers in late summer and autumn. These are followed by pretty, silky seed heads. ♈

Clematis 'Jackmanii'
CLEMATIS
☼ ❄❄❄   ↕ ↔ 3m (10ft)

A long-established garden favourite, this climbs by twining leaf stalks. Masses of large, velvety, dark purple flowers, turning violet with age, appear in summer. ♈

Rosa 'Dublin Bay'
CLIMBING ROSE
☼ ❄❄❄   ↕ ↔ 2.2m (7ft)

'Dublin Bay' is a climbing floribunda rose of dense growth, with glossy, dark green leaves and clusters of cupped, fragrant flowers from summer to early autumn. ♈

Vitis vinifera 'Purpurea'
CLARET VINE
☼ ❄❄❄   ↕↔7m (22ft)

A vigorous form of the grape vine, with young leaves that mature to wine-purple. These colour richly in autumn, when small bunches of blue-black grapes ripen. ♔

SELF-CLINGING CLIMBERS FOR SUNNY WALLS AND FENCES

Campsis radicans
Cissus striata
Decumaria barbara
Decumaria sinensis, see p.105
Ficus pumila
Parthenocissus tricuspidata 'Lowii'
Trachelospermum asiaticum, see p.107
Trachelospermum jasminoides, see p.104
Trachelospermum jasminoides
  'Variegatum'

Rosa 'Mme Gregoire Staechelin'
CLIMBING ROSE
☼ ❄❄❄   ↕↔3m (10ft)

One of the most beautiful climbing roses, this is vigorous, with shining green leaves and abundant clusters of rounded, slightly fragrant flowers in summer. ♔

OTHER CLIMBERS FOR SUN

Araujia sericofera
Campsis x *tagliabuana* 'Madame Galen'
Clematis armandii, see p.104
Dregea sinensis
Jasminum officinale 'Affine'
Lonicera periclymenum 'Graham
  Thomas', see p.103
Mandevilla suaveolens
Mutisia ilicifolia
Rosa banksiae 'Lutea'
Solanum jasminoides, see p.95
Sollya heterophylla
Wisteria sinensis, see p.105

Rosa 'Maigold'
CLIMBING ROSE
☼ ❄❄❄   ↕↔4m (12ft)

This vigorous climber has thorny stems and lush foliage. Fragrant bronze-yellow blooms, reddish in bud, appear in early summer, and less profusely in autumn. ♔

Solanum jasminoides 'Album'
SOLANUM
☼ ❄❄   ↕↔6m (20ft)

Semi-evergreen and slender-stemmed, this climber will grow vigorously through any support. Loose clusters of star-flowers occur from summer into autumn. ♔

Wisteria floribunda 'Alba'
WHITE JAPANESE WISTERIA
☼ ❄❄❄   ↕↔9m (28ft)

The handsome leaves of this powerful climber are divided. Long spikes of white pea-flowers emerge in early summer. Thrives in neutral to slightly acid soils. ♔

CLIMBERS

Climbers for Sunless Walls and Fences

THE COOLER CONDITIONS normally found in places that do not receive the sun's glare directly suit a good number of climbers, many of which grow naturally in woodland, or similarly shaded places in the wild. Most need to be tied to a wire or trellis support, and even the self-clinging ones, such as ivy, benefit from this for a year or two after planting.

CLIMBERS

Berberidopsis corallina
CORAL PLANT
☀ ☀ ✻✻✻ PH ▽   ↕ ↔ 4.5m (14ft)

Coral Plant's long, rambling stems, with heart-shaped evergreen leaves, need tying to a support. Pendent, globular flowers are carried from summer into autumn.

Clematis montana f. *grandiflora*
CLEMATIS
☀ ☀ ✻✻✻   ↕ ↔ 10m (30ft)

In time, this vigorous climber will produce blankets of leafy growth, bronze-purple when the leaves are young. Large white spring flowers are borne in abundance. ▽

Hedera colchica 'Dentata Variegata'
PERSIAN IVY
☀ ☀ ✻✻✻   ↕ ↔ 5m (15ft)

A spectacular evergreen with broad-based, leathery leaves, each irregularly margined creamy white. Shoots have aerial roots that cling to the surface of a support. ▽

OTHER DECIDUOUS CLIMBERS FOR SUNLESS WALLS

Akebia trifoliata
Aristotelia tomentosa
Hydrangea anomala subsp. *petiolaris*, see p.107
Parthenocissus henryana, see p.107
Parthenocissus thomsonii
Parthenocissus tricuspidata 'Lowii'
Parthenocissus tricuspidata 'Robusta'
Schizophragma hydrangeoides
Schizophragma hydrangeoides 'Roseum'

Clematis x *jouiniana* 'Praecox'
CLEMATIS
☀ ☀ ✻✻✻   ↕ ↔ 3m (10ft)

Vigorous and sprawling, this dense-growing climber should be trained to a support. Its coarse foliage backs masses of small, fragrant, tubular flowers in late summer. ▽

Clematis 'Nelly Moser'
CLEMATIS
☀ ✻✻✻   ↕ ↔ 3.5m (11ft)

Large, single, pale mauve flowers, with a carmine stripe on each petal, cover this popular twining clematis in early summer. Their colour fades in strong sunlight. ▽

Hedera colchica 'Sulphur Heart'
PERSIAN IVY
☀ ☀ ✻✻✻   ↕ ↔ 5m (15ft)

This dramatic ivy, with its boldly splashed leaves, is similar in growth to *H. colchica* 'Dentata Variegata' *(above)*. They are most effective when grown together. ▽

Hedera helix 'Eva'
IVY
☼ ☀ ✻✻✻   ↕ ↔ 1.2m (4ft)

The evergreen leaves of this very popular,
variegated common ivy cultivar are green
and grey-green with broad, creamy white
margins. It is self-clinging.   ♆

Lapageria rosea
CHILEAN BELLFLOWER
☼ ☀ ✻✻   ↕ ↔ 5m (15ft)

Strongly twining stems support leathery
evergreen leaves and, from summer into
late autumn, beautiful, pendulous, tubular
flowers with fleshy petals.   ♆

Lonicera japonica 'Halliana'
JAPANESE HONEYSUCKLE
☼ ☀ ☀ ✻✻✻   ↕ ↔ 10m (30ft)

Evergreen or semi-evergreen, this prolific,
twining climber produces loose clusters of
fragrant flowers, emerging white and aging
to yellow, from summer into autumn.   ♆

Hedera helix 'Green Ripple'
IVY
☼ ☀ ✻✻✻   ↕ ↔ 1.2m (4ft)

This is a distinct cultivar of common ivy
in which the bright evergreen leaves, with
pale veins, are deeply lobed and pointed.
Self-clinging, it is ideal for low walls.   ♆

Humulus lupulus 'Aureus'
GOLDEN HOP
☼ ☀ ✻✻✻   ↕ ↔ 6m (20ft)

A strong-growing herbaceous climber, this
has hairy, twining stems and boldly lobed
yellow-green leaves. Clusters of green
fruits (hops) are produced in autumn.   ♆

**OTHER EVERGREEN CLIMBERS
FOR SUNLESS WALLS**

Hedera pastuchovii
Holboellia latifolia
Lardizabala biternata
Pileostegia viburnoides, see p.104

Schizophragma integrifolium
SCHIZOPHRAGMA
☼ ☀ ✻✻✻   ↕ ↔ 12m (40ft)

In time, this slow-growing, self-clinging
climber will reach great heights. Flattened
heads of creamy white flowers appear in
summer, among pointed green leaves.   ♆

Shrubs for Warm, Sunny Walls and Fences

SUNNY WALLS AND FENCES are a bonus to the gardener as they offer both the warmth and shelter necessary for less hardy plants. They are also ideal for shrubs with trailing or fragile stems that need some support. Most will greatly increase their average height when grown against a wall. Careful pruning and training onto wires or a trellis may be necessary.

Abutilon megapotamicum
ABUTILON

☼ ❋❋❋   ↕ ↔ 3m (10ft)

This free-growing shrub is of virtually pendulous habit with slender stems and, from late spring to autumn, flowers that resemble colourful Chinese lanterns.

Callistemon pallidus
BOTTLEBRUSH

☼ ❋❋❋ PH   ↕ ↔ 3m (10ft)

In flower, bottlebrushes are among the most exotic of evergreen shrubs. This is certainly no exception, with its brushes of creamy yellow flowers, borne in summer.

Ceanothus arboreus 'Trewithen Blue'
CATALINA CEANOTHUS

☼ ❋❋❋   ↕ ↔ 6m (20ft)

This strong-growing evergreen shrub is ideal for covering a large surface. It flowers for many weeks in late winter and spring. Prefers well-drained, lime-free soils.

Buddleja crispa
BUDDLEJA

☼ ❋❋   ↕ ↔ 2.5m (8ft)

The oval leaves of this choice shrub are all covered in a woolly pelt of soft, greyish white down. Its small, fragrant flowers are carried in dense clusters in summer.

OTHER DECIDUOUS SHRUBS FOR WARM, SUNNY WALLS AND FENCES

Abelia floribunda
Abeliophyllum distichum
Buddleja officinalis
Caesalpinia japonica
Chimonanthus praecox 'Grandiflorus', see p.166
Clianthus puniceus
Colquhounia coccinea
Edgeworthia chrysantha
Indigofera heterantha, see p.126
Lagerstroemia indica
Lavatera maritima
Prunus mume 'Alphandii'
Prunus mume 'Beni-shidore'
Punica granatum 'Flore Pleno'
Ribes speciosum
Viburnum macrocephalum 'Sterile'
Xanthoceras sorbifolium, see p.127

Cytisus battandieri
MOROCCAN BROOM

☼ ❋❋   ↕ ↔ 4m (12ft)

Moroccan Broom is worth growing for its leaves alone, each divided into three parts, and covered in soft, silky silvery hairs. Its summer flowers are pineapple-scented.

Feijoa sellowiana
PINEAPPLE GUAVA
☼ ❄❄ ‡↔ 3m (10ft)

The summer flowers of this interesting
evergreen shrub have fleshy, edible petals
and crimson stamens. Edible, egg-shaped
fruits are produced after a hot summer.

Robinia hispida
ROSE ACACIA
☼ ❄❄❄ ‡↔ 2.5m (8ft)

Large rose-pink pea-flowers are borne in
drooping clusters from late spring into
summer. The leaves, with numerous lush
green leaflets, are held on fragile stems. ♛

Fremontodendron 'California Glory'
FREMONTODENDRON
☼ ❄❄ ‡↔ 8m (25ft)

This fast-growing evergreen has beautiful
yellow flowers from spring into autumn.
Prune regularly if it is on a small fence or
wall, and ensure the roots are not too wet.

Rosa x *odorata* 'Mutabilis'
CHINA ROSE
☼ ❄❄ ‡↔ 3m (10ft)

This vigorous China rose is popular for its
dark purple shoots, coppery young leaves,
and lovely fragrant summer flowers. It will
grow taller than usual against a wall. ♛

**OTHER EVERGREEN SHRUBS FOR
WARM, SUNNY WALLS AND FENCES**

Acacia dealbata, see p.158
Carpenteria californica, see p.158
Ceanothus 'Concha'
Viburnum odoratissimum

Desmodium tiliifolium
DESMODIUM
☼ ❄❄ ‡↔ 2m (6ft)

From late summer into autumn, loose
heads of pea-flowers are borne above large,
downy leaves. Except in warm areas, old
growth is best pruned back every spring.

Itea ilicifolia
ITEA
☼ ❄❄ ‡↔ 5m (15ft)

On warm evenings from late summer into
autumn, long greenish catkins give off a
honey-like aroma. The dark green, glossy,
holly-like leaves are evergreen. ♛

Solanum crispum 'Glasnevin'
SOLANUM
☼ ❄❄ ‡↔ 6m (20ft)

Vigorous and scrambling, this shrub is
evergreen in warmer areas. Loose clusters
of star-shaped flowers appear over a long
period in summer. Needs support. ♛

Shrubs for Sunless Walls and Fences

SOME GARDENERS may perceive a wall or fence that does not receive direct sunlight as a curse, and consider it unsightly. It need not be a problem, however, as long as it receives some light. Many shrubs (and climbers) will thrive, and some even prefer the normally cooler conditions of such a site, while others flower freely in or out of the sun.

Azara microphylla
AZARA
☼ ☼ ✻✻   ↕↔6m (20ft)

This elegant evergreen will grow to small tree size if allowed. Arching branchlets are clothed with leaves and, in late winter or spring, tiny vanilla-scented flowers. ♈

Chaenomeles speciosa 'Moerloosei'
ORNAMENTAL QUINCE
☼ ☼ ☼ ✻✻✻   ↕↔2.5m (8ft)

A reliable, adaptable, and vigorous shrub, this carries large flower clusters in spring and early summer, followed by aromatic fruits. Prune, and train on wires. ♈

Chaenomeles x superba 'Rowallane'
ORNAMENTAL QUINCE
☼ ☼ ☼ ✻✻✻   ↕↔1.5m (5ft)

Superb in spring, when the previous year's branches are hidden beneath brilliant red flower clusters. Like 'Moerloosei', best pruned and trained close to the wall. ♈

Euonymus fortunei 'Silver Queen'
SILVER QUEEN EUONYMUS
☼ ☼ ☼ ✻✻✻   ↕↔2.5m (8ft)

A handsome evergreen shrub, low and bushy in a bed, but rising higher against a wall if trained. Glossy dark green leaves have broad, irregular creamy margins. ♈

Forsythia suspensa
WEEPING FORSYTHIA
☼ ☼ ☼ ✻✻✻   ↕↔3m (10ft)

A vigorous, rambling shrub, this requires regular pruning and training to prevent it from becoming overpowering. Star-shaped flowers wreathe the branches in spring. ♈

Garrya elliptica (male form)
SILK-TASSEL BUSH
☼ ☼ ☼ ✻✻✻   ↕↔5m (15ft)

From midwinter through to early spring the branches are draped with long tassels, which tremble in the slightest breeze. This shrub has leathery evergreen leaves.

Illicium anisatum
CHINESE ANISE
☼ ☼ ✻✻   ↕↔2.5m (8ft)

The aromatic leaves of this slow-growing evergreen are joined by loose clusters of yellow, star-shaped flowers in spring. The wood also has a strong, agreeable aroma.

Jasminum humile
HIMALAYAN JASMINE

☼ ☼ ☀ ❄❄❄   ↕ ↔ 2m (6ft)

The numerous greenish stems of this bushy evergreen are clothed in attractive, much-divided leaves. It sports clusters of yellow flowers from spring into autumn.

> **OTHER EVERGREEN SHRUBS FOR SUNLESS WALLS AND FENCES**
>
> *Azara lancifolia*
> *Azara serrata*
> *Camellia* 'Inspiration'
> *Crinodendron hookerianum*, see p.132
> *Euonymus fortunei* 'Emerald Gaiety',
>   see p.118
> *Garrya* x *issaquahensis*
>   'Glasnevin Wine'
> *Jasminum humile* 'Revolutum'
> *Pyracantha* 'Orange Glow', see p.169

Kerria japonica 'Pleniflora'
BATCHELOR'S BUTTONS

☼ ☼ ☀ ❄❄❄   ↕ ↔ 3m (10ft)

Popular and easy to grow, this vigorous shrub has long green shoots that require support, along with sharply toothed leaves, and rich yellow spring flowers. ♔

Pyracantha rogersiana
FIRETHORN

☼ ☼ ☀ ❄❄❄   ↕ ↔ 3m (10ft)

The spiny branches of this strong-growing evergreen are clothed in narrrow, glossy leaves. Flower clusters in early summer are replaced by orange-red berries. ♔

> **OTHER DECIDOUS SHRUBS FOR SUNLESS WALLS AND FENCES**
>
> *Chaenomeles speciosa*
>   'Kermesina Semiplena'
> *Chaenomeles speciosa* 'Nivalis'
> *Chaenomeles speciosa* 'Phylis Moore'
> *Chaenomeles* x *superba*
>   'Crimson and Gold'
> *Chaenomeles* x *superba* 'Pink Lady'
> *Cotoneaster horizontalis*
> *Lonicera* x *purpusii* 'Winter Beauty',
>   see p.167

Jasminum nudiflorum
WINTER JASMINE

☼ ☼ ☀ ❄❄❄   ↕ ↔ 3m (10ft)

This is a most popular and reliable winter-flowering shrub, with long shoots bearing yellow flowers through winter into spring. Prune after flowering to keep neat. ♔

Piptanthus nepalensis
EVERGREEN LABURNUM

☼ ☼ ☀ ❄❄   ↕ ↔ 3m (10ft)

This strong-growing shrub has lush semi-evergreen or evergreen foliage. Its clusters of bright yellow pea-flowers are produced from spring into summer.

Ribes laurifolium (male form)
RIBES

☼ ☀ ❄❄   ↕ ↔ 2m (6ft)

A curious, slow-growing evergreen currant which needs training to gain height. Its bold leaves are joined by drooping flower clusters from late winter into early spring.

Climbers to Train into Trees and Shrubs

IF YOU LACK WALLS OR FENCES, encourage climbers to grow into trees or large shrubs, where they can create spectacular effects when in flower or leaf. It is important to match each climber to its supporting plant: grow strong climbers into large trees and weaker ones into small trees or shrubs.

Careful pruning may be necessary to control growth.

Clematis rehderiana
CLEMATIS
☼ ✳✳✳   ↕ ↔ 7m (22ft)

As well as a dense growth of divided leaves, loose clusters of primrose-yellow, cowslip-scented flowers cover this twining climber from late summer into autumn. ♔

OTHER FOLIAGE CLIMBERS FOR TRAINING INTO TREES

Ampelopsis aconitifolia
Aristolochia macrophylla
Hedera colchica 'Dentata Variegata', see p.96
Humulus lupulus 'Aureus', see p.97
Vitis vinifera 'Purpurea', see p.95

Akebia quinata
CHOCOLATE VINE
☼ ☼ ✳✳   ↕ ↔ 10m (30ft)

The clusters of vanilla-scented, brownish purple flowers in spring are followed by sausage-shaped fruits. This vigorous semi-evergreen climbs by twining.

Clematis 'Madame Julia Correvon'
CLEMATIS
☼ ✳✳✳   ↕ ↔ 3.5m (11ft)

This twining climber with slender stems, freely produces magnificent, four-petalled wine-red flowers with cream-coloured stamens, from summer to early autumn. ♔

Celastrus orbiculatus
ORIENTAL BITTERSWEET
☼ ☼ ✳✳✳   ↕ ↔ 20m (70ft)

The leaves of this strong-growing climber turn yellow in autumn, when capsules of orange seeds, that last into winter, first appear on pollinated female plants.   ♔

Clematis montana var. *rubens*
CLEMATIS
☼ ✳✳✳   ↕ ↔ 10m (30ft)

Dense curtains of growth, covered with masses of pink flowers in late spring and early summer, are formed by this twining climber. Many good selections exist.   ♔

Hedera colchica
PERSIAN IVY
☼ ☼ ✺ ✳✳✳   ↕ ↔ 10m (30ft)

Persian Ivy is a strong-growing, evergreen, self-clinging climber, which also makes a splendid ground cover. Its shining, dark green leaves are pointed and leathery.   ♔

Lonicera periclymenum
'Graham Thomas'
☼ ✻✻✻   ↕ ↔ 7m (22ft)

Vigorous and dense-growing, this twining climber has oval leaves and, in summer, loose clusters of freely borne, fragrant flowers that are white, ageing to yellow. ♈

Rosa 'Albertine'
CLIMBING ROSE
☼ ✻✻✻   ↕ ↔ 5m (15ft)

An old and popular vigorous rambling rose, 'Albertine' has thorny reddish stems and richly fragrant, double salmon-pink flowers, freely borne in summer. ♈

Rosa filipes 'Kiftsgate'
CLIMBING ROSE
☼ ✻✻✻   ↕ ↔ 10m (30ft)

Rampant if unpruned, this rose has fresh, glossy green foliage and branched heads of fragrant, yellow-centred white flowers in summer, followed by small red hips. ♈

Tropaeolum speciosum
FLAME NASTURTIUM
☼ ✻✻✻   ↕ ↔ 3m (10ft)

Brilliant, long-spurred flowers adorn this climber, with fleshy, twining stems and long-stalked leaves, from summer into autumn. Bright blue fruits follow. ♈

Vitis coignetiae
JAPANESE VINE
☼ ✻✻✻   ↕ ↔ 20m (70ft)

This vigorous vine climbs by means of twining tendrils, and is chiefly grown for its handsome, heart-shaped leaves, which turn crimson and scarlet in autumn. ♈

OTHER FLOWERING CLIMBERS FOR TRAINING INTO TREES

Clematis 'Jackmanii', see p.94
Clematis 'Perle d'Azur'
Clematis viticella
   'Purpurea Plena Elegans'
Hydrangea anomala subsp. *petiolaris*,
   see p.107
Jasminum officinale
Rosa brunonii 'La Mortola'
Schisandra rubrifolia
Wisteria sinensis, see p.105

Polygonum baldschuanicum
RUSSIAN VINE
☼ ✻✻✻   ↕ ↔ 12m (40ft)

Well known, popular, and rampant, this twining climber has string-like tassels of white or pink-tinged flowers in summer and early autumn. Dislikes dry soils. ♈

Wisteria floribunda 'Macrobotrys'
WISTERIA
☼ ✻✻✻   ↕ ↔ 10m (30ft)

In early summer, this vigorous, twining climber produces fragrant lilac, darker-flushed pea-flowers in handsome, pendent tassels up to 1.2m (4ft) long. ♈

Evergreen Climbers

I VIES APART, the number of evergreen climbers suitable for gardens in cool, temperate regions is relatively few, when compared with the abundance of deciduous climbers. This makes them all the more valuable, especially in winter, when their persistent foliage provides a welcome touch of colour, and they can be used to hide unsightly structures, as well as providing useful shelter for wildlife. Most evergreen climbers need support; but self-clinging plants are specified here.

OTHER EVERGREEN CLIMBERS

Cissus striata
Clematis cirrhosa var. *balearica*
Clematis fasciculiflora
Hedera canariensis 'Gloire de Marengo'
Hedera colchica 'Sulphur Heart', see p.96
Holboellia coriacea
Holboellia latifolia
Lapageria rosea, see p.97
Lonicera japonica
Rosa bracteata
Rubus henryi

Clematis armandii
CLEMATIS
☼ ❄❄❄　　　　　↕ ↔ 5m (15ft)

The leaflets of this vigorous climber are dark, glossy green. Fragrant white or pink-flushed flowers are borne in bold clusters in early spring. Best in a sheltered position.

Pileostegia viburnoides
PILEOSTEGIA
☼ ☀ ❄❄　　　　　↕ ↔ 6m (20ft)

This slow-growing hydrangea relative is self-clinging, climbing by aerial roots. Its branched heads of tiny creamy flowers open in late summer and early autumn. ♔

Clematis cirrhosa
CLEMATIS
☼ ❄❄❄　　　　　↕ ↔ 3m (10ft)

Slender, twining stems and small, fern-like leaves form a dense curtain. Loose clusters of nodding, bell-shaped, creamy flowers open from late winter into early spring.

Hedera helix 'Buttercup'
GOLDEN IVY
☼ ☀ ❄❄❄　　　　　↕ ↔ 6m (20ft)

The three-lobed leaves of this self-clinging climber form a dense cover. They become a rich yellow in summer, though excessive sun can scorch them. ♔

Trachelospermum jasminoides
STAR, OR CONFEDERATE, JASMINE
☼ ❄❄　　　　　↕ ↔ 6m (20ft)

Best started on supporting wires, this self-clinging climber has dark green leaves that may turn red in winter. Clusters of creamy white summer flowers are fragrant. ♔

Climbers with Fragrant Flowers

MENTION FRAGRANT CLIMBERS, and most people instantly picture honeysuckle scrambling over a hedge or framing a cottage door. No one would deny its attraction, but there are many other climbers whose flowers produce fragrances which, once experienced, are not forgotten.

Rosa 'Wedding Day'
CLIMBING ROSE
☼ ✻✻✻   ↕ ↔ 8m (25ft)

The yellow buds of this climbing rose, with glossy green leaves and thorny stems, open in summer to richly scented, creamy white flowers. Blooms age to pale pink.

Clematis flammula
CLEMATIS
☼ ✻✻✻   ↕ ↔ 5m (15ft)

The herbaceous stems of this vigorous climber are clothed with deeply divided green leaves and, in late summer and early autumn, almond-scented white flowers.

Jasminum officinale
'Argenteovariegatum'
☼ ✻✻✻   ↕ ↔ 5m (15ft)

Strong-growing and semi-evergreen, this climber has twining stems, much-divided cream-margined leaves, and richly fragrant, pink-budded, white summer flowers. ♔

Wisteria sinensis
CHINESE WISTERIA
☼ ✻✻✻   ↕ ↔ 20m (70ft)

Pruning is required if this twining climber is grown against a wall. Its leaves are fresh green, and the crowded tassels of fragrant summer flowers, lilac and pale violet. ♔

Decumaria sinensis
DECUMARIA
☼ ✻✻   ↕ ↔ 4m (12ft)

This self-clinging evergreen climber has aerial roots, fairly narrow, pointed leaves, and heads of tiny, greenish white, honey-scented flowers, borne freely in spring.

Lonicera periclymenum 'Serotina'
LATE DUTCH HONEYSUCKLE
☼ ☼ ✻✻✻   ↕ ↔ 5m (15ft)

Vigorous and twining, with young purple shoots, this climber produces long-tubed, fragrant purple flowers, fading to yellow within, in summer. Bears red berries. ♔

> **OTHER CLIMBERS WITH FRAGRANT FLOWERS**
>
> *Clematis maximowicziana*
> *Clematis montana* 'Fragrant Spring'
> *Clematis montana* var. *wilsonii*
> *Clematis rehderiana*, see p.102
> *Dregea sinensis*
> *Jasminum* x *stephanense*
> *Lonicera caprifolium*
> *Mandevilla laxa*
> *Rosa polyantha grandiflora*
> *Trachelospermum jasminoides*, see p.104

Climbing Annuals and Biennials

M OST OF THE CLIMBERS commonly grown from seed, and treated as annuals in cool gardens, are actually perennial in the wild, or when cultivated in warmer climates. When they are planted in containers, many of these can be overwintered under glass, and some may survive for several years outside in a warm, sheltered spot, especially where winters are mild.

Rhodochiton atrosanguineum
PURPLE-BELL VINE
☼ ❄   ↕ ↔ 5m (15ft)

Borne from spring to autumn, the curious, pendulous blooms of this strong-growing climber each have a rose-pink, bell-like calyx and a maroon-black tubular flower.

Cobaea scandens
CUP AND SAUCER VINE
☼ ❄   ↕ ↔ 6m (20ft)

Climbing by tendrils, this vigorous, leafy perennial has curious yellow-green, cup-shaped flowers that turn purple with age. Each rests on a saucer-like green calyx. ♆

Ipomoea 'Heavenly Blue'
MORNING GLORY
☼ ❄   ↕ ↔ 3m (10ft)

Sporting lovely, large sky-blue flowers from summer into autumn, this vigorous annual or perennial has twining stems and long-pointed, heart-shaped leaves. ♆

OTHER CLIMBING ANNUALS
Asarina barclayana
Dicentra torulosa
Ipomoea alba
Lablab purpureus
Tropaeolum peregrinum

Eccremocarpus scaber
CHILEAN GLORY FLOWER
☼ ❄   ↕ ↔ 3m (10ft)

This vigorous evergreen, scrambling sub-shrub climbs by means of tendrils. It has ferny leaves and spikes of orange, red, or yellow tubular flowers in summer. ♆

SWEET PEAS
Lathyrus odoratus 'Annabelle'
Lathyrus odoratus 'Anniversary'
Lathyrus odoratus 'Painted Lady'
Lathyrus odoratus 'White Supreme'
Lathyrus odoratus 'World's Children'

Thunbergia alata
BLACK-EYED SUSAN
☼ ❄   ↕ ↔ 3m (10ft)

A succession of striking, dark-eyed, orange-yellow flowers covers this vigorous, twining annual through summer and into autumn. It bears abundant, heart-shaped leaves.

Self-clinging Climbers

FEW SELF-CLINGING CLIMBERS, apart from the ubiquitous ivies, are hardy enough for cool, temperate gardens, especially when compared with the large number that climb by other means. Hardy, self-clinging species, therefore, have a value of their own, not only for clothing walls and fences, but also for growing up the stems or trunks of suitable trees. This selection includes climbers that cling by means of aerial roots and those that have tendrils tipped with sucker pads.

Parthenocissus henryana
PARTHENOCISSUS
☼ ☼ ☼ ✲✲✲   ↕↔6m (20ft)

This free-growing ornamental vine clings by adhesive tendrils tips. Leaves, divided into five, silver-veined, velvety green or bronze leaflets, colour richly in autumn. ♉

Hedera helix 'Goldheart'
IVY
☼ ☼ ☼ ✲✲✲   ↕↔3m (10ft)

Striking and easy to recognize, this ivy has dark, glossy evergreen leaves with a gold central splash. Green-leaved reversions should be removed as soon as they appear.

Hydrangea anomala subsp. *petiolaris*
CLIMBING HYDRANGEA
☼ ☼ ☼ ✲✲✲   ↕↔10m (30ft)

The stems of this robust shrub, which will climb by means of aerial roots, have rich brown peeling bark. Its white flowers, in lace-cap flowerheads, open in summer. ♉

Parthenocissus tricuspidata 'Veitchii'
BOSTON IVY
☼ ☼ ☼ ✲✲✲   ↕↔15m (50ft)

Commonly, but incorrectly, referred to as Virginia Creeper, this vigorous vine soon clothes walls with its ivy-like green leaves. These colour brilliantly in autumn. ♉

OTHER SELF-CLINGING CLIMBERS

Campsis radicans
Decumaria barbara
Decumaria sinensis, see p.105
Euonymus fortunei 'Coloratus'
Ficus pumila
Hedera canariensis 'Gloire de Marengo'
Hedera colchica, see p.102
Hedera colchica 'Sulphur Heart', see p.96
Hedera helix 'Cavendishii'
Hedera helix 'Pedata'
Hedera nepalensis
Hydrangea anomala
Hydrangea seemannii
Hydrangea serratifolia
Parthenocissus tricuspidata 'Lowii'
Pileostegia viburnoides, see p.104
Schizophragma hydrangeoides
Schizophragma hydrangeoides 'Roseum'
Schizophragma integrifolium

Trachelospermum asiaticum
☼ ✲✲   ↕↔6m (20ft)

Self-clinging in a wind-free situation, the slender stems of this climber twine round any support. Clusters of fragrant, creamy white flowers in summer age to yellow. ♉

SHRUBS

ORNAMENTAL SHRUBS in the garden are the bridge between trees and perennials, forming the middle layer in mixed borders or beds. Their flexibility is legendary. Many shrubs are so distinctive in habit or impressive in flower or leaf that they make excellent single specimens in a lawn or border, where they can freely develop to their fullest potential.

△ *Aucuba japonica* 'Crotonifolia'

△ INSECT PARADISE *The nectar-filled flowers of the Butterfly Bush* (Buddleja davidii) *attract bees and other insects too.*

The range of shrubs stretches from small carpeting plants, right through to the larger stalwarts. Between is a host of shrubs whose habits make a substantial contribution to garden design. Horizontally extending branches such as *Viburnum plicatum* 'Mariesii', arching or weeping growth such as the brooms *(Cytisus)*, and those of upright habit such as *Viburnum sargentii* 'Onondaga' can all play a part in creating pleasing and useful architectural effects.

SOME TOUGH, SOME TENDER

Most shrubs in this section are winter hardy, but some prefer to be planted in warmer sites. In cold areas, grow tender shrubs in pots and bring them under cover for the winter. Some shrubs flourish during summer, but are cut back by winter frost. These plants are known as subshrubs, and any dead growth should be removed when re-growth commences in spring.

STABILITY OR DIVERSITY

Evergreens bring an important sense of stability and continuity to the garden, most notably when deciduous or herbaceous plants are leafless or below ground. Shrubs in this section are deciduous unless described as evergreen. Numerous deciduous shrubs are worth growing for their foliage alone, especially those having bold or otherwise dramatic leaves, perhaps variegated or coloured. Some produce brilliant autumn tints, of which just one can make a real impact in the garden.

THE BEAUTY OF SHRUBS

- Flowering and fruiting shrubs attract wildlife, birds, and insects.
- Offer numerous forms and shapes.
- Provide flowers for every season of the year, including winter.
- Evergreens are attractive in winter.
- Ideal specimens for lawns or beds.
- Excellent in mixed plantings with perennials, climbers, and/or conifers.
- Useful for massed spring effect.
- Provide good ground cover.

△ GROUND COVER *The Partridge-berry* (Gaultheria procumbens) *is an effective and attractive lime-free ground cover.*

◁ SPRING PAGEANT *Rhododendrons and evergreen azaleas grow together in the wild, and combine well in the garden.*

▷ LATE SUMMER MAGIC *This mop-headed form of* Hydrangea macrophylla *provides a reliable show late in the season.*

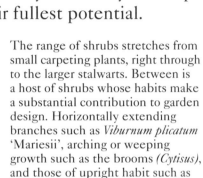

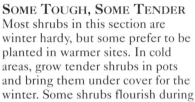

Large Shrubs for Specimen Planting

M OST GARDENS have at least one situation suitable for planting something particularly special – maybe in a lawn, a courtyard, or as a border feature. A tree is frequently chosen for this role, but a refreshing alternative is to consider one of the following ultimately large and impressive shrubs instead. All have character and presence as well as flowers.

Magnolia liliiflora 'Nigra'
MAGNOLIA
☼ ☀ ❋❋❋ 🌡️PH   ↕3m (10ft) ↔3m (10ft)

One of the most satisfactory and reliable magnolias, this forms a compact mound of glossy leaves. Flowers appear from spring into summer, and in early autumn. ♈

Aesculus parviflora
BOTTLEBRUSH BUCKEYE
☼ ☀ ❋❋❋   ↕3m (10ft) ↔5m (15ft)

A bold thicket or mound of leaves, bronze-red when young, and turning yellow in autumn, will form in time. Long, tapering flower spikes are produced in summer. ♈

Clerodendrum trichotomum
GLORY TREE
☼ ❋❋❋   ↕3m (10ft) ↔4m (12ft)

The leaves of this spreading shrub are aromatic. Pink or greenish buds open into clusters of fragrant white flowers from late summer. Turquoise-blue berries follow. ♈

Pieris formosa var. *forrestii* 'Wakehurst'
PIERIS
☼ ❋❋❋ PH   ↕3m (10ft) ↔3m (10ft)

The young, new leaves of this handsome, mounded evergreen emerge brilliant red in spring. These follow drooping sprays of white lily-of-the-valley flowers. ♈

Chionanthus virginicus
FRINGE TREE
☼ ❋❋❋   ↕3m (10ft) ↔4m (12ft)

This large, bushy shrub bears bold, deep green leaves that turn yellow in autumn. Sprays of fragrant white flowers drape the branches in summer. Dislikes dry soils.

Ligustrum sinense
CHINESE PRIVET
☼ ☀ ❋❋❋   ↕5m (15ft) ↔5m (15ft)

Upright at first, this strong-growing semi-evergreen spreads with age. Its arching, leafy branches terminate in large heads of tiny, sweet-scented white summer flowers.

OTHER LARGE SHRUBS FOR SPECIMEN PLANTING

Aesculus californica
Camellia x *williamsii* 'Brigadoon'
Elaeagnus 'Quicksilver', see p.220
Genista aetnensis
Hydrangea paniculata 'Pink Diamond'
Hydrangea plicatum 'Mariesii'
Mahonia x *media* 'Lionel Fortescue'
Malus sargentii
Photinia x *fraseri* 'Red Robin'
Syringa x *josiflexa* 'Bellicent'

Shrubs with Bold Leaves

EXPERIENCED GARDENERS sensibly choose plants as much for their foliage effect as for their attractive flowers. This is particularly important with large plants such as shrubs that occupy a greater area than the average perennial. Where a shrub has both flowers and leaves worthy of attention, then give serious consideration to its inclusion; these dual-purpose plants certainly earn their place in the garden. The following is but a small selection; there are many more.

Paeonia delavayi var. *ludlowii*
TREE PEONY
☼ ☀ ❋❋❋   ↕ 2.5m (8ft) ↔ 2.5m (8ft)

Loose-stemmed, with boldly cut, bright green leaves, this shrub has yellow flowers in late spring and early summer. *P. delavayi*, with deep red flowers, is similar in leaf. ♔

Fatsia japonica
FATSIA
☼ ☀ ❋❋❋   ↕ 3m (10ft) ↔ 3m (10ft)

This domed evergreen bears handsome, long-stalked, deeply lobed, shining green leaves. Branched clusters of white flowers in autumn precede black berries. ♔

OTHER SHRUBS WITH BOLD LEAVES

Aralia elata
Decaisnea fargesii
Hydrangea sargentiana
Magnolia delavayi
Mahonia lomariifolia
Prunus laurocerasus 'Magnoliifolia'
Rhamnus imeritina
Rhus x *pulvinata* 'Red Burgundy Lace'
Rubus odoratus
Sambucus canadensis 'Maxima'
Yucca recurvifolia

SHRUBS

Eriobotrya japonica
LOQUAT
☼ ❋❋   ↕ 4m (12ft) ↔ 4m (12ft)

Leathery, prominently veined, dark green leaves distinguish this evergreen shrub or small tree. Fragrant white autumn flowers are followed by orange-yellow fruits. ♔

Hydrangea quercifolia
OAK-LEAVED HYDRANGEA
☼ ❋❋❋   ↕ 1.5m (5ft) ↔ 2.5m (8ft)

Boldly lobed leaves, that colour richly in autumn, cover this bushy shrub and form a broad mound. Dense white flowerheads occur from summer into autumn. ♔

Rhus glabra
SMOOTH SUMACH
☼ ❋❋❋   ↕ 2.5m (8ft) ↔ 2.5m (8ft)

Smooth shoots support regularly divided, deep blue-green leaves that colour richly in autumn. Summer flowers are followed by red-brown fruits on female plants. ♔

Large Shrub Roses for Specimen Planting

MOST SHRUB ROSES in the wild occur as single, scattered specimens, with space to expand and show their flowers to advantage. In gardens where space permits, shrub roses should be grown in the same way, either singly, or in groups as highlights in mixed borders. Grow spreading kinds alone on the lawn, where their display can be admired from all sides.

Rosa 'Mme Isaac Pereire'
BOURBON ROSE
☼ ✽✽✽   ↕ 2.2m (7ft) ↔ 2m (6ft)

This lovely bourbon rose has a vigorous, prickly, arching growth. Richly fragrant flowers, deep rose with magenta shading, appear from summer into autumn. ♔

Rosa 'Complicata'
GALLICA ROSE
☼ ✽✽✽   ↕ 2.2m (7ft) ↔ 2.5m (8ft)

A bold, reliable gallica rose with vigorous, thorny, arching branches. Lightly scented, single, white-centred pink flowers occur in summer. May also be trained into trees. ♔

OTHER SHRUB ROSES WITH FRUITS
Rosa davidii
Rosa 'Hillieri'
Rosa macrophylla
Rosa macrophylla 'Master Hugh'
Rosa moyesii
Rosa prattii
Rosa roxburghii
Rosa rugosa 'Scabrosa'
Rosa setipoda
Rosa sweginzowii
Rosa 'Wintonensis'

Rosa 'Alexander'
HYBRID TEA ROSE
☼ ✽✽✽   ↕ 1.7m (5½ft) ↔ 75cm (30in)

This strong-growing hybrid tea rose with erect stems makes an excellent informal hedge. Lightly fragrant, double red flowers are carried from summer into autumn. ♔

Rosa 'Iceberg'
FLORIBUNDA ROSE
☼ ✽✽✽   ↕ 1.5m (5ft) ↔ 1.2m (4ft)

'Iceberg' is a popular, reliable floribunda rose with strong, upright growth, glossy foliage, and clusters of fully double, lightly scented flowers in summer and autumn. ♔

Rosa 'Marguerite Hilling'
SHRUB ROSE
☼ ✽✽✽   ↕ 2.2m (7ft) ↔ 2.2m (7ft)

This is a vigorous shrub with dense, leafy growth. In summer, and to a lesser degree autumn, it is crowded with large, fragrant, deep pink flowers with pale centres. ♔

Rosa moyesii 'Geranium'
SPECIES ROSE
☼ ✹✹✹   ↕3m (10ft) ↔ 2.2m (7ft)

This tall, vigorous species rose is upright.
Its branches arch widely and sport small,
saucer-shaped summer flowers that are
followed by flagon-shaped red hips. ♈

Rosa 'Roseraie de l'Hay'
RUGOSA ROSE
☼ ✹✹✹   ↕2.2m (7ft) ↔ 2m (6ft)

A strong-growing rugosa rose of dense
habit, this has attractive green foliage and
richly scented, velvety, deep crimson
flowers from summer into autumn. ♈

Rosa 'Tour de Malakoff'
PROVENCE ROSE
☼ ✹✹✹   ↕2m (6ft) ↔ 1m (3ft)

Provence rose of vigorous, open growth,
and bearing fragrant, loose rosette flowers
in summer. The magenta blooms fade to a
greyish purple. May require support. ♈

Rosa 'Nevada'
SHRUB ROSE
☼ ✹✹✹   ↕2.2m (7ft) ↔ 2.2m (7ft)

This vigorous, leafy shrub rose produces
an abundance of scented, creamy white
flowers in summer – fewer in autumn.
The flowers turn pink in hot weather. ♈

Rosa soulieana
SPECIES ROSE
☼ ✹✹✹   ↕3m (10ft) ↔ 3m (10ft)

The distinct stems of this rose are prickly,
and its foliage is bluish green. Numerous
scented summer flowers are yellow in bud
and open white. May need support. ♈

Rosa
'Pink Grootendorst'
☼ ✹✹✹   ↕2m (6ft) ↔ 1.5m (5ft)

A rugosa hybrid of bushy, upright growth,
this has prickly stems and wrinkled leaves.
Dense clusters of rosette flowers occur
from summer, continuing into autumn. ♈

OTHER LARGE SHRUB ROSES
FOR SPECIMEN PLANTING

Rosa 'Alba Maxima'
Rosa 'Alba Semiplena'
Rosa 'Blanc Double de Coubert'
Rosa 'Dupontii'
Rosa eglanteria, see p.169
Rosa 'Frühlingsgold'
Rosa glauca, see p.153
Rosa 'Madame Hardy'
Rosa 'White Grootendorst'
Rosa willmottiae

Rosa xanthina 'Canary Bird'
SPECIES ROSE
☼ ✹✹✹   ↕2.2m (7ft) ↔ 2.2m (7ft)

The arching branches of this vigorous
species rose carry small, fern-like foliage.
Musk-scented yellow flowers appear in
spring, fewer in autumn. ♈

S
H
R
U
B
S

Medium-sized Shrubs

SOME OF THE LOVELIEST and most desirable of all shrubs are found in the medium size range of 1.5–2.5m (5–8ft) in height. Where space is no object, many of these can be planted to glorious effect in groups, or even drifts. In smaller gardens where space is limited, any of the shrubs featured here makes an impressive single specimen in the lawn. They may also be used in combination with smaller shrubs or ground cover to create informal groups in beds or borders.

Hydrangea macrophylla 'Lilacina'
LACE-CAP HYDRANGEA
☼ ❋❋❋   ↕ 1.5m (5ft) ↔ 2m (6ft)

This shrub is particularly lovely when in flower in late summer. Its lace-cap flowerheads are carried above mounds of slender, pointed leaves. Dislikes dry soils.

Clerodendrum bungei
CLERODENDRUM
☼ ❋❋❋   ↕ 2m (6ft) ↔ indefinite

From late summer into autumn, fragrant, deep pink flowerheads nestle among the aromatic, heart-shaped leaves. A suckering shrub, this has erect purple shoots. ♔

Exochorda x *macrantha* 'The Bride'
EXOCHORDA
☼ ❋❋❋   ↕ 1.5m (5ft) ↔ 2.5m (8ft)

Wider than it is tall, this mounded shrub is covered by pure white blossoms in spring and early summer. Its arching or weeping branches are densely leafy. ♔

OTHER DECIDUOUS MEDIUM-SIZED SHRUBS

Berberis linearifolia 'Orange King'
Cytisus scoparius 'Cornish Cream'
Deutzia x *hybrida* 'Pink Pompon'
Lavatera 'Barnsley', see p.129
Neillia thibetica, see p.123
Paeonia delavayi var. *ludlowii*, see p.111
Philadelphus 'Belle Etoile'
Spiraea x *vanhouttei*, see p.135
Syringa x *persica*, see p.139
Weigela 'Mont Blanc'

Deutzia x *elegantissima* 'Rosealind'
DEUTZIA
☼ ❋❋❋   ↕ 1.5m (5ft) ↔ 1.5m (5ft)

This is among the best flowering shrubs for smaller gardens. Its mound of arching, leafy branches are wreathed in clusters of pink flower in summer. ♔

Hydrangea aspera
HYDRANGEA
☼ ❋❋❋   ↕ 2.5m (8ft) ↔ 2.5m (8ft)

The large, downy leaves of this impressive shrub are an excellent foil for the lace-cap flowerheads with marginal florets in late summer and autumn. Dislikes dry soils.

Lavatera 'Rosea'
TREE MALLOW
☼ ❋❋❋   ↕ 2m (6ft) ↔ 2m (6ft)

Tree Mallow is one of the most continuous and free-flowering of all garden shrubs, with its pink blooms opening throughout summer. The lobed leaves are downy. ♔

Syringa microphylla 'Superba'
LILAC
☼ ❋❋❋   ↕ 2m (6ft) ↔ 2m (6ft)

Slender-stemmed and spreading, with
pointed leaves, this lilac produces fragrant
pink flowerheads, darker in bud, from late
spring right through to early autumn. ♈

Viburnum plicatum 'Pink Beauty'
VIBURNUM
☼ ☼ ❋❋❋   ↕ 2m (6ft) ↔ 1.5m (5ft)

Elegant, spreading, layered branches carry
neat, pleated leaves and, in early summer,
lace-cap flowerheads that are white when
they emerge, and mature to pink. ♈

OTHER EVERGREEN
MEDIUM-SIZED SHRUBS

Daphne bholua 'Jacqueline Postill',
  see p.166
Escallonia 'Apple Blossom', see p.138
Jasminum humile 'Revolutum'

Philadelphus coronarius 'Variegatus'
MOCK ORANGE
☼ ❋❋❋   ↕ 2.5m (8ft) ↔ 2.5m (8ft)

Striking, white-margined leaves are the
main attraction of this dense, bushy shrub.
Its richly fragrant flower clusters, in late
spring and early summer, are a bonus. ♈

Paeonia delavayi
TREE PEONY
☼ ☼ ❋❋❋   ↕ 2m (6ft) ↔ 1.5m (5ft)

Cup-shaped, dark crimson flowers, each
with a leafy bract beneath it, are borne on
long stalks in early summer, above bold,
deeply cut, bright green leaves. ♈

Pieris japonica
PIERIS
☼ ☼ ❋❋❋❋ ᴾᴴ   ↕ 2m (6ft) ↔ 2m (6ft)

This compact evergreen shrub has narrow,
leathery leaves, which are bronze when
young. Drooping tassels of white flowers
appear in late winter and early spring.

Viburnum sargentii
'Onondaga'
☼ ☼ ❋❋❋   ↕ 2.5m (8ft) ↔ 1.5m (5ft)

The maple-like foliage of this vigorous
shrub are bronze when young, and colour
richly in autumn. Its beautiful spring lace-
cap flowers are white, but pink in bud. ♈

S H R U B S

Small Shrubs

THE VARIETY OF ATTRACTIVE small shrubs available to gardeners is exciting, if potentially bewildering. In large gardens, many of these can be planted in groups of three to five or more, but where space is more limited, any of the following will make an attractive and satisfying feature as a single plant, either alone or used as a centrepiece in a mixed border. They include some of the best small shrubs, and most are sun-loving.

Cytisus x *praecox* 'Warminster'
WARMINSTER BROOM
☼ ❋❋❋   ↕ 1.2m (4ft) ↔ 1.5m (5ft)

This is one of the most reliable of all small flowering shrubs. In late spring, its slender green branches are wreathed with small, scented, creamy yellow pea-flowers. ♔

Caryopteris x *clandonensis*
'Arthur Simmonds'
☼ ❋❋❋   ↕ 75cm (30in) ↔ 75cm (30in)

Numerous clusters of small lavender-blue flowers adorn this bushy, mound-forming shrub in late summer and early autumn. It has slender stems and grey-green leaves.

Cistus x *aguilari* 'Maculatus'
SUN ROSE
☼ ❋❋   ↕ 1.2m (4ft) ↔ 1.2m (4ft)

Magnificent white flowers, each with dark red blotches and a yellow eye, appear in summer. Wavy-edged leaves, clammy to the touch, cover this bushy evergreen. ♔

OTHER SMALL DECIDUOUS SHRUBS

Acer palmatum 'Garnet', see p.154
Berberis sieboldii
Berberis thunbergii 'Aurea', see p.150
Caryopteris x *clandonensis*
  'Heavenly Blue'
Cytisus 'Boskoop Ruby'
Daphne x *burkwoodii* 'Somerset'
Daphne mezereum
Hydrangea involucrata 'Hortensis'
Prunus glandulosa 'Alba Plena'
Spiraea japonica 'Genpei'

Ceratostigma willmottianum
HARDY PLUMBAGO
☼ ❋❋   ↕ 1m (3ft) ↔ 1m (3ft)

This loosely domed shrub carries cobalt-blue flowers from late summer through to autumn, when its neat, pointed leaves turn red. Dies down in severe winters. ♔

Cistus x *corbariensis*
SUN ROSE
☼ ❋❋❋   ↕ 75cm (30in) ↔ 1.2m (4ft)

A broad mound of wrinkled, wavy-edged leaves is obscured in summer by masses of white, yellow-eyed flowers, pink when in bud. Among the hardiest sun roses. ♔

Deutzia gracilis
DEUTZIA
☼ ❋❋❋   ↕ 1m (3ft) ↔ 1m (3ft)

The bright green leaves of this elegant shrub form a most attractive backdrop for its white flower clusters that last from late spring to early summer.

SHRUBS

Fuchsia 'Mrs Popple'
FUCHSIA
☼ ❄❄   ↕ 1.2m (4ft) ↔ 1.2m (4ft)

One of the hardiest fuchsias, this vigorous shrub has glossy foliage, and a continuous supply of flowers that resemble Chinese lanterns from summer into autumn.   ⚱

Philadelphus 'Manteau d'Hermine'
MOCK ORANGE
☼ ❄❄❄   ↕ 75cm (30in) ↔ 1.5m (5ft)

When the clusters of long-lasting, fragrant, double, creamy white flowers are borne in summer, they cover this broad, low shrub of compact, bushy habit.   ⚱

Potentilla 'Abbotswood'
SHRUBBY POTENTILLA
☼ ❄❄❄   ↕ 75cm (30in) ↔ 1.2m (4ft)

In summer and early autumn, this low-domed bush is plastered with small white flowers, resembling miniature roses. Its deeply divided leaves are grey-green.   ⚱

Rhododendron yakushimanum
RHODODENDRON
☼ ☼ ❄❄❄❄ ᴾᴴ   ↕ 1m (3ft) ↔ 1.5m (5ft)

One of the most popular and reliable small rhododendrons, it forms a tight evergreen dome. Its trusses of pink flowers, in late spring and early summer, turn to white. ⚱

Hebe recurva
HEBE
☼ ❄❄   ↕ 60cm (24in) ↔ 1.2m (4ft)

This low, dome-shaped evergreen hebe produces narrow blue-grey leaves, and an abundance of white flowers, carried on small, slender spikes in summer.

OTHER SMALL EVERGREEN SHRUBS

Artemisia arborescens, see p.50
Aucuba japonica 'Rozannie', see p.146
Choisya 'Aztec Pearl', see p.144
Daphne retusa
Erica terminalis
Halimium ocymoides 'Susan'
Hedera helix 'Poetica Arborea'
Phlomis italica, see p.131
Pieris japonica 'Little Heath', see p.145
Prostanthera cuneata, see p.160
Sarcococca confusa

Phygelius x *rectus* 'Moonraker'
PHYGELIUS
☼ ❄❄   ↕ 1.5m (5ft) ↔ 1.5m (5ft)

Long, upright spires of pendulous, tubular, creamy yellow flowers are held by this striking evergreen or semi-evergreen from summer into autumn. Of suckering habit.

Salix hastata 'Wehrhahnii'
WILLOW
☼ ❄❄❄   ↕ 1m (3ft) ↔ 1.5m (5ft)

This handsome, shrubby little willow is well worth growing for the dumpy silvery catkins that emerge in spring, before its leaves unfurl. Dislikes dry soils.   ⚱

SHRUBS

Shrubs for Ground Cover

THE NUMBER OF SHRUBS that make good ground cover is enormous. Some have far-reaching, trailing, or creeping stems that lie close to the soil surface, while others produce short ascending or arching branches that give a low, mounded effect. Yet more are of a suckering nature. To achieve good results as quickly as possible, ground cover shrubs should be planted in groups of three or five, or even more, depending on the area to be covered. Remove weeds before planting.

Euonymus fortunei 'Emerald 'n' Gold'
EVERGREEN EUONYMUS
☼ ☼ ✿ ❄❄❄ ↕60cm (24in) ↔ 1.2m (4ft)

This adaptable, bright-foliaged evergreen forms dense hummocks of green shoots and gold-margined leaves, usually pink-tinted in winter. Climbs if supported. ♈

Cornus canadensis
CREEPING DOGWOOD
☼ ✿ ❄❄❄ PH ↕13cm (5in) ↔ 30cm (12in)

In late spring and early summer, the starry, white-bracted flowerheads of this carpeting perennial are borne above ruffs of oval leaves. Red berries follow. ♈

OTHER EVERGREEN SHRUBS FOR GROUND COVER
Arctostaphylos uva-ursi 'Vancouver Jade'
Ceanothus gloriosus
Ceanothus griseus 'Yankee Point'
Ceanothus thyrsiflorus var. *repens*
Cistus salviifolius 'Avalanche'
Cotoneaster cochleatus
Daboecia cantabrica
Gaultheria procumbens
Rubus tricolor
Ulex gallii 'Mizen'

Cotoneaster dammeri
COTONEASTER
☼ ✿ ❄❄❄ ↕8cm (3in) ↔ 2m (6ft)

This is one of the best evergreen ground-covering shrubs. Its densely leafy, trailing stems are studded with white flowers in summer and red berries in winter. ♈

Euonymus fortunei 'Emerald Gaiety'
EVERGREEN EUONYMUS
☼ ☼ ✿ ❄❄❄ ↕1m (3ft) ↔ 1.5m (5ft)

Tough, adaptable, and easy to grow, this shrub forms a dense, low cover of rounded leaves, margined white and marbled grey. Leaves are often pink-tinted in winter. ♈

x *Halimiocistus sahucii*
SUN ROSE
☼ ❄❄❄ ↕30cm (12in) ↔ 1.2m (4ft)

Crowded with narrow, dark green leaves, this dense, low, bushy evergreen is covered with small, rose-like, yellow-eyed, white flowers in late spring and early summer. ♈

Hedera helix 'Glacier'
IVY

☼ ☼ ☼ ❋❋❋ ↕ 10cm (4in) ↔ 3m (10ft)

One of the best variegated ivies suitable
for ground cover, this will climb if given
support. The evergreen silver-grey leaves
each have an irregular white margin. ♔

Hedera helix 'Ivalace'
IVY

☼ ☼ ☼ ❋❋❋ ↕ 10cm (4in) ↔ 1.5m (5ft)

Dense hummocks or patches of glossy
dark green are formed by this good-looking
ground cover. Leaves are shallowly lobed
and crinkled. Will climb with support. ♔

Hypericum calycinum
ROSE OF SHARON

☼ ☼ ❋❋❋ ↕ 30cm (12in) ↔ 1.5m (5ft)

The creeping roots of this evergreen form
a close green carpet of leafy shoots, topped
by golden yellow flowers, with red-tipped
stamens, from summer into autumn.

Leptospermum rupestre
LEPTOSPERMUM

☼ ❋❋❋ ↕ 8cm (3in) ↔ 2m (6ft)

This evergreen shrub will create a packed
carpet of tiny, deep green leaves, studded
in summer with small white flowers. Its
leaves turn bronze in the winter cold. ♔

**OTHER DECIDUOUS SHRUBS
FOR GROUND COVER**

Cotoneaster adpressus
Prunus pumila var. *depressa*
Salix nakamurana var. *yezoalpina*
Salix uva-ursi

Viburnum davidii
VIBURNUM

☼ ❋ ❋❋❋ ↕ 1m (3ft) ↔ 1.5m (5ft)

Broad mounds of boldly veined evergreen
leaves need space. The white flowers are
small, and pollinated female plants bear
striking blue berries from autumn. ♔

Vinca minor
LESSER PERIWINKLE

☼ ❋ ❋❋❋ ↕ 10cm (4in) ↔ 1.5m (5ft)

Long, slender, prostrate stems and paired,
glossy green leaves provide reliable ground
cover. Charming blue, purple, or white
flowers open from spring into summer.

SHRUBS

119

Small Shrub Roses for Limited Space

Nᴜᴍᴇʀᴏᴜꜱ ꜱʜʀᴜʙ ʀᴏꜱᴇꜱ are medium to large in size, and require considerable space in which to develop to their full potential. Fortunately, certain roses are of lesser stature and therefore suitable for planting where space is limited. Some of the following may need support to prevent their slender stems from flopping to the ground when in flower.

Rosa gallica var. *officinalis*
Aᴘᴏᴛʜᴇᴄᴀʀʏ'ꜱ Rᴏꜱᴇ
☼ ✹✹✹   ↕ 1m (3ft) ↔ 1m (3ft)

Lush foliage and an abundant supply of scented, semi-double, deep pink flowers cover this spreading, low-branching species rose in summer. Hips are attractive. ♜

Rosa x *centifolia* 'Cristata'
Cʀᴇꜱᴛᴇᴅ Mᴏꜱꜱ Rᴏꜱᴇ
☼ ✹✹✹   ↕ 1.5m (5ft) ↔ 1.2m (4ft)

Distinct green, mossy buds open to reveal richly scented pink blooms on nodding stalks in summer. The rather lax stems of this prickly bush may need support. ♜

Rosa gallica 'Versicolor'
Rᴏꜱᴀ Mᴜɴᴅɪ, Gᴀʟʟɪᴄᴀ Rᴏꜱᴇ
☼ ✹✹✹   ↕ 1m (3ft) ↔ 1m (3ft)

This well-known rose began as a mutation of *R. gallica* var. *officinalis*, and differs in its flowers, which are pale pink with crimson stripes. Prune to maintain its size. ♜

Rosa 'Buff Beauty'
Hʏʙʀɪᴅ Mᴜꜱᴋ Rᴏꜱᴇ
☼ ✹✹✹   ↕ 1.2m (4ft) ↔ 1.2m (4ft)

A popular and reliable rose with shining green foliage that is coppery brown when young. Deliciously scented, fully double flowers are freely borne in summer. ♜

Rosa x *centifolia* 'Muscosa'
Cᴏᴍᴍᴏɴ Mᴏꜱꜱ Rᴏꜱᴇ
☼ ✹✹✹   ↕ 1.5m (5ft) ↔ 1.2m (4ft)

Coarse foliage provides a good backdrop for the richly scented pink flowers opening from mossy buds in summer. This loose-stemmed bush may need support. ♜

Oᴛʜᴇʀ Sᴍᴀʟʟ Sʜʀᴜʙ Rᴏꜱᴇꜱ

Rosa carolina
Rosa 'Cecile Brunner'
Rosa 'Chianti'
Rosa 'Comte de Chambord'
Rosa damascena 'Versicolor'
Rosa 'Jacques Cartier'
Rosa 'Little White Pet'
Rosa 'Lutea Maxima'
Rosa 'Perle d'Or'
Rosa 'Rose de Rescht'
Rosa 'The Fairy'

Low-growing Roses for Ground Cover

I N SUNNY SITUATIONS, low-spreading roses or those with trailing stems provide a useful and charming ground cover. They are particularly suited to steep banks, wall tops, or beneath plantings of other roses, especially those whose stems become unsightly with age. In recent years, a host of new, free-flowering cultivars has become available. Where space permits, you can achieve impressive displays with generous plantings, but in small gardens a single plant can give as much pleasure.

Rosa 'Grouse'
GROUND COVER ROSE
☼ ❋❋❋ ‡ 45cm (18in) ↔ 3m (10ft)

In summer, this free-growing rose, with its long, trailing stems and shining foliage, produces a succession of small, fragrant, pale pink blooms.

Rosa 'Max Graf'
RUGOSA HYBRID
☼ ❋❋❋ ‡ 45cm (18in) ↔ 3m (10ft)

Large, single flowers have an apple scent, and are carried in summer. The shining, bright green foliage of this dense rose is carried on long, trailing stems.

Rosa 'Nozomi'
GROUND COVER ROSE
☼ ❋❋❋ ‡ 45cm (18in) ↔ 1.2m (4ft)

This charming creeping rose has arching stems clothed with small, neat, dark green leaves, and bears single blush-pink and white flowers in summer. ♈

OTHER GROUND COVER ROSES
Rosa macrantha
Rosa nitida
Rosa 'Paulii'
Rosa 'Pheasant'
Rosa 'Pink Wave'
Rosa x *polliniana*
Rosa 'Sea Foam'
Rosa 'Snow Fairy'
Rosa 'The Fairy'
Rosa virginiana
Rosa 'William Baffin'

Rosa 'Partridge'
GROUND COVER ROSE
☼ ❋❋❋ ‡ 45cm (18in) ↔ 3m (10ft)

The pure white flowers of this rose, borne in abundance throughout summer, are small and fragrant. It is similar in growth to *R*. 'Grouse', to which it is related.

MINIATURE ROSES
Rosa 'Anytime'
Rosa 'Baby Gold Star'
Rosa 'Chelsea Pensioner'
Rosa 'Hokey Pokey'
Rosa 'Little Sir Echo'
Rosa 'Petit Four'
Rosa 'Popcorn'
Rosa 'Robin Redbreast'
Rosa 'Roulettii'
Rosa 'Snowball'
Rosa 'Stacey Sue'

Rosa 'Seagull'
CLIMBING ROSE
☼ ❋❋❋ ‡ 60cm (24in) ↔ 4m (12ft)

'Seagull' is a strong-growing climbing rose, good for ground cover where space allows. Large, branched clusters of fragrant, semi-double white flowers open in summer. ♈

Shrubs for Heavy Clay Soils

I F YOU HAVE A CLASSIC clay soil; one that is heavy and sticky when wet, shrinking and cracking when it is dry, then it is a good idea to try to improve it by careful drainage and by adding liberal and frequent amounts of coarse grit, together with rough, especially fibrous, organic matter. Avoid working clay soil when it is wet. Despite the doom and gloom that is commonly associated with heavy clay, however, a large and diverse selection of shrubs can thrive in such soils.

SHRUBS

Cytisus 'Killiney Red'
BROOM
☼ ✳✳✳ PH   ↕ 1m (3ft) ↔ 1.2m (4ft)

One of many brooms tolerant of clay soils, 'Killiney Red' is a dwarf, compact variety. Slender green shoots carry many flowers in late spring and early summer.

Berberis darwinii
DARWIN'S BARBERRY
☼ ✳✳✳   ↕ 3m (10ft) ↔ 4m (12ft)

This large, mounded evergreen shrub is densely covered with small, dark green leaves. Clusters of orange-yellow flowers in spring are followed by black berries. ♈

OTHER DECIDUOUS SHRUBS FOR HEAVY CLAY SOILS

Colutea x *media* 'Copper Beauty'
Cotinus coggygria 'Royal Purple', see p.154
Cytisus x *praecox* 'Allgold', see p.128
Deutzia x *elegantissima* 'Rosealind', see p.114
Kerria japonica 'Pleniflora', see p.101
Magnolia 'Susan'
Prunus glandulosa 'Alba Plena'
Rhododendron occidentale, see p.134
Ribes sanguineum 'White Icicle'
Sambucus nigra 'Guincho Purple', see p.155
Spiraea x *vanhouttei*, see p.135
Syringa vulgaris 'Charles Joly'
Viburnum sargentii 'Onondaga' see p.115
Weigela 'Fiesta'

Escallonia 'Langleyensis'
ESCALLONIA
☼ ✳✳✳   ↕ 2m (6ft) ↔ 2m (6ft)

Evergreen and wind-tolerant, this tried and tested shrub has arching stems, small, glossy leaves on weeping branches, and tiny bunches of pink summer flowers. ♈

Chaenomeles x *superba* 'Nicoline'
ORNAMENTAL QUINCE
☼ ◐ ✳✳✳   ↕ 1m (3ft) ↔ 1.5m (5ft)

The branches of this tough, reliable shrub are studded in spring with a profusion of large scarlet flowers. These are followed by small yellow, apple-like fruits. ♈

Hydrangea arborescens 'Grandiflora'
HYDRANGEA
☼ ◐ ✳✳✳   ↕ 1.5m (5ft) ↔ 2m (6ft)

Large heads of white flowers appear from summer through to early autumn. Broad, oval leaves clothe this tough and reliable, mounded shrub. Dislikes dry soils. ♈

Magnolia stellata 'Waterlily'
STAR MAGNOLIA
☼ ✸✸✸   ↕ 3m (10ft) ↔ 4m (12ft)

Eventually broader than it is high, this
charming shrub is slow-growing. Fragrant,
multi-petalled blooms cover the branches
in spring. Leaves are yellow in autumn. ♚

Neillia thibetica
NEILLIA
☼ ✸✸✸   ↕ 2.5m (8ft) ↔ 2.5m (8ft)

The flowers of this strong-growing shrub
are held in lax, tail-like spikes, on arching
branches amid its jagged, pointed leaves,
from late spring into early summer. ♚

Philadelphus 'Virginal'
MOCK ORANGE
☼ ✸✸✸   ↕ 3m (10ft) ↔ 2.5m (8ft)

A strong-growing shrub, this is deservedly
one of the most popular, due to its great
abundance of large, richly fragrant, double
or semi-double white summer flowers. ♚

Potentilla 'Elizabeth'
SHRUBBY POTENTILLA
☼ ✸✸✸   ↕ 75cm (30in) ↔ 1.5m (5ft)

A broad, low mound of densely crowded
branches and small, deeply divided leaves,
this is covered, from late spring through to
autumn, with bright yellow flowers. ♚

Rhododendron 'Mrs. G.W. Leak'
RHODODENDRON
☼ ☼ ✸✸✸   ↕ 4m (12ft) ↔ 4m (12ft)

This large evergreen shrub is particularly
striking in late spring, when it is covered
with bold trusses of pink, funnel-shaped
flowers, splashed brown and crimson.

**OTHER EVERGREEN SHRUBS
FOR HEAVY CLAY SOILS**

Aucuba japonica 'Crotonifolia',
  see p.148
Berberis sargentiana
Choisya ternata, see p.158
Escallonia rubra 'Crimson Spire'
Osmanthus x *burkwoodii*, see p.159
Pyracantha 'Orange Glow', see p.169
Skimmia x *confusa* 'Kew Green',
  see p.137
Viburnum davidii, see p.119

Spiraea japonica 'Anthony Waterer'
SPIRAEA
☼ ✸✸✸   ↕ 1.2m (4ft) ↔ 1.2m (4ft)

Erect and compact, this is an extremely
popular flowering shrub. It produces dark
green, jaggedly toothed leaves, and flat
crimson-pink flowerheads in summer. ♚

Spiraea nipponica 'Snowmound'
SPIRAEA
☼ ✸✸✸   ↕ 2m (6ft) ↔ 2m (6ft)

Tufts of white flowers are carried all along
the upper sides of densely leafy, arching
stems, making this a spectacular shrub at
its peak in early summer. ♚

S H R U B S

Shrubs for Lime-free Soils

THE SHRUBS PREFERRING, if not demanding, lime-free or acid soils are relatively few in number, but encompass some of the loveliest, most popular shrubs. Rhododendrons, camellias, and heathers are well-known lime-haters, but many other shrubs have similar requirements. Although they thrive in naturally acid soils, many of these plants will grow reasonably well in specially prepared beds, or in containers filled with lime-free compost.

Daboecia cantabrica 'Bicolor'
ST DABEOC'S HEATH
☼ ❄❄❄ PH ↕45cm (18in) ↔60cm (24in)

This low, bushy evergreen shrub is dense and wiry, with nodding white, purple, or purple-striped flowers, held in loose spikes, from late spring into autumn. ♇

Desfontainea spinosa
DESFONTAINEA
☼ ❄❄❄ PH ↕2m (6ft) ↔1.5m (5ft)

Tubular red flowers are borne in the leaf axils of this slow-growing evergreen, from midsummer to autumn. The leaves are small, and holly-like. Dislikes dry soils. ♇

Camellia x *williamsii* 'Donation'
CAMELLIA
☼ ❄❄❄❄ PH ↕3m (10ft) ↔2m (6ft)

One of the best camellias for general cultivation, this free-growing, upright evergreen carries an abundance of large flowers from late winter into spring. ♇

Calluna vulgaris 'Annemarie'
HEATHER, LING
☼ ❄❄❄❄ PH ↕45cm (18in) ↔45cm (18in)

Reliable and free-flowering, this heather forms a compact bush. Long spires of double, light pink flowers rise above dark evergreen foliage in autumn. ♇

Camellia japonica 'Adolphe Audusson'
JAPANESE CAMELLIA
☼ ❄❄❄❄ PH ↕3m (10ft) ↔2.5m (8ft)

This reliable camellia is a dense, bushy evergreen with glossy, dark green leaves. Large, deep red, gold-stamened flowers appear from late winter into spring. ♇

Clethra delavayi
CLETHRA
☼ ❄❄❄ PH ↕4m (12ft) ↔3m (10ft)

Dense, horizontal spikes of fragrant white flowers, pink when in bud, give this shrub a most distinguished appearance when they open in summer. Dislikes dry soil. ♇

Enkianthus cernuus var. *rubens*
ENKIANTHUS
☼ ❄❄❄❄ PH ↕2.5m (8ft) ↔2m (6ft)

In late spring, bunches of fringed, bell-shaped, deep red flowers hang beneath its neat rosettes of leaves. The leaves colour richly in autumn. Dislikes dry soils. ♇

S
H
R
U
B
S

124

Erica cinerea 'C.D. Eason'
BELL HEATHER
☼ ✳✳✳ PH ↕30cm (12in) ↔60cm (24in)

From summer to autumn, this dense, low-growing evergreen is covered by crowded spikes of carmine pink, pitcher-shaped flowers. It has needle-like leaves. 🏆

Pieris 'Forest Flame'
PIERIS
☼ ✳✳✳ PH ↕4m (12ft) ↔2m (6ft)

The leaves of this erect evergreen emerge crimson, and then pale to pink and cream before turning glossy green. Its sprays of white flowers appear in spring. 🏆

Rhododendron 'May Day'
RHODODENDRON
☼ ☼ ✳✳✳ PH ↕1.5m (5ft) ↔1.5m (5ft)

Excellent for all but the very coldest areas, this flat-topped or domed evergreen bears dark green leaves, and is covered in spring with trusses of red trumpet-flowers. 🏆

OTHER EVERGREEN SHRUBS FOR LIME-FREE SOIL

Calluna vulgaris 'Kinlochruel'
Camellia 'Spring Festival'
Camellia x *williamsii* 'St. Ewe'
Crinodendron hookerianum, see p.132
Erica australis 'Riverslea'
Grevillea juniperina f. *sulphurea*
Kalmia latifolia 'Ostbo Red'
Leptospermum scoparium 'Red Damask'
Rhododendron 'P.J. Mezitt'
Rhododendron yakushimanum, see p.117

Kalmia latifolia
CALICO BUSH
☼ ☼ ✳✳✳ PH ↕3m (10ft) ↔3m (10ft)

Free-flowering and impressive, this shrub, clad in cheerful glossy evergreen leaves, bears clusters of small pink flowers, darker when in bud, in early summer. 🏆

OTHER DECIDUOUS SHRUBS FOR LIME-FREE SOIL

Clethra alnifolia 'Paniculata'
Enkianthus campanulatus
Enkianthus perulatus
Fothergilla gardenii, see p.157
Menziesia ciliicalyx
Rhododendron 'Homebush', see p.145
Rhododendron 'Hotspur'
Rhododendron schlippenbachii
Vaccinium corymbosum, see p.135
Zenobia pulverulenta

Rhododendron 'Hino-mayo'
EVERGREEN AZALEA
☼ ☼ ✳✳✳ PH ↕1.5m (5ft) ↔1.5m (5ft)

This dense, twiggy evergreen is crowded with small leaves, and plastered in spring by little funnel-shaped pink flowers. It will not tolerate dry soils. 🏆

Rhododendron 'Narcissiflorum'
GHENT AZALEA
☼ ✳✳✳ PH ↕2m (6ft) ↔2m (6ft)

A vigorous shrub that produces masses of pale yellow, darker-flushed flowers with a sweet scent in spring and early summer. Leaves often colour bronze in autumn. 🏆

SHRUBS

Shrubs for Alkaline Soils

FAR FROM BEING PROBLEMATIC, alkaline soils are suitable for a huge variety of shrubs, many of which actually thrive in the high pH, and the warmer, free-draining conditions that prevail there. A number of these plants are also drought-tolerant, although this does not mean moisture is not essential. Such soils need to be given organic matter as well, in the form of a mulch. Sufficient water and enough organic matter improves the ability of most garden shrubs to grow well, and keeps leaves a healthy green.

Indigofera heterantha
INDIGOFERA
☼ ❄❄❄   ↕ 1.5m (5ft) ↔ 1.7m (5½ft)

This multi-stemmed shrub has arching branches clothed in fern-like leaves. Small, rich mauve-pink pea-flowers are produced all through summer into autumn.   ♈

Buddleja davidii 'Dartmoor'
BUTTERFLY BUSH
☼ ❄❄❄   ↕ 2.5m (8ft) ↔ 2.5m (8ft)

In late summer and autumn, distinctive flowerheads, popular with butterflies and bees, cover this vigorous shrub. Its arching branches carry long, pointed leaves.   ♈

Deutzia longifolia 'Veitchii'
DEUTZIA
☼ ❄❄❄   ↕ 2.2m (7ft) ↔ 1.7m (5½ft)

One of the most reliable of all deutzias, this has arching branches, narrow leaves, and large clusters of star-shaped summer flowers that are rich, lilac-stained pink.   ♈

Hibiscus syriacus 'Red Heart'
HIBISCUS
☼ ❄❄❄   ↕ 2.2m (7ft) ↔ 2.2m (7ft)

The branches of this slow-growing shrub spread with age. Boldly lobed leaves unfurl late in the season. Large flowers are carried from late summer into autumn.   ♈

Kolkwitzia amabilis 'Pink Cloud'
BEAUTY BUSH
☼ ❄❄❄   ↕ 3m (10ft) ↔ 3m (10ft)

A vigorous shrub of mounded habit, this has small, oval leaves, and masses of bell flowers in spring and early summer. Pale, bristly seed clusters follow.   ♈

OTHER EVERGREEN SHRUBS
FOR ALKALINE SOIL

Berberis darwinii, see p.122
Choisya 'Aztec Pearl', see p.144
Escallonia 'Iveyi'
Itea ilicifolia, see p.99
Jasminum humile, see p.101
Mahonia x *media* 'Buckland', see p.167
Olearia macrodonta, see p.146
Osmanthus x *burkwoodii*, see p.159
Sarcococca hookeriana var. *digyna*,
    see p.167

Osmanthus delavayi
OSMANTHUS
☼ ☼ ❄❄❄   ↕ 2.2m (7ft) ↔ 2.2m (7ft)

Mounded, evergreen shrub, with slender, arching stems packed with small, dark green leaves. In spring, clusters of small, sweet-smelling, tubular flowers appear. ♀

Santolina pinnata subsp. *neapolitana* 'Sulphurea'
☼ ❄❄❄   ↕ 70cm (28in) ↔ 1m (3ft)

Long-stalked, button-shaped clusters of tiny flowers top narrow, feathery leaves in midsummer. This is a low, dome-shaped evergreen shrub of dense habit.

Weigela 'Looymansii Aurea'
WEIGELA
☼ ❄❄❄   ↕ 1.5m (5ft) ↔ 1.1m (3½ft)

This shrub is principally grown for its golden foliage, which later becomes yellowish green. Funnel-shaped flowers open in late spring and early summer.

Philadelphus 'Boule d'Argent'
MOCK ORANGE
☼ ❄❄❄   ↕ 1.5m (5ft) ↔ 1.5m (5ft)

One of several mock oranges suitable for small gardens, this has a bushy habit and arching branches. Striking clusters of lightly fragrant flowers appear in summer.

Spiraea canescens
SPIRAEA
☼ ❄❄❄   ↕ 2.2m (7ft) ↔ 1.7m (5½ft)

The arching stems of this graceful shrub are covered, for much of their length, with clusters of tiny white summer flowers, set above small grey-green leaves.

Xanthoceras sorbifolium
XANTHOCERAS
☼ ❄❄❄   ↕ 3m (10ft) ↔ 2.2m (7ft)

An uncommon, unusual shrub of upright growth, with much-divided leaves and erect flower spikes from late spring. It may produce large fruits after a hot summer. ♀

Prunus tenella
DWARF RUSSIAN ALMOND
☼ ❄❄❄   ↕ 70cm (28in) ↔ 1.2m (4ft)

This low, bushy shrub has many slender stems, narrow, glossy green leaves, and bright pink flowers crowding the branches in spring. 'Fire Hill' is a superb selection.

Syringa x *persica*
PERSIAN LILAC
☼ ❄❄❄   ↕ 2.2m (7ft) ↔ 2.2m (7ft)

A reliable and justifiably popular lilac, this forms a large bush in time. Slender branches bear spectacular conical heads of fragrant flowers in late spring. ♀

OTHER DECIDUOUS SHRUBS FOR ALKALINE SOILS

Abelia triflora
Buddleja alternifolia 'Argentea'
Chaenomeles speciosa 'Moerloosii', see p.100
Cotinus coggygria 'Notcutt's Variety'
Dipelta floribunda
Forsythia x *intermedia* 'Lynwood', see p.136
Hydrangea paniculata 'Pink Diamond'
Rubus 'Benenden', see p.165

SHRUBS

Shrubs for Sandy Soils

NUMEROUS SHRUBS favour sandy soils because they are usually warm and free-draining. In times of drought, however, sandy soils can turn to dust, and plants growing in them may require a great deal of irrigation. Such soils can, of course, be improved by changing their structure with the addition of peat substitutes, or liberal and regular amounts of moisture-retentive organic matter, but it is still a good idea to plant shrubs tolerant of drought and rapid drainage.

Cytisus x *praecox* 'Allgold'
BROOM
☼ ❄❄❄   ↕ 2m (6ft) ↔ 2m (6ft)

The slender, arching shoots of this shrub form a compact mound. Its grey-green branchlets are crowded with small, long-lasting yellow pea-flowers in spring. ♗

Callistemon citrinus 'Splendens'
BOTTLEBRUSH
☼ ❄❄   ↕ 2m (6ft) ↔ 2m (6ft)

Brilliant red, tightly packed, brush-like spikes adorn this evergreen in summer. It has many arching stems, and branches of narrow, leathery, glossy green leaves. ♗

Ballota acetabulosa
BALLOTA
☼ ❄❄   ↕ 60cm (24in) ↔ 75cm (30in)

This grey-green, woolly plant has erect stems with rounded leaves, and bears tiny, two-lipped pink flowers in summer. Prune back hard, if damaged in cold winters.

OTHER SHRUBS FOR SANDY SOIL
Atraphaxis frutescens
Brachyglottis 'Sunshine', see p.136
Cistus populifolius var. *lasiocalyx*
Coronilla emerus
Cytisus nigricans
Genista tenera 'Golden Showers'
Halimodendron halodendron
Indigofera ambylantha
Potentilla 'Elizabeth' see p.123
Robinia hispida 'Macrophylla'
Santolina chamaecyparissus, see p.153

Brachyglottis monroi
SHRUBBY SENECIO
☼ ❄❄❄   ↕ 1m (3ft) ↔ 1.5m (5ft)

Low-domed and compact, this evergreen shrub is crowded with small, wavy-edged, dark green, white-backed leaves. It carries yellow daisy-flowers in summer. ♗

Cistus x *purpureus*
SUN ROSE
☼ ❄❄   ↕ 1m (3ft) ↔ 1m (3ft)

In early summer, this rounded, bushy evergreen carries single, rose-like flowers. Narrow grey-green leaves are a perfect foil for its deep purplish pink blooms. ♗

Dorycnium hirsutum
DORYCNIUM
☼ ❄❄❄   ↕ 60cm (24in) ↔ 60cm (24in)

This small, mounded shrub is entirely covered with silvery grey down. Clusters of little white pea-flowers in summer are followed by attractive reddish seed pods.

SHRUBS

Grevillea 'Canberra Gem'
GREVILLEA
☼ ✻✻ ↕ 2m (6ft) ↔ 2m (6ft)

One of the hardiest grevilleas, 'Canberra
Gem' forms an evergreen mound of green,
needle-like leaves. Loose flower clusters
are borne from late winter into spring. ♈

Hibiscus syriacus 'Woodbridge'
HIBISCUS
☼ ✻✻✻ ↕ 2.5m (8ft) ↔ 3m (10ft)

Slow-growing and late-leafing, this shrub
is upright at first, spreading as it matures.
Beautiful, saucer-shaped
pink flowers are produced in
late summer and autumn. ♈

Lespedeza thunbergii
LESPEDEZA
☼ ✻✻✻ ↕ 1.5m (5ft) ↔ 2.5m (8ft)

This is one of the best autumn-flowering
shrubs. Its long, arching stems become
weighed down with large sprays of purple
pea-flowers. May require support. ♈

Lavatera 'Barnsley'
TREE MALLOW
☼ ✻✻ ↕ 2m (6ft) ↔ 2m (6ft)

All through summer, this semi-evergreen
carries a succession of lovely, pale blush-
pink, almost white, red-eyed flowers. Its
lobed leaves are sage-green and downy. ♈

Potentilla fruticosa var. *mandshurica*
'Manchu'
☼ ✻✻✻ ↕ 45cm (18in) ↔ 60cm (24in)

Twiggy branches, clothed with silver-grey
leaves, form a low mound. The bush is
densely packed with small, single white
flowers from late spring into early autumn.

Romneya coulteri
CALIFORNIA POPPY
☼ ✻✻✻ ↕ 2m (6ft) ↔ 2m (6ft)

This strong-growing plant, with blue-grey
stems and deeply cut foliage, produces
large, fragrant white poppy-flowers in late
summer. These have golden stamens. ♈

Shrubs for Dry, Sunny Sites

COUNTLESS SHRUBS thrive in situations that are sunny and relatively dry; if your winters are mild, then the choice is both immense and exciting. Where winter temperatures are not as favourable, make use of any shelter available, be it a backing wall or protection provided by more hardy plants nearby. Many of the shrubs thriving in dry, sunny situations hail from regions such as the Mediterranean, where sun, heat, and stony, well-drained soils often go hand in hand.

Euphorbia characias subsp. *wulfenii*
SHRUBBY EUPHORBIA
☼ ❄❄❄   ↕ 1m (3ft) ↔ 1m (3ft)

This evergreen produces erect, biennial stems, with grey-green leaves in one year, followed the next spring by large heads of little yellow-green, cup-shaped flowers. ♈

Cistus x *cyprius*
SUN ROSE
☼ ❄❄❄   ↕ 2m (6ft) ↔ 1.5m (5ft)

Large white flowers, with yellow stamens and red blotches, open in early summer. Both the shoots and leaves of this vigorous evergreen are sticky to the touch.   ♈

OTHER SHRUBS FOR DRY SUN

Abutilon x *suntense* 'Violetta'
Carpenteria californica, see p.158
Caryopteris incana
Cistus x *hybridus*
Colquhounia coccinea
Fremontodendron 'California Glory', see p.99
Grevillea 'Canberra Gem', see p.129
Grevillea juniperina f. *sulphurea*
Xanthoceras sorbifolium, see p.127
Zauschneria californica 'Dublin'

Erythrina crista-galli
CORAL TREE
☼ ❄   ↕ 2m (6ft) ↔ 2m (6ft)

Eye-catching spikes of waxy coral-red flowers open in late summer. The prickly shoots bear leaves, each composed of three leaflets. Dies right back in cold winters. ♈

Euryops pectinatus
EURYOPS
☼ ❄   ↕ 1m (3ft) ↔ 1m (3ft)

An evergreen mound of deeply cut grey-green leaves is topped with long-stalked, bright yellow, daisy-like flowers, from late winter through to early summer.   ♈

Grindelia chiloensis
GRINDELIA
☼ ✻✻ ↕75cm (30in) ↔60cm (24in)

Reminiscent of a golden cornflower, this evergreen bears long-stalked, bright yellow daisy-flowers from late winter into early summer. It is sticky to the touch. ⚱

Phlomis fruticosa
JERUSALEM SAGE
☼ ✻✻ ↕1m (3ft) ↔1m (3ft)

This low, mound-forming evergreen shrub is worth growing for its downy, aromatic grey-green leaves alone; golden flowers during summer are an added bonus. ⚱

Hibiscus syriacus 'Blue Bird'
HIBISCUS
☼ ✻✻✻ ↕2.5m (8ft) ↔2m (6ft)

Erect at first, this slow-growing and late-leafing shrub spreads with age, and carries a wealth of large lilac-blue flowers in late summer and autumn.

Phlomis italica
PHLOMIS
☼ ✻✻ ↕1m (3ft) ↔60cm (24in)

The stems and leaves of this low, upright evergreen are covered with grey-green, woolly hairs. Whorls of two-lipped summer flowers are a lovely shade of lilac-pink.

Fabiana imbricata 'Violacea'
FABIANA
☼ ✻✻ ↕2.5m (8ft) ↔2m (6ft)

The stems of this upright to vase-shaped evergreen are clothed with tiny, heath-like leaves, and crowded in early summer with pale violet, tubular flowers. ⚱

Olearia stellulata
DAISY BUSH
☼ ✻✻ ↕1.5m (5ft) ↔1.5m (5ft)

During late spring, the stems and narrow, wavy-edged leaves of this dense evergreen are almost completely obscured by masses of white, daisy-like flowers. ⚱

Sophora davidii
SOPHORA
☼ ✻✻✻ ↕1.5m (5ft) ↔2m (6ft)

Loose-stemmed when young, this shrub becomes dense and spiny with age. Bluish white pea-flowers are produced among its small, deeply divided leaves in summer.

S H R U B S

131

Shrubs Tolerant of Shade

YOU MAY BE SURPRISED at the range of shrubs suitable for growing in shade. Many are woodlanders in the wild, preferring to grow where they are not directly exposed to the sun's rays. This does not mean they can survive without any light – all green-leaved plants need light to photosynthesize. Some, however, are more tolerant of lower light levels than others, and it is these that are most successful when planted in the shade of deciduous trees, or that cast by buildings.

SHRUBS

Euonymus fortunei 'Emerald Gaiety'
EVERGREEN EUONYMUS
☼ ☀ ❆❆❆ ↕ 1.5m (5ft) ↔ 1.5m (5ft)

Strong-growing and bushy, this upright evergreen shrub has leathery, dark green, glossy-topped leaves. In autumn, creamy white capsules encase orange seeds.

Euonymus fortunei   'Vegetus'
EVERGREEN EUONYMUS
☼ ☀ ❆❆❆ ↕ 30cm (12in) ↔ 2m (6ft)

The presence of both creeping and erect stems enable this tough, bushy evergreen to form extensive patches. Its green leaves and pinkish seed capsules are numerous.

Crinodendron hookerianum
LANTERN TREE
☼ ☀ ❆❆❆^{PH} ↕ 3m (10ft) ↔ 2m (6ft)

From late spring through to early summer, the branches of this handsome evergreen are strung with beautiful red flowers that resemble lanterns. Dislikes dry soils. ♈

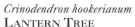

OTHER DECIDUOUS SHRUBS
TOLERANT OF SHADE

Cornus canadensis, see p.118
Euonymus obovatus
Hydrangea macrophylla
  'Generale Vicontessa de Vibraye'
Hypericum androsaemum
Kerria japonica
Rhodotypos scandens, see p.135
Rubus odoratus
Rubus spectabilis 'Olympic Double'
Symphoricarpos x *chenaultii* 'Hancock'

Daphne laureola var. *philippi*
SPURGE LAUREL
☼ ☀ ☀ ❆❆❆ ↕ 30cm (12in) ↔ 60cm (2ft)

A dwarf variety of a woodland evergreen, this is just as effective when grown in full sun. Crowded light green flower clusters emerge in late winter and early spring.

Hydrangea macrophylla 'Veitchii'
LACE-CAP HYDRANGEA
☼ ☀ ❆❆ ↕ 1.5m (5ft) ↔ 2.5m (8ft)

Broader than it is high, this bold-foliaged bush carries heads of tiny flowers, each surrounded by a ring of larger florets, from mid- to late summer. Dislikes dry soils. ♈

Hydrangea serrata 'Bluebird'
LACE-CAP HYDRANGEA
☼ ☀ ❄❄   ↕1.2m (4ft) ↔ 1.5m (5ft)

The pointed leaves of this dense, bushy
shrub often colour well in autumn. Violet-
blue, lace-cap flowers in summer have
pale marginal florets. Dislikes dry soils. ♈

Pachysandra terminalis
JAPANESE SPURGE
☼ ☀ ❄❄❄   ↕10cm (4in) ↔ 20cm (8in)

This evergreen, suckering shrublet likes
moist soils, and makes a superb ground
cover for shade. Its dark green leaves back
little white flower spikes in spring. ♈

Skimmia japonica 'Fructu-albo'
SKIMMIA
☼ ☀ ❄❄❄   ↕75cm (30in) ↔ 75cm (30in)

If you plant a male variety of this dense,
low evergreen nearby to effect pollination,
this spring-flowering skimmia cultivar will
produce an abundance of white berries.

Lonicera pileata
SHRUBBY HONEYSUCKLE
☼ ☀ ❄❄❄   ↕60cm (24in) ↔ 2m (6ft)

Its low and wide-spreading habit makes
this an excellent evergreen ground cover.
Tiny, inconspicuous late spring flowers
are occasionally followed by violet berries.

Prunus laurocerasus 'Otto Luyken'
CHERRY LAUREL
☼ ☀ ❄❄❄   ↕75cm (30in) ↔ 1.2m (4ft)

The branches of this low evergreen shrub
are clothed with narrow, glossy, leathery
leaves. Erect spikes of white flowers in
late spring are followed by black fruits. ♈

Mahonia nervosa
CASCADES MAHONIA
☼ ☀ ❄❄❄❄ PH   ↕60cm (24in) ↔ 1m (3ft)

This evergreen, suckering shrub produces
short, erect stems with handsome leaves
that turn red or purplish in winter. Spikes
of yellow flowers appear in early summer.

**OTHER EVERGREEN SHRUBS
TOLERANT OF SHADE**

Aucuba japonica 'Rozannie', see p.146
Buxus sempervirens 'Latifolia Maculata'
Daphne pontica
x *Fatshedera lizei*, see p.144
Fatsia japonica, see p.111
Osmanthus heterophyllus
Rubus tricolor
Ruscus hypoglossum
Sarcococca confusa
Viburnum davidii, see p.119

Vinca major 'Variegata'
VARIEGATED LARGE PERIWINKLE
☼ ☀ ❄❄❄   ↕30cm (12in) ↔ 1.5m (5ft)

Striking, variegated leaves are margined
creamy white, and form a superb ground
cover that is rampant if unchecked. Blue
flowers last from spring to autumn. ♈

S H R U B S

Shrubs Tolerant of Damp Sites and Watersides

PERMANENTLY MOIST SOILS, or sites that occasionally flood, are not ideal planting spots. This makes shrubs tolerant of wet conditions valuable to gardeners faced with damp or boggy areas. Where practical and desirable, you can improve such soils by draining, but if you decide to leave them alone, the following plants can generally be relied upon to thrive.

Myrica gale
SWEET GALE, BOG MYRTLE
☼ ✹✹✹ PH   ↕1m (3ft) ↔ 1m (3ft)

Catkins crowd this small, aromatic shrub in spring, before its blue-green leaves unfurl. Fruiting spikes, seen here, follow. Tolerant of extremely boggy conditions.

Aronia arbutifolia
RED CHOKEBERRY
☼ ☼ ✹✹✹   ↕3m (10ft) ↔ 2m (6ft)

This vigorous shrub forms clumps of erect stems that eventually arch widely. Small white spring flowers are followed by red berries. Its leaves turn red in autumn.

Lindera benzoin
SPICE BUSH
☼ ✹✹✹ PH   ↕3m (10ft) ↔ 3m (10ft)

The bright green foliage of this free-growing shrub is aromatic and turns clear yellow in autumn. Clusters of small, greenish yellow flowers appear in spring.

Physocarpus opulifolius 'Dart's Gold'
NINE-BARK
☼ ✹✹✹   ↕2m (6ft) ↔ 2m (6ft)

Golden yellow leaves, carried from spring and all through summer, eclipse the late spring flowers of this tough and adaptable shrub. The bark on older stems peels. ♆

OTHER SHRUBS TOLERANT OF DAMP SITES AND WATERSIDES

Amelanchier canadensis
Aronia melanocarpa
Calycanthus floridus
Cephalanthus occidentalis
Clethra tomentosa
Cornus alba 'Aurea', see p.150
Cornus alba 'Elegantissima', see p.148
Cornus alba 'Gouchaultii'
Cornus stolonifera 'Flaviramea', see p.168
Hamamelis vernalis
Myrica cerifera
Neillia thibetica, see p.123
Photinia villosa, see p.228
Sorbaria aitchisonii
Viburnum lantanoides
Viburnum opulus 'Xanthocarpum'
Viburnum sieboldii

Clethra alnifolia
SWEET PEPPER BUSH
☼ ☼ ✹✹✹ PH   ↕2m (6ft) ↔ 1.5m (5ft)

Spikes of small, sweetly scented white flowers are produced in late summer. The toothed leaves of this upright, frequently suckering shrub give yellow autumn tints.

Rhododendron occidentale
AZALEA
☼ ✹✹✹ PH   ↕2m (6ft) ↔ 2m (6ft)

Bold clusters of fragrant, funnel-shaped flowers appear in early summer, and vary from white to pink or pale yellow. Glossy green leaves colour richly in autumn. ♆

Rhodotypos scandens
RHODOTYPOS
☼ ☀ ❊❊❊   ↕ 2m (6ft) ↔ 2m (6ft)

Pure white flowers, borne from late spring through summer, are followed by small, shining black fruits. This vigorous shrub has toothed, conspicuously veined leaves.

> **SHRUBBY WILLOWS TOLERANT OF DAMP OR WATERSIDES**
>
> *Salix acutifolia*
> *Salix discolor*
> *Salix elaeagnos*
> *Salix exigua*, see p.153
> *Salix gracilistyla* 'Melanostachys'
> *Salix irrorata*
> *Salix japonica*
> *Salix purpurea* 'Nana'
> *Salix triandra*
> *Salix udensis* 'Sekka'

Spiraea x *vanhouttei*
BRIDAL WREATH
☼ ❊❊❊   ↕ 1.5m (5ft) ↔ 1.5m (5ft)

The arching stems of this strong-growing shrub form a dense mound. Clusters of white flowers are carried all along the upper sides of its branches in summer. ♈

Salix daphnoides
VIOLET WILLOW
☼ ❊❊❊   ↕ 6m (20ft) ↔ 6m (20ft)

This vigorous shrub is grown for its pale violet winter shoots. Male forms such as 'Aglaia' have attractive catkins in spring, silver at first, then turning to yellow.

Vaccinium corymbosum
SWAMP BLUEBERRY
☼ ☀ ❊❊❊❊ ᴾᴴ   ↕ 1.5m (5ft) ↔ 1.5m (5ft)

Clusters of small flowers in late spring are white or pale pink in colour, and followed by edible black berries. In autumn, the leaves of this bushy shrub turn crimson. ♈

Viburnum opulus
GUELDER ROSE
☼ ☀ ❊❊❊   ↕ 4m (12ft) ↔ 4m (12ft)

White, lace-cap flowerheads opening in summer give way to clusters of glistening red berries. The leaves of this vigorous shrub are orange, purple, or red in autumn.

135

Shrubs Tolerant of Air Pollution

OTHER EVERGREEN SHRUBS
TOLERANT OF AIR POLLUTION

Aucuba japonica 'Rozannie', see p.146
Camellia japonica 'Adolphe Audusson',
   see p.124
Cotoneaster sternianus, see p.162
Elaeagnus x *ebbingei* 'Gilt Edge',
   see p.149
Euonymus fortunei 'Emerald Gaiety',
   see p.118
Sarcococca hookeriana var. *digyna*,
   see p.167

THE DAYS WHEN INDUSTRIAL POLLUTION was common-place in most, if not all, manufacturing towns and cities are thankfully now ended. Other forms of pollution, however, remain a problem, particularly from vehicle exhausts, hence the value of shrubs showing some degree of tolerance. The following are among the most successful.

Brachyglottis 'Sunshine'
SHRUBBY SENECIO
☼ ❋❋❋   ↕ 1m (3ft) ↔ 1.5m (5ft)

Of all flowering shrubs, this is one of the most reliable and popular, with its striking grey-green foliage, silvery when young, and bright yellow summer flowers. ⏀

Forsythia x *intermedia* 'Lynwood'
FORSYTHIA, GOLDEN BELL
☼ ☀ ❋❋❋   ↕ 3m (10ft) ↔ 2.5m (8ft)

Spectacular in flower, and thus deservedly popular; the branches of this robust shrub are wreathed with masses of rich yellow bell-shaped, star-like flowers in spring. ⏀

Buddleja davidii 'Royal Red'
BUTTERFLY BUSH
☼ ❋❋❋   ↕ 4m (12ft) ↔ 4m (12ft)

The arching branches of this vigorous shrub produce silvery leaves that become green in summer, when its fragrant flower spikes, lasting into autumn, appear. ⏀

Hypericum 'Hidcote'
SHRUBBY HYPERICUM
☼ ☀ ❋❋❋   ↕ 1.2m (4ft) ↔ 1.5m (5ft)

From summer into autumn, this vigorous evergreen or semi-evergreen shrub carries a long succession of large, golden yellow flowers amid neat, dark green foliage. ⏀

Mahonia aquifolium 'Smaragd'
OREGON GRAPE
☼ ☀ ❋❋❋   ↕ 75cm (30in) ↔ 1.5m (5ft)

This low-growing, spreading evergreen bears glossy green, spine-toothed leaves, bronze when young. Bright yellow flower clusters are produced in spring.

SHRUBS

Skimmia x *confusa* 'Kew Green'
SKIMMIA
☼ ☀ ☀ ✽✽✽ ↕75cm (30in) ↔1.2m (4ft)

Deep green, aromatic leaves are topped in spring by dense, conical heads of fragrant, creamy white flowers. An excellent and adaptable, mounded evergreen shrub. ♔

Olearia x *haastii*
DAISY BUSH
☼ ✽✽✽ ↕2m (6ft) ↔2m (6ft)

Crowded heads of fragrant white, daisy-like flowers cover this tough, reliable, compact evergreen in summer. Its small, oval leaves have white-felted undersides.

OTHER DECIDUOUS SHRUBS
TOLERANT OF AIR POLLUTION

Amelanchier lamarckii, see p.222
Buddleja 'Pink Delight'
Colutea x *media* 'Copper Beauty'
Lonicera ledebourii
Sambucus nigra 'Guincho Purple',
   see p.155
Sorbaria aitchisonii
Spartium junceum, see p.139
Viburnum opulus 'Notcutt's Variety'
Weigela coraeensis

Rhododendron 'Susan'
RHODODENDRON
☼ ✽✽✽ PH ↕3m (10ft) ↔3m (10ft)

Compact, bushy, and quite vigorous, this evergreen bears rounded flower trusses in spring. The flowers, with dark margins and purple spots, fade to near-white. ♔

Syringa vulgaris 'Mme Lemoine'
LILAC
☼ ✽✽✽ ↕4m (12ft) ↔3m (10ft)

Spectacular, crowded heads of fragrant white flowers are produced in late spring and early summer. Upright when young, it spreads with age. ♔

Philadelphus 'Beauclerk'
MOCK ORANGE
☼ ✽✽✽ ↕2.5m (8ft) ↔2m (6ft)

This lovely shrub is well worth growing for its abundance of large, broad-petalled white flowers, carried from early to mid-summer. The blooms are fragrant. ♔

Ribes sanguineum 'Pulborough Scarlet'
FLOWERING CURRANT
☼ ✽✽✽ ↕2.5m (8m) ↔2m (6ft)

Fairly upright when young, and spreading as it matures, this vigorous shrub's aromatic leaves are preceded, or accompanied, by pendent red flower clusters in spring. ♔

Tamarix tetrandra
TAMARISK
☼ ✽✽✽ ↕4m (12ft) ↔4m (12ft)

The dark shoots of this loose-stemmed shrub all are clothed with scale-like green leaves. In late spring and early summer, crowded plumes of tiny flowers appear. ♔

SHRUBS

Shrubs Tolerant of Coastal Exposure

CONTRARY TO POPULAR BELIEF, a great number of shrubs can be grown in gardens near the sea. Some are more than happy to take the full blast of coastal winds and even salt spray. Others, however, while tolerant to a degree, prefer some shelter to thrive. Those listed here are among the most reliable for seaside gardens.

Escallonia 'Apple Blossom'
ESCALLONIA
☼ ❄❄❄   ↕ 2m (6ft) ↔ 2m (6ft)

Shining, dark green foliage clothes this dense evergreen shrub. Clusters of pink and white flowers, the colour of apple blossom, adorn it in summer.

OTHER DECIDUOUS SHRUBS
TOLERANT OF COASTAL EXPOSURE

Colutea x *media* 'Orange Beauty'
Cytisus 'Killiney Red', see p.122
Elaeagnus angustifolia
Elaeagnus 'Quicksilver', see p.220
Halimodendron halimifolium
Hydrangea macrophylla 'Ayesha'
Lycium barbarum
Rosa rugosa, see p.141
Tamarix ramosissima 'Rubra'
Tamarix tetrandra, see p.137

Atriplex halimus
TREE PURSLANE
☼ ❄❄❄   ↕ 2m (6ft) ↔ 2m (6ft)

This bushy evergreen shrub, with its attractive, silvery grey foliage, is partially deciduous in cold areas. It is excellent as a specimen, or as an informal hedge.

Bupleurum fruticosum
SHRUBBY HARE'S-EAR
☼ ❄❄   ↕ 2m (6ft) ↔ 2m (6ft)

A bushy evergreen shrub, this is mainly grown for its shining, dark bluish green leaves, though it does carry tiny yellowish flowerheads from summer into autumn.

Buddleja globosa
ORANGE BALL TREE
☼ ❄❄❄   ↕ 3m (10ft) ↔ 3m (10ft)

When in flower in summer, the tiny, tight, globular orange-yellow heads make this shrub stand out. Robust, with bold leaves, it is semi-evergreen in mild areas. ♈

Colutea arborescens
BLADDER SENNA
☼ ❄❄❄   ↕ 2.5m (8ft) ↔ 2.5m (8ft)

A vigorous shrub of open habit, this has small, much-divided leaves. The clusters of yellow pea-flowers in summer are replaced by inflated seed capsules. ♈

Fuchsia magellanica
LADY'S EARDROPS
☼ ❄❄❄   ↕ 2m (6ft) ↔ 2m (6ft)

Dense, leafy mounds make this ideal as a specimen plant or an informal hedge. Its lantern-like flowers hang freely from the shoots from midsummer into autumn.

SHRUBS

Hebe x *franciscana* 'Blue Gem'
HEBE
☼ ❄❄❄   ↕60cm (24in) ↔ 1.2m (4ft)

This evergreen shrub is a familiar sight on promenades in coastal towns. Short violet flower spikes are carried from summer through to early winter. ♈

Hydrangea macrophylla
'Lanarth White'
☼ ◐ ❄❄❄   ↕1.5m (5ft) ↔ 2m (6ft)

In summer, long-lasting, domed heads of dark blue, fertile flowers and starry white, sterile florets cover this reliable, compact, mounded shrub. Light green leaves. ♈

Olearia nummulariifolia
DAISY BUSH
☼ ❄❄❄   ↕2m (6ft) ↔ 2m (6ft)

Stiff shoots crowded with tiny, leathery evergreen leaves characterize this rounded shrub. Small, fragrant flowers open near the ends of the branches in summer. ♈

Spartium junceum
SPANISH BROOM
☼ ❄❄❄   ↕2.5m (8ft) ↔ 2.5m (8ft)

Spanish Broom is a vigorous shrub with smooth, dark green, almost leafless shoots, and sprays of fragrant yellow pea-flowers, lasting from early summer into autumn. ♈

OTHER EVERGREEN SHRUBS TOLERANT OF COASTAL EXPOSURE

Brachyglottis 'Sunshine', see p.136
Elaeagnus macrophylla
Escallonia 'Iveyi'
Olearia macrodonta 'Major'

Lupinus arboreus
TREE LUPIN
☼ ❄❄❄   ↕1m (3ft) ↔ 1m (3ft)

This vigorous, mounded semi-evergreen, with the fingered leaves typical of lupins, bears numerous tapered spikes of fragrant yellow flowers in early summer. ♈

Tamarix ramosissima
TAMARISK
☼ ❄❄❄   ↕4m (12ft) ↔ 4m (12ft)

Openly branched and vigorous, this shrub has feathery blue-green foliage on long branches, and plumes of tiny pink flowers from late summer into early autumn.

SHRUBS

139

Shrubs for Screening or Hedges

SHRUBS SUITABLE FOR HEDGING can be pruned or clipped annually for a formal effect, or allowed to develop a more natural appearance. Those of stronger growth and ultimately large habit are useful for screening, to hide intrusive views, filter noise, or lessen the effect of wind. Sizes given refer to the average ultimate size of a single plant without pruning.

OTHER SHRUBS FOR SMALL HEDGES
Berberis thunbergii 'Red Pillar'
Buxux sempervirens 'Suffruticosa', see p.170
Hebe x *franciscana* 'Blue Gem', see p.139
Ilex cornuta 'Burfordii'
Ilex crenana 'Convexa'
Lavandula angustifolia 'Hidcote', see p.164
Myrtus communis var. *tarentina*

Berberis x *stenophylla*
BERBERIS
☼ ✳✳✳   ↕ 2.5m (8ft) ↔ 2.5m (8ft)

Popular as an informal hedge, this tough, adaptable evergreen has slender, arching stems, narrow, dark green leaves, and tiny, golden yellow flowers in spring. ♀

Cotoneaster lacteus
COTONEASTER
☼ ✳✳✳   ↕ 4m (12ft) ↔ 3m (10ft)

One of the best evergreens for a formal hedge or an informal screen, this bears veined leaves, white summer flowers, and red berries from autumn into winter. ♀

OTHER EVERGREEN SHRUBS FOR SCREENING OR HEDGES
Berberis darwinii, see p.122
Elaeagnus macrophylla
Escallonia rubra 'Crimson Spire'
Escallonia rubra var. *macrantha*
Euonymus japonicus
Ilex aquifolium
Olearia macrodonta, see p.146
Pittosporum colensoi
Pittosporum crassifolium
Viburnum tinus

Buxus sempervirens 'Handsworthensis'
HANDSWORTH BOX
☼ ◐ ✳✳✳   ↕ 3m (10ft) ↔ 3m (10ft)

This evergreen is upright, densely leafy, and strong-growing, making it reliable as a formal hedge or screen. Its leathery deep green leaves are rounded or oblong.

Cotoneaster simonsii
COTONEASTER
☼ ✳✳✳   ↕ 2.5m (8ft) ↔ 2m (6ft)

Shiny deciduous or semi-evergreen leaves cover this vigorous shrub, ideal as a formal hedge. White flowers open in summer, and red berries ripen from autumn. ♀

S H R U B S

Elaeagnus x *ebbingei*
ELAEAGNUS
☼ ❊❊❊   ↕4m (12ft) ↔4m (12ft)

Small, fragrant, silvery white flowers crowd the branches in autumn, among shining green leaves. This vigorous evergreen is suitable for formal and informal screens.

Griselinia littoralis
BROADLEAF
☼ ❊❊   ↕6m (20ft) ↔5m (15ft)

This vigorous evergreen shrub, with bright green leaves, is excellent grown alone, or mixed, as it is here, with *Prunus cerasifera* 'Nigra'. Well-suited to seaside gardens. ♈

Prunus laurocerasus 'Rotundifolia'
CHERRY LAUREL
☼ ◐ ● ❊❊❊   ↕3m (10ft) ↔2m (6ft)

Cherry Laurel is the most commonly used laurel for formal hedging, with its striking, glossy green evergreen leaves, and upright growth. Can also be grown informally. ♈

Prunus lusitanica
PORTUGAL LAUREL
☼ ◐ ❊❊❊   ↕6m (20ft) ↔6m (20ft)

Particularly impressive in spring, when it produces white flower tassels, this bushy evergreen shrub carries shining, slender, pointed green leaves on red stalks. ♈

Ilex aquifolium 'Argentea Marginata'
SILVER-MARGINED HOLLY
☼ ❊❊❊   ↕8m (25ft) ↔4m (12ft)

One of the best formal hedges or screens, this shrub or tree has cream-margined, prickly toothed, evergreen leaves, and red fruits when pollinated by a male holly. ♈

OTHER DECIDUOUS SHRUBS FOR SCREENING OR HEDGES

Amelanchier canadensis
Berberis thunbergii 'Atropurpurea'
Carpinus betulus
Chaenomeles speciosa 'Moerlooseii', see p.100
Crataegus monogyna
Fagus sylvatica, see p.215
Hydrangea macrophylla 'Joseph Banks'
Prunus spinosa
Symphoricarpos 'White Hedge'

Fuchsia magellanica 'Riccartonii'
FUCHSIA
☼ ❊❊   ↕2m (6ft) ↔2m (6ft)

Superb as an informal hedge, particularly in coastal areas, this vigorous shrub soon forms a dense bush, and is strung with lantern-like flowers from late summer. ♈

Rosa rugosa
RAMANAS ROSE
☼ ❊❊❊   ↕1.5m (5ft) ↔1.5m (5ft)

This species rose is popular as an informal hedge, with its large, wrinkled leaves and purplish red flowers opening from summer into autumn, followed by tomato-red hips.

S H R U B S

141

Shrubs for Rock Gardens, Raised Beds, and Screes

NUMEROUS SHRUBS NEAT IN HABIT, and attractive in flower, foliage, and fruit are prevented by their small size from being used in a mixed border, unless it is well away from the domination of larger, stronger-growing neighbours. Such shrubs are ideal for planting in rock gardens or raised beds where their special, smaller charms can better be appreciated.

Genista lydia
GENISTA
☼ ✹✹✹ ↕ 55cm (22in) ↔ 75cm (30in)

This shrub is a superb sight in late spring and early summer, when it is covered with clusters of tiny pea-flowers. Ideal for a dry wall top, where its stems can tumble. ♔

OTHER ROCK GARDEN SHRUBS

Anthyllis hermanniae
Berberis x *stenophylla* 'Corallina Compacta'
Convolvulus cneorum, see p.152
Crassula sarcocaulis
Daphne collina
Helichrysum selago
Hypericum olympicum 'Citrinum'
Penstemon pinifolius
Sorbus poteriifolia
Teucrium polium

Acer palmatum 'Corallinum'
JAPANESE MAPLE
☼ ☼ ✹✹✹ ↕ 75cm (30in) ↔ 45cm (18in)

A striking, slow-growing, compact shrub, capable of twice the above size in moist, rich, well-drained soils. Grown mainly for its brilliant coral-pink growths in spring.

Daphne retusa
DAPHNE
☼ ☼ ✹✹✹ ↕ 70cm (28in) ↔ 70cm (28in)

A domed shrub with leathery evergreen leaves, this bears fragrant flowers, purple when in bud, in clusters from late spring, followed by bright red berries. ♔

Berberis empetrifolia
BERBERIS
☼ ✹✹✹✹ ᴾᴴ ↕ 30cm (12in) ↔ 45cm (18in)

The stems of this dwarf evergreen are wiry and prickly, and its branches clothed with small, narrow, spine-tipped leaves. Tiny golden flowers appear in late spring.

Euryops acraeus
EURYOPS
☼ ✹✹✹✹ ↕ 30cm (12in) ↔ 30cm (12in)

Distinctive shrub, forming a small mound of narrow silvery leaves, above which late spring flowers rise on thin, downy stalks. Thrives in sun and well-drained soils. ♔

Hebe cupressoides 'Boughton Dome'
HEBE
☼ ✹✹ ↕ 30cm (12in) ↔ 45cm (18in)

This attractive evergreen mound of tiny, dark grey-green leaves resembles a dwarf juniper and produces clusters of white summer flowers. Needs good drainage. ♔

S H R U B S

Helianthemum 'Fire Dragon'
ROCK ROSE
☼ ❄❄❄   ↕ 28cm (11in) ↔ 55cm (22in)

This evergreen carpet-forming shrub has
narrow grey-green leaves and is plastered
with brilliant orange-scarlet flowers from
late spring, continuing into summer.   ♈

Penstemon serrulatus
PENSTEMON
☼ ❄❄❄   ↕ 60cm (24in) ↔ 30cm (12in)

A loose semi-evergreen shrub, this forms
clumps of dark green foliage, and erect
stems that bear branched heads of tubular
blue to purple flowers in summer.   ♈

Punica granatum var. *nana*
DWARF POMEGRANATE
☼ ❄❄❄   ↕ 60cm (24in) ↔ 60cm (24in)

The glossy leaves of this charming little
pomegranate turn gold in autumn. Funnel-
shaped flowers appear in early autumn.
Appreciates warmth and good drainage.

Linum arboreum
TREE FLAX
☼ ❄❄❄   ↕ 28cm (11in) ↔ 30cm (12in)

Clusters of bright yellow flowers appear
throughout summer, whenever the sun
shines. This low, dome-shaped evergreen
needs warmth and good drainage.   ♈

Parahebe catarractae
PARAHEBE
☼ ❄❄   ↕ 30cm (12in) ↔ 30cm (12in)

This choice, reliable plant forms loose
mounds of evergreen leaves and, in late
summer and early autumn, sprays of small
flowers with crimson and white centres. ♈

OTHER CARPETING SHRUBS

Cistus salviifolius 'Avalanche'
Cytisus purpureus 'Atropurpureus'
Genista sagittalis
Helianthemum apenninum 'Roseum'
Hypericum empetrifolium var. *oliganthum*

Salix reticulata
RETICULATE WILLOW
☼ ❄❄❄   ↕ 4cm (1½in) ↔ 30cm (12in)

Carpets of prostrate stems are clothed in
oval leaves that are pale beneath and net-
veined above. Male plants have pretty
spring catkins. Best in moist soils.   ♈

SHRUBS

Shrubs for Containers

JUST ABOUT ANY SHRUB can be planted in a container, although some are more suitable than others. Generally, large and vigorous shrubs are best avoided unless you prune them regularly. Pots and tubs are particularly useful on patios, terraces, and in courtyards; or for growing tender shrubs, to move to shelter in cold weather. For those who garden on a particular soil type and who wish to grow a plant unsuited to it, containers provide a practical solution to this problem.

Felicia amelloides 'Santa Anita'
FELICIA
☼ ❈   ↕ 30cm (12in) ↔ 30cm (12in)

Long-stalked, yellow-eyed, blue daisy-like flowers rise above a bushy mound of oval evergreen leaves, from late spring through to autumn.   ♗

OTHER TENDER SHRUBS FOR CONTAINERS

Abutilon 'Canary Bird'
Brugmansia x *candida* 'Knightii'
Cestrum nocturnum
Nerium oleander

Choisya 'Aztec Pearl'
CHOISYA
☼ ☼ ❈❈❈   ↕ 1.2m (4ft) ↔ 1.2m (4ft)

The fingered leaves of this free-growing evergreen are aromatic. Its fragrant white flower clusters, pink in bud, occur in late spring, and again in late summer.   ♗

Aloysia triphylla
LEMON VERBENA
☼ ❈❈❈   ↕ 2m (6ft) ↔ 2m (6ft)

Mainly grown for its deliciously lemon-scented leaves, this slender-stemmed bush produces flimsy flower spikes in summer. Prune in late winter to control size.

Cestrum elegans
CESTRUM
☼ ❈   ↕ 3m (10ft) ↔ 2m (6ft)

The arching stems and leafy branches of this vigorous evergreen shrub bow beneath its freely produced clusters of tubular red flowers from spring through summer.   ♗

x *Fatshedera lizei*
FATSHEDERA
☼ ☼ ❈❈   ↕ 2m (6ft) ↔ 2m (6ft)

This handsome evergreen shrub forms a loose mound of boldly lobed, shining, dark green leaves. Loose heads of small cream flowers are carried in autumn.

Fuchsia 'Celia Smedley'
FUCHSIA
☼ ❈❈   ↕ 1.5m (5ft) ↔ 1m (3ft)

Vigorous and upright, this is one of the more hardy fuchsias. Pendulous, pinkish white and red flowers, with greenish white tubes, open throughout summer.   ♗

S H R U B S

Fuchsia 'Thalia'
FUCHSIA
☼ ❈   ↕ 1m (3ft) ↔ 1m (3ft)

Deservedly popular, this erect shrub bears
drooping clusters of long, slender flowers,
carried in summer above dark reddish
green, velvety leaves. ♀

Lantana camara
LANTANA
☼ ❈   ↕ 1.5m (5ft) ↔ 1.5m (5ft)

This prickly-stemmed, summer-flowering
evergreen is rampant in hot climates, but
easily controlled by tip-pruning. Several
colours, changing with age, are available.

OTHER HARDY SHRUBS FOR CONTAINERS

Camellia japonica 'Adolphe Audusson',
  see p.124
Camellia 'Spring Festival'
Camellia x *williamsii* 'Debbie'
Hydrangea macrophylla 'Munster'
Mahonia aquifolium 'Apollo'
Prunus laurocerasus 'Otto Luyken',
  see p.133
Rhododendron 'Hydon Dawn'
Rhododendron 'Vuyk's Scarlet'
Skimmia x *confusa* 'Kew Green',
  see p.137

Prostanthera rotundifolia
ROUND-LEAVED MINT BUSH
☼ ❈   ↕ 1.5m (5ft) ↔ 1.5m (5ft)

When they are bruised, the tiny leaves of
this dense, rounded evergreen are sweetly
aromatic. Masses of bell-shaped flowers
open from spring into early summer. ♀

Mimulus aurantiacus
SHRUBBY MIMULUS
☼ ❈   ↕ 60cm (24in) ↔ 1m (3ft)

A succession of two-lipped orange-yellow
flowers are borne from late spring through
to autumn. The narrow evergreen leaves
of this low bush are sticky to the touch. ♀

Pieris japonica 'Little Heath'
PIERIS
☼ ☼ ❈❈❈   ↕ 1.2m (4ft) ↔ 1m (3ft)

A choice, compact evergreen, this pieris is
grown mainly for its small, slender, white-
margined leaves, which are red when they
emerge in spring. Slow-growing. ♀

Rhododendron 'Homebush'
KNAPHILL AZALEA
☼ ☼ ❈❈❈   ↕ 1.5m (5ft) ↔ 1.5m (5ft)

This charming, relatively compact shrub
is popular on account of its tight, rounded
heads of trumpet-shaped flowers that are
produced in late spring. ♀

Evergreen Shrubs

WHERE WINTER TEMPERATURES are not low enough to severely inhibit their growth, shrubs having evergreen foliage provide some of the most worthwhile ornamental subjects for the garden. They come in an impressive range of shapes, sizes, textures, and colours, adding variety as well as permanence to the mixed bed or border. Most have flowers and perhaps fruit as a bonus. Some evergreen shrubs are so distinguished that they are ideal as courtyard or lawn specimens, while others with a low spreading habit make effective ground cover in sun or shade. Less hardy ever-greens are usually more successful when grown in the shelter of other shrubs or a wall.

Elaeagnus pungens 'Maculata'
ELAEAGNUS
☼ ✳✳✳   ↕2.5m (8ft) ↔ 3m (10ft)

Robust and dense with brown, scaly branchlets, this shrub has gold-splashed green leaves. Clusters of tiny, scented, creamy white flowers occur in autumn. ♔

Aucuba japonica   'Rozannie'
JAPANESE LAUREL
☼ ☼ ✳✳✳   ↕75cm (30in) ↔ 75cm (30in)

The tiny female flowers of this compact dwarf shrub appear in spring, and produce red fruits when pollinated. This cultivar is excellent in a bed or in a container.

Olearia macrodonta
NEW ZEALAND HOLLY
☼ ☼ ✳✳   ↕3.5m (11ft) ↔ 3.5m (11ft)

This sturdy shrub has attractive, pale brown, ultimately shaggy, bark and holly-like leaves. Fragrant, daisy-like white flowerheads appear in early summer. ♔

Buxus sempervirens 'Vardar Valley'
BOX
☼ ☼ ✳✳✳   ↕75cm (30in) ↔ 1.2m (4ft)

This valuable cultivar of the Common Box has a low, wide-spreading habit. With its glossy, densely packed leathery leaves, it is superb for ground cover in most soils.

Daphne odora 'Aureo-marginata'
WINTER DAPHNE
☼ ✳✳   ↕1.1m (3½ft) ↔ 1.2m (4ft)

For a warm, sheltered corner, this is a most reliable evergreen. Sweetly scented flowers are borne from winter into spring, and its leaves have narrow yellow margins.

OTHER EVERGREEN SHRUBS

Berberis 'Goldilocks', see p.169
Camellia japonica 'Magnoliiflora'
Choisya ternata, see p.158
Cleyera japonica
Danae racemosa
Elaeagnus macrophylla
Fatsia japonica, see p.111
Mahonia x *media* 'Buckland', see p.167
Rhododendron bureaui
Skimmia x *confusa* 'Kew Green', see p.137

S H R U B S

Ozothamnus rosmarinifolius
OZOTHAMNUS
☼ ❄❄ ↕2m (6ft) ↔1.5m (5ft)

The erect stems of this vigorous shrub are crowded with thread-like leaves. Its tiny, scented flowers occur in early summer. Needs a warm, well-drained site.

Prunus lusitanica subsp. *azorica*
PORTUGAL LAUREL
☼ ◐ ❄❄ ↕6m (20ft) ↔6m (20ft)

This vigorous form of the Portugal Laurel is densely branched with light green leaves, red at first. Shining, dark purple fruits follow fragrant summer flowers. ♔

EVERGREEN GROUND COVER
SHRUBS

Arctostaphylos uva-ursi 'Vancouver Jade'
Ceanothus gloriosus
Ceanothus thyrsiflorus var. *repens*
Gaultheria shallon
Hypericum calycinum, see p.119
Mahonia nervosa, see p.133
Rubus tricolor
Sarcococca hookeriana var. *humilis*
Vaccinium vitis-idaea
Viburnum davidii, see p.119

Pittosporum tenuifolium
'Irene Paterson'
☼ ❄❄ ↕2.5m (8ft) ↔1.1m (3½ft)

A broadly columnar shrub, this has thin black stems and small, wavy green leaves, marbled white when mature, pink-tinted in winter. Excellent for containers. ♔

Vaccinium glaucoalbum
VACCINIUM
☼ ❄❄❄ ᴾᴴ ↕60cm (24in) ↔75cm (30in)

Handsome and compact, this low-growing shrub has leathery green leaves. Drooping clusters of pink-tinted white spring flowers are followed by blue-black berries. ♔

Prunus laurocerasus 'Zabeliana'
CHERRY LAUREL
☼ ◐ ❄❄❄ ↕80cm (32in) ↔2.2m (7ft)

A tough, wide-spreading form of the Cherry Laurel, with narrow, glossy leaves. Flower spikes in late spring are followed by red, ripening to shiny black, fruits.

Rhododendron 'Dora Amateis'
RHODODENDRON
☼ ◐ ❄❄❄ ᴾᴴ ↕60cm (2ft) ↔60cm (2ft)

This free-flowering dwarf rhododendron of compact habit has glossy foliage, and terminal trusses of funnel-shaped, pink-tinged white flowers in late spring. ♔

Viburnum 'Pragense'
VIBURNUM
☼ ❄❄❄ ↕2.5m (8ft) ↔2.5m (8ft)

The narrow green leaves of this vigorous shrub are boldly veined on top. Creamy white flowers, pink-tinged in bud, are produced in domed heads in spring. ♔

SHRUBS

Variegated-leaved Shrubs

VARIEGATION COMES in a number of forms. Generally a green leaf has a white or yellow margin; occasionally a white or yellow leaf has a green margin. There are, however, a host of shrubs with green, grey, or purple leaves, that are spotted, blotched, or streaked a lighter shade. Two-colour variegation may be joined by paler or darker shades of the dominant colours. The bolder the variegation, the more dramatic the effect when planted with foliage of one colour.

Buxus sempervirens 'Elegantissima'
VARIEGATED BOX
☼ ✳✳✳   ↕ 1.7m (5½ft) ↔ 1.1m (3½ft)

Neat and slow-growing, this is easily the best variegated form of the Common Box. The bush is dome-shaped, with small evergreen, white-margined leaves. ♈

Cornus alba 'Elegantissima'
SILVER VARIEGATED DOGWOOD
☼ ✳✳✳   ↕ 2.2m (7ft) ↔ 2.2m (7ft)

A reliable, variegated dogwood that bears white-margined grey-green leaves on reddish shoots. Prune hard in late winter for brighter stems and larger leaves. ♈

Buddleja davidii 'Harlequin'
BUTTERFLY BUSH
☼ ✳✳✳   ↕ 2.5m (8ft) ↔ 2.5m (8ft)

A vigorous and attractive shrub, this has arching stems and creamy white-margined leaves. Large, dense spikes of red-purple flowers occur from summer into autumn.

OTHER DECIDUOUS
VARIEGATED SHRUBS

Berberis thunbergii 'Rose Glow'
Cornus alba 'Spaethii'
Daphne x *burkwoodii* 'Carol Mackie'
Fuchsia magellanica 'Sharpitor'
Hypericum x *moserianum* 'Tricolor'
Ligustrum sinense 'Variegatum'
Lonicera nitida 'Silver Beauty'
Sambucus nigra 'Pulverulenta'
Stachyurus chinensis 'Magpie'
Weigela praecox 'Variegata'

Aucuba japonica 'Crotonifolia'
SPOTTED LAUREL
☼ ☼ ✳✳✳   ↕ 2m (6ft) ↔ 1.7m (5½ft)

The jade green shoots of this spectacular, dense, bushy shrub develop into shiny, leathery green leaves, blotched yellow. This laurel is a most reliable evergreen. ♈

Cornus mas 'Variegata'
VARIEGATED CORNELIAN CHERRY
☼ ☼ ✳✳✳   ↕ 4m (12ft) ↔ 4m (12ft)

This dense, bushy shrub has leaves with bold white margins. Small clusters of tiny yellow flowers stud the twigs in late winter, before the leaves unfurl. ♈

Cotoneaster atropurpureus 'Variegatus'
VARIEGATED COTONEASTER
☼ ❄❄❄   ↕ 45cm (18in) ↔ 1.2m (4ft)

Also known as *C. horizontalis* 'Variegatus',
the low, wide-spreading stems are densely
clothed with tiny, cream-margined leaves.
These are tinted red in autumn.   ♚

Ilex aquifolium 'Ferox Argentea'
SILVER HEDGEHOG HOLLY
☼ ☼ ❄❄❄   ↕ 4m (12ft) ↔ 1.5m (5ft)

An attractive, bushy evergreen holly, with
small, prickly leaves that have creamy
white margins. This is a male form, useful
as a pollinator for berrying hollies.   ♚

Rhamnus alaternus 'Argenteovariegata'
VARIEGATED BUCKTHORN
☼ ❄❄❄   ↕ 2.5m (8ft) ↔ 1.7m (5½ft)

A handsome, bushy evergreen, this has
small, glossy grey-green leaves, margined
creamy white. Discreet yellow flowers will
produce red berries in a hot   summer. ♚

Viburnum tinus 'Variegatum'
VARIEGATED LAURUSTINUS
☼ ☼ ❄❄   ↕ 2.5m (8ft) ↔ 2m (6ft)

The leaves of this mounded or conical
evergreen are boldly and irregularly
margined. Red-budded, fragrant white
flowers occur from autumn through winter.

Elaeagnus x *ebbingei* 'Gilt Edge'
ELAEAGNUS
☼ ❄❄❄   ↕ 2.5m (8ft) ↔ 2.5m (8ft)

This robust evergreen shrub has brown,
scaly stems and shining green leaves, with
golden yellow margins. Its small sweetly
fragrant flowers open in autumn.   ♚

**OTHER EVERGREEN
VARIEGATED SHRUBS**

Coronilla valentina subsp. *glauca*
 'Variegata'
Euonymus fortunei 'Silver Queen',
 see p.100
Euonymus japonicus
 'Latifolius Albomarginatus'
Pieris japonica 'Little Heath', see p.145
Pittosporum 'Garnettii'
Prunus laurocerasus 'Marbled White',
 see p.163

Osmanthus heterophyllus 'Variegatus'
VARIEGATED FALSE HOLLY
☼ ☼ ❄❄❄   ↕ 2.2m (7ft) ↔ 1.2m (4ft)

This evergreen bush of relatively slow
growth has small, white-margined, holly-
like leaves. Clusters of little, sweetly
scented white flowers occur in autumn. ♚

Weigela florida 'Variegata'
VARIEGATED WEIGELA
☼ ❄❄❄   ↕ 1.5m (5ft) ↔ 1.5m (5ft)

One of the most popular and easily grown
variegated shrubs, with distinctly edged
leaves that provide a perfect foil for pink
flowers in late spring and early summer.♚

SHRUBS

Shrubs with Golden or Yellow Leaves

THERE IS NOTHING like a bright splash of yellow or gold foliage to bring a most welcome touch of warmth to the garden, especially in the depths of winter. An abundance of shrubs, both evergreen and deciduous, have leaves in varying shades of yellow. Careful use of these can create striking contrasts with green- or purple-leaved plants.

Berberis thunbergii 'Aurea'
BARBERRY
☼ ✳✳✳   ↕75cm (30in) ↔75cm (30in)

The low, dense, compact mound of small, rounded leaves is vivid yellow at first, and becomes yellow-green later. It is liable to scorch in full sun, except in cool summers.

Calluna vulgaris 'Gold Haze'
HEATHER, LING
☼ ✳✳✳   ↕50cm (20in) ↔45cm (18in)

One of many similar heathers available from nurseries, 'Gold Haze' has packed foliage of a golden hue, brighter in winter. White flowers appear in late summer. ♈

Choisya ternata 'Sundance'
MEXICAN ORANGE-BLOSSOM
☼ ☼ ✳✳✳   ↕1.5m (5ft) ↔2m (6ft)

The bright yellow, aromatic leaves of this evergreen, mounded shrub fade with age. Fragrant white flowers are produced in late spring. Dislikes cold winds. ♈

Cornus alba 'Aurea'
GOLDEN-LEAVED DOGWOOD
☼ ☼ ✳✳✳✳   ↕3m (10ft) ↔3m (10ft)

This vigorous dogwood forms a sizeable mound of dark red branches, clothed, all through summer and into autumn, with broad leaves of a lovely soft yellow colour.

Erica arborea 'Albert's Gold'
TREE HEATH
☼ ✳✳✳   ↕2m (6ft) ↔2m (6ft)

The twiggy branches are densely crowded with tiny leaves, giving plumes of golden yellow throughout the year. Masses of honey-scented white flowers in spring. ♈

Fuchsia 'Genii'
FUCHSIA
☼ ☼ ✳✳✳   ↕1.4m (4½ft) ↔75cm (30in)

This small, colourful, upright shrub has red shoots and bright lime-yellow foliage. It carries small, pendulous violet and red flowers from summer into autumn. ♈

Ligustrum 'Vicaryi'
VICARY GIBBS GOLDEN PRIVET
☼ ☀ ✽✽✽   ↕ 3m (10ft) ↔ 3m (10ft)

This is a vigorous semi-evergreen shrub of dense, bushy habit. The sweetly scented white flowers and bright yellow leaves are carried throughout the summer.

OTHER DECIDUOUS SHRUBS WITH GOLDEN OR YELLOW LEAVES

Acer palmatum 'Aureum'
Caryopteris x *clandonensis* 'Worcester Gold'
Cornus mas 'Aurea'
Fuchsia 'Golden Marinka'
Physocarpus opulifolius 'Dart's Gold', see p.134
Ptelea trifoliata 'Aurea', see p.219
Ribes alpinum 'Aureum'
Rubus cockburnianus 'Golden Vale'
Rubus parviflorus 'Sunshine Spreader'
Sambucus nigra 'Aurea', see p.171
Sambucus racemosa 'Plumosa Aurea'
Spiraea japonica 'Candle Light'
Syringa vulgaris 'Aureum'
Viburnum lantana 'Aurea'
Weigela 'Looymansii Aurea', see p.127
Weigela 'Rubidor'

Sambucus racemosa 'Sutherland Gold'
☼ ✽✽✽   ↕ 3m (10ft) ↔ 3m (10ft)

The large, deeply divided yellow leaves of this vigorous golden elder do not readily scorch. Clusters of yellow flowers, borne in spring, are followed by red berries. ♈

Lonicera nitida 'Baggesen's Gold'
BAGGESEN'S GOLD LONICERA
☼ ✽✽✽   ↕ 5m (15ft) ↔ 5m (15ft)

Attractive, tiny yellow leaves crowd the slender, arching shoots of this dense, bushy evergreen. Capable of greater height when trained against a wall. ♈

Ribes sanguineum 'Brocklebankii'
GOLDEN FLOWERING CURRANT
☼ ✽✽✽   ↕ 1m (3ft) ↔ 1.2m (4ft)

Although clusters of pink flowers decorate this bushy shrub in spring, the aromatic golden yellow leaves, liable to scorch in full sun, are its main attraction. ♈

Spiraea japonica 'Goldflame'
SPIRAEA
☼ ✽✽✽   ↕ 75cm (30in) ↔ 1m (3ft)

Leaves on a low, dense mound of twiggy branches emerge orange-red, then turn to golden yellow, and finally to green. Small summer flowerheads are rose-pink. ♈

OTHER EVERGREEN SHRUBS WITH GOLDEN OR YELLOW LEAVES

Aucuba japonica 'Sulphurea'
Calluna vulgaris 'Beoley Gold'
Erica erigena 'Golden Lady'
Erica vagans 'Valerie Proudley'
Escallonia laevis 'Gold Brian'
Escallonia laevis 'Gold Ellen'
Euonymus japonicus 'Ovatus Aureus'
Ilex x *attenuata* 'Sunny Foster'
Ilex crenata 'Golden Gem'
Ligustrum ovalifolium 'Aureum'

Philadelphus coronarius 'Aureus'
GOLDEN MOCK ORANGE
☼ ✽✽✽   ↕ 2.5m (8ft) ↔ 1.5m (5ft)

The yellow spring leaves of this shrub fade to greenish in late summer, and can scorch in full sun. Creamy white flowers in late spring and early summer, are fragrant. ♈

Viburnum opulus 'Aureum'
GOLDEN GUELDER ROSE
☼ ✽✽✽   ↕ 2.5m (8ft) ↔ 2m (6ft)

Bright yellow, maple-like leaves are red-bronze when young. Its white flowerheads appear in summer, followed by red berries in autumn. Leaves scorch in hot sun.

151

Shrubs with Silver or Blue-grey Leaves

THE SILVERY FLASH of blue-grey leaves when the sunlight catches them shifting in a breeze is a pleasing sight in any garden. Silver-foliaged shrubs can also be grown for their softening effect near leaves of a darker or brighter hue. The silvery colour may be due to a silky or woolly coating of hairs, silvery scales, or a white, powdery bloom.

Convolvulus cneorum
CONVOLVULUS
☼ ❄❄❄   ↕ 75cm (30in) ↔ 1m (3ft)

Silky, silvery leaves and stems make this one of the loveliest dwarf evergreen shrubs. White, yellow-throated flowers cover it from late spring to late summer. ⚱

Berberis dictyophylla
BARBERRY
☼ ❄❄❄   ↕ 2m (6ft) ↔ 2m (6ft)

This graceful shrub has striking stems and leaves with a whitish bloom. Light yellow summer flowers give way to berries that, with the leaves, turn scarlet in autumn. ⚱

Calluna vulgaris 'Silver Queen'
HEATHER, LING
☼ ❄❄❄ ᴾᴴ   ↕ 40cm (16in) ↔ 45cm (18in)

Although it produces mauve-pink flower spikes in late summer and early autumn, this dwarf evergreen is popular mainly for its silver-grey, downy foliage. ⚱

Hebe pimeleoides 'Quicksilver'
HEBE
☼ ❄❄❄   ↕ 25cm (10in) ↔ 60cm (24in)

The dark, wiry stems and branches of this low, spreading evergreen shrub bear small silver-blue leaves, and short spikes of pale lilac flowers in summer. ⚱

OTHER EVERGREEN SHRUBS WITH SILVER OR BLUE-GREY LEAVES

Acacia baileyana
Artemisia arborescens, see p.50
Artemisia 'Powis Castle', see p.72
Ballota pseudodictamnus
Brachyglottis 'Sunshine', see p.136
Cassinia leptophylla
Cistus albidus
Dendromecon rigida
Elaeagnus macrophylla
Euryops acraeus, see p.142
Olearia x *mollis*
Rhododendron campanulatum
  subsp. *aeruginosum*
Rhododendron cinnabarinum
  Concatenans Group
Teucrium fruticans
Yucca glauca
Yucca gloriosa, see p.67

Cistus
'Peggy Sammons'
SUN ROSE
☼ ❄❄   ↕ 1m (3ft) ↔ 1m (3ft)

The pale pink flowers of this lovely, bushy evergreen are freely produced in summer, and resemble small, single roses. Grey-green leaves and stems are downy. ⚱

OTHER DECIDUOUS SHRUBS WITH SILVER OR BLUE-GREY LEAVES

Buddleja alternifolia 'Argentea'
Buddleja nivea
Dorycnium hirsutum, see p.128
Elaeagnus 'Quicksilver', see p.220
Hippophae rhamnoides, see p.214
Romneya coulteri, see p.129
Rosa fedtschenkoana
Rubus thibetanus 'Silver Fern', see p.169
Salix elaeagnos
Salix lanata

Helichrysum italicum
CURRY PLANT
☼ ✽✽ ↕ 60cm (24in) ↔ 1m (3ft)

Thread-like leaves crowd the erect stems
of this low, aromatic evergreen subshrub.
Its leaves and stems are silvery grey and
downy, and summer flowers are yellow. ♔

Leptospermum lanigerum
LEPTOSPERMUM
☼ ✽✽ ↕ 3m (10ft) ↔ 2m (6ft)

The reddish shoots of this evergreen bush
are clothed in narrow grey or silvery grey
leaves. Its small white flowers are freely
produced in early summer. ♔

Perovskia atriplicifolia 'Blue Spire'
RUSSIAN SAGE
☼ ✽✽✽ ↕ 1.2m (4ft) ↔ 1.2m (4ft)

Spires of small violet-blue flowers open in
late summer and autumn, from grey-white
upright stems. These are all clothed with
deeply cut grey-green leaves. ♔

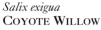

Rosa glauca
SPECIES ROSE
☼ ✽✽✽ ↕ 2m (6ft) ↔ 2m (6ft)

The leaves of this rose, on reddish violet
stems, are glaucous purple in sun, mauve-
tinted grey-green in shade. Early summer
flowers and autumn fruits are a bonus. ♔

Salix exigua
COYOTE WILLOW
☼ ✽✽✽ ↕ 4m (12ft) ↔ 1.5m (5ft)

This tall, upright shrub has long flexuous
stems, each clothed with beautiful leaves,
narrow, silvery and silky, ever-shifting and
shimmering in the slightest breeze.

Santolina chamaecyparissus
COTTON LAVENDER
☼ ✽✽✽ ↕ 75cm (30in) ↔ 1m (3ft)

Narrow, aromatic, woolly whitish leaves
crowd this evergreen shrub, forming a low,
dense dome. Long-stalked, button-like
yellow flowerheads occur in summer. ♔

153

Shrubs with Purple, Red, or Bronze Leaves

PURPLE OR REDDISH foliage in spring or summer can be extremely useful in the garden, providing that it is not overdone. These relatively sombre colours are particularly effective when contrasted with silver or grey foliage; even more dramatic effects can be achieved when they are placed alongside plants with yellow or gold foliage.

Berberis thunbergii 'Red Chief'
BARBERRY
☼ ❄❄❄ ↕1.2m (4ft) ↔1.2m (4ft)

'Red Chief' is a vigorous, upright or vase-shaped shrub, spreading as it matures. It has bright red, arching shoots and narrow, glossy-topped, red-purple leaves. 🏆

Acer palmatum 'Garnet'
JAPANESE MAPLE
☀ ❄❄❄ ↕4m (12ft) ↔4m (12ft)

This strong-growing shrub, with an open, spreading habit, has slender, dark shoots clothed in large, deep garnet-red leaves with finely cut lobes. Dislikes dry soils. 🏆

Corylus maxima 'Purpurea'
PURPLE-LEAF FILBERT
☼ ❄❄❄ ↕6m (20ft) ↔6m (20ft)

Vase-shaped at first, spreading later, this popular form of the filbert is planted for its large, deep purple leaves. Purplish catkins drape branches in late winter. 🏆

Acer palmatum 'Red Pygmy'
JAPANESE MAPLE
☀ ❄❄❄ ↕1.5m (5ft) ↔1.2m (4ft)

The dark purple leaves of this densely branched, slow-growing shrub turn green with age. Leaves on mature plants differ from the juvenile leaves shown here. 🏆

Berberis thunbergii 'Atropurpurea Nana'
BARBERRY
☼ ❄❄❄ ↕60cm (24in) ↔60cm (24in)

This dwarf, dome-shaped shrub of dense, twiggy habit has small, rounded, reddish purple leaves and is particularly suitable for growing on the rock garden. 🏆

Cotinus coggygria 'Royal Purple'
SMOKE TREE
☼ ❄❄❄ ↕↔4m (12ft)

One of the most popular shrubs for foliage, this will form a dense mound of rounded, deep red-purple leaves. Plumes of tiny, smoky pink flowers appear in summer. 🏆

Hebe 'Amy'
HEBE
☼ ✳   ↕ 1m (3ft) ↔ 1m (3ft)

The glossy, dark coppery purple leaves of
this small, rounded evergreen shrub turn
green in time. Rich violet-purple flowers
are borne in short spikes in summer.

**OTHER EVERGREEN SHRUBS WITH
PURPLE, RED, OR BRONZE LEAVES**

Daphne x *houtteana*
Leucothoe 'Scarletta'
Lonicera nitida 'Red Tips'
Nandina domestica 'Nana Purpurea'

Pittosporum tenuifolium 'Tom Thumb'
PITTOSPORUM
☼ ✳✳   ↕ 60cm (24in) ↔ 60cm (24in)

The dark shoots of this dome-shaped
dwarf evergreen shrub are crowded with
shining, crinkly-edged leaves of a deep
reddish purple. These emerge green. ♈

**OTHER DECIDUOUS SHRUBS WITH
PURPLE, RED, OR BRONZE LEAVES**

Acer palmatum 'Bloodgood'
Berberis x *ottawensis* 'Superba'
Itea virginica 'Henry's Garnet'
Weigela florida 'Foliis Purpureis'

Prunus cerasifera 'Hessei'
PURPLE-LEAVED PLUM
☼ ✳✳✳   ↕ 4m (12ft) ↔ 4m (12ft)

In spring, snow-white blossom precedes
the leaves, which emerge green and then
turn bronze-purple with cream or pink
variegation. Bushy form of the cherry plum.

Prunus x *cistena*
PURPLE-LEAF SAND CHERRY
☼ ✳✳✳   ↕ 1.5m (5ft) ↔ 1.5m (5ft)

The Purple-leaf Sand Cherry is a small,
erect shrub with glossy leaves, red at first,
maturing to deep reddish purple. Small
blush-white flowers appear in spring. ♈

Prunus spinosa 'Purpurea'
PURPLE-LEAF SLOE
☼ ✳✳✳   ↕ 4m (12ft) ↔ 4m (12ft)

This is a dense, bushy shrub or small tree,
with spiny branches and bright red leaves,
that change to a deep reddish purple.
Small, pale pink flowers
open in spring.

Sambucus nigra 'Guincho Purple'
PURPLE-LEAF ELDER
☼ ✳✳✳   ↕ 4m (12ft) ↔ 4m (12ft)

The deeply divided leaves of this vigorous
shrub are green at first, maturing to dark
purple, then red in autumn. Its pink-
budded summer flowers open white. ♈

SHRUBS

Shrubs with Colourful Leaf Tints in Autumn

GIVEN FAVOURABLE CONDITIONS, most deciduous shrubs will produce colourful tints before their leaves are shed in autumn; those here have been chosen for their quality and reliability. The impact of a group of shrubs in autumn colour is spectacular, but even a single well-selected and sited shrub can provide eye-catching effects in a small garden.

Cotinus 'Flame'
SMOKE BUSH
☼ ✳✳✳   ↕ 4m (12ft) ↔ 4m (12ft)

Strong-growing and bushy, this shrub has plumes of purplish pink summer flowers. Its bold leaves turn fiery orange and red in autumn. The sap may cause a rash. ♛

OTHER SHRUBS WITH COLOURFUL LEAF TINTS IN AUTUMN

Acer palmatum 'Osakazuki', see p.222
Acer palmatum 'Seiryu'
Aronia arbutifolia 'Brilliant'
Berberis sieboldii
Cornus alba
Enkianthus perulatus
Fothergilla major
Rhododendron 'Corneille'
Vaccinium corymbosum, see p.135
Viburnum opulus 'Notcutt's Variety'

Berberis thunbergii
JAPANESE BARBERRY
☼ ✳✳✳   ↕ 1.4m (5ft) ↔ 1.4m (5ft)

Arching, thorny branches are clothed with small leaves, orange and red in autumn. Tiny yellow flowers are produced in spring and scarlet berries follow in autumn. ♛

Acer palmatum var. *heptalobum*
JAPANESE MAPLE
☼ ◐ ✳✳✳   ↕ 6m (20ft) ↔ 6m (20ft)

Most Japanese maples are worth growing for their impressive autumn tints. The large, seven-lobed green leaves of this one turn red or orange-red. Dislikes dry soils.

Callicarpa japonica
BEAUTY BERRY
☼ ✳✳✳   ↕ 1.4m (4½ft) ↔ 1.4m (4½ft)

The leaves of this bushy shrub turn mauve or rose-madder in autumn. When planted in groups, small violet berries are usually produced at the same time.

Disanthus cercidifolius
DISANTHUS
◐ ✳✳✳✳ PH   ↕ 3m (10ft) ↔ 3m (10ft)

This spreading shrub is grown principally for its rounded blue-green leaves. During autumn, they turn a rich wine-purple, then crimson and orange. Dislikes dry soils. ♛

Ribes odoratum
BUFFALO CURRANT
☼ ☀ ❄❄❄   ↕ 2m (6ft) ↔ 1.5m (5ft)

This open-habited shrub has upright stems
loosely clothed with lobed and rounded
leaves that turn red and purple in autumn.
Golden spring flowers are clove-scented.

Euonymus alatus
WINGED SPINDLE
☼ ❄❄❄   ↕ 2m (6ft) ↔ 3m (10ft)

Compact, and with curious corky, winged
branches, this is a spectacular autumn
shrub. The leaves turn every shade from
pink through to brilliant crimson. ♈

Fothergilla gardenii
FOTHERGILLA
☼ ☀ ❄❄❄ ᴾᴴ   ↕ 1m (3ft) ↔ 1m (3ft)

Although the small white flowerheads in
spring are pretty enough, autumn leaves in
brilliant orange, red, and purple are surely
this fothergilla's most impressive feature.

Hamamelis vernalis 'Sandra'
OZARK WITCH HAZEL
☼ ☀ ❄❄❄ ᴾᴴ   ↕ 3m (10ft) ↔ 3m (10ft)

Young purple leaves mature green, then
become yellow, orange, red, and purple in
autumn. Tiny, crowded, spidery, scented
yellow flowers follow in late winter. ♈

**EVERGREEN SHRUBS WITH
COLOURFUL WINTER LEAF TINTS**

Calluna vulgaris 'Boskoop'
Eurya japonica 'Winter Wine'
Mahonia nervosa, see p.133
Nandina domestica 'Firepower'

Shrubs with Fragrant Flowers

WHEN PRESENTED with a lovely flower, most people will instinctively take a sniff, assuming that a pleasing scent accompanies a beautiful blossom. Sadly, this is not always the case. Numerous shrubs do have fragrant flowers though, and these include some whose fragrance is far more noticeable or appealing than the appearance of the flower itself.

Coronilla valentina subsp. *glauca*
CORONILLA
☼ ✻✻   ↕ 1.4m (4½ft) ↔ 1.4m (4½ft)

The leaves of this bushy evergreen are blue-green and fleshy. Clusters of small yellow pea-flowers are borne continuously from winter into early summer.   ♈

Acacia dealbata
MIMOSA, SILVER WATTLE
☼ ✻✻✻ ᴾᴴ   ↕ 6m (20ft) ↔ 6m (20ft)

Popular with florists, this fast-growing evergreen has feathery blue-green leaves and plumes of bright yellow flower-heads from winter into spring.   ♈

Carpenteria californica
CARPENTERIA
☼ ✻✻   ↕ 2m (6ft) ↔ 2m (6ft)

The evergreen leaves of this bushy shrub are leathery and dark green, and the bark is papery and peeling. Its summer flowers are white with yellow centres.   ♈

Daphne x *burkwoodii* 'Somerset'
DAPHNE
☼ ✻✻✻   ↕ 1.2m (4ft) ↔ 1.2m (4ft)

This narrow-leaved, bushy shrub is one of the best daphnes for general cultivation. In late spring, it is plastered with clusters of small, starry pink and white flowers.

Buddleja 'Lochinch'
BUTTERFLY BUSH
☼ ✻✻✻   ↕ 3m (10ft) ↔ 3m (10ft)

This vigorous shrub, with softly hairy, pointed, grey-green leaves, bears tapered plumes of tubular, orange-eyed, lilac-blue flowers from summer into autumn.   ♈

Choisya ternata
MEXICAN ORANGE-BLOSSOM
☼ ☼ ✻✻✻   ↕ 2m (6ft) ↔ 2m (6ft)

This good-looking evergreen forms a dense mound of glossy, aromatic leaves. White flowers are freely borne in late spring and again, less abundantly, in autumn.   ♈

OTHER HARDY SHRUBS WITH
FRAGRANT FLOWERS

Abelia triflora
Berberis julianae
Buddleja crispa, see p.98
Ceanothus 'Gloire de Versailles'
Clethra alnifolia 'Paniculata'
Colletia hystrix 'Rosea'
Daphne mezereum
Dipelta floribunda
Elaeagnus 'Quicksilver', see p.220
Genista tenera 'Golden Shower'
Osmanthus delavayi, see p.127
Philadelphus 'Belle Etoile'
Philadelphus 'Sybille'
Rhododendron 'Exquisitum'
Ribes odoratum, see p.157
Sarcococca confusa
Skimmia japonica 'Fragrans'
Syringa villosa

Erica arborea var. *alpina*
TREE HEATH
☼ ✻✻✻ PH ↕ 2m (6ft) ↔ 2m (6ft)

Bright green, needle-like evergreen leaves crowd this dense, compact, upright shrub. Plumes carrying masses of tiny, honey-scented flowers are produced in spring. ♈

Osmanthus x *burkwoodii*
OSMANTHUS
☼ ✻✻✻ ↕ 3m (10ft) ↔ 3m (10ft)

This strong-growing, compact evergreen shrub is densely packed with small, dark green, leathery leaves, and carries masses of small white flowers in spring. ♈

OTHER SEMI-HARDY SHRUBS
WITH FRAGRANT FLOWERS

Azara petiolaris
Buddleja asiatica
Buddleja auriculata
Buddleja officinalis
Cytisus 'Porlock'
Daphe bholua 'Jacqueline Postill',
  see p.166
Edgeworthia chrysantha
Elaeagnus macrophylla
Erica x *veitchii* 'Exeter'
Euphorbia mellifera
Hoheria lyallii
Itea ilicifolia, see p.99
Lomatia myricoides
Myrtus communis
Olearia solandri
Pittosporum tobira
Rhododendron 'Lady Alice Fitzwilliam'

Rhododendron luteum
COMMON YELLOW AZALEA
☼ ✻✻✻ PH ↕ 2.5m (8ft) ↔ 2.5m (8ft)

Rounded trusses of funnel-shaped flowers in spring are a lovely yellow colour. Rich green leaves turn to shades of crimson, purple, and orange in autumn. ♈

Syringa 'Mme Antoine Buchner'
LILAC
☼ ✻✻✻ ↕ 4m (12ft) ↔ 4m (12ft)

Upright at first, this bushy shrub spreads later. Pink-mauve flowers, in magnificent crowded heads, are purple-red in bud and open in late spring and early summer. ♈

Viburnum x *carlcephalum*
VIBURNUM
☼ ✻✻✻ ↕ 3m (10ft) ↔ 3m (10ft)

This vigorous, bushy shrub bears white flowers, pink in bud, in rounded and crowded heads in spring. Its dark green leaves often colour richly in autumn. ♈

S
H
R
U
B
S

Shrubs with Aromatic Leaves

GARDENERS ARE NORMALLY aware of fragrance in flowers, but the aroma of foliage is all too often neglected. The leaves of many shrubs are aromatic, but for most the scent is subtle, and only detectable when leaves are bruised. Some, such as the gummy leaves of cistus, are more obvious when it is hot and sunny.

S H R U B S

Rosmarinus officinalis 'Roseus'
ROSEMARY
☼ ✷✷   ↕ 1.5m (5ft) ↔ 1.5m (5ft)

Of dense habit when pruned, this is a pink-flowered version of a popular evergreen. Narrow leaves crowd its stems, as do the flowers in late spring and early summer.

Cistus ladanifer
GUM CISTUS
☼ ✷✷   ↕ 1.2m (4ft) ↔ 1.2m (4ft)

The narrow, willow-like, dark green leaves of this evergreen shrub are coated, like the branches, in a sticky, aromatic gum. Large white flowers open in summer. ♉

Elsholtzia stauntonii
MINT BUSH
☼ ✷✷✷   ↕ 1.5m (5ft) ↔ 1.5m (5ft)

This bushy subshrub has sharply toothed leaves that smell of mint when bruised. Dense spikes of mauve flowers are carried in late summer and early autumn.

Salvia microphylla var. *neurepia*
SAGE
☼ ✷✷   ↕ 1.2m (4ft) ↔ 1m (3ft)

The slender, upright stems of this bushy shrub are clothed with apple-green leaves. Spikes of brilliant scarlet flowers are borne from summer into early autumn.

OTHER DECIDUOUS SHRUBS
WITH AROMATIC LEAVES

Artemisia abrotanum
Citronella triphylla
Comptonia peregrina
Myrica gale, see p.134

Prostanthera cuneata
PROSTANTHERA
☼ ✷✷✷   ↕ 1m (3ft) ↔ 1.4m (4½ft)

The branches of this shrub are crowded with tiny, glossy, dark green leaves that smell of wintergreen. It produces masses of white flowers in spring. ♉

OTHER EVERGREEN SHRUBS
WITH AROMATIC LEAVES

Drimys lanceolata
Escallonia laevis
Eucalyptus urnigera
Gaultheria procumbens, see p.108
Helichrysum italicum, see p.153
Illicium anisatum, see p.100
Lavandula 'Hidcote Giant'
Myrtus communis
Rhododendron cinnabarinum
Santolina chamaecyparissus, see p.153

160

Shrubs with Ornamental Fruit

MOST SHRUBS with ornamental fruit, especially the many berrying kinds, bring a welcome touch of colour to the garden, and provide birds and small rodents with a useful source of food. Many fruit freely, but some need to be planted in groups to effect pollination, while others, such as holly and pernettya require only a single male in a group of females.

Callicarpa bodinieri var. *giraldii*
CALLICARPA
☼ ❄❄❄   ↕ 2.2m (7ft) ↔ 2m (6ft)

The shoots are clustered with small, bright mauve or pale violet berries in autumn, when the leaves are mauve-tinted. Plant several together for good pollination.

Cotoneaster frigidus 'Fructuluteo'
TREE COTONEASTER
☼ ☀ ❄❄❄   ↕ 6m (20ft) ↔ 6m (20ft)

This large, strong-growing shrub or small, multi-stemmed tree has bold foliage, white flowers in summer, and bunches of long-lasting yellow berries in autumn.

Euonymus hamiltonianus var. *sieboldianus* 'Red Elf'
☼ ☀ ❄❄❄   ↕ 3m (10ft) ↔ 3m (10ft)

Upright at first, this strong-growing shrub spreads with age. It is mainly grown for the clusters of deep pink capsules that split to reveal orange seeds in autumn.

Gaultheria mucronata 'Wintertime'
PERNETTYA
☼ ❄❄❄❄ PH   ↕ 1m (3ft) ↔ 1.2m (4ft)

Include a male plant in a group for good pollination, and this suckering evergreen will bear white berries from autumn into winter. Forms dense clumps in time. ⚆

Ilex x *meserveae* 'Blue Princess'
BLUE HOLLY
☼ ☀ ❄❄❄   ↕ 3m (10ft) ↔ 1.2m (4ft)

This is a dense, upright evergreen with spiny, purple-tinged leaves. Red berries are freely borne when its spring flowers are pollinated by those of a male form. ⚆

OTHER SHRUBS WITH ORNAMENTAL FRUIT

Berberis 'Rubrostilla'
Cotoneaster 'Rothschildianus'
Decaisnea fargesii
Euonymus europaeus 'Red Cascade'
Viburnum opulus 'Xanthocarpum'

Viburnum wrightii 'Hessei'
VIBURNUM
☼ ☀ ❄❄❄   ↕ 1m (3ft) ↔ 1m (3ft)

Heads of small white flowers are produced in early summer, and form bunches of red berries in autumn. The broad, veined leaves often colour richly in autumn.

S H R U B S

Shrubs that Provide Berries for Birds

MANY WOULD SAY A GARDEN is incomplete without the presence of birds, be they resident or just regular visitors. Songbirds are particularly desirable. In spring and summer, there is plenty of food to attract them, but in autumn and winter it can be scarce, so it is best to entice the birds by planting some shrubs that produce reliable crops of berries.

SHRUBS

Cotoneaster 'Cornubia'
COTONEASTER

☼ ☼ ❋❋❋   ↕ 6m (20ft) ↔ 6m (20ft)

This strong-growing semi-evergreen shrub has clusters of tiny white flowers in early summer, and ample bunches of large red berries from autumn into early winter. ♔

Ilex aquifolium 'J.C. van Tol'
VAN TOL'S HOLLY

☼ ☼ ❋❋❋   ↕ 6m (20ft) ↔ 4m (12ft)

This extremely popular holly carries few-spined leaves, and red berries that crowd the purple shoots in winter. It will fruit even when no male plant is present. ♔

OTHER LARGE SHRUBS THAT PROVIDE BERRIES FOR BIRDS

Amelanchier 'Ballerina'
Aralia spinosa
Aronia arbutifolia 'Erecta'
Berberis jamesiana
Cornus mas, see p.166
Cotoneaster bullatus
Cotoneaster frigidus, see p.202
Cotoneaster moupinensis
Elaeagnus multiflora
Prunus laurocerasus
Rubus spectabilis
Sambucus canadensis 'Maxima'
Sambucus racemosa
Viburnum opulus, see p.135

Cotoneaster sternianus
COTONEASTER

☼ ☼ ❋❋❋   ↕ 3m (10ft) ↔ 3m (10ft)

The branches of this evergreen or semi-evergreen shrub are clothed with small grey-green leaves, and covered in autumn with clusters of orange-red berries. ♔

Crataegus x *schraderiana*
HAWTHORN

☼ ☼ ❋❋❋❋   ↕ 5m (15ft) ↔ 5m (15ft)

A mass of white flowers covers this large shrub or small tree, in late spring or early summer. These blooms are followed by drooping clusters of dark purple-red haws.

Leycesteria formosa
HIMALAYAN HONEYSUCKLE

☼ ☼ ❋❋❋   ↕ 2m (6ft) ↔ 1.5m (5ft)

An upright shrub (or subshrub in colder climates), this carries drooping clusters of white flowers with claret-coloured bracts in summer. Reddish purple berries follow.

Lonicera xylosteum
FLY HONEYSUCKLE
☼ ☼ ❋❋❋   ↕ 3m (10ft) ↔ 3m (10ft)

Strong-growing and bushy, this shrub has
spreading or arching branches, and bears
creamy white flowers in spring or early
summer, followed by red berries.

Mahonia aquifolium
OREGON GRAPE
☼ ☼ ☀ ❋❋❋   ↕ 1m (3ft) ↔ 1.5m (5ft)

The glossy green leaves of this dense, low
evergreen shrub are prickly. Its bloomy
blue-black berries are preceded in spring
by crowded yellow flower clusters.

Sambucus nigra
ELDERBERRY
☼ ☼ ❋❋❋   ↕ 6m (20ft) ↔ 6m (20ft)

This, the typical wild elderberry, produces
flattened heads of fragrant, creamy white
flowers in early summer, followed by its
heavy bunches of tiny black berries.

Prunus laurocerasus 'Marbled White'
VARIEGATED CHERRY LAUREL
☼ ☼ ❋❋❋   ↕ 5m (15ft) ↔ 5m (15ft)

Dense and compact, this bright-foliaged
evergreen has green- and cream-marbled
leaves. White flower spikes in late spring
are followed by shining black fruits.

**OTHER SMALL SHRUBS THAT
PROVIDE BERRIES FOR BIRDS**

Aronia melanocarpa
Berberis 'Rubrostilla'
Berberis wilsoniae
Coriaria terminalis
Cotoneaster horizontalis
Daphne longilobata
Daphne mezereum
Daphne tangutica
Gaultheria mucronata 'Bell's Seedling'
Gaultheria mucronata 'Pink Pearl'
Gaultheria shallon
Hedera helix 'Arborescens', see p.164
Mahonia nervosa, see p.133
Rubus illecebrosus
Sorbus reducta
Vaccinium corymbosum, see p.135
Vaccinium parviflorum
Vaccinium vitis-idaea 'Koralle'

Viburnum opulus 'Compactum'
GUELDER ROSE
☼ ☼ ❋❋❋   ↕ 1.5m (5ft) ↔ 1.5m (5ft)

The maple-like leaves of this dense shrub
colour richly in autumn, when its bunches
of bright red berries appear. Lace-cap
heads of white flowers open in spring. ♈

SHRUBS

Shrubs Attractive to Butterflies

Flowering shrubs that appeal to butterflies offer a bonus that few gardeners would wish to ignore. Many are also sweetly scented. The nectar of their flowers is attractive to butterflies, as well as to a host of other insect beneficiaries, including hoverflies and bees. All these industrious creatures help to make the garden a more interesting and lively place.

Buddleja davidii 'Peace'
BUTTERFLY BUSH
☼ ❄❄❄   ↕4m (12ft) ↔ 4m (12ft)

Buddlejas come in many colours, and are among the most popular plants with bees and butterflies. 'Peace' has fragrant white flower spikes from summer into autumn.

Calluna vulgaris 'Anthony Davis'
HEATHER, LING
☼ ❄❄❄ PH↓   ↕45cm (18in) ↔ 50cm (20in)

This fine, bushy heather is crowded with grey-green evergreen foliage. Long sprays of white flowers are produced from late summer into early autumn. ♈

Escallonia 'Donard Seedling'
ESCALLONIA
☼ ❄❄❄   ↕3m (10ft) ↔ 3m (10ft)

A long-time favourite, this reliable shrub has arching stems, each densely clothed in glossy evergreen leaves. Masses of pale pink buds open white or blush in summer.

Hebe albicans
HEBE
☼ ❄❄❄   ↕60cm (24in) ↔ 1m (3ft)

In summer, spikes crowded with white flowers grow from the upper leaf axils of this dwarf, mounded, compact hebe. Its evergreen leaves are blue-green. ♈

Hedera helix 'Arborescens'
TREE IVY
☼ ◐ ☀ ❄❄❄   ↕1.4m (4½ft) ↔ 2m (6ft)

This ivy forms a dense evergreen mound of glossy leaves. Heads of brownish green flowers in autumn are a veritable honey pot for late-flying insects.

Lavandula angustifolia 'Hidcote'
LAVENDER
☼ ❄❄❄   ↕60cm (24in) ↔ 75cm (30in)

Long-stalked spikes with small, fragrant violet flowers rise above the narrow grey-green leaves of this aromatic evergreen in summer. A deservedly popular plant. ♈

S H R U B S

Pyracantha 'Watereri'
FIRETHORN

☼ ☼ ❈❈❈   ↕ 2.5m (8ft) ↔ 2.5m (8ft)

The spreading branches of this vigorous evergreen bear narrow, glossy, dark green leaves. White flower clusters occur in early summer, and red berries in winter. ♈

Rubus 'Benenden'
RUBUS

☼ ❈❈❈   ↕ 3m (10ft) ↔ 3m (10ft)

The strong, upright stems of this shrub are arching, and eventually wide-spreading. Lovely flowers, like small white roses, are borne in late spring and early summer. ♈

Syringa x *hyacinthiflora* 'Esther Staley'
LILAC

☼ ❈❈❈   ↕ 4m (12ft) ↔ 3m (10ft)

Upright at first, and spreading later, this is a strong-growing, bushy shrub. Striking, dense heads of fragrant lilac-pink flowers appear from spring into early summer. ♈

OTHER LARGE SHRUBS ATTRACTIVE TO BUTTERFLIES

Buddleja 'Lochinch', see p.158
Buddleja 'Pink Delight'
Clerodendrum bungei, see p.114
Cotoneaster lacteus, see p.140
Cotoneaster sternianus, see p.162
Escallonia 'Edinensis'
Escallonia 'Langleyensis', see p.122
Ligustrum sinense, see p.110
Rubus cockburnianus
Syringa microphylla

OTHER SMALL SHRUBS ATTRACTIVE TO BUTTERFLIES

Aster albescens
Cotoneaster conspicuus 'Decorus'
Lavandula stoechas
Salvia lavandulifolia

S H R U B S

Ligustrum quihoui
PRIVET

☼ ☼ ❈❈❈   ↕ 2.5m (8ft) ↔ 2.5m (8ft)

A most elegant privet, this has slender, arching branches, glossy evergreen leaves, and branched, conical heads of tiny white flowers from late summer into autumn. ♈

Salvia officinalis
COMMON SAGE

☼ ❈❈❈   ↕ 60cm (24in) ↔ 1m (3ft)

Sage is a popular culinary herb. It forms a mound of semi-evergreen, aromatic grey-green leaves, and produces spikes of two-lipped purple-blue flowers in summer.

Thymus vulgaris
COMMON THYME

☼ ❈❈   ↕ 30cm (12in) ↔ 25cm (10in)

Most often used in the herb garden, this dwarf subshrub has narrow, aromatic grey-green leaves, and slender spikes of pale purplish pink flowers all through summer.

Winter-flowering Shrubs

FLOWERING SHRUBS are at no time more welcome and more valued than during the winter months. This is partly due to their being few in number and, having fewer rivals, they command our full attention, particularly when planted where their flowers are easily seen against a darker background such as a wall or an evergreen hedge. If the blooms have an attractive fragrance as well, this makes them all the more desirable, especially to the blind or partially sighted.

Daphne bholua 'Jacqueline Postill'
DAPHNE
☼ ◐ ❄❄   ↕2m (6ft) ↔ 1.5m (5ft)

Best in a sheltered position, this vigorous, upright evergreen bears clusters of richly fragrant flowers that bloom over a long period. Dislikes dry soils.

Erica carnea 'Springwood White'
WINTER HEATH
☼ ◐ ❄❄❄   ↕15cm (6in) ↔45cm (18in)

This reliable, scented evergreen shrublet forms a good, low ground cover with its dense, needle-like foliage. Spikes of small white bell-flowers continue into spring. ♛

Cornus mas
CORNELIAN CHERRY
☼ ◐ ❄❄❄   ↕5m (15ft) ↔5m (15ft)

The twigs of this broad, rounded shrub or small tree are studded with little clusters of tiny yellow flowers. These twigs are also useful for cutting to display inside. ♛

OTHER WINTER-FLOWERING
SHRUBS

Abeliophyllum distichum
Camellia sasanqua 'Narumigata'
Daphne odora 'Aureo-marginata',
  see p.146
Erica carnea 'Myretoun Ruby'
Erica x *darleyensis* 'Kramer's Rote'
Erica x *darleyensis* 'Silberschmelze'
Garrya elliptica 'James Roof'
Hamamelis mollis 'Pallida'
Rhododendron dauricum 'Midwinter'

Chimonanthus praecox 'Grandiflorus'
WINTERSWEET
☼ ❄❄❄   ↕2.5m (8ft) ↔3m (10ft)

This large, slow-growing, spreading shrub is justly famous for its deliciously fragrant, small, cup-shaped flowers. These are pale yellow with a purple heart. ♛

Hamamelis x *intermedia* 'Jelena'
WITCH HAZEL
☼ ◐ ❄❄❄ ᴾᴴ   ↕4m (12ft) ↔4m (12ft)

In autumn, the large, softly hairy leaves turn orange-red and scarlet, and in winter, spidery orange flowers densely crowd the bare twigs. Dislikes dry soils. ♛

Sycopsis sinensis
SYCOPSIS

☼ ☀ ✳✳✳ ↕5m (15ft) ↔4m (12ft)

This uncommon, erect evergreen shrub
carries glossy, dark green, pointed leaves,
and produces compact clusters of tiny
flowers. Grows best in a sheltered site.

Mahonia x *media* 'Buckland'
MAHONIA

☼ ☀ ✳✳✳ ↕3m (10ft) ↔3m (10ft)

Erect at first, this big and bold evergreen
spreads with age. Long, cylindrical spikes
of tiny, fragrant yellow flowers are borne
above divided, prickle-toothed leaves. ♈

Viburnum x *bodnantense* 'Dawn'
WINTER-FLOWERING VIBURNUM

☼ ☀ ✳✳✳ ↕3m (10ft) ↔2.5m (8ft)

From autumn all through to spring, the
leafless twigs of this popular and reliable
shrub are studded with clusters of strongly
fragrant pink flowers, darker in bud. ♈

Lonicera x *purpusii* 'Winter Beauty'
WINTER HONEYSUCKLE

☼ ☀ ✳✳✳ ↕2m (6ft) ↔4m (12ft)

Vigorous, and with a spreading habit, this
honeysuckle is mainly grown for its small,
sweetly fragrant white flowers. These are
carried over a very long period. ♈

Sarcococca hookeriana var. *digyna*
CHRISTMAS BOX, SWEET BOX

☼ ☀ ☀ ✳✳✳ ↕1.2m (4ft) ↔1m (3ft)

This suckering evergreen in time forms
dense clumps of upright shoots. Clusters
of tiny, sweetly scented white flowers are
carried in the axils of its narrow leaves. ♈

Viburnum tinus 'Eve Price'
LAURUSTINUS

☼ ☀ ✳✳✳ ↕2.5m (8ft) ↔2.5m (8ft)

Heads of reddish buds open into many
white flowers with a subtle fragrance from
autumn onwards. Neat and rounded, this
shrub has glossy, dark evergreen leaves. ♈

SHRUBS

Shrubs with Ornamental Twigs in Winter

ORNAMENTAL FEATURES that enliven a garden in winter are to be welcomed. In addition to the indisputable attraction of winter flowers and evergreen foliage, the stems and twigs of many plants offer surprisingly decorative colours and forms. The dramatic effect of some, such as dogwood and willow, can be improved by hard pruning.

S H R U B S

Cornus stolonifera 'Flaviramea'
GOLDEN-TWIGGED DOGWOOD
☼ ☼ ✻✻✻   ↕ 2m (6ft) ↔ 3m (10ft)

The greenish yellow winter shoots of this vigorous suckering and layering shrub are brighter if regularly pruned, and in full sun. Leaves turn yellow in autumn. ♔

Corylus avellana 'Contorta'
CORKSCREW HAZEL
☼ ☼ ✻✻✻   ↕ 5m (15ft) ↔ 5m (15ft)

Charming lamb's tail catkins enliven the coiled and twisted shoots of this strong-growing shrub in late winter. Prune suckers out from stock as soon as they appear. ♔

Cornus alba 'Sibirica'
WESTONBIRT DOGWOOD
☼ ☼ ✻✻✻   ↕ 2m (6ft) ↔ 2m (6ft)

This dogwood is the best in cultivation for coloured stems. It produces red winter shoots, and large summer leaves when pruned. These give rich autumn tints. ♔

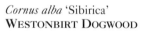

SHRUBS WITH ORNAMENTAL BARK FOR WINTER EFFECT
Abelia triflora
Clethra barbinervis
Deutzia x *wilsonii*
Dipelta floribunda
Euonymus alatus, see p.157
Euonymus phellomanus
Prunus tomentosa
Rhododendron barbatum
Rhododendron thomsonii
Rosa sericea f. *pteracantha*

Cornus sanguinea 'Winter Beauty'
DOGWOOD
☼ ☼ ✻✻✻   ↕ 1.5m (5ft) ↔ 2m (6ft)

With regular pruning, this shrub produces winter stems that are a fiery orange-yellow at the base, shading to pink and red at the tips. Leaves turn golden yellow in autumn.

OTHER COLOURED-STEMMED SHRUBS FOR WINTER EFFECT
Cornus alba 'Kesselringii'
Kerria japonica 'Pleniflora', see p.101
Leycesteria formosa, see p.162
Rubus biflorus
Rubus thibetanus, see p.169
Salix alba var. *vitellina*
Salix alba var. *vitellina* 'Britzensis'
Salix fargesii
Salix irrorata
Stephanandra tanakae

Shrubs with Spines or Thorny Branches

FOR MANY GARDENERS, shrubs whose stems or branches are spiny or thorny have a positive security value as they can deter prowlers and other uninvited individuals. Others find they are at best a nuisance, and at worst a danger. Whatever your attitude to plants that happen to be hostile to the touch, they undeniably include some very fine ornamental shrubs.

Rubus thibetanus
WHITE-STEMMED BRAMBLE
☼ ☀ ✻✻✻   ↕ 2.5m (8ft) ↔ 3m (10ft)

Clumps of thorny, bloomy-white, purple-barked winter stems become clothed with prettily divided, fern-like, silvery-hairy leaves. Small summer flowers are pink. ♈

OTHER SHRUBS WITH SPINES OR THORNY BRANCHES

Berberis pruinosa
Chaenomeles x *californica* 'Enchantress'
Colletia cruciata
Colletia hystrix
Pyracantha 'Mohave'
Rosa roxburghii
Rosa soulieana, see p.113
Rubus cockburnianus
Rubus ulmifolius 'Bellidiflorus'
Ulex europaeus 'Flore Pleno'

Berberis 'Goldilocks'
BARBERRY
☼ ☀ ✻✻✻   ↕ 4m (12ft) ↔ 4m (12ft)

The stems and arching branches of this bushy evergreen are viciously spiny. It has shiny, dark green, prickle-toothed leaves, and golden yellow flowers in spring. ♈

Pyracantha 'Orange Glow'
FIRETHORN
☼ ☀ ✻✻✻   ↕ 4m (12ft) ↔ 4m (12ft)

This vigorous evergreen shrub has spiny branches, glossy green oblong leaves, clusters of white flowers in summer, and orange berries in autumn and winter. ♈

Rosa eglanteria
SWEET BRIAR, EGLANTINE
☼ ✻✻✻   ↕ 2.5m (8ft) ↔ 2.5m (8ft)

The arching, thorny stems of this vigorous shrub are clothed in apple-scented leaves. It produces single pink flowers in summer, and small red hips in autumn. ♈

Zanthoxylum piperitum
JAPAN PEPPER
☼ ☀ ✻✻✻   ↕ 2.5m (8ft) ↔ 2.5m (8ft)

The erect, ascending, spiny stems of this bushy shrub bear aromatic, glossy green leaves that become yellow in autumn. Red fruits in autumn contain peppery seeds.

SHRUBS

Rabbit-proof Shrubs

S HRUBS THAT RABBITS IGNORE are surely all worthy of consideration, particularly by gardeners in rural areas. It may be the taste of the leaves and shoots, or their texture, that is unpalatable to rabbits, but whatever it is, such plants are extremely valuable where these furry creatures are a problem. It may be assumed that most other forms of the shrubs featured here, as well as their immediate relatives, are also rabbit-proof.

Hypericum kouytchense
SHRUBBY HYPERICUM
☼ ❄❄❄　　　‡ 75cm (30in) ↔ 1.2m (4ft)

From summer into autumn, the arching stems of this mounded semi-evergreen carry numerous yellow flowers. These are followed by bronze-red seed capsules. ♉

Aucuba japonica
DOG LAUREL
☼ ◐ ● ❄❄❄　‡ 2.5m (8ft) ↔ 2m (6ft)

Long, pointed, glossy, dark green leaves cover this dense evergreen. Female plants produce red berries when pollinated by a male. Several forms exist, some variegated.

Fuchsia 'Tom Thumb'
FUCHSIA
☼ ❄❄　　　‡ 50cm (20in) ↔ 50cm (20in)

Dwarf and upright, this neat fuchsia has small, glossy green leaves, and showers of charming, pendent red and purple flowers, through summer and into early autumn. ♉

Kalmia angustifolia f. *rubra*
SHEEP LAUREL
☼ ❄❄❄❄ ᴾᴴ♉　‡ 45cm (18in) ↔ 1m (3ft)

Sheep Laurel forms a low, bushy mound of narrow evergreen leaves. It produces clusters of small, deep red flowers in early summer. Dislikes dry soils.　♉

Buxus sempervirens 'Suffruticosa'
EDGING BOX
☼ ❄❄❄　　　‡ 75cm (30in) ↔ 75cm (30in)

All forms of box are unpalatable to rabbits. This dense and compact cultivar has long been used as a low, evergreen edging to beds and borders, as well as in parterres. ♉

Gaultheria mucronata 'Mulberry Wine'
PERNETTYA
☼ ❄❄❄❄ ᴾᴴ♉　‡ 1m (3ft) ↔ 1m (3ft)

This low evergreen with pointed, leathery leaves on wiry branches, spreads in time. When pollinated by a male, large berries are borne from autumn through winter. ♉

Rhododendron 'Strawberry Ice'
EXBURY AZALEA
☼ ❄❄❄❄ ᴾᴴ♉　‡ 2.5m (8ft) ↔ 2.5m (8ft)

Showy clusters of yellow-throated, pale pink trumpet-flowers are carried in spring. The leaves of this bushy azalea may colour attractively before they fall in autumn. ♉

Sambucus nigra   'Aurea'
GOLDEN ELDER
☼ ✳✳✳   ↕ 4m (12ft) ↔ 4m (12ft)

This large, bushy shrub has golden yellow leaves, and bears flattened heads of tiny, fragrant white flowers in summer. Shining black berries follow in autumn. ♈

Rosa 'Rosy Cushion'
SHRUB ROSE
☼ ✳✳✳   ↕ 1m (3ft) ↔ 1.2m (4ft)

Glossy green foliage offsets clusters of scented pink flowers, with white centres, throughout summer. A strong-growing rose, this is low, dense, and spreading. ♈

DEER-PROOF SHRUBS

Berberis x *stenophylla*, see p.140
Buddleja 'Lochinch', see p.158
Hypericum forrestii
Mahonia x *media* 'Buckland', see p.167
Rhododendron 'Exquisitum'
Romneya coulteri, see p.129
Spiraea nipponica 'Snowmound', see p.123
Viburnum sargentii 'Onondaga', see p.115
Weigela 'Victoria'

Skimmia japonica
SKIMMIA
☼ ◐ ✳✳✳   ↕ 1.2m (4ft) ↔ 1.2m (4ft)

This bushy mound of aromatic evergreen leaves is dotted with white flower clusters in spring and, if both sexes are present, female plants then produce red berries.

OTHER RABBIT-PROOF SHRUBS

Ceanothus thyrsiflorus var. *repens*
Cornus sanguinea 'Winter Beauty', see p.168
Cotoneaster horizontalis
Daphne tangutica
Prunus laurocerasus 'Otto Luyken', see p.133
Spiraea japonica 'Anthony Waterer', see p.123
Vinca major 'Variegata', see p.133
Vinca minor, see p.119

Rosmarinus officinalis
ROSEMARY
☼ ✳✳   ↕ 1.5m (5ft) ↔ 1.5m (5ft)

Rosemary is a popular, aromatic evergreen bush. Small, purplish blue flowers clothe the branches all through summer, along with its narrow grey-green leaves.

Ruscus aculeatus
BUTCHER'S BROOM
☼ ◐ ● ✳✳✳   ↕ 75cm (30in) ↔ 1m (3ft)

Tough and adaptable, this evergreen shrub forms clumps of erect stems, crowded with spine-tipped leaves. When pollinated, the female plants produce long-lasting fruits.

S H R U B S

CONIFERS

ALL CONIFERS ARE EITHER trees or shrubs but, as is usual, I have chosen to treat them separately. They comprise a distinct and primitive group of woody plants and add an individual element to the garden. All but a few are evergreen. The deciduous kinds, specified in the descriptions, offer the interesting feature of autumn colour.

△ Tsuga heterophylla

△ DOMED SPECIMEN *Chamaecyparis pisifera 'Filifera Aurea' makes an ideal golden yellow specimen for a larger lawn.*

Conifers are extremely versatile, due to their great variety in size, form, colour, and texture. You can use them for countless effects and situations. Many are of such noble proportions and elegance of form that they can make magnificent specimens for important positions.

DECORATIVE FOLIAGE
Conifer foliage tends to be either small and scale-like, as in cypress and *Thuja*, or long and needle-like, as in pine, spruce, and cedar. Junipers have needle-like or scale-like leaves and, in some cases, both. Yew, for example, has narrow, strap-shaped leaves, and many conifer cultivars have lovely mossy or soft, feathery juvenile foliage. Add to this all the shades of blue,

green, and yellow, as well as the interesting variegations, and it is obvious why conifers occupy such a special place among garden plants. Deciduous conifers such as larch, *Metasequoia*, and *Ginkgo* brighten the autumn with a final flash of gold or yellow before their leaves fall.

TOO BIG, TOO SOON
As with broad-leaved trees, consider the vigour, ultimate height and shape, and intended purpose of your chosen conifer. Some species used as hedging, for instance, grow rapidly and require regular pruning to achieve the best results. Do not plant fast-growing hedges if you cannot maintain them – there are numerous small- to medium-sized conifers for limited space.

THE BEAUTY OF CONIFERS
- Large conifers are linchpins, giving a feeling of permanence to a garden.
- Offer a wonderfully wide selection of shapes, colours, and textures.
- Contribute evergreen foliage effects, especially valuable in winter.
- Deciduous foliage changes seasonally.
- Dwarf and slow-growing conifers are ideal for rock gardens, patios, screes.
- Provide shelter in the garden when used as screens, hedges, windbreaks.

△ WINTER APPEAL *The rich reddish brown bark of deciduous* Metasequoia glyptostroboides *is impressive.*

◁ CONIFERS AND HEATHERS *This is an excellent example of the use of conifers with late winter-flowering ericas.*

▷ COLOUR AND TEXTURE *Just a few well-chosen conifers combine to create a colourful and extremely effective feature.*

Large Conifers

SOME OF THE MOST SPECTACULAR large trees in the world are conifers. Given the evergreen nature of all but a small minority, they bring a sense of permanence and continuity to the large garden or estate. Most conifers are comparatively long-lived. They generally thrive best on deep, moist, but well-drained soils, although they are remarkably adaptable to most sites. A handful are tolerant of wet sites, but few will survive in completely waterlogged conditions.

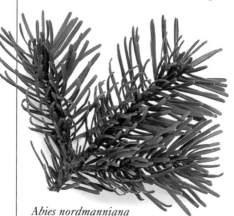

Abies nordmanniana
CAUCASIAN FIR
☼ ☼ ❋❋❋   ↕ 25m (80ft) ↔ 9m (28ft)

The spreading branches of this columnar to conical fir are packed with slender green leaves. Erect, greenish brown cones appear in summer on the upper branches. ♛

Cedrus libani
CEDAR OF LEBANON
☼ ❋❋❋   ↕ 24m (78ft) ↔ 15m (50ft)

This conifer is a familiar sight in parks. Conical when young, it later assumes the typical flat-topped and tiered cedar-habit. Sharp leaves are green to blue-green. ♛

Cryptomeria japonica
JAPANESE RED CEDAR
☼ ☼ ❋❋❋   ↕ 20m (70ft) ↔ 7m (22ft)

The narrow leaves of this columnar to conical tree are arranged spirally on the shoots. Fibrous bark is reddish brown, and its small green cones mature to brown. ♛

Araucaria araucana
CHILE PINE, MONKEY PUZZLE
☼ ❋❋❋   ↕ 18m (60ft) ↔ 12m (40ft)

When young, this tree is conical, and has whorled branches to ground level. Finally, it is mop-headed with a tall stem. Broad, sharp leaves densely clothe the branches.

OTHER LARGE COLUMNAR OR
NARROW, CONICAL CONIFERS

Abies grandis
Abies magnifica
Calocedrus decurrens
Cedrus libani
  subsp. *atlantica* 'Fastigiata'
Chamaecyparis lawsoniana 'Alumii'
Chamaecyparis lawsoniana 'Intertexta'
Chamaecyparis lawsoniana 'Wisselii',
  see p.178
x *Cupressocyparis leylandii* 'Naylor's Blue'
Cupressus abramsiana
Cupressus sempervirens
Juniperus virginiana 'Canaertii'
Metasequoia glyptostroboides, see p.182
Picea abies 'Cupressina'
Pinus strobus 'Fastigiata'
Taxodium ascendens 'Nutans', see p.181
Taxodium distichum 'Pendens'

Ginkgo biloba
MAIDENHAIR TREE
☼ ☼ ❋❋❋   ↕ 20m (70ft) ↔ 7m (22ft)

This distinctive deciduous conifer has an ancient pedigree. Conical when young, with rising branches, it later spreads. Fan-shaped leaves turn yellow in autumn. ♛

Picea abies
NORWAY SPRUCE
☼ ☀ ❄❄❄   ↕ 25m (80ft) ↔ 7m (22ft)

Norway Spruce, the traditional Christmas tree, is conical at first, but broadens and spreads with age. Its layered branches are closely packed with dark green needles.

OTHER LARGE CONIFERS OF ULTIMATELY SPREADING HABIT

Cedrus libani subsp. *atlantica* f. *glauca*,
   see p.193
Cupressus macrocarpa, see p.184
Larix decidua
Larix x *eurolepis*
Larix kaempferi
Larix kaempferi 'Blue Rabbit'
Larix x *pendula*
Picea sitchensis
Pinus ayacahuite
Pinus x *holfordiana*
Pinus nigra, see p.187
Pinus radiata, see p.187
Pinus x *schwerinii*
Pinus sylvestris
Pinus wallichiana
Pseudotsuga menziesii
Tsuga heterophylla, see p.183

Pinus jeffreyi
JEFFREY PINE
☼ ❄❄❄   ↕ 20m (70ft) ↔ 9m (28ft)

This robust, distinguished pine is conical or rounded at first, then broad-columnar later. Its fissured bark is dark grey-brown, and its long needles are blue-green. ♈

Sequoia sempervirens
REDWOOD, COAST REDWOOD
☼ ☀ ❄❄❄   ↕ 30m (100ft) ↔ 8m (25ft)

Conical when it is young, this distinctive conifer becomes columnar later. It has rich red, fibrous, spongy bark, and its branches are clothed with lush, yew-like foliage. ♈

Sequoiadendron giganteum
WELLINGTONIA, BIG TREE
☼ ❄❄❄   ↕ 30m (100ft) ↔ 11m (35ft)

Renowned worldwide for its longevity, this species will form a tall column of down-curved branches, clothed with blue-green foliage. Bark is reddish brown. ♈

Wide-spreading and Vase-shaped Conifers

CONIFERS WITH ASCENDING or wide-spreading branches, ultimately wider than they are high, are numerous. They make excellent single specimens where a severe or formal line, such as the straight edge of a long border, needs to be broken or softened. Alternatively, consider them as a feature in a lawn, where their full spread can be admired.

Cupressus macrocarpa 'Gold Spread'
MONTEREY CYPRESS
☼ ✻✻　　　　　↕ 1m (3ft) ↔ 2.5m (8ft)

This ornamental form of the Monterey Cypress is low and compact. Horizontal or slightly ascending branches are densely crowded with bright yellow foliage. ♈

Juniperus x *media* 'Blue and Gold'
JUNIPER
☼ ✻✻✻　　　　　↕ 1.5m (5ft) ↔ 1.5m (5ft)

The stems crowding the base of this fine juniper are packed with intense blue-grey foliage, scattered with sprays of creamy yellow. Whole shoots can be creamy yellow.

Juniperus x *media* 'Pfitzeriana Glauca'
JUNIPER
☼ ✻✻✻　　　　　↕ 2m (6ft) ↔ 4m (12ft)

'Pfitzeriana Glauca' is a strong-growing juniper of dense habit, whose ascending and spreading stems are densely crowded with prickly blue-grey foliage.

Juniperus davurica
'Expansa Variegata'
☼ ✻✻✻　　　　　↕ 75cm (30in) ↔ 2m (6ft)

Low and wide-spreading, this is a vigorous juniper with virtually horizontal branches, crowded by prickly, bluish green foliage, interspersed with creamy white sprays.

Juniperus x *media* 'Pfitzeriana Aurea'
GOLDEN PFITZER JUNIPER
☼ ✻✻✻　　　　　↕ 2m (6ft) ↔ 4m (12ft)

The terminal shoots and closely packed foliage of this strong-growing juniper are suffused golden yellow in summer, and become yellowish green in winter.

Juniperus x *media* 'Plumosa Aurea'
JUNIPER
☼ ✻✻✻　　　　　↕ 1.5m (5ft) ↔ 2m (6ft)

The many stems of this compact juniper are crowded with plume-like sprays, each crammed with yellow, scale-like foliage that turns bronze-gold in winter. ♈

CONIFERS

OTHER WIDE-SPREADING
CONIFERS

Cephalotaxus fortunei
  'Prostrate Spreader'
Chamaecyparis lawsoniana
  'Tamariscifolia'
Picea abies 'Tabuliformis'
Picea bicolor 'Howell's Dwarf'
Pinus strobus 'Prostrata'
Taxus baccata 'Dovastoniana'
Taxus baccata 'Ingeborg Nellemen'
Torreya californica 'Spreadeagle'

Juniperus virginiana 'Grey Owl'
JUNIPER

☼ ✳✳✳   ↕ 2.5m (8ft) ↔ 4m (12ft)

A handsome and strong-growing juniper, its ascending branches are densely clothed with soft, silvery grey foliage. A most effective, and ultimately large, shrub. ▽

Juniperus squamata 'Blue Carpet'
JUNIPER

☼ ✳✳✳   ↕ 30cm (12in) ↔ 2m (6ft)

The wide-spreading stems of this vigorous juniper form a large, low carpet of prickly glaucous-blue foliage. It is one of the most effective plants of its kind. ▽

OTHER WIDE-SPREADING JUNIPERS

Juniperus chinensis 'Kaizuka'
Juniperus x *media* 'Blaauw'
Juniperus x *media* 'Gold Coast'
Juniperus x *media* 'Old Gold'
Juniperus x *media* 'Pfitzeriana'
Juniperus x *media*
  'Pfitzeriana Compacta'
Juniperus x *media* 'Sulphur Spray'
Juniperus virginiana 'Blue Cloud'
Juniperus virginiana 'Frosty Morn'

Juniperus sabina var. *tamariscifolia*
JUNIPER

☼ ✳✳✳   ↕ 1m (3ft) ↔ 2m (6ft)

This effective and low-growing form of the Savin juniper produces close-packed layers of spreading branches, each densely clothed in bright green, prickly leaves.

OTHER WEEPING, WIDE-
SPREADING CONIFERS

Cedrus deodora 'Pendula'
Cedrus libani subsp. *atlantica*
  'Glauca Pendula'
Larix kaempferi 'Pendula'

Taxus baccata 'Dovastonii Aurea'
YEW

☼ ☼ ✳✳✳   ↕ 5m (15ft) ↔ 6m (20ft)

This elegant shrub or small tree has tiers of horizontal branches and long, sweeping branchlets. Leaves on golden shoots have bright yellow margins. Non-fruiting. ▽

C O N I F E R S

Columnar or Narrowly Conical Conifers

SLENDER OR NARROW CROWNS are great assets in conifers, allowing them to be planted in restricted spaces. Their generally compact nature means that they very rarely, if ever, need to be pruned, and their strong, vertical lines make them ideal for breaking or lifting otherwise low plantings, as well as providing a striking focal point.

Austrocedrus chilensis
CHILEAN CEDAR
☼ ❅❅❅   ↕ 12m (40ft) ↔ 3m (10ft)

The short, ascending branches of this uncommon, dense conifer are clothed in feathery sprays of green or blue-green, scale-like foliage. Small terminal cones.

OTHER COLUMNAR CONIFERS

Calocedrus decurrens
Cupressus sempervirens
  'Swane's Golden', see p.192
Juniperus chinensis 'Aurea'
Juniperus virginiana 'Glauca'
Sequoiadendron giganteum 'Glaucum'
Taxus baccata 'Standishii'
Taxus x *media* 'Sentinel'
Thuja occidentalis 'Holmstrup'
Thuja occidentalis 'Malonyana'
Thuja occidentalis 'Spiralis'

OTHER COLUMNAR CYPRESSES

Chamaecyparis lawsoniana
  'Alumii Magnificent'
C. lawsoniana 'Columnaris'
C. lawsoniana 'Elwoods' Pillar'
C. lawsoniana 'Fraseri'
C. lawsoniana 'Grayswood Pillar'
C. lawsoniana 'Green Pillar', see p.186
C. lawsoniana 'Hillieri'
C. lawsoniana 'Kilmacurragh'
C. lawsoniana 'Pottenii'
C. lawsoniana 'Winston Churchill'

Chamaecyparis lawsoniana 'Wisselii'
LAWSON CYPRESS
☼ ❅❅❅   ↕ 15m (50ft) ↔ 3m (10ft)

A distinctive form of Lawson cypress, this has erect, close-packed branches and blue-green foliage in three-dimensional sprays. Tiny cones in spring are brick-red.   ♈

Cupressus sempervirens
ITALIAN CYPRESS
☼ ❅❅   ↕ 15m (50ft) ↔ 3m (10ft)

The grey-green, scale-like leaves that form this characteristic narrow column are held in erect sprays. Fairly large, shiny grey-brown cones ripen in their second year.   ♈

Juniperus chinensis 'Keteleeri'
CHINESE JUNIPER
☼ ❅❅❅   ↕ 15m (50ft) ↔ 5m (15ft)

This columnar to narrowly conical tree of dense, compact habit has closely packed sprays of grey-green, scale-like foliage. Excellent and reliable for formal planting.

Juniperus communis 'Hibernica'
IRISH JUNIPER
☼ ❄❄❄   ↕ 4m (12ft) ↔ 50cm (20in)

This popular, much-planted juniper forms
a slender column composed of crowded,
needle-like leaves. Each of these has a
silver line on its inside face.   ♈

Pinus omorika
SERBIAN SPRUCE
☼ ☼ ❄❄❄   ↕ 18m (60ft) ↔ 5m (15ft)

The downswept branches of this spire-like
spruce arch at their tips, and are crowded
with narrow, dark green leaves. Clusters of
long purple cones mature to brown.   ♈

Taxus baccata 'Fastigiata Robusta'
YEW
☼ ☼ ❄❄❄   ↕ 10m (30ft) ↔ 1.5m (5ft)

In habit, this yew is erect, columnar, and
eventually cigar-shaped, with ascending,
close-packed branches. Narrow, dark green
leaves are arranged all round the shoots.

Juniperus scopulorum 'Skyrocket'
JUNIPER
☼ ❄❄❄   ↕ 8m (25ft) ↔ 75cm (30in)

One of the narrowest of all conifers, this
is a tall, slender, columnar juniper with a
compact habit. Crowded sprays of blue-
grey, scale-like foliage pack the branches.

Pinus sylvestris 'Fastigiata'
SCOTS PINE
☼ ❄❄❄   ↕ 6m (20ft) ↔ 1m (3ft)

This is a columnar form of the Scots pine.
The bark is reddish brown and its erect,
close-packed branches are clothed with
blue-green needles. Dislikes exposed sites.

Thuja occidentalis 'Smaragd'
AMERICAN ARBOR-VITAE
☼ ☼ ❄❄❄   ↕ 2.5m (8ft) ↔ 75cm (30in)

The branches of this dense, narrowly
conical conifer are clothed with flattened
sprays of rich green foliage, which has a
pleasant "fruity" scent when bruised.   ♈

CONIFERS

179

Medium-sized Conifers

A WIDE SELECTION of conifers exists in the height range of 6–15m (20–50ft), including many wild species that have both botanical interest and ornamental merit. Even more abundant are the numerous cultivars of conifers such as the Lawson Cypress, Hinoki Cypress, and the various Thuja species. Any of these is worth considering in all but very small gardens. Most are winter hardy, but those that are less so will grow happily in milder areas or in a sheltered site.

Cupressus cashmeriana
KASHMIR CYPRESS
☼ ☀ ✳✳   ↕12m (40ft) ↔ 5.5m (18ft)

This beautiful conical tree, which spreads with age, is perfect for a sheltered site. Its bloomy blue-green foliage is carried in elegant, drooping sprays. Dislikes dry soils.

Abies koreana
KOREAN FIR
☼ ☀ ✳✳✳   ↕10m (30ft) ↔ 5m (15ft)

The ascending or spreading branches of this broad, conical tree are densely clothed with dark green, silvery-backed needles. Even small plants bear violet-blue cones.

Chamaecyparis obtusa
'Tetragona Aurea'
☼ ✳✳✳   ↕10m (30ft) ↔ 5m (15ft)

Easily recognized and popular, this Hinoki cypress is bushy when young, becoming loosely conical. Moss-like sprays of yellow foliage clothe its angular branches. ♔

OTHER MEDIUM-SIZED CONIFERS
Athrotaxis laxifolia
Chamaecyparis lawsoniana 'Columnaris'
Chamaecyparis nootkatensis 'Pendula'
Cupressus arizonica 'Pyramidalis'
Juniperus chinensis 'Aurea'
Pinus parviflora
Pinus sylvestris 'Aurea', see p.192
Pseudolarix amabilis
Sciadopitys verticillata
Thuja occidentalis 'Spiralis'
Tsuga mertensiana

Chamaecyparis obtusa 'Crippsii'
HINOKI CYPRESS
☼ ✳✳✳   ↕10m (30ft) ↔ 5m (15ft)

This popular, colourful, loosely conical conifer has bright golden, aromatic foliage borne in large, flattened sprays. Rounded cones are brown. Dislikes dry soils. ♔

Cunninghamia lanceolata
CHINA FIR
☼ ☀ ✳✳✳   ↕13m (43ft) ↔ 5m (15ft)

The branches of this columnar conifer are all lined with two rows of narrow, glossy green leaves, silvery beneath, and sharp. Does not like exposed sites, or dry soils.

Fitzroya cupressoides
PATAGONIAN CYPRESS
☀ ✳✳✳   ↕10m (30ft) ↔ 5m (15ft)

Columnar when young, this bushy, juniper-like tree becomes more lax in habit later. It has peeling, reddish brown bark and sprays of white-banded, scale-like leaves.

Taxodium ascendens 'Nutans'
POND CYPRESS
☼ ❄❄❄　　　　　$\updownarrow$ 15m (50ft) ↔ 5m (15ft)

Pond Cypress is a deciduous, columnar
tree. Its ascending branches are crowded
above with slender sprays of bright green
foliage. Ideal in deep or moist soils. ☙

Pinus aristata
BRISTLECONE PINE
☼ ❄❄❄　　　　　$\updownarrow$ 8m (25ft) ↔ 5m (15ft)

Suitable for any but the smallest gardens,
this slow-growing, dense, bushy pine has
branches crowded with dark blue-green,
white-flecked needles. Cones are whiskery.

Picea breweriana
BREWER SPRUCE
☼ ☼ ❄❄❄❄　$\updownarrow$ 12m (40ft) ↔ 6m (20ft)

This is one of the most distinctive of the
spruces. Its spreading branches support
long, pendulous branchlets, clothed with
narrow leaves. Cylindrical brown cones. ☙

Podocarpus salignus
PODOCARPUS
☼ ❄❄　　　　　　$\updownarrow$ 10m (30ft) ↔ 6m (20ft)

A most attractive columnar tree (broadly
conical later), this podocarpus has stringy,
reddish brown bark and narrow, shiny,
willow-like leaves. Dislikes dry soils. ☙

Tsuga canadensis
EASTERN HEMLOCK
☼ ☼ ❄❄❄　$\updownarrow$ 15m (50ft) ↔ 10m (30ft)

This multi-stemmed tree has pendent or
arching sprays of small, dark green, silver-
backed leaves. Cones are freely borne and
ripen to brown. Dislikes dry soils.

181

Conifers for Heavy Clay Soil

A LARGE NUMBER OF CONIFERS will grow in heavy clay soil, providing it is not always waterlogged. They encompass an extremely wide selection of sizes and shapes, and have foliage of great variety, both in colour and texture. These are hardy, easy to grow, and evergreen unless specified deciduous.

Pinus peuce
MACEDONIAN PINE
☼ ❋❋❋   ↕ 18m (60ft) ↔ 6m (20ft)

Worth growing where space is available, this impressive pine has densely crowded grey-green needles and pendent, rounded and curved, resin-flecked cones.

Cryptomeria japonica
'Elegans Compacta'
☼ ❋❋❋   ↕ 3m (10ft) ↔ 2m (6ft)

This is a dense, billowy, bushy form of the Japanese Red Cedar. The fresh green foliage is soft to touch, and turns a rich reddish bronze colour in winter.   ♈

Pinus leucodermis
BOSNIAN PINE
☼ ❋❋❋   ↕ 18m (60ft) ↔ 9m (28ft)

A handsome tree of dense, conical habit, this pine broadens as it ages. Its special features include rich green needles, white hairy buds, and cobalt-blue cones.   ♈

OTHER EVERGREEN CONIFERS FOR HEAVY CLAY SOIL

Abies koreana, see p.150
Chamaecyparis lawsoniana
  'Triomf van Boskoop'
Picea likiangensis
Picea purpurea
Pinus aristata, see p.181
Pinus coulteri
Pinus ponderosa
Saxegothaea conspicua
Thuja occidentalis

Metasequoia glyptostroboides
DAWN REDWOOD
☼ ☼ ❋❋❋   ↕ 20m (70ft) ↔ 5m (15ft)

The feathery leaves of this magnificent deciduous conifer turn tawny pink in autumn. An ancient and vigorous tree, it is narrowly conical to columnar.   ♈

Pinus mugo 'Mops'
MOUNTAIN PINE
☼ ❋❋❋   ↕ 1m (3ft) ↔ 1.2m (4ft)

This dwarf mountain pine in time forms a compact mound of dark green needles. Ideal for a large rock garden, or a big pot, but it is slow-growing.   ♈

Pinus strobus
WEYMOUTH PINE
☼ ❋❋❋   ↕ 20m (70ft) ↔ 9m (28ft)

A well-known conical pine, this broadens with age. Open branches bear slender grey-green needles and pendulous cones. Will not tolerate air pollution.

C O N I F E R S

Pinus thunbergii
JAPANESE BLACK PINE
☼ ✳✳✳ ↕13m (43ft) ↔8m (25ft)

Its dark green needles and hairy silvery
buds distinguish this easy-to-grow pine.
Conical when young, and broadening with
age, this makes an excellent coastal tree.

Taxodium distichum
SWAMP CYPRESS
☼ ✳✳✳ ↕20m (70ft) ↔9m (28ft)

This attractive deciduous, conical conifer
is excellent for a damp site. It has fibrous,
reddish brown bark and feathery green
leaves that turn gold in autumn. ♔

Thuja koraiensis
KOREAN ARBOR-VITAE
☼ ✳✳✳ ↕7m (22ft) ↔3m (10ft)

Loose and slow-growing, this columnar
conifer has broad sprays of bright green,
scaly foliage, silver-white beneath. When
bruised, the foliage smells of almonds.

OTHER DECIDUOUS CONIFERS
FOR HEAVY CLAY SOILS

Ginkgo biloba, see p.174
Larix decidua
Larix kaempferi
Taxodium ascendens 'Nutans', see p.181

Taxus baccata 'Aurea'
GOLDEN YEW
☼ ◐ ✳✳✳ ↕5m (15ft) ↔3m (10ft)

The leaves of this striking golden form of
the Common Yew become green in their
second year. Trim it annually to obtain a
neat, rounded habit, as seen here.

Tsuga heterophylla
WESTERN HEMLOCK
☼ ◐ ✳✳✳ ᴾᴴ ↕20m (70ft) ↔10m (30ft)

Slender branches, crowded with green,
silver-backed needles and drooping at
the tips, form graceful layers. This fast-
growing conical conifer has small cones. ♔

Conifers for Dry, Sunny Sites

Many CONIFERS ARE NATIVE to warm, dry regions of the world, and a good number of these are readily available for planting in gardens where warm, dry summers are a regular feature. Some are vigorous, and soon create shade; others are slow-growing. All are evergreen, and best planted when small to give them the best chance of establishing.

Pinus cembroides
MEXICAN PINYON
☼ ❄❄❄   ↕6m (20ft) ↔5m (15ft)

This unusual and attractive, slow-growing pine is bushy and conical when young, becoming rounded with age. Stout, stiff grey-green needles crowd its branches.

OTHER PINES FOR DRY, SUNNY SITES

Pinus aristata, see p.181
Pinus armandii
Pinus brutia
Pinus bungeana
Pinus contorta
Pinus coulteri
Pinus edulis
Pinus pinaster
Pinus sylvestris
Pinus yunnanensis

Cedrus deodara
DEODAR
☼ ❄❄❄   ↕25m (80ft) ↔12m (40ft)

A handsome, vigorous conifer, this has long, drooping branches when young, and ultimately assumes a typical flat-topped cedar shape, with layered branches. ♟

Juniperus drupacea
SYRIAN JUNIPER
☼ ❄❄❄   ↕12m (40ft) ↔1.5m (5ft)

Distinctive and very easily recognized, this juniper of close columnar habit is superb as a specimen in the lawn or in a border. It has bright green, needle-like leaves.

Cupressus macrocarpa
MONTEREY CYPRESS
☼ ❄❄❄   ↕20m (70ft) ↔22m (76ft)

This popular, fast-growing conifer, with its sprays of feathery green foliage, is often grown in coastal areas as a screen. When young it is columnar, but spreads with age.

Juniperus rigida
TEMPLE JUNIPER
☼ ❄❄❄   ↕8m (25ft) ↔5m (15ft)

Loosely branched, and often sprawling, this tree or large bush has drooping sprays of needle-like green leaves that become bronze in winter, and peeling bark.

Pinus halepensis
ALEPPO PINE
☼ ❄❄❄   ↕14m (46ft) ↔6m (20ft)

Excellent for growing in sandy soils, this pine rounds with age. Needles on juvenile trees are blue-green; bright green on older trees. Egg-shaped cones are glossy orange.

CONIFERS

Pinus muricata
BISHOP PINE
☼ ✲✲✲   ↕18m (60ft) ↔9m (28ft)

This tough and adaptable, fast-growing
pine is columnar at first, broadening and
often becoming flat-topped later. It is very
good on poor, or lime-free, sandy soils. ♈

Pinus pinea
STONE PINE, UMBRELLA PINE
☼ ✲✲✲   ↕12m (40ft) ↔10m (30ft)

Conical when young, Stone Pine gradually
develops its characteristic head of packed,
radiating branches. Mature trees have dark
green foliage, juveniles have blue-green. ♈

Pinus virginiana
SCRUB PINE, VIRGINIA PINE
☼ ✲✲✲✲ ᴾᴴ▽   ↕14m (46ft) ↔9m (28ft)

Loose and often untidy, this is a pine with
densely crowded grey to yellow-grey
needles on pinkish white shoots. It bears
small, prickly orange-brown winter cones.

Taxus cuspidata
JAPANESE YEW
☼ ☀ ✲✲✲   ↕5m (15ft) ↔5m (15ft)

This multi-branched shrub opens out and
spreads with age. Yellowish green leaves,
sometimes red-brown in winter, clothe its
branches. Female plants bear red fruits.

Torreya californica
CALIFORNIAN NUTMEG
☼ ✲✲   ↕18m (60ft) ↔8m (25ft)

An impressive, upright conifer, this has
whorled branches and long, narrow, spine-
tipped leaves. If pollinated, female trees
produce pendent, olive-like fruits.

**OTHER CONIFERS FOR DRY,
SUNNY SITES**

Abies concolor
Abies pinsapo 'Glauca'
Abies vejarii
Cupressus duclouxiana
Cupressus glabra
Cupressus glabra 'Pyramidalis'
Cupressus lusitanica
Cupressus macnabiana
Cupressus sempervirens
Juniperus chinensis
Juniperus chinensis 'Aurea'
Juniperus deppeana
Juniperus oxycedrus
Juniperus virginiana 'Canaertii'
Picea likiangensis
Picea purpurea
Tetraclinis articulata
Tsuga heterophylla, see p.183

C O N I F E R S

Conifers for Hedges, Windbreaks, or Screening

CONIFERS ARE SUPERB subjects for hedging and screens as most are evergreen, and provide an attractive permanent effect once established. The filtering effect on winds, and subsequent benefit to plants they are sheltering, has also long been recognized. Most conifers used for formal hedges or screening are ultimately big and need regular trimming.

OTHER CONIFERS FOR HEDGES AND SCREENING

Chamaecyparis lawsoniana 'Blue Jacket'
Chamaecyparis lawsoniana 'Fraseri'
Chamaecyparis lawsoniana 'Golden Wonder'
Chamaecyparis lawsoniana 'Pembury Blue', see p.193
x *Cupressocyparis leylandii* 'Gold Rider'
Thuja occidentalis 'Pyramidalis'
Thuja plicata 'Atrovirens'
Tsuga heterophylla, see p.183

Chamaecyparis 'Green Hedger'
LAWSON CYPRESS
☼ ❄❄❄   ↕15m (50ft) ↔6m (20ft)

Well clothed down to its base with sprays of rich green foliage, this is one of the best cypresses for screening. It is conical as a single specimen. Dislikes dry soils. ♛

x *Cupressocyparis leylandii* 'Castlewellan'
☼ ❄❄❄   ↕25m (80ft) ↔5.5m (18ft)

'Castlewellan' is commonly planted as a hedge or screen. It grows rapidly but can be cut back hard. Densely packed bronze-yellow foliage is golden on young plants.

Chamaecyparis lawsoniana 'Green Pillar'
☼ ❄❄❄   ↕15m (50ft) ↔3m (10ft)

Good for screens or hedges, this columnar cypress is moderately sized, and requires little clipping. Its vertical sprays of green foliage are gold-tinged in early spring.

x *Cupressocyparis leylandii*
LEYLAND CYPRESS
☼ ❄❄❄   ↕24m (78ft) ↔5.5m (18ft)

One of the fastest growing of all conifers – too fast for many gardens – this is ideal as a temporary screen or tall hedge. Its foliage is dark green or grey-green.

Picea asperata
CHINESE SPRUCE
☼ ❄❄❄   ↕15m (50ft) ↔10m (30ft)

The yellow-brown shoots of this tough, conical spruce are all crowded with blue-grey, needle-like foliage. Adaptable to most soils, it makes a useful windbreak.

CONIFERS

Pinus nigra
AUSTRIAN PINE
☼ ✳✳✳   ↕ 25m (80ft) ↔ 20m (70ft)

This tough, rugged, ultimately large tree
is excellent as a windbreak for exposed
sites. It has a domed crown and spreading
branches. Dislikes dry soils.   ▽

Taxus baccata
YEW
☼ ◐ ● ✳✳✳   ↕ 12m (40ft) ↔ 10m (30ft)

Yew, with its narrow, blackish green leaves,
is popular for hedging. Regular clipping
will encourage a dense habit, which is
particularly effective in topiary.   ▽

Taxus x *media* 'Hicksii'
HICK'S YEW
☼ ◐ ● ✳✳✳   ↕ 6m (20ft) ↔ 2m (6ft)

Tough, adaptable, and slow-growing, this
yew is very good for screening or hedging.
Columnar when young, it matures to vase-
shaped. Bears red fruit if pollinated.   ▽

OTHER CONIFERS FOR WINDBREAKS

Cupressus macrocarpa, see p.184
Larix decidua
Larix kaempferi
Picea sitchensis
Pinus cembra
Pinus contorta
Pinus contorta var. *latifolia*
Pinus leucodermis, see p.182
Pinus sylvestris
Pinus thunbergii, see p.183
Sequoiadendron giganteum, see p.175

Pinus radiata
MONTEREY PINE
☼ ✳✳✳ ᴾᴴ   ↕ 25m (80ft) ↔ 20m (70ft)

An impressive, large pine for shelter on
exposed sites, except in cold inland areas,
this has bold bunches of green needles,
and attractive male cones in spring.   ▽

CONIFERS FOR SMALL HEDGES

Chamaecyparis lawsoniana 'Globosa'
Chamaecyparis thyoides 'Ericoides'
Cryptomeria japonica 'Elegans Nana'
Thuja occidentalis 'Sunkist'
Thuja orientalis 'Rosedalis'

Thuja plicata
WESTERN RED CEDAR
☼ ◐ ✳✳✳   ↕ 25m (80ft) ↔ 8m (25ft)

This handsome, conical conifer makes a
first-rate hedge or screen, with its close-
packed sprays of glossy, scale-like foliage
that smells of pineapple when bruised.

C O N I F E R S

Slow-growing or Dwarf Conifers

$\mathbb{S}$LOW-GROWING CONIFERS, or those with a naturally dwarf habit, are ideal for small gardens, rock gardens, raised beds, or containers. Most are mutations of a normal-sized tree and are propagated by grafting onto seedling stock. Few other hardy, woody plants offer such a range of shape, form, and colour, all year round.

Chamaecyparis lawsoniana 'Gnome'
DWARF CYPRESS
☼ ❄❄❄   ‡ 30cm (12in) ↔ 30cm (12in)

Dense, slow-growing form of the Lawson Cypress, this has flat sprays of scale-like foliage. Occasional tufts of coarse growth should be cut away to maintain shape.

OTHER DWARF CONIFERS OF ROUNDED OR DOMED HABIT

Picea abies 'Gregoryana'
Pinus mugo 'Ophir'
Pinus strobus 'Minima'
Pinus sylvestris 'Beuvronensis'
Pinus wallichiana 'Umbraculifera'
Thuja occidentalis 'Sunkist'
Thuja occidentalis 'Tiny Tim'
Thuja orientalis 'Meldensis'
Thujopsis dolabrata 'Nana'
Tsuga canadensis 'Jeddeloh'

Abies balsamea 'Nana'
DWARF FIR
☼ ❄❄❄   ‡ 50cm (20in) ↔ 75cm (30in)

This low-domed form of the Balsam Fir is dense and compact. The short, spreading, glossy green leaves have two greyish bands beneath, and crowd the branchlets.

Abies nordmanniana
'Golden Spreader'
☼ ❄❄❄   ‡ 45cm (18in) ↔ 1.2m (4ft)

This form of the Caucasian Fir is low-spreading and flat-topped. The crowded leaves are yellow above, yellowish-white beneath, and golden yellow in winter. ♈

Abies concolor 'Glauca Compacta'
DWARF FIR
☼ ❄❄❄   ‡ 1.1m (3½ft) ↔ 1.3m (4½ft)

Ideal for larger rock gardens, this is a handsome, compact form of the Colorado Fir. Its habit is irregular, with branches of narrow, spreading, greyish blue leaves. ♈

Cedrus libani 'Sargentii'
DWARF CEDAR
☼ ❄❄❄   ‡ 75cm (30in) ↔ 2.5m (8ft)

This splendid, low-domed form of the Cedar of Lebanon has long, weeping branches, with needle-like blue-green leaves. Train the main stem to give height.

Chamaecyparis obtusa 'Nana Aurea'
DWARF CYPRESS
☼ ❄❄❄   ‡ 1.3m (4½ft) ↔ 65cm (26in)

An excellent golden dwarf conifer for general cultivation, this slow-growing, conical form of the Hinoki Cypress has fan-shaped sprays of scale-like foliage. ♈

CONIFERS

Juniperus squamata 'Blue Star'
DWARF JUNIPER
☼ ✽✽✽　　　↕ 45cm (18in) ↔ 50cm (20in)

The branches of this slow-growing juniper of squat habit are densely crowded with needle-like, silvery blue leaves. A most satisfactory blue-grey dwarf conifer. ♈

Picea pungens 'Montgomery'
DWARF SPRUCE
☼ ✽✽✽　　　↕ 1.1m (3½ft) ↔ 1.1m (3½ft)

This reliable, dome-shaped form of the Colorado Spruce is ideal for larger rock gardens or as a specimen. Sharp, pointed greyish needles crowd its branches. ♈

Pinus leucodermis 'Schmidtii'
DWARF PINE
☼ ✽✽✽　　　↕ 1m (3ft) ↔ 75cm (30in)

A slow-growing form of the Bosnian Pine that forms a globular or conical bush, this is compact in habit. Its short branches are crowded with needle-like green leaves. ♈

OTHER DWARF CONIFERS OF COLUMNAR OR CONICAL HABIT
Abies lasiocarpa 'Compacta' *Chamaecyparis lawsoniana* 　'Ellwood's Gold' x *Cupressocyparis leylandii* 'Hyde Hall' *Juniperus communis* 'Compressa' *Juniperus communis* 'Sentinel' *Picea abies* 'Remontii' *Picea glauca* var. *albertiana* 'Laurin' *Pinus parviflora* 'Negishi' *Thuja plicata* 'Rogersii'

Picea glauca var. *albertiana* 'Conica'
DWARF SPRUCE
☼ ✽✽✽　　　↕ 1.3m (4½ft) ↔ 60cm (24in)

This popular form of the Alberta White Spruce develops a tight, conical habit if stray side shoots are removed. Needle-like green leaves crowd the branchlets. ♈

OTHER SLOW OR DWARF CONIFERS
Chamaecyparis obtusa 'Caespitosa' *Chamaecyparis obtusa* 'Rigid Dwarf' *Cryptomeria japonica* 'Vilmoriniana' *Thuja orientalis* 'Elegantissima' *Tsuga canadensis* 'Horstmann'

Thuja plicata 'Stoneham Gold'
DWARF RED CEDAR
☼ ✽✽✽　　　↕ 1.7m (5½ft) ↔ 75cm (30in)

A choice form of the Western Red Cedar, developing a conical habit. The aromatic, scale-like leaves are borne in flat sprays and become darker as they mature. ♈

CONIFERS

189

Conifers for Ground Cover

A RANGE OF MUTATIONS from taller growing conifers is available, in addition to the many conifers, including several junipers, of naturally creeping or trailing habit. These are grafted or, in some cases, grown from cuttings, and spread low over the ground to form a dense, carpet-like cover. Found in several colours, their foliage may also vary in arrangement and shape. Where space permits, plant several together to create a striking tapestry effect.

Picea abies 'Reflexa'
NORWAY SPRUCE
☼ ❄❄❄   ↕ 45cm (18in) ↔ 5m (15ft)

The branches of this unusual, irregular, low-growing form of the Norway Spruce are long, prostrate, and crowded in green needle-like leaves that form a dense mat.

Juniperus communis 'Green Carpet'
JUNIPER
☼ ❄❄❄   ↕ 12cm (5in) ↔ 1.2m (4ft)

This prostrate juniper makes an excellent ground cover, and blends well with others of its kind. Its branches are crowded with prickly, needle-like, bright green leaves. ♛

Juniperus procumbens 'Nana'
CREEPING JUNIPER
☼ ❄❄❄   ↕ 30cm (12in) ↔ 2m (6ft)

Slightly raised mats or carpets, are formed by the tightly packed, prostrate branches of this dwarf juniper. Bristly blue-green leaves crowd its shoots.

OTHER CONIFERS FOR
GROUND COVER

Juniperus horizontalis 'Blue Chip'
Juniperus horizontalis 'Jade River'
Juniperus horizontalis
  'Turquoise Spreader'
Picea abies 'Repens'
Picea pungens 'Procumbens'
Taxus baccata 'Cavendishii'
Taxus baccata 'Repandens'
Taxus baccata
  'Summergold'

Juniperus horizontalis 'Plumosa'
CREEPING JUNIPER
☼ ❄❄❄   ↕ 15cm (6in) ↔ 2m (6ft)

Seen here next to *J. horizontalis* 'Glauca', with which it combines well, this reliable ground cover has sprays of grey-green foliage that turn bronze-purple in winter.

Microbiota decussata
MICROBIOTA
☼ ☼ ❄❄❄   ↕ 30cm (12in) ↔ 2m (6ft)

The arching, spray-like branches of this low-growing, wide-spreading conifer are densely clothed with bright green, scale-like leaves, which turn bronze in winter.

Taxus baccata
'Repandens Aurea'
☼ ☼ ❄❄❄   ↕ 45cm (18in) ↔ 2m (6ft)

Short, overlapping branchlets, crowded with yellow-margined leaves, dark green in shade, fill the long branches of this low-spreading form of the Common Yew. ♛

CONIFERS

Variegated Conifers

T HE VARIEGATION IN CONIFERS usually takes the form of white or yellow sprays scattered in otherwise green foliage. Occasionally, however, the additional colour is banded, such as in *Thuja plicata* 'Zebrina' *(see right)*, or the overall effect may appear speckled. These variegations may not appeal to all gardeners, but they can provide a pleasing contrast to greens, especially in winter. Such conifers also make interesting single specimens for the lawn.

x *Cupressocyparis leylandii* 'Harlequin'
VARIEGATED LEYLAND CYPRESS
☼ ❋❋❋   ↕ 20m (70ft) ↔ 6m (20ft)

This variegated cultivar is just as easy and vigorous as the species, but its packed, plume-like, grey-green foliage is relieved by scattered, creamy white sprays.

Thuja plicata 'Zebrina'
WESTERN ARBOR-VITAE
☼ ❋❋❋   ↕ 20m (70ft) ↔ 12m (40ft)

A striking conical conifer, this is easily recognised by the dark green sprays of pineapple-scented foliage, boldly banded cream-yellow, and its reddish, fibrous bark.

OTHER VARIEGATED CONIFERS
Chamaecyparis lawsoniana 'Argenteovariegata'
Chamaecyparis lawsoniana 'Ellwood's White'
Chamaecyparis lawsoniana 'Fletcher's White'
Chamaecyparis lawsoniana 'Konijn's Silver'
Chamaecyparis lawsoniana 'Luna'
Pinus mugo 'Pal Maleter'
Sequoia sempervirens 'Adpressa'

Calocedrus decurrens 'Aureovariegata'
INCENSE CEDAR
☼ ❋❋❋   ↕ 12m (40ft) ↔ 3m (10ft)

The short, spreading branches of this slow-growing cedar are covered by sprays of aromatic green foliage, interspersed with yellow sprigs.

Chamaecyparis nootkatensis 'Variegata'
VARIEGATED NOOTKA CYPRESS
☼ ❋❋❋   ↕ 15m (50ft) ↔ 6m (20ft)

Pendulous sprays of pungent green foliage are coarse to the touch, and interspersed with creamy white sprays. Nootka Cypress is loosely conical and dislikes dry soils. ♈

Juniperus chinensis 'Kaizuka Variegata'
☼ ❋❋❋   ↕ 3m (10ft) ↔ 2m (6ft)

The protruding branches of this distinctly angular, slow-growing juniper are crowded with bright green, almost mossy foliage, marked with patches of creamy white.

Thujopsis dolabrata 'Variegata'
VARIEGATED HIBA
☼ ❋❋❋   ↕ 10m (30ft) ↔ 6m (20ft)

Broad, flattened sprays of aromatic green foliage have silvery marks beneath, and random sprays are splashed creamy white. It is slow-growing, and dislikes dry soils.

Conifers with Golden or Yellow Foliage

A WIDE VARIETY of conifers with golden or yellow foliage is available for both the large or small garden. In some cases, only the growing tips show yellow; in others, the entire foliage retains this cheerful colour throughout the year, adding a warm glow to the garden during the drab winter months. All those illustrated here are reliable.

OTHER MEDIUM-SIZED TO LARGE
CONIFERS WITH GOLDEN FOLIAGE

Cedrus deodara 'Aurea'
Chamaecyparis lawsoniana 'Lane'
Chamaecyparis lawsoniana 'Lutea'
Chamaecyparis obtusa 'Crippsii',
  see p.180
Juniperus chinensis 'Aurea'
Picea orientalis 'Skylands'
Thuja occidentalis 'Europe Gold'
Thuja plicata 'Aurea'
Thuja plicata 'Irish Gold'

Chamaecyparis pisifera 'Filifera Aurea'
SAWARA CYPRESS
☼ ❄❄❄   ↕12m (40ft) ↔5m (15ft)

This dense, conical or mounded conifer produces numerous long, thread-like branches clothed with tiny, bright yellow leaves. It only slowly increases in size. ⚊

Cupressus macrocarpa 'Goldcrest'
MONTEREY CYPRESS
☼ ❄❄   ↕10m (30ft) ↔3m (10ft)

Still one of the best of its colour, this is a vigorous, columnar or slender, conical tree. It is dense and compact, with crowded, plume-like foliage. Avoid clipping. ⚊

Cupressus sempervirens
'Swane's Golden'
☼ ❄❄❄   ↕10m (30ft) ↔60cm (24in)

For very small gardens, this is probably the best conifer of its shape and colour. It forms a tall, slender column of golden-tinged foliage in dense, crowded sprays. ⚊

OTHER SMALL OR SLOW-GROWING
CONIFERS WITH GOLDEN FOLIAGE

Cedrus deodara 'Golden Horizon'
Chamaecyparis occidentalis 'Rheingold'
Cryptomeria japonica 'Sekkan-sugi'
Cupressus macrocarpa 'Gold Spread'
Juniperus communis 'Gold Cone'
Pinus contorta 'Frisian Gold'
Pinus sylvestris 'Moseri', in winter
Thuja occidentalis 'Golden Globe'
Thuja occidentalis 'Trompenburg'
Thuja plicata 'Stoneham Gold', see p.189

Pinus sylvestris 'Aurea'
GOLDEN SCOTS PINE
☼ ❄❄❄   ↕12m (40ft) ↔5m (15ft)

The normally blue-green needles of this slow-growing, broad, columnar tree turn a rich yellow from winter into spring. The colder the winter, the richer the colour. ⚊

Thuja plicata 'Collyer's Gold'
WESTERN RED CEDAR
☼ ❄❄❄   ↕2m (6ft) ↔1m (3ft)

This is a slow-growing conifer of compact, dense, dome-shaped or conical habit. Its crowded sprays of foliage emerge a rich golden yellow colour, and turn light green.

C O N I F E R S

Conifers with Silver or Blue-grey foliage

WHEN SEEN AGAINST a darker background, blue-grey or silvery conifers have a striking effect in the garden. The Blue Atlas Cedar and the Colorado Spruce, or Blue Spruce, are perhaps the two most well known in general cultivation but, happily, there are many others of similar effect and equal merit, some suitable for small gardens.

Picea glauca 'Coerulea'
WHITE SPRUCE
☼ ❄❄❄ ↕13m (43ft) ↔6m (20ft)

This vigorous, conical spruce has branches that are ascending at first, and spread with age. They are crowded with short blue-grey to silver needles. Dislikes dry soils.

Abies concolor 'Candicans'
COLORADO WHITE FIR
☼ ❄❄❄ ↕20m (70ft) ↔7m (22ft)

The branches of this handsome conical conifer are clothed with spreading, needle-like leaves, coloured a striking silver-white or blue-grey. Dislikes dry soils. 🏆

Chamaecyparis lawsoniana 'Pembury Blue'
☼ ❄❄❄ ↕15m (50ft) ↔6m (20ft)

An excellent blue-grey cypress, 'Pembury Blue' is a conical tree, bearing numerous sprays of scale-like foliage on its loosely arching branches. Dislikes dry soils. 🏆

OTHER CONIFERS WITH SILVER OR BLUE-GREY FOLIAGE

Cedrus deodora 'Karl Fuchs'
Chamaecyparis lawsoniana 'Chilworth Silver'
Chamaecyparis lawsoniana 'Pelt's Blue'
Cupressus glabra 'Pyramidalis'
Picea engelmannii 'Glauca'
Picea pungens 'Fat Albert'
Pinus pumila 'Glauca'
Pinus sylvestris 'Bonna'
Pinus wallichiana 'Nana'

Cedrus libani subsp. *atlantica* f. *glauca*
BLUE ATLAS CEDAR
☼ ❄❄❄ ↕24m (78ft) ↔15m (50ft)

This spectacular conifer is recognizable by its fast growth when young, its wide-spreading habit, barrel-shaped cones, and silver-blue needles. Dislikes dry soils. 🏆

Juniperus sabina 'Blue Danube'
SAVIN
☼ ❄❄❄ ↕25cm (10in) ↔1.5m (5ft)

Its low, wide-spreading habit makes this a most effective conifer for the rock garden or scree. Branches have ascending tips and are crowded with light blue-grey foliage.

Picea pungens 'Koster'
COLORADO, OR BLUE, SPRUCE
☼ ❄❄❄ ↕13m (43ft) ↔5m (15ft)

A striking spruce, this is one of several similar selections. It has scaly grey bark, whorled branches, and prickly, needle-like, silver-blue fading to green leaves. 🏆

TREES

I BELIEVE THAT ALL PLANTS, no matter how small, are important but, I confess, trees are to me the most inspirational. This is partly due to their size, but more significant is the sense of continuity and permanence that they bring to the garden; to plant a tree, particularly a potentially large or long-lived one, is to express a belief in the future.

△ CRAB-APPLE CHEER *The cherry-like crab apples of* Malus *'Red Sentinel', an excellent small tree, last well into winter.*

△ *Quercus canariensis*

THE BEAUTY OF TREES

• Provide a framework or backbone to the garden to tie in other plants.
• Large trees give permanence and continuity to the garden.
• Give shade for plants and humans.
• Deciduous trees change seasonally.
• Offer a variety of shapes and sizes.
• Some make excellent specimens.
• Offer protection from the elements, pollution, noise, and prying eyes.
• Give food and/or shelter for wildlife.

Trees are the linchpins in many gardens, holding together diverse design elements. They can offer a seasonal display of flowers, fruit, or foliage, or an attractive habit, as well as provide a useful focal point for one's neighbours. The mountain ash *(Sorbus)*, thorn *(Crataegus)*, and ornamental crab apple *(Malus)* are examples that boast several of these attractive features.

ANNUAL ANTICIPATION

In cooler temperate climates, the number and variety of deciduous trees far exceeds their evergreen counterparts. Evergreen trees do, however, provide an excellent foil, often being used as background trees, screens, or windbreaks, though they should be considered

for prime sites where conditions suit. The miracle of renewal – bud flush, flowering, fruiting, and leaf fall – that deciduous trees annually enact, is something we never tire of. All the trees in this section are deciduous unless otherwise stated.

BIG IS NOT ALWAYS BETTER

Trees vary in height and shape, providing plenty of candidates for every type and size of garden. Small trees need not be confined to small gardens, while a single large tree in place of several small ones can provide a welcome focus for all nearby. Whatever your priorities, available space should always be paramount. Large trees need space to develop; it is foolhardy to plant one where space is limited.

△ GLORIOUS GOLD *Popular and very reliable, golden* Robinia pseudocacacia *'Frisia' brightens dull corners in summer.*

◁ DUAL DELIGHT Amelanchier lamarckii's *lovely snow white spring blossom is matched by its autumn tints.*

▷ NOBLE AUTUMN SPECIMEN *This Tulip Tree (*Liriodendron tulipifera *'Fastigiatum') is ideal for a large lawn.*

Bold Specimens for Large Gardens

TREES THAT ultimately grow to a large size – many native to forests – form an impressive sight in gardens big enough to accommodate them. Where conditions suit, some live to a great age, and may be enjoyed for years to come by future generations.

Catalpa speciosa
WESTERN CATALPA
☼ ❄❄❄   Vigorous growth
↕ 20m (70ft) ↔ 15m (50ft)

The glossy, dark green leaves of this imposing tree are broad at the base, and each has a slender point. Bell-shaped white flowers, spotted lightly inside, are carried in large heads in summer, and followed by slender, pendulous pods.

Acer saccharinum
SILVER MAPLE
☼ ❄❄❄   Vigorous growth
↕ 25m (80ft) ↔ 15m (50ft)

This handsome, broadly columnar tree spreads with age. Slender branchlets carry jagged leaves with silvery undersides that flash when disturbed by the wind. These turn yellow in autumn. Pendulous selections with more finely cut leaves are available. ♔

Fagus sylvatica 'Aspleniifolia'
FERN-LEAVED BEECH
☼ ❄❄❄   Vigorous growth
↕ 25m (80ft) ↔ 25m (80ft)

A tree that combines impressive stature and grace, this beech is often broader than it is tall, and eventually forms a large, dome-shaped crown. The slender, spreading branchlets are clothed in narrow, toothed leaves that turn gold, then brown, in autumn. ♔

Castanea sativa
SWEET, OR SPANISH, CHESTNUT
☼ ☼ ❄❄❄   Vigorous growth
↕ 25m (80ft) ↔ 15m (50ft)

A magnificent tree that develops reddish brown, ridged bark in time. Clusters of slender summer flower spikes precede prickly capsules that contain the familiar edible chestnuts, and the leaves turn yellow in autumn. Best in rich lime-free soils. ♔

Liriodendron tulipifera
TULIP TREE, TULIP POPLAR
☼ ❄❄❄   Vigorous growth
↕ 25m (80ft) ↔ 15m (50ft)

This is one of the noblest ornamental trees, its impressive conical habit spreading with age. Tulip-like flowers appear around mid-summer and its distinctively shaped leaves turn yellow in autumn. Seed-grown trees rarely flower until they are 15–20 years old. ♔

Nothofagus obliqua
ROBLÉ BEECH
☼ ❄❄❄ PH ▽
↕ 20m (70ft) ↔ 18m (60ft)
Vigorous growth

This elegant relative of the beech tree comes from the southern hemisphere, and it develops a domed crown of slightly drooping branches. The deep green leaves turn red and orange in autumn. Happiest in moist but well-drained soils, in a sheltered site. ▽

Quercus frainetto
HUNGARIAN OAK
☼ ❄❄❄
↕ 20m (70ft) ↔ 18m (60ft)
Vigorous growth

One of the most handsome and distinct of all oaks in leaf, this species has large, glossy green leaves that are boldly and regularly lobed, and borne on stout shoots. Its habit is spreading, and the bark is darkly and deeply fissured. Tolerates most sites and soils.

OTHER BOLD SPECIMEN TREES

Acer cappadocicum subsp. *lobelii*
Aesculus flava
Aesculus hippocastanum 'Baumannii', see p.202
Carpinus betulus
Carya ovata, see p.222
Corylus colurna
Eucalyptus gunnii
Fraxinus americana
Juglans nigra
Magnolia acuminata
Platanus x *acerifolia*, see p.213
Platanus orientalis
Quercus canariensis, see p.209
Quercus cerris
Quercus petraea
Quercus robur, see p.203
Tilia 'Petiolaris'
Tilia tomentosa

Quercus palustris
PIN OAK
☼ ❄❄❄ PH ▽
↕ 20m (70ft) ↔ 12m (40ft)
Vigorous growth

Good-looking and dome-shaped, Pin Oak is a superb tree for a large lawn. Spreading branches, the lowest of which are pendent, bear beautiful, sharply lobed leaves. Shining green in summer, they turn spectacular bronze, russet, or red in autumn. ▽

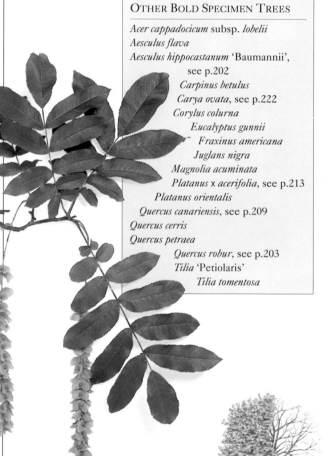

Pterocarya x *rehderiana*
HYBRID WINGNUT
☼ ❄❄❄
↕ 20m (70ft) ↔ 20m (70ft)
Vigorous growth

In summer, the branchlets of this walnut relative are draped with long catkins that are replaced by even longer strings of green, winged fruits. Its leaves turn a clear yellow in autumn. Thrives in deep soils, or in a moist situation. An imposing tree at all times.

Zelkova carpinifolia
CAUCASIAN ELM
☼ ❄❄❄
↕ 30m (100ft) ↔ 25m (80ft)
Slow growth

This slow-growing tree is one to plant for your grandchildren to enjoy. Mature specimens develop a characteristic dense, broad-topped crown with strongly upswept branches and a short, stout stem. Its green leaves often turn orange-brown in autumn. ▽

TREES

197

Medium-sized Trees

SOME OF THE LOVELIEST trees are found in the medium size range of 6–15m (20–50ft); they are suitable for all but very small gardens. This selection encompasses the full variety of ornamental effects, from spring flowers, through autumn foliage, to attractive winter bark. All these are winter hardy, but others, requiring a sheltered site, are also available.

Magnolia x *loebneri* 'Leonard Messel'
MAGNOLIA   Moderate growth
☼ ✳✳✳   ↕ 10m (30ft) ↔ 6m (20ft)

One of the loveliest of its kind, this magnolia is upright to vase-shaped in habit, becoming conical to rounded in maturity. The leafless branches are flooded during spring with fragrant, multi-petalled, pale lilac-pink flowers, a deeper colour when in bud. ♉

Aesculus x *neglecta* 'Erythroblastos'
SUNRISE HORSE CHESTNUT   Moderate growth
☼ ◑ ✳✳✳   ↕ 10m (30ft) ↔ 6m (20ft)

Grown principally for its spring foliage, this is a choice tree of upright habit, spreading later. The leaves are bright pink when they emerge, changing to yellow and then to green. In autumn the leaves turn orange and yellow. Not suitable for exposed sites. ♉

Magnolia 'Wada's Memory'
MAGNOLIA   Moderate growth
☼ ✳✳✳   ↕ 10m (30ft) ↔ 7m (22ft)

This tree has a conical or oval crown. The fragrant white flowers that crowd its dense branches in spring are large, lax, and multi-petalled. Its leaves, aromatic when bruised, are dark green above, paler beneath. Spectacular when in full bloom. ♉

Cornus macrophylla
DOGWOOD   Moderate growth
☼ ◑ ✳✳✳   ↕ 12m (40ft) ↔ 10m (30ft)

The branches of this uncommon spreading tree grow in glossy, leafy layers. Flattened clusters of small, creamy white flowers are held above the foliage during summer, and are followed by blue-black berries in autumn. An attractive tree of loosely tiered habit.

> ### OTHER MEDIUM-SIZED TREES GROWN FOR FLOWERS
>
> *Cornus kousa* var. *chinensis*
> *Fraxinus ornus*, see p.207
> *Koelreuteria paniculata*, see p.207
> *Magnolia* x *loebneri* 'Merrill'
> *Oxydendrum arboreum*, see p.205
> *Prunus padus* 'Watereri'
> *Pterostyrax hispida*
> *Pyrus ussuriensis*
> *Sorbus alnifolia*, see p.203
> *Stewartia pseudocamellia*, see p.205

Malus hupehensis
HUPEH CRAB
☼ ✳✳✳   Vigorous growth
↕ 8m (25ft) ↔ 8m (25ft)

The spreading branches of this dense, round-headed tree are crowded in spring with large, fragrant white flowers, pink in bud. Small, dark red fruits held on slender stalks follow, and remain after the leaves have fallen, eventually to be eaten by birds. ♈

Prunus avium 'Plena'
DOUBLE GEAN
☼ ✳✳✳   Vigorous growth
↕ 12m (40ft) ↔ 12m (40ft)

In spring, the rounded to spreading crown of this popular, strong-growing, flowering cherry is heavily laden with drooping clusters of clear white, double flowers. The leaves turn an attractive red and yellow in autumn. Makes an excellent specimen tree. ♈

OTHER MEDIUM-SIZED TREES GROWN FOR FOLIAGE

Acer triflorum, see p.200
Alnus glutinosa 'Imperialis'
Betula maximowicziana
Cladrastis lutea, see p.208
Meliosma veitchiorum
Parrotia persica, see p.223
Quercus cerris 'Variegata', see p.218
Robinia pseudoacacia 'Frisia', see p.219
Sorbus cuspidata
Tilia mongolica

Prunus jamasakura
HILL CHERRY
☼ ✳✳✳   Moderate growth
↕ 12m (40ft) ↔ 12m (40ft)

This beautiful cherry has a vase-shaped, later spreading, crown. In spring, the branches are crowded with white or pink blossom. The leaves are bronze at first, and colour richly in autumn. When in full bloom, this tree is visible from a considerable distance.

Styrax japonica
JAPANESE SNOWBELL
☼ ✳✳✳   Moderate growth
↕ 10m (30ft) ↔ 10m (30ft)

    Neat, bright green leaves pack the spreading branches of this dense-headed tree. The undersides of its branches are crowded in early summer with drooping white, star-shaped flowers, each with a yellow beak of stamens. ♈

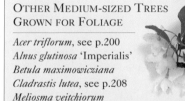

Small Trees for Limited Space

SELECTING a single tree for a small space is a pleasant but difficult task because there are so many attractive candidates. Plant any of the suggestions here, alone as a specimen, or perhaps in a boundary bed, where it can be enjoyed by neighbours or passers-by.

Aesculus pavia 'Atrosanguinea'
DARK RED BUCKEYE   Slow growth
☼ ✻✻✻   ↕ 5m (15ft) ↔ 4m (12ft)

Because of its slow growth and compact, dome-shaped habit, this tree makes an ideal lawn specimen. The dark green leaves form an excellent backdrop for its red, tubular summer flowers. These are followed by smooth-skinned, pale brown fruits.

Acer palmatum var. *coreanum*
JAPANESE MAPLE   Vigorous growth
☼ ☼ ✻✻✻   ↕ 5m (15ft) ↔ 5m (15ft)

The slender branches of this reliable and easily grown tree are clothed with attractive green leaves that become a spectacular red-orange in autumn. Tiny, reddish purple flower clusters emerge with the leaves in spring. Dislikes dry soils. ♔

Acer triflorum
ROUGH-BARKED MAPLE   Slow growth
☼ ✻✻✻   ↕ 8m (25ft) ↔ 7m (22ft)

The rugged, peeling grey-brown bark of this handsome maple is especially noticeable in winter. Its leaves, comprising three hairy leaflets, give brilliant gold, orange, and red autumn tints. The small, greenish yellow flowers appear in clusters in late spring.

Cornus alternifolia   'Argentea'
VARIEGATED PAGODA DOGWOOD   Moderate growth
☼ ✻✻✻   ↕ 3m (10ft) ↔ 2m (6ft)

In time, distinct layers of slender branches with narrow leaves create a pagoda-effect, making this a perfect specimen tree. You can prune and train it on a single stem or leave it with branches to the base. Its small clusters of white flowers appear in spring. ♔

Cornus florida 'White Cloud'
FLOWERING DOGWOOD   Moderate growth
☼ ✳✳✳   ↕ 5m (15ft) ↔ 6m (20ft)

This low, bushy tree with a spreading crown needs space to expand. It has two main seasons of interest – the first in spring, when distinctive white flowerheads appear, and the second in autumn, when dark green leaves become suffused red and purple.

Eucalyptus pauciflora subsp. *niphophila*
SNOW GUM   Moderate growth
☼ ✳✳✳   ↕ 10m (30ft) ↔ 8m (25ft)

One of the most popular of all eucalypts, this is worth growing for its evergreen grey-green leaves, and its fluffy clusters of white summer flowers. It is best known, however, for its beautiful bark – green, grey, cream, and silver create a marbled effect. ♈

Eucryphia glutinosa
EUCRYPHIA   Moderate growth
☼ ✳✳✳ PH   ↕ 6m (20ft) ↔ 5m (15ft)

This much-branched, rather bushy tree has shining, dark green leaflets that turn orange and red in autumn. Clusters of fragrant, rose-like flowers occur from mid- to late summer. It prefers a moist but well-drained soil with its roots shaded from the sun. ♈

Rhus trichocarpa
RHUS   Moderate growth
☼ ✳✳✳✳   ↕ 7m (22ft) ↔ 7m (22ft)

In autumn, the large, deeply divided, ash-like green leaves of this spreading tree provide purplish, then orange and red tints, alongside the drooping clusters of bristly yellow fruits. The sap of this rhus is poisonous and may cause an allergic reaction.

OTHER SMALL TREES

Acer shirasawanum 'Aureum', see p.219
Amelanchier lamarckii, see p.222
Aralia elata
Crataegus orientalis, see p.206
Fraxinus mariesii
Magnolia 'Wada's Memory', see p.198
Malus 'Red Sentinel', see p.224
Mespilus germanica 'Nottingham'
Prunus 'Kursar'
Prunus 'Pink Shell'
Sorbus forrestii, see p.225

△ *Sorbus vilmorinii*
'Pearly King'

Sorbus vilmorinii
CHINESE ROWAN   Moderate growth
☼ ✳✳✳✳   ↕ 4m (12ft) ↔ 5m (15ft)

The arching branches of this elegant tree are clothed in neat sprays of fern-like leaves that colour orange or red in autumn. It bears white flowers in late spring, and loose clusters of small pink berries from autumn into early winter. 'Pearly King' is similar. ♈

T R E E S

Trees Tolerant of Heavy Clay Soils

CLAY SOILS are frequently among the most fertile in gardens, although their physical characteristics do cause problems. Gardeners can take heart from the following selection of trees, all of which will grow happily in heavy clay, as long as it is not waterlogged.

Alnus incana
GREY ALDER
☼ ✳✳✳   Moderate growth
                          ↕ 18m (60ft) ↔ 10m (30ft)

This is a tough and adaptable tree with a loosely conical habit. Its dark green leaves are strongly veined, and each has a downy grey underside. Drooping yellow catkins drape the branches in late winter or early spring. The Grey Alder dislikes dry soils.

Catalpa bignonioides
INDIAN BEAN TREE
☼ ✳✳✳   Moderate growth
                          ↕ 12m (40ft) ↔ 15m (50ft)

Often broader than it is high, this is a bold, spreading tree. It has light-green, heart-shaped leaves, purple-tinged when young, and bears large, loose heads of bell-flowers with purple and yellow spots in summer. These are followed by long, thin seed pods. ♈

Aesculus hippocastanum 'Baumannii'
DOUBLE HORSE CHESTNUT
☼ ✳✳✳   Vigorous growth
                          ↕ 30m (100ft) ↔ 15m (50ft)

A large tree with a spreading crown, the Double Horse Chestnut has bold leaves, each divided into broad, finger-like leaflets. It produces erect, conical spires of double white flowers in spring, which have red or yellow markings. Non-fruiting. ♈

Cotoneaster frigidus
TREE COTONEASTER
☼ ◐ ✳✳✳   Vigorous growth
                          ↕ 10m (30ft) ↔ 10m (30ft)

Although it is most often multi-stemmed with a spreading crown, this cotoneaster can be trained on a single stem. It carries large leaves, and white flowerheads in early summer, to be followed in autumn and early winter by bold bunches of red berries.

TREES

+ Laburnocytisus adamii
ADAM'S LABURNUM
☼ ✳✳✳   Moderate growth
↕ 8m (25ft) ↔ 7m (22ft)

This tree resembles a laburnum in habit and leaf, but the tassels of both yellow and pink flowers that are produced in late spring or early summer, are accompanied by the occasional fuzzy clump of purple-flowered broom.

Quercus robur
ENGLISH OAK
☼ ✳✳✳   Slow growth
↕ 25m (80ft) ↔ 25m (80ft)

A famous tree, and one that is very popular in folk culture, the English Oak fully justifies its position as a symbol of toughness and longevity. Its rugged bark, wavy-lobed green leaves, and long-stalked acorns contribute to its credentials. ♛

Magnolia x soulangeana ▷

Magnolia x *soulangeana*
MAGNOLIA
☼ ✳✳✳   Moderate growth
↕ 6m (20ft) ↔ 7m (22ft)

Fragrant, goblet-shaped, white, pink, or purple-flushed blooms grace this magnolia from spring through to summer, making it a magnificent tree when in flower. It has a spreading, low-branched crown and bold foliage. There are many excellent cultivars.

OTHER TREES TOLERANT OF HEAVY CLAY SOILS

Acer pseudoplatanus 'Brilliantissimum'
Betula utilis 'Jermyns'
Carpinus betulus 'Fastigiata'
Crataegus x *persistens* 'Prunifolia'
Eucalyptus glaucescens
Ilex x *koehneana*
Malus hupehensis, see p.199
Platanus acerifolia, see p.213
Prunus padus 'Watereri'
Quercus palustris, see p.197
Salix pentandra
Sorbus intermedia
Tilia mongolica

Populus maximowiczii
POPLAR
☼ ✳✳✳   Vigorous growth
↕ 20m (70ft) ↔ 10m (30ft)

This poplar is a tall tree with ascending, then shortly spreading, branches. Its bold, heart-shaped, bright green leaves turn yellow in autumn. The spring catkins produced by female trees ripen to fluffy white in late summer. Dislikes dry soils.

Sorbus alnifolia
SORBUS
☼ ☼ ✳✳✳✳   Moderate growth
↕ 11m (35ft) ↔ 8m (25ft)

The crown of this tough and adaptable tree is conical or oval, and spreads later. Its bright green leaves become orange and red in autumn. White flower clusters are produced in late spring, and these are followed by bright red fruits in autumn.

Trees for Lime-free Soils

EW TREES WILL ACTUALLY FAIL to grow
on alkaline soils, but several perform
poorly in such places, preferring soils of an
acid, or neutral reaction. The trees shown
here grow best in lime-free soils, provided
sufficient moisture is available in summer.

Magnolia fraseri
FRASER'S MAGNOLIA
☼ ✳✳✳✳ PH   Moderate growth
                    ↕ 10m (30ft) ↔ 8m (25ft)

Uncommon in general cultivation, this attractive, loose-spreading
magnolia is easily distinguished by its enormous green leaves.
The large, fragrant flowers are carried from late spring into early
summer, and may be followed by cylindrical red fruit clusters.

Cornus nuttallii
PACIFIC DOGWOOD
☼ ☀ ✳✳✳✳ PH   Vigorous growth
                    ↕ 13m (43ft) ↔ 8m (25ft)

The dark green leaves of this beautiful, free-growing tree become
yellow or red in autumn. Tight clusters of tiny spring flowers are
surrounded by large white bracts, and followed, in a hot summer,
by red fruit clusters. Thrives in moist but well-drained soils.

TREES TOLERANT OF BOTH HIGH ACIDITY AND HIGH ALKALINITY
Betula pendula
Crataegus monogyna
Fagus sylvatica, see p.215
Ilex aquifolium
Populus alba, see p.214
Populus canescens
Quercus cerris
Quercus robur, see p.203
Sorbus x hybrida
Sorbus intermedia

Eucryphia x *nymansensis*
EUCRYPHIA
☼ ☀ ✳✳✳ PH   Moderate growth
                    ↕ 13m (43ft) ↔ 6m (20ft)

From late summer into early autumn, the shoots of this compact,
columnar evergreen tree are crowded with clusters of white, rose-
like flowers. Its leaves are typically divided into glossy green
leaflets. Enjoys moist, well-drained soils, with its roots shaded. ♛

Nothofagus procera
RAULI
☼ ☀ ✳✳✳✳ PH   Vigorous growth
                    ↕ 20m (70ft) ↔ 12m (40ft)

A straight-stemmed, good-looking tree, with its shoots clothed in
large, conspicuously veined leaves. These emerge bronze, then
become green in summer, and give attractive orange and red
tints in autumn. Rauli is not suitable for exposed sites.

T R E E S

OTHER TREES FOR
LIME-FREE SOILS

Acer rubrum
Embothrium coccineum
Eucryphia glutinosa, see p.201
Liquidambar styraciflua
Lyonothamnus floribundus
  subsp. *aspleniifolius*
Magnolia 'Heaven Scent'
Nothofagus dombeyi
Nyssa sylvatica
Picrasma quassioides

Oxydendrum arboreum
SORREL TREE
☼ ☼ ✻✻✻ ᴾᴴ   Moderate growth
↕ 12m (40ft) ↔ 8m (25ft)

This conical, later spreading, tree produces handsome, glossy
green leaves that turn brilliant yellow, red, or purple in autumn.
Tiny, scented flowers appear in late summer and last into
autumn. Thrives in moist, well-drained soils with its roots shaded.

Sassafras albidum
SASSAFRAS
☼ ☼ ✻✻✻ ᴾᴴ   Moderate growth
↕ 20m (70ft) ↔ 8m (25ft)

Famous for a medicinal tea brewed from its aromatic root bark,
this handsome tree is clothed with leaves, often lobed, that turn
yellow, orange, or purple in autumn. Its rugged bark and pale
branches are an attraction in winter.   ♈

Quercus rubra
RED OAK
☼ ✻✻✻ ᴾᴴ   Vigorous growth
↕ 25m (80ft) ↔ 20m (70ft)

Suitable for planting as a specimen or a large screen, this bold-
foliaged, spreading oak is free-growing. Its large, often deeply
lobed leaves turn a deep bronze or brownish red in autumn, and
sometimes change to a brighter red before they fall.   ♈

Stewartia pseudocamellia
JAPANESE STEWARTIA
☼ ☼ ✻✻✻ ᴾᴴ   Moderate growth
↕ 12m (40ft) ↔ 6m (20ft)

This superb decorative tree has many garden qualities. Spreading
in habit, its reddish brown bark flakes with age to form patches
that are attractive in winter. White flowers open from midsummer,
and the leaves turn a striking orange or red in autumn.   ♈

T R E E S

Trees for Alkaline Soils

FREE-DRAINING, and warming faster than most other soils in spring, alkaline soils suit a wide range of ornamental trees, some of them very popular and reliable flowering trees. Many hail from regions enjoying warm summers and so appreciate sun and warmth to help ripen their wood and promote flowering.

Albizia julibrissin
PINK SIRIS, SILK TREE
☼ ✻✻   Moderate growth
                                         ↕ 10m (30ft) ↔ 10m (30ft)

As a young tree, Pink Siris is more broad than tall, with spreading branches and finely divided, fern-like leaves. Its clusters of fluffy, pink-stamened flowers are produced in late summer and autumn. *A. julibrissin* 'Rosea' is a more hardy selection. ♈

Cercis siliquastrum
JUDAS TREE
☼ ✻✻✻   Moderate growth
                                         ↕ 10m (30ft) ↔ 10m (30ft)

Occasionally multi-stemmed, this more often single-stemmed, spreading tree has heart-shaped blue-green leaves. Rosy lilac pea-flowers emerge in spring and are followed by flattened red seed pods. 'Bodnant' is a form with deep purple flowers. ♈

OTHER TREES FOR
ALKALINE SOILS

Acer campestre
Acer negundo 'Flamingo'
Acer platanoides, see p.215
Aesculus hippocastanum 'Baumannii',
    see p.202
Arbutus x *andrachnoides*
Fraxinus mariesii
Ligustrum lucidum
Malus 'Red Sentinel', see p.224
Morus nigra
Paulownia tomentosa
Prunus 'Mount Fuji'
Prunus 'Shogetsu'
Prunus 'Ukon'
Robinia x *slavinii* 'Hillieri'
Sophora japonica 'Violacea', see p.209
Sorbus intermedia
Tilia tomentosa 'Brabant'

△ *Crategus orientalis*

Crataegus orientalis
ORIENTAL THORN
☼ ✻✻✻   Slow growth
                                         ↕ 5.5m (18ft) ↔ 5.5m (18ft)

This slow-growing ornamental thorn tree will eventually develop a dense, rounded crown clothed in deeply lobed, dark green leaves. Clusters of pretty white blossoms emerge in late spring, and its large, downy red fruits are produced in autumn. ♈

TREES

Fraxinus ornus
MANNA ASH
☼ ❄❄❄ Moderate growth
↕ 15m (50ft) ↔ 13m (43ft)

Typically round-headed, this attractive tree has much-divided, pale green leaves and produces large, branched heads of scented, creamy white flowers from late spring into early summer. Bronze-tinted fruits follow. A reliable tree of compact habit. ♈

Malus floribunda
JAPANESE CRAB
☼ ❄❄❄ Moderate growth
↕ 8m (25ft) ↔ 10m (30ft)

This is one of the most popular and reliable of all the flowering crab apples. Its dense, rounded crown is flooded in spring with pale pink flowers. Masses of pea-sized yellow, red-cheeked fruits are borne in autumn. One of the first crabs to flower. ♈

Koelreuteria paniculata
PRIDE OF INDIA, GOLDEN-RAIN TREE
☼ ❄❄❄ Moderate growth
↕ 10m (30ft) ↔ 10m (30ft)

The leaves of this domed tree, which is sometimes broader than it is tall, are regularly divided into numerous toothed leaflets, and turn yellow in autumn. Large, branched yellow flowerheads, in late summer, are followed by conspicuous, inflated seed pods. ♈

Prunus x *yedoensis*
YOSHINO CHERRY
☼ ❄❄❄ Moderate growth
↕ 8m (25ft) ↔ 10m (30ft)

Eventually broad-domed, this cherry has wide-spreading, arching branches. In early spring, these are profusely hung with drooping clusters of almond-scented, white or pale blush blossoms, pink in bud. One of the earliest, most reliable of all flowering cherries. ♈

Laburnum alpinum
SCOTCH LABURNUM
☼ ❄❄❄ Moderate growth
↕ 7m (22ft) ↔ 7m (22ft)

Scotch Laburnum is broad-headed, with a short, stocky stem and lush, deep green, three-parted leaves. Long, pendent chains of bright yellow pea-flowers appear in late spring or early summer and are deliciously fragrant. All parts are poisonous if eaten.

Sorbus aria 'Lutescens'
WHITEBEAM
☼ ❄❄❄ Moderate growth
↕ 11m (35ft) ↔ 8m (25ft)

This is a popular ornamental tree with an erect to oval crown at first, later spreading. Its leaves are creamy white when they first emerge in spring, and become grey-green as they mature. White flowers are produced from late spring into early summer. ♈

T R E E S

207

Trees for Dry, Sunny Sites

THOSE WITH gardens in dry, sunny places will be all too familiar with the problems that a summer drought can bring to trees. A fast-draining sandy or gravelly soil can be an added difficulty. Fortunately, some trees tolerate, if not relish, such conditions.

Eucalyptus dalrympleana
MOUNTAIN GUM
☼ ❄❄❄   Vigorous growth
                              ↕ 20m (70ft) ↔ 9m (28ft)

Columnar when young, the handsome Mountain Gum broadens later. Its evergreen leaves are rounded on younger trees, and elongated and drooping later. Leaves are joined by white flower clusters in late summer. Young creamy white bark is attractive. ♔

Celtis australis
SOUTHERN NETTLE TREE
☼ ❄❄❄   Moderate growth
                              ↕ 18m (60ft) ↔ 15m (50ft)

Uncommon, but easy to grow, this ornamental tree has smooth, pale grey bark. It is broadly columnar with a dome-shaped crown, although the branches on older trees are often pendulous. The surfaces of its slender, pointed leaves are rough to the touch.

Cladrastis lutea
YELLOW-WOOD
☼ ❄❄❄   Moderate growth
                              ↕ 12m (40ft) ↔ 12m (40ft)

This excellent ornamental tree has numerous attractive features: a rounded or dome-shaped crown, ash-like leaves that become clear yellow in autumn, and large, branched, drooping heads of fragrant white pea-flowers that are produced in summer. ♔

Gleditsia triacanthos 'Sunburst'
HONEY LOCUST
☼ ❄❄❄   Moderate growth
                              ↕ 12m (40ft) ↔ 12m (40ft)

The stem and branches of this broad-spreading tree are grey-brown. Its pretty, much-divided, glossy leaves are golden yellow when they emerge, darken to green later, then turn pale yellow in autumn. Honey locusts are tolerant of extreme air pollution. ♔

T R E E S

Maackia amurensis
MAACKIA
☼ ❄❄❄   Slow growth   ↕7m (22ft) ↔7m (22ft)

This wide-spreading tree with greyish brown bark has ash-like, deep green leaves, silver-blue when young. Dense, stubby spikes of flowers, white, tinged the palest slate-blue, are produced in summer, and held in clusters above the branches.

Sophora japonica 'Violacea'
PAGODA TREE
☼ ❄❄❄   Vigorous growth   ↕18m (60ft) ↔18m (60ft)

The grey-brown bark of this round-headed tree is prominently ridged. Its ash-like leaves emerge late in the season, and the loose heads of small white, lilac-tinged pea-flowers are borne from late summer into early autumn. Drooping seed pods follow.

Pittosporum crassifolium 'Variegatum'
VARIEGATED KARO
☼ ❄   Moderate growth   ↕5m (15ft) ↔3m (10ft)

Unless it is trained to a single stem, this evergreen tree, with its dense, bushy crown, will remain shrubby. The leathery leaves are grey-green with a white margin. Small, scented, reddish purple flowers appear in spring. Karo is excellent for mild coastal areas.

OTHER TREES FOR DRY, SUNNY SITES

Arbutus x *andrachnoides*
Cercis siliquastrum, see p.206
Fraxinus velutina
Genista aetnensis
Juglans microcarpa
Koelreuteria paniculata, see p.207
Ligustrum lucidum
Phillyrea latifolia, see p.214
Quercus agrifolia
Quercus suber

Quercus canariensis
ALGERIAN OAK
☼ ❄❄❄   Moderate growth   ↕20m (70ft) ↔12m (40ft)

The habit of this distinct and handsome oak is broadly columnar when young, and becomes more rounded with age. Its upswept branches are densely covered with large, regularly lobed leaves, which are usually retained into late winter.

Umbellularia californica
CALIFORNIA BAY, HEADACHE TREE
☼ ❄❄   Moderate growth   ↕12m (40ft) ↔10m (30ft)

A relative of the bay *(Laurus nobilis)*, this dense, bushy-headed evergreen tree produces clusters of delicate yellowish flowers in spring. Its bright green, leathery leaves are pungent if crushed and this vapour may cause nausea if inhaled.

TREES

Trees for Watersides

FEW SIGHTS, to me, are more appealing than a weeping willow growing on a river bank. Not many of us are fortunate enough to have a river running through our garden, but there is no reason why a suitable tree should not be planted next to a pool or stretch of water. As long as you maintain a sense of scale, the possibilities are endless.

Pterocarya fraxinifolia
CAUCASIAN WINGNUT
☼ ❄❄❄   Moderate growth
‡ 25m (80ft) ↔ 20m (70ft)

Eventually a large, broad-spreading tree, this has much-divided, ash-like leaves and long, drooping tassels of green flowers. Its green, winged fruits follow. Suckers that appear should always be removed, unless you want to encourage a grove.

Alnus rubra
RED ALDER
☼ ❄❄❄   Vigorous growth
‡ 15m (50ft) ↔ 10m (30ft)

This is a fast-growing tree of conical habit. In early spring, before the leaves unfurl, its branches are draped with yellowish orange male catkins that can be up to 15cm (6in) long. Its toothed leaves are boldy veined. Older trees have pale grey bark.

OTHER TREES FOR WATERSIDES
Alnus firma
Alnus glutinosa 'Imperialis'
Populus alba 'Richardii'
Populus maximowiczii, see p.203
Salix alba subsp. *vitellina*
Salix daphnoides, see p.135
Salix matsudana 'Tortuosa', see p.227
Salix pentandra

△ *Salix* x *sepulcralis* 'Chrysocoma'

Betula nigra
RIVER BIRCH   Moderate growth
☼ ❄❄❄   ‡ 15m (50ft) ↔ 15m (50ft)

The River Birch is distinctive, and quite unlike the more usual white-stemmed kinds. The bark of the stem and main branches is peeling and shaggy, pinkish grey in colour, maturing to dark brown. Its leaves are diamond-shaped and pale beneath.

Salix x *sepulcralis* 'Chrysocoma'
GOLDEN WEEPING WILLOW   Vigorous growth
☼ ❄❄❄   ‡ 20m (70ft) ↔ 25m (80ft)

This is a popular subject for the waterside, but it is too large for the small gardens in which it is often planted. It has long curtains of weeping, golden yellow branches in winter. These are covered with slender, bright green leaves in spring and summer.

Weeping Trees

NOT EVERY GARDENER likes weeping trees. Some find them too untidy or sad, but a well-sited weeping tree on a lawn, or by water or a border edge, can add both interest and dramatic effect. To attain a good height, such trees generally require further training to a cane or stake for a few years, especially when bought as young, grafted plants.

Prunus pendula 'Pendula Rubra'
WEEPING SPRING CHERRY
☼ ✳✳✳　　　　　　　Moderate growth
　　　　　　　　　　↕ 5m (15ft) ↔ 6m (20ft)

The dome-shaped crown of this beautiful, elegant cherry can be trained to a greater height than 5m (15ft) if desired. Masses of small, deep rose pink, single blossoms, carmine in bud, crowd its slender, weeping branches in spring. ♈

Fagus sylvatica 'Pendula'
WEEPING BEECH
☼ ✳✳✳　　　　　　　Vigorous growth
　　　　　　　　　　↕ 18m (60ft) ↔ 20m (70ft)

A magnificent tree for a large lawn, the Weeping Beech is normally broader than it is high. Its arching or spreading branches are all draped with long, hanging branchlets, and it remains attractive throughout the year. Several other forms are also in cultivation. ♈

OTHER WEEPING TREES

Betula pendula 'Youngii'
Ilex aquifolium 'Pendulum'
Morus alba 'Pendula'
Pyrus salicifolia 'Pendula', see p.220
Sophora japonica 'Pendula'

Salix caprea
'Kilmarnock' ▷

Prunus 'Cheal's Weeping'
CHEAL'S WEEPING CHERRY
☼ ✳✳✳　　　　　　　Moderate growth
　　　　　　　　　　↕ 2.5m (8ft) ↔ 3m (10ft)

Normally low-domed, this small, weeping Japanese cherry tree is very popular in gardens where space is at a premium. In spring, the arching and pendent branches are crowded with bright pink, double flowers. It looks particularly effective by a small pool. ♈

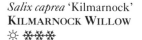

Salix caprea 'Kilmarnock'
KILMARNOCK WILLOW
☼ ✳✳✳　　　　　　　Vigorous growth
　　　　　　　　　　↕ 2m (6ft) ↔ 1.4m (4½ft)

This dense-crowned form of the Common Sallow or Goat Willow is suitable for even the smallest garden. It has numerous weeping branches, which, in spring, are studded with silver-grey male catkins that turn yellow as they mature. ♈

T R E E S

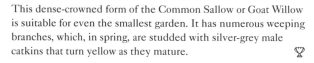

Trees Tolerant of Air Pollution

SITES SUBJECT to air pollution would not seem to be ideal areas for growing trees. Given adequate soil preparation and after-care, however, a good variety of trees, both large and small, will perform just as they would well as in places enjoying clean air.

Fraxinus angustifolia
NARROW-LEAVED ASH
☼ ❆❆❆   Vigorous growth
                          ↕ 20m (70ft) ↔ 12m (40ft)

More elegant in habit than the Common Ash *(Fraxinus excelsior)*, this large tree has spreading branches that form an attractive oval to rounded crown. Its leaves are regularly divided into narrow, smooth, glossy green leaflets, that become yellow in autumn.

Amelanchier laevis
ALLEGHENY SERVICEBERRY
☼ ☼ ❆❆❆   Moderate growth
                          ↕ 6m (20ft) ↔ 6m (20ft)

Clusters of white flowers flood the branches of this small, often multi-stemmed tree or large shrub in spring. It has a dense, spreading habit, and leaves which are bronze in spring, changing to green in summer, and then red or orange in autumn.

Ilex x *altaclerensis* 'Belgica Aurea'
SILVER SENTINEL
☼ ☼ ❆❆❆   Moderate growth
                          ↕ 8m (25ft) ↔ 3m (10ft)

The bold leaves of this evergreen holly are lance-shaped, with occasional spines. They are a mottled grey-green in colour, and irregularly edged pale or creamy yellow. From autumn onwards, this dense, compact columnar tree also carries red berries. ♈

Crataegus laevigata 'Paul's Scarlet'
PAUL'S SCARLET THORN
☼ ❆❆❆   Moderate growth
                          ↕ 6m (20ft) ↔ 8m (25ft)

This is a popular tree, with a dense, rounded or spreading crown. In late spring and early summer, the branches are covered in numerous clusters of double red flowers. The leaves are glossy dark green. 'Punicea' is similar, with single crimson flowers. ♈

OTHER TREES TOLERANT OF AIR POLLUTION

Acer pseudoplatanus 'Brilliantissimum'
Aesculus x *carnea* 'Briotii'
Ailanthus altissima
Alnus cordata, see p.215
Amelanchier lamarckii, see p.222
Catalpa bignonioides, see p.202
Crataegus persimilis 'Prunifolia'
Magnolia x *soulangeana*, see p.203
Malus baccata var. *mandschurica*, see p.228
Malus 'Profusion'
Phellodendron amurense
Populus 'Robusta'
Prunus 'Pink Perfection'
Quercus ilex
Sorbus aria 'Majestica'
Tilia 'Euchlora'
Tilia platyphyllos 'Rubra'

△ *Crataegus laevigata* 'Paul's Scarlet'

TREES

Prunus dulcis 'Roseoplena'
DOUBLE ALMOND
☼ ✽✽✽   Moderate growth
                          ↕ 8m (25ft) ↔ 8m (25ft)

In late winter and early spring, the spreading branches of this tree are studded with double, pale pink flowers. These emerge ahead of the dark green, lance-shaped, long and pointed leaves and brighten the dullest of late winter days.

Laburnum x *waterei* 'Vossii'
VOSS'S LABURNUM
☼ ✽✽✽   Moderate growth
                          ↕ 7m (22ft) ↔ 7m (22ft)

The crown of this tree, the most commonly planted laburnum, is spreading and crowded with leaves composed of three leaflets. Long, tapering chains of pea-flowers hang from its branches in late spring or early summer. All parts are poisonous if eaten. ♈

Pyrus calleryana 'Chanticleer'
ORNAMENTAL PEAR
☼ ✽✽✽   Moderate growth
                          ↕ 12m (40ft) ↔ 6m (20ft)

Tough and hardy, this compact, conical tree has rounded, glossy green leaves that turn reddish purple in autumn. The branches are flooded with beautiful white blossoms in spring, at which time the tree is clearly visible from afar.

Platanux acerifolia
LONDON PLANE
☼ ✽✽✽   Moderate growth
                          ↕ 30m (100ft) ↔ 20m (70ft)

This enormous tree develops a massive piebald stem and a large spreading crown. Broad, maple-like leaves with five big, toothed lobes are carried in summer. From the summer onwards, strings of bristly, spherical fruits hang on single stalks, like baubles. ♈

Robinia pseudoacacia
BLACK LOCUST, FALSE ACACIA
☼ ✽✽✽   Vigorous growth
                          ↕ 20m (7
0ft) ↔ 12m (40ft)

The shoots of this tough and adaptable tree are prickly, and its leaves ash-like, with oval leaflets. Drooping clusters of white pea-flowers are fragrant, and occur from late spring into early summer. Develops rugged bark in time, and will sucker if hard pruned. ♈

TREES

Trees Tolerant of Coastal Exposure

ONLY THE TOUGHEST TREES will survive the twin problems of strong winds and salt spray in seaside gardens. The following are among the most tolerant, and are well worth considering if only as an outer planting to provide shelter for shrubs and perennials.

Populus alba
WHITE POPLAR, ABELE
☼ ✻✻✻ — Vigorous growth — ↕ 20m (70ft) ↔ 13m (43ft)

This well-known spreading tree has imposing, grey-fissured bark. The leaves, which vary in shape from rounded and toothed to lobed and maple-like, are dark green above and covered below with a white felt, making a striking contrast when blown by wind.

Hippophae rhamnoides
SEA BUCKTHORN
☼ ✻✻✻ — Moderate growth — ↕ 6m (20ft) ↔ 6m (20ft)

Due to its bushy habit, careful pruning and training are needed to make a single- or few-stemmed tree. Narrow, silver-grey leaves crowd the thorny branches. Plant both male and female plants to produce brilliant orange berries that last all winter. ♔

Salix alba
WHITE WILLOW
☼ ✻✻✻ — Vigorous growth — ↕ 20m (70ft) ↔ 13m (43ft)

A handsome willow of conical habit at first, this soon spreads to be as broad as it is tall. Its narrow silvery leaves shimmer in the sun. Suited to damp places, but do not plant near underground drains or water systems, or buildings because of its invasive roots.

OTHER TREES TOLERANT
OF COASTAL EXPOSURE

Alnus rubra, see p.210
Alnus rubra, see p.210
Populus x *canadensis* 'Robusta'
Quercus ilex
Tilia cordata 'Rancho'

Phillyrea latifolia
PHILLYREA
☼ ✻✻✻ — Slow growth — ↕ 8m (25ft) ↔ 8m (25ft)

This little known, but valuable, evergreen tree is rather like a small version of the Holm Oak (*Quercus ilex*). The narrow, glossy, dark green leaves are leathery and toothed. Its tiny cream-yellow flowers are borne in dense clusters from late spring into summer.

Sorbus aucuparia
ROWAN OR MOUNTAIN ASH
☼ ☼ ✻✻✻ — Moderate growth — ↕ 10m (30ft) ↔ 7m (22ft)

The leaves of this grey-barked tree of spreading habit resemble those of an ash, often turning red or yellow in autumn. Clusters of white spring flowers are followed by drooping bunches of orange-red berries, maturing to bright red. Tough and adaptable.

T R E E S

Trees for Screening or Windbreaks

IN ADDITION TO CONIFERS, various medium-sized to large, broad-leaved trees make a good line of defence against persistent winds, and can screen unattractive views or unsightly objects. Many also have ornamental features.

Acer platanoides
NORWAY MAPLE
☼ ❅❅❅   Vigorous growth
↕ 25m (80ft) ↔ 15m (50ft)

One of the most adaptable and reliable of all trees, the Norway Maple develops a rounded crown. Yellow flower clusters emerge in mid-spring, before the leaves appear, followed by green, winged fruits. The leaves turn a rich yellow, red, or orange in autumn. ♈

Fagus sylvatica
COMMON BEECH
☼ ❅❅❅   Moderate growth
↕ 35m (120ft) ↔ 15m (50ft)

One of the temperate world's most beautiful trees, this matures to form a dome-shaped crown. Smooth grey bark in winter and pale green leaves in spring, turning shiny mid-green in summer and golden yellow in autumn, make this a tree for all seasons. ♈

OTHER TREES FOR SCREENING OR WINDBREAKS

Acer pseudoplatanus
Fraxinus excelsior 'Westhof's Glorie'
Populus nigra 'Italica'
Populus 'Robusta'
Quercus robur, see p.203
Tilia cordata

△ *Prunus serotina*

Alnus cordata
ITALIAN ALDER
☼ ❅❅❅   Vigorous growth
↕ 25m (80ft) ↔ 11m (35ft)

This handsome, columnar tree becomes conical later. Bunches of long yellow male catkins drape the branches in late winter or early spring. In summer, its cone-like fruits develop among the large, rounded leaves with shining, dark green upper surfaces. ♈

Prunus serotina
RUM, OR BLACK, CHERRY
☼ ◑ ❅❅❅   Moderate growth
↕ 15m (50ft) ↔ 13m (43ft)

A free-growing tree with an oval crown of pendulous or arching branches, its deep green, glossy leaves are deciduous, becoming yellow or red in autumn. Small white spring flowers are carried in drooping tassels, and give way to shining black fruits. ♈

TREES

215

Evergreen Trees

IN TEMPERATE AREAS, evergreen trees (apart from conifers) are greatly outnumbered by deciduous ones. This makes evergreens all the more desirable in the garden, especially in winter when their rich green, coloured, or variegated foliage offers a striking contrast to bare twigs or winter-flowering shrubs. They also provide effective year-round screening.

Maytenus boaria
MAITEN
☼ ◐ ❄❄❄ Moderate growth
↕10m (30ft) ↔8m (25ft)

An unusual and elegant tree, this is not unlike a weeping willow in effect. Erect when young, it gradually broadens into a round-headed tree, its branches well-clothed with narrow, glossy green, toothed leaves. Tiny spring flowers are of little ornamental merit.

Myrtus luma
LUMA
☼ ◐ ❄❄ Vigorous growth
↕7m (22ft) ↔5m (15ft)

Luma is a splendid all-year-round performer. From midsummer into autumn, the glossy, dark green leaves of this dense-habited tree are interspersed with masses of small white flowers. Golden brown bark peels with age to reveal patches of creamy new bark.

Pittosporum tenuifolium
KOHUHU
☼ ❄❄ Moderate growth
↕6m (20ft) ↔5m (15ft)

Columnar when young, it is later dome-shaped and compact, with slender branchlets bearing glossy leaves. Small, honey-scented, bell-shaped purple flowers appear in late spring. It is excellent as a screen or single specimen, especially in coastal areas. 🏆

OTHER EVERGREEN TREES

- *Arbutus unedo*
- *Castanopsis cuspidata*
- *Drimys winteri*
- *Eucalyptus glaucescens*
- *Ilex latifolia*
- *Ligustrum lucidum*
- *Magnolia grandiflora*
- *Phillyrea latifolia*, see p.214
- *Prunus lusitanica*, see p.141
- *Quercus ilex*
- *Trachycarpus fortunei*, see p.217

Rhododendron arboreum
TREE RHODODENDRON
☼ ❄❄❄ Slow growth
↕12m (40ft) ↔3m (10ft)

This magnificent, slow-growing species rhododendron broadens in later life. The leaves are leathery and dark green on top, silver or brownish beneath. Red, pink, or occasionally white, bell-shaped flowers are carried in dense, globular heads in spring.

Trees with Bold Leaves

YOU CAN TRANSFORM your garden by growing a
tree with bold foliage. A single specimen with
leaves of impressive size is worth planting in its own
right, bringing a touch of the tropics to the most
mundane planting. Bold foliage can also be effective
when contrasted with smaller-leaved subjects. Many
bold-foliaged trees have the further
bonus of attractive
flowers and fruits.

Toona sinensis
TOON, CEDRELA
☼ ❄❄❄   Vigorous growth
              ↕ 15m (50ft) ↔ 10m (30ft)

This fast-growing tree has large, much-divided leaves that can
grow up to 60cm (24in) long. These are bronze-red when young,
and turn yellow in autumn. In summer, mature trees carry large,
drooping heads of small, fragrant white flowers.

OTHER TREES WITH BOLD LEAVES

Aralia elata 'Variegata'
Catalpa bignonioides, see p.202
Juglans ailantifolia
Juglans nigra
Meliosma veitchiorum

Kalopanax pictus
PRICKLY CASTOR OIL TREE
☼ ❄❄❄   Moderate growth
              ↕ 12m (40ft) ↔ 10m (30ft)

A handsome tree, this has prickly stems and trunk, and maple-
like leaves that turn yellow in autumn. Rounded clusters of tiny
whitish flowers in late summer are replaced, after a hot summer,
by blue-black berries. Thrives in moist, well-drained soils.

Magnolia hypoleuca
JAPANESE BIG-LEAF MAGNOLIA
☼ ❄❄❄ ᴾᴴ ⬇   Vigorous growth
                   ↕ 20m (70ft) ↔ 10m (30ft)

The large, firm leaves of this magnificent conical tree, broadest
in their upper halves, are carried in impressive whorls at the ends
of the branches. Strongly fragrant, bowl-shaped flowers are borne
in summer, and followed by cylindrical red fruit clusters. ♈

Trachycarpus fortunei
CHUSAN PALM, WINDMILL PALM
☼ ❄❄   Slow growth
            ↕ 8m (25ft) ↔ 2.5m (8ft)

This is probably the hardiest palm suitable for cool, temperate
regions, especially in coastal areas. It is a familiar sight, with its
shaggy, fibrous bark, rounded head of fan-shaped, many-fingered
leaves, and sprays of fragrant creamy flowers in early summer. ♈

Trees with Variegated Leaves

BESIDES the novelty appeal they afford, trees with variegated leaves are valuable when used as a contrast against plain green or darker-leaved subjects. This is particularly true of foliage whose variegation consists of a strong white or yellow margin against green.

Ilex x *altaclerensis* 'Camelliifolia Variegata'
HIGHCLERE HOLLY
☼ ☀ ❋❋❋   Slow growth
                                    ↕ 8m (25ft) ↔ 3m (10ft)

This broadly columnar evergreen is densely packed with short-spreading branches that reach all the way down to the base. Its oblong leaves are glossy dark green colour, and each has a broad yellow margin. Bears red berries when pollinated.

Liriodendron tulipifera 'Aureomarginatum'
VARIEGATED TULIP TREE
☼ ❋❋❋   Vigorous growth
                                    ↕ 18m (60ft) ↔ 11m (35ft)

Strong-growing and erect, this tree spreads with age. Its peculiarly shaped leaves are dark green with yellow margins in full sun, and pale to light green in shade. They turn a golden colour in autumn. Established trees produce cup-shaped, greenish white flowers. ♈

Cornus controversa 'Variegata'
WEDDING-CAKE TREE
☼ ❋❋❋   Slow growth
                                    ↕ 10m (30ft) ↔ 10m (30ft)

As a lawn specimen, this beautiful tree is unmatched. Frequently broader than it is high, it develops a tabulated, or tiered, crown of spreading branches, ideally to ground level. These are clothed with slender-pointed leaves, broadly margined creamy white. ♈

OTHER VARIEGATED TREES
Acer negundo 'Flamingo'
Acer platanoides 'Drummondii'
Ligustrum lucidum
'Excelsum Superbum'
Populus x *candicans* 'Aurora'

Quercus cerris 'Variegata'
VARIEGATED TURKEY OAK
☼ ❋❋❋   Moderate growth
                                    ↕ 10m (30ft) ↔ 12m (40ft)

This broad-spreading oak needs to be given plenty of space to develop and is one of the most effective hardy, variegated trees. Its branches are crowded with bristle-toothed, deeply lobed, dark green, glossy leaves, each with an irregular, creamy white margin.

TREES

Trees with Golden or Yellow Leaves

FLOWERING DISPLAYS APART, no trees bring a brighter effect to the garden than those with golden or yellow foliage. A single tree of this kind, especially in a lawn, immediately attracts the attention, as well as providing a bold contrast to a plain or dark background.

Ptelea trifoliata 'Aurea'
GOLDEN HOP TREE
☼ ☀ ❋ ❋ ❋   Moderate growth
↕ 3m (10ft) ↔ 3m (10ft)

The aromatic, three-parted leaves of this small, round-headed or bushy tree are soft yellow when young, maturing through yellow-green to green. It is less harsh on the eye than most other golden trees. Greenish summer flowers are followed by winged fruits. ♆

Acer shirasawanum 'Aureum'
GOLDEN FULL MOON MAPLE
☼ ☀ ❋ ❋ ❋   Slow growth
↕ 5.5m (18ft) ↔ 5m (15ft)

This beautiful maple is upright to begin with, and spreads later. Its rounded, many-lobed leaves are golden yellow, often with a thin scarlet edge. It is one of the best golden-leaved trees, but may be susceptible to sun-scorch, particularly in hot, dry sites. ♆

Quercus rubra 'Aurea'
GOLDEN RED OAK
☼ ☀ ❋ ❋ ❋ PH   Slow growth
↕ 15m (50ft) ↔ 10m (30ft)

Although it is seldom planted, the Golden Red Oak is a lovely tree, with a spreading crown of large, boldly lobed leaves. These are a clear, soft yellow when they emerge, becoming green later. It prefers a site that is sheltered from cold winds.

Catalpa bignonioides 'Aurea'
GOLDEN INDIAN-BEAN TREE
☼ ❋ ❋ ❋   Moderate growth
↕ 10m (30ft) ↔ 10m (30ft)

Eventually, the Golden Indian-bean Tree grows to be domed or round-headed. The large, heart-shaped leaves are bronze-purple when young, and mature to bright yellow. Its bell-shaped white flowers with purple and yellow spots are produced in summer. ♆

Robinia pseudoacacia 'Frisia'
GOLDEN ACACIA
☼ ☀ ❋ ❋ ❋   Moderate growth
↕ 15m (50ft) ↔ 8m (25ft)

This is one of the most popular and commonly planted golden-leaved trees. Its much-divided, ash-like leaves are a rich golden colour when young, maturing through yellow to greenish yellow. They then become orange-yellow in autumn. ♆

Trees with Silver or Blue-grey Leaves

COMPARED with the abundance of shrubs, there are very few trees with blue-grey or silver leaves suitable for gardens in cool, temperate climates. Fortunately, the few that are encompass a wide range of sizes. Their presence can contribute much to the garden.

Pyrus salicifolia 'Pendula'
WEEPING WILLOW-LEAVED PEAR
☀ ❄❄❄
Vigorous growth
↕ 8m (25ft) ↔ 6m (20ft)

This is a popular small tree that will form a domed or mushroom-shaped crown of arching and weeping branches, each clothed in narrow grey, downy leaves. The white flowers produced in spring are followed by small green fruits. Easy and reliable. ♈

Elaeagnus 'Quicksilver'
OLEASTER
☀ ❄❄❄
Moderate growth
↕ 5m (15ft) ↔ 5m (15ft)

Although it has a bushy habit, this oleaster can be trained on a single stem to form a small tree (as can many large shrubs), with a loose, spreading crown of narrow silver-grey leaves. Fragrant, star-shaped, creamy yellow flowers open in late spring or summer. ♈

OTHER TREES WITH SILVER OR BLUE-GREY LEAVES
Eucalyptus coccifera
Eucalyptus glaucescens
Eucalyptus gunnii
Populus alba, see p.214
Populus alba 'Raket'
Pyrus nivalis
Salix alba f. *argentea*
Salix exigua, see p.153
Salix x *seringeana*
Sorbus aria 'Lutescens'

△ *Sorbus thibetica* 'John Mitchell'

Eucalyptus perriniana
SPINNING GUM
☀ ❄❄
Vigorous growth
↕ 6m (20ft) ↔ 4m (12ft)

The stems of this small evergreen tree are darkly blotched and they have a white sheen. The leaves on juvenile trees are round, and a shimmering silver-blue, but as the tree matures, its leaves are larger and longer, and their colour more blue-green.

Sorbus thibetica 'John Mitchell'
HIMALAYAN WHITEBEAM
☀ ☀ ❄❄❄
Vigorous growth
↕ 12m (40ft) ↔ 10m (30ft)

This broad, eventually round-headed, tree produces large leaves that are grey-green above, and become green and white-felted beneath. Leaves of young, vigorous trees can be more than 15cm (6in) long. Clusters of white flowers appear in late spring. ♈

Trees with Purple, Red, or Bronze Leaves

PURPLE- OR BRONZE-LEAVED trees in a garden do not appeal to all gardeners, and there is no doubt that such a strong colour can be an eye-sore in the wrong place. Used with discretion, however, purple foliage can be very effective, especially when contrasted with shades of silver or blue-grey.

Fagus sylvatica f. *purpurea*
PURPLE BEECH
☼ ✳✳✳   Vigorous growth
↕ 30m (100ft) ↔ 22.5m (75ft)

This striking, round-headed beech is the largest tree of its colour. The oval, wavy-margined leaves are shiny purple, turning a rich coppery colour in autumn. 'Riversii' is also an excellent selection, with rich autumn tints. It is one of the most commonly planted. ♈

Acer platanoides 'Crimson King'
NORWAY MAPLE
☼ ✳✳✳   Vigorous growth
↕ 18m (60ft) ↔ 15m (50ft)

One of the most commonly planted trees of this colour, Norway maple is a large tree with sharply-toothed, deep crimson-purple leaves. Even the clusters of small, deep yellow flowers that occur in spring have a reddish tinge. Displays rich autumn colour. ♈

> **OTHER TREES WITH PURPLE, RED, OR BRONZE LEAVES**
>
> *Acer palmatum* 'Trompenburg'
> *Fagus sylvatica* 'Roseomarginata'
> *Malus* 'Lizet'
> *Prunus virginiana* 'Schubert'

△ *Prunus cerasifera* 'Nigra'

Cercis canadensis 'Forest Pansy'
REDBUD
☼ ✳✳✳   Moderate growth
↕ 8m (25ft) ↔ 8m (25ft)

This is a small, often multi-stemmed, tree with a broad, rounded crown. It has relatively large, heart-shaped leaves that are a rich reddish purple. The small pink pea-flowers, which are borne in spring, are not always freely produced in temperate climates. ♈

Prunus cerasifera 'Nigra'
PURPLE-LEAVED PLUM
☼ ✳✳✳   Moderate growth
↕ 10m (30ft) ↔ 10m (30ft)

In spring, the branches of this commonly planted, dense-headed tree are flooded with pink flowers. These are followed by its red leaves that turn to blackish purple. 'Pissardii' is very similar, and an equally popular cultivar, with white, pink-budded blooms. ♈

Trees for Autumn Colour

FEW SIGHTS warm the heart more than a Japanese maple in autumn, its canopy a blaze of colour. The foliage of many other trees, however, offers equally rich tints, and also more subtle shades of yellow, pink, and purple. These are some of the most reliable.

Amelanchier lamarckii
SNOWY MESPILUS
☼ ☀ ❋❋❋   Moderate growth
‡ 20m (70ft) ↔ 15m (50ft)

A superb tree, Snowy Mespilus has two main seasons of interest: spring, when the bushy crown is a cloud of white blossom, and autumn, when it is ablaze with red and orange foliage. Dislikes dry soils. One of the most reliable trees for autumn colour. ▽

Acer palmatum 'Osakazuki'
JAPANESE MAPLE
☼ ☀ ❋❋❋   Moderate growth
‡ 6m (20ft) ↔ 6m (20ft)

This beautiful tree is commonly acknowledged to be one of the most impressive and reliable of its kind. It is rounded and bushy, with seven-lobed leaves that turn a brilliant scarlet in autumn. All the Japanese maples dislike exposed sites and dry soils. ▽

Carya ovata
SHAGBARK HICKORY
☼ ☀ ❋❋❋   Moderate growth
‡ 20m (70ft) ↔ 15m (50ft)

The bold, divided, ash-like leaves of this robust tree with an ultimately spreading crown, turn a rich golden yellow in autumn. Its greyish brown bark peels in vertical plates. This is the most reliable member of a colourful group of hickories. ▽

Acer rubrum 'Schlesingeri'
RED MAPLE
☼ ❋❋❋   Moderate growth
‡ 15m (50ft) ↔ 12m (40ft)

'Schlesingeri' is an old selection, but still one of the earliest and best of its colour. The three- to five-lobed leaves turn wine-red and have contrasting pale undersurfaces, which are eye-catching even when shed and lying on the ground.

Cercidiphyllum japonicum
KATSURA
☼ ☀ ❋❋❋   Vigorous growth
‡ 18m (60ft) ↔ 15m (50ft)

This is a lovely tree of graceful, spreading habit, with slender branches. Its neatly rounded, paired leaves are bronze when they first unfurl, changing through blue-green in summer to yellow, pink, or purple in autumn. Dislikes dry soils. ▽

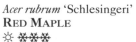

Nyssa sinensis
CHINESE TUPELO   Moderate growth
☼ ☀ ❅❅❅   ↕ 12m (40ft) ↔ 10m (30ft)

Erect or conical when young, this lovely tree spreads later. Its long, narrow leaves emerge purplish, turn green, and finish off a brilliant scarlet in autumn; at least equal to the American Tupelo *(N. sylvatica)* in autumn effect. Dislikes dry soils. ♈

Cotinus 'Grace'
SMOKE TREE   Vigorous growth
☼ ☀ ❅❅❅   ↕ 5m (15ft) ↔ 5m (15ft)

This can be a small, bushy, round-headed tree, or a large, multi-stemmed shrub. The striking leaves are wine-purple in summer, colouring to a brilliant orange-red later. Large plumes of purplish pink flowers are produced in summer. ♈

OTHER TREES FOR
AUTUMN COLOUR

Crataegus persimilis 'Prunifolia'
Fraxinus angustifolia 'Raywood'
Malus tschonoskii
Prunus sargentii
Sorbus commixta
   'Embley'

Parrotia persica
PERSIAN IRONWOOD   Moderate growth
☼ ☀ ❅❅❅   ↕ 7m (22ft) ↔ 12m (40ft)

The Persian Ironwood will eventually become a broad, spreading tree with piebald bark. It produces small red flower clusters in late winter or early spring, and its glossy green leaves turn yellow, orange, and red-purple in autumn. Dislikes dry soils. ♈

Liquidambar styraciflua 'Lane Roberts'
SWEET GUM   Moderate growth
☼ ☀ ❅❅❅   ↕ 20m (70ft) ↔ 11m (35ft)

One of the darkest and most reliable of all the autumn-colouring trees, this handsome specimen of conical, later spreading, habit has shining green maple-like leaves that turn through a range of colours from pale orange to deep red-purple. Dislikes dry soils. ♈

Rhus typhina 'Dissecta'
STAG'S-HORN SUMACH   Vigorous growth
☼ ❅❅❅   ↕ 3m (10ft) ↔ 5m (15ft)

Generally wider than it is tall, this low-crowned tree has deeply divided, fern-like leaves that are large and downy. They turn orange-red in autumn, when dense, conical clusters of red fruits are borne. Sensitive skins may react to the sap of this sumach. ♈

T R E E S

223

Trees with Autumn-to-winter Fruit

Μ ANY TREES produce attractive fruits in autumn, but few carry them through into winter, when they are of most ornamental value to gardeners, frequently hanging from or clinging to the often leafless branches. Birds, too, appreciate fruits during the winter months.

Malus 'John Downie'
CRAB APPLE   Moderate growth
☼ ❄❄❄   ↕ 8m (25ft) ↔ 5m (15ft)

One of the most popular of all ornamental crabs, 'John Downie' is upright at first, and spreads later. White blossom is carried in spring. The slightly elongated, red-flushed orange crab apples that crowd the branches from autumn onwards are edible. ♈

Malus 'Professor Sprenger'
CRAB APPLE   Moderate growth
☼ ❄❄❄   ↕ 5.5m (18ft) ↔ 5.5m (18ft)

From autumn onwards, this free-fruiting crab apple, with a dense, dome-shaped crown, bears little, rounded orange-red crab apples. Its pink-budded white flowers open in spring, and the glossy green leaves become yellow in autumn.

Ilex x *altaclerensis* 'Lawsoniana'
HIGHCLERE HOLLY   Moderate growth
☼ ☼ ❄❄❄   ↕ 10m (30ft) ↔ 5m (15ft)

This is a dense evergreen holly, with a wide, columnar habit that broadens further with age. It has large, yellow-splashed leaves, and a heavy crop of red berries from autumn onwards. Plant a male form nearby to effect pollination. ♈

Malus 'Red Sentinel'
CRAB APPLE   Moderate growth
☼ ❄❄❄   ↕ 5.5m (18ft) ↔ 5.5m (18ft)

One of the best fruiting crab apples for the smaller garden, this develops a compact, rounded crown. White flowers are borne in spring, and the autumn clusters of glossy-skinned, cherry-like fruits mature to bright red, lasting well into winter. ♈

OTHER TREES WITH AUTUMN-TO-WINTER FRUIT
Arbutus unedo
Crataegus x *lavallei* 'Carrierei'
Crataegus phaenopyrum
Idesia polycarpa (female)
Ilex x *altaclerensis* 'Wilsonii'
Ilex aquifolium 'Bacciflava'
Melia azedarach
Oxydendrum arboreum, see p.205
Pterostyrax hispida
Sorbus hupehensis 'Pink Pagoda'

Photinia davidiana
STRANVAESIA
☼ ☀ ❄❄❄   Moderate growth
     ↕ 5m (15ft) ↔ 5m (15ft)

Although it is often grown as a large evergreen shrub, this can be trained on a single stem to form a small tree. White flowers are produced in early summer, and the clusters of bright red berries that appear in autumn last all through the winter months.

Sorbus forrestii
ROWAN
☼ ☀ ❄❄❄   Moderate growth
     ↕ 6m (20ft) ↔ 6m (20ft)

Each leaf of this small, rounded tree is composed of numerous leaflets – blue-green in colour. Flattened heads of white flowers are carried in late spring, and the large bunches of small white berries that emerge in the autumn persist all through winter.

Sorbus cashmiriana
KASHMIR ROWAN
☼ ☀ ❄❄❄   Moderate growth
     ↕ 8m (25ft) ↔ 8m (25ft)

Erect when young, this openly branched tree has divided leaves that become gold or russet in autumn. Blush-pink flowers open in early summer, and the clusters of marble-sized white berries decorate the branches from autumn onwards. ▽

Sorbus 'Joseph Rock'
ROWAN
☼ ☀ ❄❄❄   Vigorous growth
     ↕ 10m (30ft) ↔ 5.5m (18ft)

One of the most popular of all rowans, 'Joseph Rock' has the characteristic vase-shaped crown that spreads with age. Its rich green, regularly divided leaves colour brilliantly in autumn, when the yellow berries, carried in drooping bunches, ripen. ▽

Sorbus commixta
JAPANESE ROWAN
☼ ☀ ❄❄❄   Vigorous growth
     ↕ 10m (30ft) ↔ 5.5m (18ft)

This is a handsome rowan with ascending, eventually spreading, branches. It has white flowers in spring, and regularly divided leaves that colour richly in autumn. Large bunches of red berries are borne from autumn onwards. 'Embley' is a superb cultivar.

Sorbus scalaris
ROWAN
☼ ☀ ❄❄❄   Moderate growth
     ↕ 10m (30ft) ↔ 10m (30ft)

The glossy green leaves of this wide-spreading tree grow in neat rosettes, and turn red and purple in autumn. Flattened white flowerheads appear in late spring, and its large, densely packed bunches of red berries persist from autumn into winter. ▽

T R E E S

Ornamental Bark or Shoots in Winter

HE BARK of many trees is attractive or interesting when examined closely, but some trees have coloured or peeling bark that is especially ornamental. Others boast coloured or unusually twisted shoots that have visual appeal, particularly in winter.

Arbutus menziesii
MADRONE   Moderate growth
☼ ✳✳✳   ↕ 15m (50ft) ↔ 12m (40ft)

Madrone is a handsome evergreen tree with a spreading crown of dark green leaves. The smooth reddish bark peels away to reveal its pea-green, new bark. White, urn-shaped flowers are produced in early summer; these are followed by orange-red fruits.   ♈

Acer griseum
CHINESE PAPERBARK MAPLE   Moderate growth
☼ ☼ ✳✳✳   ↕ 10m (30ft) ↔ 8m (25ft)

Famous for its peeling, papery orange-brown bark, this maple has the characteristic three-parted leaves that turn orange and red in autumn. The branches are ascending at first, spreading later. It is excellent for growing in a border or a large lawn.   ♈

△ *Betula utilis* var. *jacquemontii*

Acer palmatum 'Senkaki'
CORAL-BARK MAPLE   Moderate growth
☼ ☼ ✳✳✳   ↕ 6m (20ft) ↔ 6m (20ft)

In their first year, the winter shoots of this stunning Japanese maple, borne on ascending branches, are an attractive coral-pink, darkening later. The prettily lobed leaves are orange-yellow in spring, mature to green, and then turn yellow in autumn.   ♈

Betula utilis var. *jacquemontii*
WEST HIMALAYAN BIRCH   Vigorous growth
☼ ☼ ✳✳✳   ↕ 15m (50ft) ↔ 8m (25ft)

This strong-growing birch is popular for the white bark of its stem and branches. Its leaves turn yellow in autumn. 'Silver Shadow' and 'Grayswood Ghost' are selections with similarly white bark, as is 'Jermyns', whose catkins drape the branches in spring.

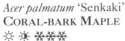

TREES

OTHER TREES WITH ORNAMENTAL
BARK OR SHOOTS IN WINTER

Acer pensylvanicum 'Erythrocladum'

Acer tegmentosum

Arbutus x *andrachnoides*

Betula albosinensis var. *septentrionalis*

Betula ermanii 'Grayswood Hill'

Betula nigra, see p.210

Fraxinus excelsior 'Allgold'

Myrtus luma, see p.216

Salix alba var. *vitellina*

Stewartia sinensis

△ *Prunus serrula*

△ *Eucalyptus pauciflora* subsp. *niphophila*

Prunus serrula
TIBETAN CHERRY

☼ ❄❄❄   Moderate growth
↕ 10m (30ft) ↔ 10m (30ft)

Its mahogany-red, polished and peeling bark makes this one of the most popular of all cherry trees. Small, inconspicuous white flowers are produced in spring. Its slender, lance-shaped, pointed green leaves become yellow in autumn. 🏆

Eucalyptus pauciflora subsp. niphophila
SNOW GUM

☼ ❄❄❄   Moderate growth
↕ 10m (30ft) ↔ 8m (25ft)

The leathery grey-green leaves of this evergreen grow on glossy shoots, bloomy white when young. The bark of its main branches and stem flakes to form a patchwork of grey, cream, and green. Fluffy summer flowerheads are white. Plant when small. 🏆

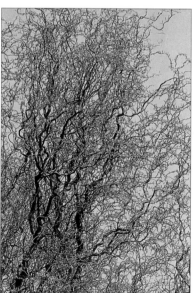

△ *Salix matsudana* 'Tortuosa'

Prunus maackii
MANCHURIAN BIRD CHERRY

☼ ❄ ❄❄❄   Moderate growth
↕ 12m (40ft) ↔ 10m (30ft)

Conical at first, this tree eventually spreads. Its smooth, glossy, yellowish brown or amber bark peels in bands like that of a birch. Small white flower spikes are produced in spring, and its leaves turn yellow in autumn. 'Amber Beauty' also has attractive bark.

Salix matsudana 'Tortuosa'
DRAGON'S CLAW WILLOW

☼ ❄❄❄   Vigorous growth
↕ 15m (50ft) ↔ 10m (30ft)

Erect when young, and spreading later, this willow is easy to recognize. Its long, twisted branches and shoots are clothed with narrow, contorted leaves. When the branches are bare in winter, the dramatic outline of this tree is very striking. 🏆

T R E E S

Multi-purpose Trees

WHEN CHOOSING a suitable tree for your garden, it makes sense to consider those offering more than one attraction. This is particularly relevant in small gardens, where space is limited. Fortunately, many trees offer a combination of ornamental features such as attractive flowers, fruit, and foliage, or impressive autumn colour and winter bark.

△ *Acer capillipes*

Acer capillipes
SNAKE-BARK MAPLE
☼ ✳✳✳

Moderate growth
↕ 10m (30ft) ↔ 8m (25ft)

Bark and autumn colour are the principal attributes of this most attractive maple with spreading branches, and three-lobed leaves that colour richly. The bark on its stems and main branches is a dark green colour, with silvery or pale green striations. ♈

Malus baccata var. *mandschurica*
MANCHURIAN CRAB
☼ ✳✳✳

Vigorous growth
↕ 12m (40ft) ↔ 12m (40ft)

The slender branches of this round-headed tree are flooded with scented white blossom in spring. Its small, rounded red fruits are carried from autumn into winter, and the mottled, flaking bark provides yet another attraction. Reliable and tough.

Photinia villosa
PHOTINIA
☼ ☼ ✳✳✳✳ PH ♈

Moderate growth
↕ 5m (15ft) ↔ 5m (15ft)

This small, versatile, wide-spreading tree has dark green leaves that are bronze-tinted when young, and turn a magnificent fiery orange-red in autumn. Clusters of white flowers open in spring and small red fruits are produced from late summer onwards. ♈

Stewartia monadelpha
STEWARTIA
☼ ✳✳✳✳ PH ♈

Moderate growth
↕ 10m (30ft) ↔ 8m (25ft)

Upright and conical when it is young, this stewartia spreads with age. Small white flowers are carried among the green leaves in summer. The foliage becomes orange and red in autumn, and its bark peels giving a piebald effect. Dislikes dry soils. ♈

△ *Malus baccata* var. *mandschurica*

OTHER MULTI-PURPOSE TREES

Acer griseum, see p.226
Aesculus flava
Arbutus unedo f. *rubra*
Cornus 'Porlock'
    Magnolia grandiflora
    Malus transitoria
Malus x *zumi*
Prunus sargentii
Pseudocydonia sinensis
Salix 'Chrysocoma', see p.210
Sassafras albidum, see p.205

TREES

Columnar Trees

TREES OF COLUMNAR habit are extremely useful. They are easily accommodated where space is at a premium, such as in small gardens or those that are long and narrow in shape. They are also effective architecturally, for breaking otherwise low or horizontal plantings, as well as for providing a focal point. Most offer other ornamental features.

OTHER COLUMNAR TREES

OTHER COLUMNAR TREES

Carpinus betulus 'Frans Fontaine'
Fagus sylvatica 'Dawyck Purple'
Liriodendron tulipifera 'Fastigiata'
Populus alba 'Raket'
Quercus petraea 'Columna'

△ *Prunus* 'Amanogawa'

Prunus 'Amanogawa'
JAPANESE CHERRY
☼ ❈❈❈   Moderate growth
                    ↕ 10m (30ft) ↔ 4m (12ft)

The branches of this cherry are closely packed at first, but they broaden as it matures. Large, fragrant, semi-double, pale pink flowers crowd its branches in spring. The leaves often give rich autumn tints. One of the most popular of all flowering cherries. ♈

Acer rubrum 'Columnare'
RED MAPLE
☼ ❈❈❈   Vigorous growth
                    ↕ 15m (50ft) ↔ 5m (15ft)

This cultivar is slender and columnar at first, and its long, upright branches are loosely packed to the stem. These branches broaden later, and are covered in leaves that turn yellow, orange, and red in autumn. *A. rubrum* 'Bowhall' is another excellent cultivar.

Acer saccharum 'Temple's Upright'
SUGAR MAPLE
☼ ❈❈❈   Slow growth
                    ↕ 12m (40ft) ↔ 5m (15ft)

The ascending branches of this broad, columnar tree are densely clothed with large, five-lobed leaves that turn yellow and orange in autumn. Performs best where summers are warm and winters cold, such as in Europe and North America.

Quercus robur f. *fastigiata*
CYPRESS OAK
☼ ❈❈❈   Slow growth
                    ↕ 18m (60ft) ↔ 6m (20ft)

The Cypress Oak is a broad, columnar form of the English Oak. Its ascending branches are thickly clothed with the bright green foliage. *Q. robur* 'Fastigiata Koster' is a very attractive compact selection. Both are long-lived. ♈

TREES

229

Index

Plants that are illustrated in the book are indicated by this symbol

A

Abele ▩ 214
Abelia floribunda 98
   A. triflora 127, 158, 168
Abeliophyllum distichum 98, 166
Abies balsamea 'Nana' ▩ 188
   A. concolor 185
   A. concolor 'Candicans' ▩ 193
   A. concolor 'Glauca Compacta' ▩ 188
   A. grandis 174
   A. koreana ▩ 150, ▩ 180, 182
   A. lasiocarpa 'Compacta' 189
   A. magnifica 174
   A. nordmanniana ▩ 174
   A. nordmanniana
      'Golden Spreader' ▩ 188
   A. pinsapo 'Glauca' 185
   A. vejarii 185
Abutilon 'Canary Bird' 144
   A. megapotamicum ▩ 92, ▩ 98
   A. x *suntense* 'Violetta' 130
Abyssinian Feathertop ▩ 37
Acacia
   False ▩ 213
   Golden ▩ 219
   Rose ▩ 99
Acacia baileyana 152
   A. dealbata 99, ▩ 158
Acaena 'Blue Haze' 28, 72
Acantholimon glumaceum 38
Acanthus hungaricus 20
   A. mollis ▩ 30
   A. mollis 'Holland's Gold' 71
   A. spinosus ▩ 18, 37, 85, 90
Acer campestre 206
   A. capillipes ▩ 228
   A. cappadocicum subsp. *lobelii* 197
   A. griseum ▩ 226, 228
   A. japonicum 'Aureum', see
      A. shirasawanum 'Aureum' ▩ 219
   A. negundo 'Flamingo' 206, 218
   A. palmatum 'Aureum' 151
   A. palmatum 'Bloodgood' 155

A. palmatum 'Corallinum' ▩ 142
A. palmatum var. *coreanum* ▩ 200
A. palmatum 'Garnet' 116, ▩ 154
A. palmatum var. *heptalobum* ▩ 156
A. palmatum 'Osakazuki' 156, ▩ 222
A. palmatum 'Red Pygmy' ▩ 154
A. palmatum 'Seiryu' 156
A. palmatum 'Senkaki' ▩ 226
A. palmatum 'Septemlobum', see
   A. palmatum var. *heptalobum* ▩ 156
A. palmatum 'Trompenburg' 221
A. pensylvanicum 'Erythrocladum' 227
A. platanoides 206, ▩ 215
A. platanoides 'Crimson King' ▩ 221
A. platanoides 'Drummondii' 218
A. pseudoplatanus 215
A. pseudoplatanus 'Brilliantissimum'
   203, 212
A. rubrum 205
A. rubrum 'Columnare' ▩ 229
A. rubrum 'Schlesingeri' ▩ 222
A. saccharinum ▩ 196
A. saccharum 'Monumentale',
   see *A. saccharum*
   'Temple's Upright' ▩ 229
A. saccharum 'Temple's Upright' ▩ 229
A. shirasawanum 'Aureum' 201, ▩ 219
A. tegmentosum 227
A. triflorum 199, ▩ 200
Achillea argentea,
   see *Tanacetum argenteum* 57, ▩ 73
   A. clavennae 28
   A. 'Coronation Gold' 37, 48, 85
   A. 'Gold Plate' ▩ 85
   A. ptarmica 'The Pearl' 48
acid soils, see lime-free soils
Aciphylla aurea 67
Aconite, Winter ▩ 60, ▩ 84
Aconitum x *bicolor*,
   see *A.* x *cammarum* 'Bicolor' ▩ 20
   A. 'Blue Sceptre' 91
   A. 'Bressingham Spire' 33
   A. x *cammarum* 'Bicolor' ▩ 20
   A. carmichaelii 'Arendsii' 90
   A. lycoctonum, see *A. vulparia* ▩ 90
   A. vulparia ▩ 90
Acorus gramineus 'Ogon' 64, 71
Actinida kolomikta ▩ 94
Adam's Laburnum ▩ 203
Adam's Needle, Variegated ▩ 69
Adiantum pedatum ▩ 34, 45
   A. pedatum var. *aleuticum* 45
Aegopodium podagraria 'Variegatum' ▩ 30
Aeonium arboreum 'Schwarzkopf',
   see *A.* 'Zwartkop' ▩ 64
   A. 'Zwartkop' ▩ 64
Aesculus californica 110
   A. x *carnea* 'Briotii' 212
   A. flava 197, 228
   A. hippocastanum 'Baumannii' 197,
      ▩ 202, 206
   A. x *neglecta* 'Erythroblastos' ▩ 198
   A. parviflora ▩ 110
   A. pavia 'Astrosanguinea' ▩ 200
Aethionema grandiflora ▩ 56

African Daisy ▩ 51, ▩ 63
African Lily ▩ 50
Agapanthus Headbourne Hybrids
   50, 63, 91
   A. inapertus var. *pendulus* 62
   A. orientalis, see *A. praecox*
      subsp. *orientalis* ▩ 50
   A. praecox subsp. *orientalis* ▩ 50
   A. praecox 'Variegatus' ▩ 68
Agave americana 'Variegata' ▩ 64
Agrostemma githago 'Milas' 22, ▩ 26
Ailanthus altissima 212
air pollution
   perennials 48–9
   shrubs 136–7
   trees 212-13
Ajuga reptans 'Atropurpurea' ▩ 74
   A. reptans 'Braunherz' 75
   A. reptans 'Catlin's Giant' 48
Akebia quinata ▩ 102
   A. trifoliata 96
Albizia julibrissin ▩ 206
Alcea rosea ▩ 22
   A. rosea 'Chater's Double' 23
Alchemilla mollis 25
Alder
   Grey ▩ 202
   Italian ▩ 215
   Red ▩ 210
Aleppo Pine ▩ 184
Algerian Oak ▩ 209
alkaline (limy) soils 12
   perennials 36–7
   shrubs 126–7
   trees 204, 206–7
Allegheny Serviceberry ▩ 212
Allium aflatunense ▩ 80
   A. albopilosum,
      see *A. christophii* ▩ 40, 50, 81
   A. christophii ▩ 40, 50, 81
   A. cyathophorum var. *farreri* ▩ 58
   A. farreri, see *A. cyathophorum*
      var. *farreri* ▩ 58
   A. karataviense 40, 59
   A. moly 41
   A. narcissiflorum 79
   A. oreophilum ▩ 58
   A. ostrowskianum,
      see *A. oreophilum* ▩ 58
   A. schoenoprasum ▩ 86
   A. schoenoprasum 'Forescate' 86
Almond
   Double ▩ 213
   Dwarf Russian ▩ 127
Alnus cordata 212, ▩ 215
   A. firma 210
   A. glutinosa 'Imperialis' 199, 210
   A. incana ▩ 202
   A. oregona, see *A. rubra* ▩ 210
   A. rubra ▩ 210, 214
Aloe arborescens 'Variegata' ▩ 64
Alopecurus pratensis 'Aureovariegatus' 70
Aloysia triphylla ▩ 144
Alpine Eryngo ▩ 39
Alpine Phlox ▩ 57

Alpine Pink □ 56
Alstroemeria 'Ligtu Hybrids' □ 80
Althaea officinalis □ 86
Alyssum saxatile, see *Aurina saxatilis* □ 54
Amaranthus caudatus □ 22
    A. caudatus 'Green Cascade' 22
    A. hybridus 22
x *Amarcrinum memoria-corsii* □ 82
Amarygia parkeri 'Alba' 83
Amaryllis belladonna □ 40
Ambrosia artemisiifolia 88
Amelanchier 'Ballerina' 162
    A. canadensis 134, 141
    A. laevis □ 212
    A. lamarckii 137, □ 194, 201,
        212, □ 222
American Arbor-vitae □ 179
Ampelopsis veitchii, see *Parthenocissus*
    tricuspidata 'Veitchii' □ 107
Anaphalis margaritacea var. *yedoensis* □ 48
    A. triplinervis 48, 72
Androsace carnea subsp. *laggeri* 57
    A. sarmentosa 54
Anemone blanda 40
    A. blanda 'Atrocaerulea' □ 60
    A. blanda 'Radar' □ 58
    A. blanda 'White Splendour' □ 78
    A. x *hybrida* 'Bressingham Glow'
        49, 52
    A. x *hybrida* 'Geant des Blanches' 52
    A. x *hybrida* 'Honorine Jobert' 33, 49,
        □ 52
    A. x *hybrida* 'Königin Charlotte' 91
    A. x *hybrida* 'Whirlwind' 49
    A. nemorosa 'Allenii' 42
    A. nemorosa 'Robinsoniana' □ 30
    A. pavonina 40, 79
Anethum graveolens □ 88
Anise, Chinese □ 100
Aniseed, Wild □ 53
annual plants
    climbers 106
    herbs 88–9
    large 22–23
    medium 22–23
    small 26–7
Anomatheca laxa 40
    A. laxa var. *alba* 40
Anthemis cupaniana, see *A. punctata*
    subsp. *cupaniana* 28, □ 50
    A. punctata subsp. *cupaniana* 28, □ 50
    A. tinctoria 'E.C. Buxton' □ 38
Anthericum liliago □ 36
Anthriscus sylvestris 'Ravenswing' □ 74
Anthyllis hermanniae 142
    A. montana □ 28
Apothecary's Rose □ 120
Apple
    Crab □ 224
    Ornamental Crab □ 194
Apple Mint, Variegated □ 69
Aquilegia vulgaris □ 52
Arabis caucasica 'Rosabella' 28, □ 54
Arachniodes standishii 45
Aralia cachemirica 18

A. elata 111, 201
A. elata 'Variegata' 217
A. japonica,
    see *Fatsia japonica* □ 111, 133, 146
A. spinosa 162
Araucaria araucana □ 174
Araujia sericofera 95
Arbor-vitae
    American □ 179
    Western □ 191
Arbutus x *andrachnoides*
    □ 202, 206, 209, 227
    A. menziesii □ 226
    A. unedo 216, 224
    A. unedo f. *rubra* 228
Archangel, Variegated □ 31
Arctostaphylos uva-ursi
    'Vancouver Jade' 118, 147
Arenaria balearica □ 54
    A. purpurascens □ 56
Argyranthemum 'Chelsea Girl' 62
    A. 'Mary Wooton' □ 62
Arisaema erubescens 44
    A. sikokianum 41, □ 44
    A. thunbergii 44
    A. triphyllum 41, 44
Arisarum proboscidium 41, □ 44
Aristolochia clematis 86
Aristotelia tomentosa 96
Armeria juniperina 38
    A. maritima 'Vindictive' 38
Armoracia rusticana 'Variegata' 68
Aronia arbutifolia □ 134
    A. arbutifolia 'Brilliant' 156
    A. arbutifolia 'Erecta' 162
    A. melanocarpa 134, 163
Artemisia absinthium 'Lambrook Silver' 86
    A. annua 88
    A. arborescens □ 50, 117, 152
    A. ludoviciana □ 72
    A. 'Powis Castle' □ 72, 152
    A. schmidtiana 'Nana' 38, □ 56
    A. stelleriana 'Mori's Form' 72
Arum creticum 40, 59
    A. italicum 'Marmoratum' 41, 60
    A. pictum 83
Aruncus dioicus □ 16
Arundinaria fortunei,
    see *Pleioblastus variegatus* □ 69
    A. viridistriatus,
    see *Pleioblastus auricomus* □ 71
Arundo donax 17, 18
    A. donax 'Variagata' 65
Asarabacca □ 30
Asarina barclayana 106
    A. procumbens □ 28, 54
Asarum caudatum 30
    A. europaeum □ 30, 86
Ash,
    Manna □ 207
    Mountain 194, □ 214
    Narrow-leaved □ 212
Asperula odorata,
    see *Galium odoratum* □ 30
Asphodel, Yellow □ 36

Asphodeline lutea □ 36
Aspidistra elatior 65
Asplenium scolopendrium 43, □ 44
    A. scolopendrium 'Crispium' 45
    A. scolopendrium 'Marginatum' 67
Astelia nervosa 'Silver Spear' 65
Aster albescens 165
    A. cordifolius 'Silver Spray' 21
    A. x *frikartii* 'Mönch' □ 48
    A. lateriflorus 'Horizontalis' 24
    A. novae-angliae 'Alma Pötschke'
        □ 32, 48
    A. novae-angliae 'Andenken an Alma
        Pötschke', see *A. novae-angliae*
        'Alma Pötschke' □ 32, 48
    A. novi-belgii 'Carnival' □ 32
    A. novi-belgii 'Marie Ballard' □ 90
    A. thomsonii 'Nanus' 24
Aster, Seaside □ 50
Astilbe 'Bressingham Beauty' □ 46
    A. 'Dunkellachs' 75
    A. 'Montgomery' □ 32
    A. 'Ostrich Plume' 20, □ 90
    A. simplicifolia 'Sprite' □ 24
    A. 'Sprite',
        see *A. simplicifolia* 'Sprite' □ 24
Astillboides tabularis 47
Astragalus augustifolius 38
Astrantia major □ 32
    A. major 'Hapsden Blood' □ 48
    A. major subsp. *involucrata* 'Shaggy' 48
    A. major 'Sunningdale Variegated' □ 68
    A. maxima 24
Athrotaxis laxifolia 180
Athyrium filix-femina 53
Athyrium nipponicum var. *pictum* 64
Atraphaxis frutescens 128
Atriplex halimus □ 138
    A. hortensis var. *rubra* 22, □ 88
Aubrieta 'Elsa Lancaster' 38
    A. 'Joy' 28, □ 54
Aucuba japonica □ 170
    A. japonica 'Crotonifolia' 123, □ 148
    A. japonica 'Rozannie' 117, 133, □ 146
    A. japonica 'Sulphurea' 151

Aurinia saxatilis ■ 54
Australian Tree Fern ■ 64
Austrian Pine ■ 187
Austrocedrus chilensis ■ 178
autumn colour 108, 156–7, 222–3
Autumn Crocus ■ 58, ■ 82
autumn-flowering bulbs, 82–3
Autumn Snowflake ■ 83
Avens, Mountain ■ 55
Award of Garden Merit 11
Azalea occidentalis,
   see *Rhododendron occidentale* 122, ■ 134
    A. pontica,
      see *Rhododendron luteum* ■ 159
Azaleas 108, 134
   Common Yellow ■ 159
   Evergreen ■ 125
   Exbury ■ 170
   Ghent ■ 125
   Knaphill ■ 145
Azara lancifolia 101
   A. microphylla ■ 100
   A. petiolaris 159
   A. serrata 101
Azorella trifurcata 38

B

Baggesen's Gold Lonicera ■ 151
Baldmoney ■ 87
Balkan Cranesbill ■ 42
Ball Tree, Orange ■ 138
Balloon Flower ■ 37
Ballota acetabulosa ■ 128
   B. pseudodictamnus 152
Bamboo ■ 66, ■ 67, ■ 71
   Chilean ■ 18
   Dwarf White-Striped ■ 69
   specimen 19
Baptisia australis ■ 20
Barberry ■ 150, ■ 152, ■ 154, ■ 169
   Darwin's ■ 122
   Japanese ■ 156
bark, ornamental 226–7
Bastard Balm ■ 87
Batchelor's Buttons ■ 101
Bay, California ■ 209
Bean Tree, Indian ■ 202
   Bearded Iris ■ 77, ■ 91
      Bear's Breeches ■ 18, ■ 30
      Beauty Berry ■ 156

Beauty Bush ■ 126
bedding, spring bulbs 78
Beech
   Common ■ 215
   Fern-leaved ■ 196
   Purple ■ 221
   Roblé ■ 197
Begonia sutherlandii ■ 62
Bell Heather ■ 125
Bell-wort ■ 45
Belladonna Lily ■ 40
Bellflower ■ 52, ■ 97
   Clustered ■ 36
   Giant ■ 52
Berberidopsis corallina ■ 96
Berberis ■ 12
   B. darwinii ■ 122, 126, 140
   B. dictyophylla ■ 152
   B. empetrifolia ■ 142
   B. 'Goldilocks' 146, ■ 169
   B. jamesiana 162
   B. julianae 158
   B. linearifolia 'Orange King' 114
   B. x *ottawensis* 'Superba' 155
   B. pruinosa 169
   B. 'Rubrostilla' 161, 163
   B. sargentiana 123
   B. sieboldii 116, 156
   B. x *stenophylla* ■ 140, 171
   B. x *stenophylla*
      'Corallina Compacta' 142
   B. thunbergii ■ 156
   B. thunbergii 'Atropurpurea' 141
   B. thunbergii
      'Atropurpurea Nana' ■ 154
   B. thunbergii 'Aurea' 116, ■ 150
   B. thunbergii 'Crimson Pygmy',
      see *B. thunbergii*
      'Atropurpurea Nana' ■ 154
   B. thunbergii 'Red Chief' ■ 154
   B. thunbergii 'Red Pillar' 140
   B. thunbergii 'Rose Glow' 148
   B. wilsoniae 163
Bergamot ■ 33, ■ 77
   Wild ■ 87
Bergenia 'Ballawley' 75, ■ 90
   B. 'Bressingham Beauty' 64
   B. 'Bressingham Ruby' 75
   B. cordifolia 'Purpurea' 37, ■ 66
   B. x *schmidtii* 48
   B. 'Silberlicht' 24, 63
Berkheya macrocephala 20
berries 162–3, 224
Beschorneria yuccoides ■ 18
Betula ■ 13
   B. albosinensis
      var. *septentrionalis* 227
   B. ermanii 'Grayswood Hill' 227
   B. maximowicziana 199
   B. nigra ■ 210, 227
   B. pendula 204
   B. pendula 'Youngii' 211
   B. utilis var. *jacquemontii* ■ 226
   B. utilis 'Jermyns' 203
Bidens ferulifolia 52, ■ 62

biennial plants
   climbers 22–3, 106
   herbs 88–9
   large 22–3
   medium 22–3
   small 24–7
Big-leaf Magnolia, Japanese ■ 217
Big Tree ■ 175
Birch ■ 13
   River ■ 210
   Weeping ■ 211
   West Himalayan ■ 226
Bird Cherry, Manchurian ■ 227
Bird-of-paradise Flower ■ 63
birds, berries for 162–3, 224
Bishop Pine ■ 185
Bishop's Hat ■ 42, ■ 90
Bistort ■ 47
Black Cherry ■ 215
Black-eyed Susan ■ 106
Black-eyed Suzy ■ 20
Black Locust ■ 213
Black Pine, Japanese ■ 183
Bladder Senna ■ 138
Blechnum chilense, see *B. tabulare* 45, ■ 66
   B. magellanicum, see *B. tabulare* 45, ■ 66
   B. spicant 34
   B. tabulare 45, ■ 66
Bleeding Heart, Wild ■ 42
Bletilla striata ■ 38
Blood-drop-emlets ■ 47
Bloody Cranesbill ■ 91
Blue Atlas Cedar ■ 193
blue-grey foliage, see silver or blue-grey
   foliage
Blue Holly ■ 161
Blue Passion Flower ■ 94
Blue Poppy ■ 35
Blue Spruce ■ 193
Bluebell, Spanish ■ 41
Blueberry, Swamp ■ 135
bog gardens 46–7
Bog Myrtle ■ 134
bold foliage,
   see also specimen plants 18, 111, 217
Borage ■ 88
Borago officinalis ■ 88
border pinks, fragrant 76
Bosnian Pine ■ 182
Bottlebrush ■ 98, ■ 128
   Buckeye ■ 110
Bourbon Rose ■ 112
Box ■ 146
   Christmas 167
   Edging ■ 170
   Handsworth ■ 140
   Sweet ■ 167
   Variegated ■ 148
Brachyglottis monroi ■ 128
   B. 'Sunshine' 128, ■ 136, 139, 152
Brachyscome iberidifolia ■ 26
Bramble, White-stemmed ■ 169
Brewer Spruce ■ 181
Bridal Wreath ■ 135
Brimeura amethystina 41

Bristlecone Pine ▣ 181
Broadleaf ▣ 141
Brodiaea laxa, see *Triteleia laxa* ▣ 40, 81
bronze foliage, see purple foliage
Broom ▣ 108, ▣ 122, ▣ 128
    Butcher's ▣ 171
    Moroccan ▣ 98
    Spanish ▣ 139
    Warminster ▣ 116
Brugmansia x *candida* 'Knightii' 144
Brunnera macrophylla 33, 52
    B. macrophylla 'Dawson's White'
        25, ▣ 68
    B. macrophylla 'Variegata',
        see *B. macrophylla*
        'Dawson's White' 25, ▣ 68
Buckeye
    Bottlebrush ▣ 110
    Dark Red ▣ 200
Buckthorn
    Sea ▣ 214
    Variegated ▣ 149
Buddleja alternifolia 'Argentea' 127, 152
    B. asiatica 159
    B. auriculata 159
    B. crispa ▣ 98, 158
    B. davidii 108
    B. davidii 'Dartmoor' ▣ 126
    B. davidii 'Harlequin' ▣ 148
    B. davidii 'Peace' ▣ 164
    B. davidii 'Royal Red' ▣ 136
    B. globosa ▣ 138
    B. 'Lochinch' ▣ 158, 165
    B. nivea 152
    B. officinalis 98, 159
    B. 'Pink Delight' 137, 165
Buffalo Currant ▣ 157
Bugbane ▣ 32
Bugele, Purple-leaved ▣ 74
bulbs
    autumn-flowering 82–3
    rock gardens, raised beds,
        and screes 58–9
    shady areas 41
    spring-flowering 78–9
    summer-flowering 80–1
    sunny sites 40
    winter-flowering 84
    wild areas 60–1
Bunnies' Ears ▣ 73
Buphthalmum salicifolium ▣ 24
Bupleurum fruticosum ▣ 138
Burning Bush ▣ 39
Butcher's Broom ▣ 171
butterflies 164–5
Butterfly Bush ▣ 108, ▣ 126, ▣ 136,
    ▣ 148, ▣ 158, ▣ 164
Buxus sempervirens
    'Elegantissima' ▣ 148
    B. sempervirens
        'Handsworthensis' ▣ 140
    B. sempervirens 'Latifolia Maculata' 133
    B. sempervirens 'Suffruticosa'
        140, ▣ 170
    B. sempervirens 'Vardar Valley' ▣ 146

C

Caesalpinia japonica 98
Calamagrostis epigejos 'Hortorum' 17
Calendula officinalis 88
    C. officinalis 'Fiesta Gitana' 88
Calico Bush ▣ 125
California Bay ▣ 209
California Nutmeg ▣ 185
California Poppy ▣ 26, ▣ 129
Callicarpa bodinieri var. *giraldii* ▣ 161
    C. japonica ▣ 156
Callistemon citrinus 'Splendens' ▣ 128
    C. pallidus ▣ 98
Calluna vulgaris 'Annemarie' ▣ 124
    C. vulgaris 'Anthony Davis' ▣ 164
    C. vulgaris 'Beoley Gold' 151
    C. vulgaris 'Boskoop' 157
    C. vulgaris 'Gold Haze' ▣ 150
    C. vulgaris 'Kinlochruel' 125
    C. vulgaris 'Silver Queen' ▣ 152
Calocedrus decurrens 174, 178
    C. decurrens 'Aureovariegata' ▣ 191
Calomeria amaranthoides 23
Calycanthus floridus 134
Camassia leichtlinii 'Alba' ▣ 60
    C. leichtlinii 'Semiplena' ▣ 80
Camellia 'Inspiration' 101
    C. japonica 'Adolphe Auduss' ▣ 124,
        136, 145
    C. japonica 'Magnoliiflora' 146
    C. sasanqua 'Narumigata' 166
    C. 'Spring Festival' 125, 145
    C. x *williamsii* 'Brigadoon' 110
    C. x *williamsii* 'Debbie' 145
    C. x *williamsii* 'Donation' ▣ 124
    C. x *williamsii* 'St. Ewe' 125
Campanula 'Burghaltii' 24
    C. cochleariifolia ▣ 54
    C. garganica 'Dickson's Gold' 70
    C. 'G. F. Wilson' 57
    C. glomerata 'Superba' ▣ 36
    C. lactiflora 'Prichard's Variety'
        ▣ 16, 52
    C. latifolia 'Brantwood' 37, ▣ 52
    C. latifolia var. *macrantha alba* 52
    C. persicifolia 'Chettle Charm' 37
    C. persicifolia 'Telham Beauty' ▣ 38
    C. poscharskyana ▣ 52
    C. pusilla, see *C. cochlearifolia* ▣ 54
    C. pyramidalis 23
    C rapunculoides 52
    C.trachelium var. *alba* 52
Campsis radicans 95, 107
    C. x *tagliabuana*
        'Madame Galen' 95
Candelabra Primula ▣ 47
Candytuft ▣ 26
Canna 'Assault' ▣ 62
    C. musifolia 65
    C. 'Striata' 65
Cape Lily ▣ 80
Cardamine trifolia 30
Cardiocrinum giganteum 81, ▣ 85
Cardoon ▣ 18

Carex elata 'Aurea' 71
    C. flagellifera ▣ 64
    C. hachijoensis 'Evergold',
        see *C. oshimensis hachijoensis*
        'Evergold' 69, ▣ 70
    C. oshimensis hachijoensis
        'Evergold' 69, ▣ 70
Carpenteria californica 99, 130, ▣ 158
carpeting shrubs 143
Carpinus betulus 141 197
    C. betulus 'Fastigiata' 203
    C. betulus 'Frans Fontaine' 229
Carthamus tinctorius ▣ 89
Carya ovata 197, ▣ 222
Caryopteris x *clandonensis*
    'Arthur Simmonds' ▣ 116
    C. x *clandonensis* 'Heavenly Blue' 116
    C. x *clandonensis* 'Worcester Gold' 151
    C. incana 130
Cascades Mahonia ▣ 133
Cassinia leptophylla 152
Castanea sativa ▣ 196
Castanopsis cuspidata 216
Castor-oil Plant ▣ 65
Castor Oil Tree, Prickly ▣ 217
Catalina Ceanothus ▣ 98
Catalpa bignonioides ▣ 202, 212, 217
    C. bignonioides 'Aurea' ▣ 219
    C. speciosa ▣ 196
Catananche coerulea 'Major' 50
Catmint ▣ 91
Caucasian Comfrey ▣ 53
Caucasian Crosswort ▣ 29
Caucasian Elm ▣ 197
Caucasian Fir ▣ 174
Caucasian Speedwell ▣ 29
Caucasian Wingnut ▣ 210
Ceanothus ▣ 92
    C. arboreus 'Trewithen Blue' ▣ 98

Ceanothus 'Concha' 99
 C. 'Gloire de Versailles' 158
 C. gloriosus 118, 147
 C. griseus 'Yankee Point' 118
 C. thyrsiflorus var. *repens* 118, 147, 171
Cedar
 Blue Atlas ▣ 193
 Chilean ▣ 178
 Dwarf ▣ 188
 Dwarf Red ▣ 189
 Incense ▣ 191
 Japanese Red ▣ 174
 of Lebanon ▣ 174
 Western Red ▣ 187, ▣ 192
Cedrela ▣ 217
Cedrela sinensis, see *Toona sinensis* ▣ 217
Cedrus deodara ▣ 184
 C. deodara 'Aurea' 192
 C. deodara 'Golden Horizon' 192
 C. deodora 'Karl Fuchs' 193
 C. deodora 'Pendula' 177
 C. libani ▣ 174
 C. libani subsp. *atlantica*
  'Fastigiata' 174
 C. libani subsp. *atlantica*
  f. *glauca* 175, ▣ 193
 C. libani subsp. *atlantica*
  'Glauca Pendula' 177
 C. libani 'Sargentii' ▣ 188
Celandine, Greater ▣ 52
Celastrus orbiculatus ▣ 102
Celmisia coriacea 34, ▣ 66
 C. spectabilis 34
 C. walkeri ▣ 34
Celtis australis ▣ 208
Centaurea cineraria 'White Diamond' 50
 C. cyanus 22
 C. gymnocarpa 50
 C. montana ▣ 48
 C. montana 'Gold Bullion' 70
 C. pulcherrima 21
Centranthus ruber ▣ 50
Century Plant,
 Variegated ▣ 64

Cephalanthus occidentalis 134
Cephalotaxus fortunei
 'Prostrate Spreader' 177
Cerastium tomentosum ▣ 28
Ceratostigma willmottianum ▣ 116
Cercidiphyllum japonicum ▣ 222
Cercis canadensis 'Forest Pansy' ▣ 221
 C. siliquastrum ▣ 206, 209
Cestrum elegans ▣ 144
 C. nocturnum 144
Ceterach officinarum 54
Chaenomeles x *californica* 'Enchantress' 169
 C. speciosa 'Kermesina Semiplena' 101
 C. speciosa 'Moerloosei' ▣ 100, 127, 141
 C. speciosa 'Nivalis' 101
 C. speciosa' Phylis Moore' 101
 C. x *superba* 'Crimson and Gold' 101
 C. x *superba* 'Moerlooseii',
  see *C. speciosa* 'Moerlooseii'
  ▣ 100, 127, 141
 C. x *superba* 'Nicoline' ▣ 122
 C. x *superba* 'Pink Lady' 101
 C. x *superba* 'Rowallane' ▣ 100
Chaerophyllum hirsutum 'Roseum' 52
Chamaecyparis 'Green Hedger' ▣ 186
 C. lawsoniana 'Alumii' 174
 C. lawsoniana 'Alumii Magnificent' 178
 C. lawsoniana 'Argenteovariegata' 191
 C. lawsoniana 'Blue Jacket' 186
 C. lawsoniana 'Chilworth Silver' 193
 C. lawsoniana 'Columnaris' 178, 180
 C. lawsoniana 'Ellwood's Gold' 189
 C. lawsoniana 'Ellwood's White' 191
 C. lawsoniana 'Ellwood's Pillar' 178
 C. lawsoniana 'Fletcher's White' 191
 C. lawsoniana 'Fraseri' 178, 186
 C. lawsoniana 'Globosa' 187
 C. lawsoniana 'Gnome' ▣ 188
 C. lawsoniana 'Golden Wonder' 186
 C. lawsoniana 'Grayswood Pillar' 178
 C. lawsoniana 'Green Pillar' 178, ▣ 186
 C. lawsoniana 'Hillieri' 178
 C. lawsoniana 'Intertexta' 174
 C. lawsoniana 'Kilmacurragh' 178
 C. lawsoniana 'Konijn's Silver' 191
 C. lawsoniana 'Lane' 192
 C. lawsoniana 'Luna' 191
  C. lawsoniana 'Lutea' 192
  C. lawsoniana 'Pelt's Blue'
   193
  C. lawsoniana 'Pembury Blue'
   186, ▣ 193
  C. lawsoniana 'Pottenii' 178
  C. lawsoniana
  'Tamariscifolia' 177
 C. lawsoniana
  'Triomf van Boskoop' 182
 C. lawsoniana 'Winston Churchill' 178
 C. lawsoniana 'Wisselii' 174, ▣ 178
 C. nootkatensis 'Pendula' 181
 C. nootkatensis 'Variegata' ▣ 191
 C. obtusa 'Caespitosa' 189
 C. obtusa 'Crippsii' ▣ 180, 192
 C. obtusa 'Nana Aurea' ▣ 188
 C. obtusa 'Rigid Dwarf' 189

 C. obtusa 'Tetragona Aurea' ▣ 180
 C. occidentalis 'Rheingold' 192
 C. pisifera 'Filifera Aurea' ▣ 172, ▣ 192
 C. thoides 'Ericoides' 187
Chamaemelum nobile 86
Cheal's Weeping Cherry ▣ 211
Cheiranthus 'Bowles Mauve',
 see *Erysimum* 'Bowles Mauve' ▣ 24
 C. cheiri 'Fire King' ▣ 26
 C. cheiri 'Harpur Crewe' ▣ 76
Chelidonium majus 'Flore Pleno' ▣ 52
Chenopodium quinoa
 Andean Hybrids Mixed 22
Cherry
 Black ▣ 215
 Cheal's Weeping ▣ 211
 Cornelian ▣ 166
 Hill ▣ 199
 Japanese ▣ 229
 Manchurian Bird ▣ 227
 Purple-leaf Sand ▣ 155
 Rum ▣ 215
 Tibetan ▣ 227
 Variegated Cornelian ▣ 148
 Weeping Spring ▣ 211
 Yoshino ▣ 207
Cherry Laurel ▣ 133, ▣ 141, ▣ 147
 Variegated ▣ 163
Chestnut
 Double Horse ▣ 202
 Sunrise Horse ▣ 198
 Spanish ▣ 196
Chiastophyllum oppositifolium ▣ 54
Chicory ▣ 86
Chile Pine ▣ 174
Chilean Bamboo ▣ 18
Chilean Bellflower ▣ 97
Chilean Cedar ▣ 178
Chilean Glory Flower ▣ 106
Chimonanthus praecox 'Grandiflorus' 98,
 ▣ 166
China Fir ▣ 180
China Rose ▣ 99
Chinese Anise ▣ 100
Chinese Juniper ▣ 178
Chinese Paperbark Maple ▣ 226
Chinese Privet ▣ 110
Chinese Rowan ▣ 201
Chinese Silver Grass ▣ 85
Chinese Spruce ▣ 186
Chinese Tupelo ▣ 223
Chinese Wisteria ▣ 105
Chionanthus virginicus ▣ 110
Chionochloa conspicua 17
Chionodoxa forbesii ▣ 78
  C. gigantea, see *C. luciliae* ▣ 58, 60
  C. luciliae 58, 60
x *Chionoscilla allenii* ▣ 78
Chives ▣ 86
Choisya 'Aztec Pearl' 117, 126, ▣ 144
 C. ternata 123, 146, ▣ 158
 C. ternata 'Sundance' ▣ 150
Chokeberry, Red ▣ 134
Christmas Box ▣ 167
Christmas Fern ▣ 45

Chrysanthemum 'Clara Curtis' ▣ 20
   C. coronarium 88
   C. frutescens 'Mary Wooton', see
     Argyranthemum 'Mary Wooton' ▣ 62
   C. 'Pennine Flute' ▣ 62
Chrysanthemum, Korean ▣ 20
Chusan Palm ▣ 217
Chusquea culeou ▣ 18
Cicerbita plumieri 52
Cichorium intybus ▣ 86
Cimicifuga racemosa 17
   C. simplex 17, ▣ 32
   C. simplex 'Brunette' 75
Circium rivulare var. *atropurpureum* 32
Cissus striata 95, 104
Cistus x *aguilari* 'Maculatus' ▣ 116
   C. albidus 152
   C. x *corbariensis* ▣ 116, 130
   C. x *cyprius* ▣ 130
   C. x *hybridus*,
     see *C.* x *corbariensis* ▣ 116, 130
   C. ladanifer ▣ 160
   C. 'Peggy Sammons' ▣ 152
   C. populifolius var. *lasiocalyx* 128
   C. x *praecox* 'Warminster' ▣ 116
   C. x *purpureus* ▣ 128
   C. salviifolius 'Avalanche' 118, 143
Cladrastis lutea 199, ▣ 208
Claret Vine ▣ 94
Clary ▣ 23
clay soils 12
   conifers 182–3
   perennials 32–3
   shrubs 122–3
   trees 202–3
Clematis armandii 95, ▣ 104
   C. 'Bill Mackenzie' ▣ 94
   C. cirrhosa ▣ 104
   C. cirrhosa var. *balaerica* 104
   C. fasciculiflora 104
   C. flammula ▣ 105
   C. 'Jackmanii' ▣ 94
   C. x *jouiniana* 'Praecox' ▣ 96
   C. 'Madame Julia Correvon' ▣ 102
   C. maximowicziana 105
   C. montana 'Fragrant Spring' 105
   C. montana f. *grandiflora* ▣ 96
   C. montana var. *rubens* ▣ 102
   C. montana var. *wilsonii* 105
   C. 'Nelly Moser' ▣ 96
   C. orientalis 'Bill Mackenzie',
     see *C.* 'Bill Mackenzie' ▣ 94
   C. recta ▣ 76
   C. recta 'Foliis Purpureis', see *C. recta*
     'Purpurea' ▣ 74
   C. recta 'Purpurea' ▣ 74
   C. rehderiana ▣ 102, 105
Cleome hassleriana 'Colour Fountain' ▣ 22
Clerodendrum bungei ▣ 114, 165
   C. trichotomum ▣ 110
Clethra alnifolia ▣ 134
   C. alnifolia 'Paniculata' 125, 158
   C. barbinervis 168
   C. delavayi ▣ 124
   C. tomentosa 134

Cleyera japonica 146
Clianthus puniceus 98
climbing plants 11, 92
   annuals and biennials 106–7
   deciduous 96
   evergreen 97, 104
   fragrant flowers 105
   self-clinging 95, 107
   shrubs 98–101
   sunless walls and fences 96–7, 100–1
   sunny walls and fences 94–5, 98–9
   training into trees and shrubs 102–3
Climbing Rose ▣ 94, ▣ 95, ▣ 105, ▣ 121
Clover, Purple-leaved ▣ 29
Clustered Bellflower ▣ 36
Cnicus benedictus 88
Coast Redwood ▣ 175
coastal exposure
   perennials 50–1
   shrubs 138–9
   trees 214
Cobaea scandens ▣ 106
Coclchium agrippinum 40, ▣ 58, 83
   C. autumnale 61, 83
   C. autumnale 'Major',
     see *C. byzantinum* ▣ 82
   C. byzantinum ▣ 82
   C. speciosum 83
   C. speciosum 'Album' ▣ 82
   C. 'The Giant' 60
   C. 'Waterlily' ▣ 82
Colletia cruciata 169
   C. hystrix 169
   C. hystrix 'Rosea' 158
Collinsia grandiflora 27
Colorado Spruce ▣ 193
Colorado White Fir ▣ 193
Colquhounia coccinea 98, 130
Columbine ▣ 52
columnar plants 178–9, 229
Colutea arborescens ▣ 138
   C. x *media* 'Copper Beauty' 122, 137
   C. x *media* 'Orange Beauty' 138
Comfrey
   Caucasian ▣ 53
   Dwarf ▣ 31
   Variegated Russian ▣ 69
Common Beech ▣ 215
Common Moss Rose ▣ 120
Common Sage ▣ 165
Common Thyme ▣ 165
Common Yellow Azalea ▣ 159
Confederate Jasmine ▣ 104
conifers 10–1, 172
   columnar 174, 178–9
   dwarf 188–9
   golden or yellow foliage 192
   ground cover 190
   heavy clay soils 182–3
   hedges, windbreaks, and screens 186
   large 174–5
   medium-sized gardens 180–1
   silver or blue-grey foliage 193
   spreading 175
   sunny sites 184–5

   variegated foliage 191
   vase-shaped 176–7
   weeping 177
   wide-spreading 176–7
Consolida ambigua ▣ 22
   C. ambigua Imperial Series 22
containers
   flowering perennials 62–3
   foliage perennials 64–5
   shrubs 144–5
Convallaria majalis ▣ 42, 76
   C. majalis 'Fortin's Giant' 91
   C. majalis 'Hardwick Hall' 69
Convolvulus ▣ 152
Convolvulus althaeoides 72
   C. cneorum 142, ▣ 152
Coral-bark Maple ▣ 226
Coral Gem ▣ 62
Coral Plant ▣ 96
Coral Tree ▣ 130
Coreopsis grandiflora 'Mayfield Giant' 22
   C. verticillata ▣ 24
Coriander ▣ 89
Coriandrum sativum ▣ 89
Coriaria terminalis 163
Corkscrew Hazel ▣ 168
Corn Cockle ▣ 26
Cornelian Cherry ▣ 166
   Variegated ▣ 148
Cornflower, Perennial ▣ 48
Cornus alba 156
   C. alba 'Aurea' 134, ▣ 150
   C. alba 'Elegantissima' 134, ▣ 148
   C. alba 'Gouchaultii' 134
   C. alba 'Sibirica' ▣ 168
   C. alba 'Spaethii' 148
Cornus alternifolia
   'Argentea' ▣ 200
   C. canadensis ▣ 118, 132
   C. controversa 'Variegata' ▣ 218
   C. florida 'White Cloud' ▣ 201
   C. kousa var. *chinensis* 198
   C. macrophylla ▣ 198

Cornus mas 162, 🔲 166
    C. mas 'Aurea' 151
  C. mas 'Variegata' 🔲 148
  C. nuttallii 🔲 204
  C 'Porlock' 228
  C. sanguinea 'Winter Beauty'
    🔲 168, 171
  C. sanguinea 'Winter Flame',
    see *C. sanguinea* 'Winter Beauty'
    🔲 168, 171
  C. stolonifera 134, 🔲 168
Coronilla emerus 128
  C. valentina subsp. *glauca* 🔲 158
  C. valentina subsp. *glauca*
    'Variegata' 149
Corsican Hellebore 🔲 66
Cortaderia fulvida 17
  C. richardii 17, 18
  C. selloana 'Albolineata' 68
  C. selloana 'Aureolineata' 69
  C. selloana 'Carnea' 17
  C. selloana 'Pumila' 37, 🔲 85
  C. selloana 'Rendatleri' 17, 18
  C. selloana 'Sunningdale Silver' 🔲 18
Corydalis flexuosa 🔲 41
  C. ochroleuca 🔲 55
  C. solida 'George Baker' 57, 79
Corylus avellana 'Contorta' 🔲 168
  C. colurna 197
  C. maxima 'Purpurea' 🔲 154
Cosmos 'Sensation' 22
Cotinus coggygria 'Notcutt's Variety' 127
  C. coggygria
    'Royal Purple' 122, 🔲 154
  C. 'Flame' 🔲 156
  C. 'Grace' 🔲 223
Cotoneaster adpressus 119
  C. atropurpureus 'Variegatus' 🔲 149
  C. bullatus 162
  C. cochleatus 118
  C. conspicuus 'Decorus' 165
  C. 'Cornubia' 🔲 162
  C. dammeri 🔲 118
  C. franchetii sternianaus,
    see *C. sternianus* 🔲 162
  C. frigidus 162, 🔲 202

C. frigidus 'Fructuluteo' 🔲 161
C. frigidus 'Xanthocarpus',
  see *C. frigidus* 'Fructuluteo' 🔲 161
C. horizontalis 101, 163, 171
C. horizontalis 'Variegatus', see
  C. atropurpureus 'Variegatus' 🔲 149
C. lacteus 🔲 140, 165
C. moupinensis 162
C. 'Rothschildianus' 161
C. simonsii 🔲 140
C. sternianus 136, 🔲 162, 165
Cotton Lavender 🔲 153
Cotton Thistle 🔲 73
Cotyledon simplicifolia, see *Chiastophyllum*
  oppositifolium 🔲 54
Cow Parsley, Purple-leaved 🔲 74
Cowslip 🔲 77
  Virginian 🔲 44
Coyote Willow 🔲 153
Crab
  Hupeh 🔲 199
  Japanese 🔲 207
  Manchurian 🔲 228
Crab Apple 🔲 224
  ornamental 🔲 194
Crambe cordifolia 17, 🔲 18, 76
Cranesbill 🔲 25, 🔲 28, 🔲 42, 🔲 48, 🔲 56
  Balkan 🔲 42
  Bloody 🔲 91
Crassula sarcocaulis 142
Crataegus 🔲 194
  C. laciniata, see *C. orientalis* 201, 🔲 206
  C. laevigata 'Paul's Scarlet' 🔲 212
  C. x *lavallei* 'Carrierei' 224
  C. monogyna 141, 204
  C. oxyacantha 'Paul's Scarlet', see
    C. laevigata 'Paul's Scarlet' 🔲 212
  C. orientalis 201, 🔲 206
  C. persimilis 'Prunifolia' 212, 223
  C. x *persistens* 'Prunifolia' 203
  C. phaenopyrum 224
  C. x *schraderiana* 🔲 162
Creeping Dogwood 🔲 118
Creeping Juniper 🔲 190
Crepis incana 37
Cress, Persian Stone 🔲 56
Crested Moss Rose 🔲 120
Crinodendron hookerianum 101, 125,
  🔲 132
x *Crinodonna corsii*, see x *Amarcrinum*
  memoria corsii 🔲 82
Crinum x *powellii* 🔲 80, 83
Crocosmia 'Bressingham Blaze' 🔲 52
  C. 'Citronella' 🔲 80
  C. 'Jackanapes' 🔲 80
  C. 'Lucifer' 33, 91
Crocus 🔲 82
  Autumn 🔲 82
Crocus banaticus 🔲 82
  C. biflorus 🔲 58
  C. dalmaticus 🔲 78
  C. 'Dutch Yellow' 61
  C. 'E. A. Bowles' 59
  C. etruscus 79
  C. kotschyanus 60, 83

C. laevigatus 'Fontenayi' 84
C. nudiflorus 83
C. pulchellus 🔲 82
C. speciosus 83
C. speciosus 'Albus' 83
C. speciosus 'Oxonian' 🔲 82
C. tommasinianus 🔲 60, 84
C. tommasinianus 'Ruby Giant' 61
C. vernus 61
C. vernus 'Princess Juliana' 🔲 78
Crosswort, Caucasian 🔲 29
Crown Imperial 🔲 79
Crucianella stylosa,
  see *Phuopsis stylosa* 🔲 29
Cryptogramma crispa 34
Cryptomeria japonica 🔲 174
  C. japonica 'Elegans
    Compacta' 🔲 182
  C. japonica 'Elegans Nana',
    see *C. japonica* 'Elegans
    Compacta' 🔲 182, 187
  C. japonica 'Sekkan-sugi' 192
  C. japonica 'Vilmoriniana' 189
Cunninghamia lanceolata 🔲 180
Cup and Saucer Vine 🔲 106
x *Cupressocyparis leylandii* 🔲 186
  x *C. leylandii* 'Castlewellan' 🔲 186
  x *C. leylandii* 'Castlewellan Gold',
    see x *C. leylandii*
    'Castlewellan' 🔲 186
  x *C. leylandii* 'Gold Rider' 186
  x *C. leylandii* 'Harlequin' 🔲 191
  x *C. leylandii* 'Hyde Hall' 189
  x *C. leylandii* 'Naylor's Blue' 174
Cupressus abramsiana 174
  C. arizonica 'Pyramidalis' 180
  C. cashmeriana 🔲 180
  C. duclouxiana 185
  C. glabra 185
  C. glabra 'Pyramidalis' 185, 193
  C. lusitanica 185
  C. macnabiana 185
  C. macrocarpa 175, 🔲 184, 187
  C. macrocarpa 'Goldcrest' 🔲 192
  C. macrocarpa 'Gold Spread'
    🔲 176, 192
  C. sempervirens 174, 🔲 178, 185
  C. sempervirens 'Swane's Golden'
    178, 🔲 192
Currant, Buffalo 🔲 157
Currant, Flowering 🔲 137
Currant, Golden Flowering 🔲 151
Curry Plant 🔲 153
Cyclamen coum 🔲 41, 60
  C. coum 'Album' 60, 🔲 84
  C. coum subsp. *coum*,
    see *C. coum* 🔲 41, 60
  C. coum (pewter-leaved) 84
  C. graecum 83
  C. hederifolium 🔲 60, 83
  C. hederifolium 'Album' 60, 🔲 83
  C. repandum 41, 60
  C. neapolitanum 'Album',
    see *C. hederifolium* 'Album' 60, 🔲 83
  C. repandum 🔲 14, 79

Cynara cardunculus □ 18, 17
  C. scolymus 'Glauca' 18, 72
Cypress
  Dwarf □ 188
  Hinoki □ 180
  Italian □ 178
  Kashmir □ 180
  Lawson □ 178, □ 186
  Leyland □ 186
  Monterey □ 176, □ 184, □ 192
  Patagonian □ 180
  Pond □ 181
  Sawara □ 192
  Swamp □ 183
  Variegated Leyland □ 191
  Variegated Nootka □ 191
Cypress Oak □ 229
Cyrtomium falcatum 65
  C. japonicum 45
Cytisus □ 108
  C. battandieri □ 98
  C. 'Boskoop Ruby' 116
  C. 'Killiney Red' □ 122, 138
  C. nigricans 128
  C. 'Porlock' 159
  C. x *praecox* □ 116
  C. x *praecox* 'Allgold' 122, □ 128
  C. x *purpureus* □ 128
  C. purpureus 'Atropurpureus' 143
  C. scoparius 'Cornish Cream' 114

D

Daboecia cantabrica 118
  D. cantabrica 'Bicolor' □ 124
Daffodil □ 79
  Hoop-petticoat □ 84
  Minature □ 59
  Tenby □ 61
Dahlia 'Bishop of Llandaff' □ 80
Daisy
  African □ 51, □ 63
  Michaelmas □ 32, □ 90
  New Zealand □ 34, □ 66
  Paris □ 62
  Swan River □ 26
Daisy Bush □ 131, □ 137, □ 139
Dame's Violet □ 77
damp sites
  perennials 44–5, 46–7
  shrubs 134–5
  trees 210
Danae racemosa 146
Daphne bholua 'Jacqueline Postill' 159, □ 166
  D. x *burkwoodii* 'Carol Mackie' 148
  D. x *burkwoodii* 'Somerset' 116, □ 158
  D. collina 142
  D. x *houtteana* 155
  D. laureola var. *philippi* □ 132
  D. longilobata 163
  D. mezereum 116, 158, 163
  D. odora 'Aureo-marginata' □ 146, 166
  D. pontica 133
  D. retusa 117, □ 142

D. tangutica 163, 171
Dark Red Buckeye □ 200
Darmera peltata,
  see *Peltiphyllum peltatum* □ 47, 64
Darwin's Barberry □ 122
Dawn Redwood □ 182
Day Lily □ 21, □ 76
Deadnettle, Spotted □ 43, □ 91
Decaisnea fargesii 111, 161
deciduous plants 10–1
  air pollution tollerant 137
  alkaline soils 127
  aromatic leaves 160
  climbers for sunless walls 96
  coastal exposure 138
  golden or yellow leaves 151
  heavy clay 122
  medium-sized 114
  perennials with golden leaves 70
  perennials with purple leaves 75
  purple, red, or bronze leaves 155
  shade tolerant 132
  shrubs 108, 122, 132
  silver or blue-grey leaves 152
  small 117
  sunless walls 101
  sunny walls 98
  trees 194
  variegated 148
decorative seed heads 85
Decumaria barbara 95, 107
  D. sinensis 95, □ 105, 107
deer-proof perennials 90
Delphinium 'Loch Leven' 17
  D. 'Fanfare' □ 16
Dendromecon rigida 152
Deodar □ 184
Desfontainea spinosa □ 124
Desmodium tiliifolium □ 99
Deutzia x *elegantissima* 'Rosealind' □ 114, 122
  D. gracilis □ 116
  D. x *hybrida* 'Pink Pompon' 114
  D. longifolia 'Veitchii' □ 126
  D. x *wilsonii* 168
Dianthus 'Becky Robinson' 76
  D. 'Devon Glow' 76
  D. 'Doris' □ 76
  D. 'Gran's Favourite' □ 36, 76
  D. 'Haytor White' 76
  D. 'Kesteven Kirkstead' 76
  D. 'La Bourboule' □ 56
  D. 'Lincolnshire Poacher' 76
  D. 'Monica Wyatt' 76
  D. 'Mrs Sinkins' 76
  D. 'Musgrave's Pink' 76
  D. 'Old Mother Hubbard' 76
  D. 'Pike's Pink' 38
Diascia 'Lilac Mist' 63
  D. rigescens □ 38
Dicentra eximea 'Spring Morning' 48
  D. formosa □ 42
  D. 'Langtrees' 42, □ 72
  D. 'Luxuriant' 42

D. spectabilis f. *alba* 63
  D. torulosa 106
Dicksonia antarctica □ 64
Dictamnus albus var. *purpureus* □ 39
Dierama pulcherrimum 18, □ 81
Digitalis Excelsior Hybrids 23
  D. x *mertonensis* □ 24
  D. purpurea □ 90
  D. purpurea 'Heywoodii' 23
  D. purpurea 'Sutton's Apricot' □ 22
Dill □ 88
Dimorphotheca barberiae,
  see *Osteospermum jucundum* □ 51
Dipelta floribunda 127, 158, 168
Diplacus glutinosus,
  see *Mimulus aurantiacus* □ 145
Dipsacus fullonum 88
Disanthus cercidifolius □ 156
Dog Laurel □ 170
Dog's Tooth Violet □ 78
Dogwood □ 168, □ 198
  Creeping □ 118
  Flowering □ 201
  Golden-leaved □ 150
  Pacific □ 204
  Silver Variegated □ 148
  Variegated Pagoda □ 200
  Westonbirt □ 168
Dorycnium hirsutum □ 128, 152
Double Almond □ 213
Double Gean □ 199
Double Horse Chestnut □ 202
Dragon's Claw Willow □ 227
Dregea sinensis 95, 105
Drimys lanceolata 160
  D. winteri 216
dry areas
  bulbs 40
  conifers 184–5
  perennials 38–9, 42–3
  shrubs 130–1
  trees 208–9
Dryas octopetala □ 55
Dryopteris affinis □ 53, 90
  D. borreri, see *D. affinis* □ 53, 90
  D. dilatata 53
  D. erythrosora 45
  D. filix-mas 53
Dutch Honeysuckle, Late □ 105
Dwarf Cedar □ 188

Dwarf Comfrey ▣ 31
dwarf conifers 188–9
Dwarf Cypress ▣ 188
Dwarf Fir ▣ 188
Dwarf Juniper ▣ 189
Dwarf Pampas Grass ▣ 85
Dwarf Pine ▣ 189
Dwarf Pomegranate ▣ 143
Dwarf Red Cedar ▣ 189
Dwarf Russian Almond ▣ 127
Dwarf Spruce ▣ 189
Dwarf White-striped Bamboo ▣ 69

E

Eastern Hemlock ▣ 181
Eccremocarpus scaber ▣ 106
Echinacea purpurea 'Robert Bloom' 21
Echinops ritro 'Veitch's Blue' ▣ 39, 48
 E. sphaerocephalus ▣ 16
Echium vulgare 'Blue Bedder' ▣ 89
Edelweiss ▣ 56
Edgeworthia chrysantha 98, 159
Edging Box ▣ 170
Eglantine ▣ 169
Elaeagnus angustifolia 138
 E. x *ebbingei* ▣ 141
 E. x *ebbingei* 'Gilt Edge' 136, ▣ 149
 E. macrophylla 140, 146, 152, 159
 E. multiflora 162
 E. pungens 'Maculata' ▣ 146
 E. 'Quicksilver' 110, 152, 158, ▣ 220
Elder, Purple-leaf ▣ 155
Elderberry ▣ 163
Elaeagnus angustifolia var. *caspica*,
 see *Elaeagnus* 'Quicksilver' ▣ 220
Elephant's Ear ▣ 66, ▣ 90
Elm, Caucasian ▣ 197
Elsholtzia stauntonii ▣ 160
Embothrium coccineum 205
English Oak ▣ 203
Enkianthus campanulatus 125
 E. cernuus var. *rubens* ▣ 124

E. perulatus 125, 156
Eomecon chionantha 31, 44
Epigaea gaultherioides 34
Epimedium acuminatum 44
 E. davidii 44
 E. x *perralchicum* 32, ▣ 42, 90
 E. perralderianum 43
 E. pinnatum subsp. *colchicum* 43
 E. pubigerum 43
 E. x *rubrum* 75, ▣ 90
 E. x *versicolor* 'Sulphureum' 24
Eranthis cilicica 84
 E. 'Guinea Gold' 84
 E. hyemalis 41, ▣ 60, 84
 E. x *tubergenii* ▣ 84
Erect Clematis ▣ 74
Eremurus himalaicus ▣ 16
Erica arborea 'Albert's Gold' ▣ 150
 E. arborea var. *alpina* ▣ 159
 E. australis 'Riverslea' 125
 E. carnea 'Myretoun Ruby' 166
 E. carnea 'Springwood White' ▣ 166
 E. cinerea 'C.D. Eason' ▣ 125
 E. x *darleyensis* 'Kramer's Rote' 166
 E. x *darleyensis* 'Silberschmelze' 166
 E. erigena 'Golden Lady' 151
 E. terminalis 117
 E. vagans 'Valerie Proudley' 151
 E. x *veitchii* 'Exeter' 159
ericas 172
Erigeron glaucus ▣ 50
 E. karvinskianus 54
Erinacea anthyllis 38
Erinus alpinus ▣ 55
Eriobotrya japonica ▣ 111
Erodium reichardii 57
Eruca sativa,
 see *E. vesicaria* subsp. *sativa* ▣ 89
 E. vesicaria subsp. *sativa* ▣ 89
Eryngium alpinum ▣ 39
 E. bourgatii 24, ▣ 36
 E. decaisneanum 18
 E. eburneum 17, 18, 67
 E. giganteum 'Silver Ghost' ▣ 23
 E. maritimum 88
 E. x *oliverianum* ▣ 51
 E. pandanifolium 67
 E. tripartitum 50
Eryngo, Alpine ▣ 39
Erysimum 'Bowles Mauve' ▣ 24
 E. cheiri 'Fire King', see *Cheiranthus*
  cheiri 'Fire King' ▣ 26
 E. cheiri 'Harpur Crew', see *Cheiranthus*
  'Harpur Crew' ▣ 76
Erythrina crista-galli ▣ 130
Erythronium californicum
 'White Beauty' 79
 E. dens-canis ▣ 78
 E. hendersonii ▣ 41
 E. oregonum 60
 E. 'Pagoda' ▣ 79
 E. revolutum 79
Escallonia 'Apple Blossom' ▣ 138
 E. 'Donard Seedling' ▣ 164
 E. 'Edinensis' 165

E. 'Iveyi' 126
E. laevis 160
E. laevis 'Gold Brian' 151
E. laevis 'Gold Ellen' 151
E. 'Langleyensis' ▣ 122, 165
E. rubra 'Crimson Spire' 123, 140
E. rubra var. *macrantha* 140
Eschscholzia californica ▣ 26
Eucalyptus coccifera 220
 E. dalrympleana ▣ 208
 E. glaucescens 203, 216, 220
 E. gunnii 197, 220
 E. niphophila, see *E. pauciflora*
  subsp. *niphophila* ▣ 201, ▣ 226
 E. pauciflora subsp. *niphophila*
  ▣ 201, ▣ 226
 E. perriniana ▣ 220
 E. urnigera 160
Eucomis bicolor 62, 83
 E. comosa ▣ 40, 81
Eucryphia glutinosa ▣ 201, 205
 E. x *nymansensis* ▣ 204
 E. pinnatifolia,
  see *E. glutinosa* ▣ 201, 205
Euonymus alatus ▣ 157, 168
 E. europaeus 'Red Cascade' 161
 E. fortunei 'Coloratus' 107
 E. fortunei 'Emerald Gaiety' 101,
  ▣ 118, ▣ 132, 136
 E. fortunei 'Emerald 'n' Gold' ▣ 118
 E. fortunei 'Silver Queen' ▣ 100, 149
 E. fortunei 'Vegetus' ▣ 132
 E. hamiltonianus var. *sieboldianus*
  'Red Elf' ▣ 161
 E. japonicus 140
 E. japonicus 'Latifolius
  Albomarginatus' 149
 E. japonicus 'Ovatus Aureus' 151
 E. obvatus 132
 E. phellomanus 168
Eupatorium maculatum
 'Atropurpureum' 33
 E. purpureum ▣ 16
Euphorbia amygdaloides 'Purpurea',
 see *E. amygdaloides* 'Rubra' ▣ 74
 E. amygdaloides subsp. *robbiae* 30, ▣ 53
 E. amygdaloides 'Rubra' ▣ 74
 E. characias 'Lambrook Gold' 18
 E. characias subsp. *wulfenii* ▣ 14, ▣ 130
 E. cyparissias 28
 E. dulcis 'Chameleon' ▣ 74
 E. epithymoides, see *E. polychroma* ▣ 25
 E. griffithii 'Dixter' 20
 E. marginata 27
 E. x *martinii* 67
 E. mellifera 159
 E. myrsinites 28, ▣ 36
 E. nicaeensis 37
 E. palustre , see *E. palustris* ▣ 46
 E. palustris ▣ 46
 E. polychroma ▣ 25
Eurya japonica 'Winter Wine' 157
Euryops acreus ▣ 142, 152
 E. hybridus, see *E. pectinatus* ▣ 130
 E. pectinatus ▣ 130

Evening Primrose 39
Evergreen Azalea 125
Evergreen Euonymus 118, 132
Evergreen Laburnum 101
evergreen plants 10–1
    air pollution tolerant 136
    alkaline soils 126
    autumn colour 157
    clay soils 123
    climbers 97, 104
    coastal exposure 139
    conifers 182
    golden leaves 151
    ground cover 118
    ornamental fruit 160
    perennials 66–5, 86
    purple, red, or bronze leaves 75, 155
    shade tolerant 133
    shrubs 108, 146–7
    silver or blue-grey leaves 152
    small 117
    sunless walls 101
    sunny walls 99
    trees 194, 216
    variegated 149
Everlasting, Pearly 48
Exbury Azalea 170
Exochorda x *macrantha* 'The Bride' 114

F

Fabiana imbricata 'Violacea' 131
Fagus sylvatica 141, 204, 215
    F. sylvatica 'Aspleniifolia' 196
    F. sylvatica 'Dawyck Purple' 229
    F. sylvatica 'Pendula' 211
    F. sylvatica f. *purpurea* 221
    F. sylvatica 'Roseomarginata' 221
Fairy Foxglove 55
Fairy's Thimbles 54
Fallopia baldschuanica, see *Polygonum baldschuanicum* 103
False Acacia 213
False Holly, Variegated 149
False Indigo 20
False Spikenard 35
Fargesia nitida 19
    F. spathacea 19
Fascicularia pitcairniifolia 50
x *Fatshedera lizei* 144
Fatsia japonica 111, 133, 146
Feathertop, Abyssinian 37
Feijoa sellowiana 99
Felicia amelloides 'Santa Anita' 144
fences, climbers for 94–101
Fennel 87
    Purple-leaved 74
Fern, Australian Tree 64
    Christmas 45
    Golden Male 53
    Hart's Tongue 44
    Northern Maidenhair 34
    Soft Shield 67
    Sword 45
Fern-leaved Beech 196

ferns for hedge bottoms 53
Ferula tingitana 18
Ficus pumila 95, 107
Figwort, Variegated Water 69
Filbert, Purple-leaf 154
Filipendula kamtschatica 18
    F. purpurea 18, 46,
    F. rubra 17
    F. ulmaria 'Aurea' 70
Fir
    Causican 174
    China 180
    Colorado White 193
    Dwarf 188
    Firethorn 101
    Korean 180
Firethorn 165, 169
Fitzroya cupressoides 180
    F. patagonica,
    see *F. cupressoides* 180
Five-spot 27
Flax 39
    Common 89
    Mountain 65, 66
    New Zealand 85
    Tree 143
Floribunda Rose 112
Flower of Jove 72
Flowering Currant 137, 151
Flowering Dogwood 201
flowering plants
    climbers for training into trees 103
    containers 62–3
    medium-sized flowering trees 198
    perennials 20, 24, 76–7
    scented flowers 76–7, 105, 158–9
    shrubs for butterflies 164–5
    winter-flowering 166–7
Fly Honeysuckle 163
Foam Flower 31
Foeniculum vulgare 87
    F. vulgare 'Purpureum' 74, 86
foliage 9
    aromatic leaves 160
    autumn colours 156–7
    bold-leaves 111, 217
    climbers for training into trees 102
    container plants 64–5
    evergreen perennials 64–5
    golden or yellow-leaves 68–71, 150–1, 192, 219
    medium-sized trees 199
    shrubs 108
    silver or blue-grey leaves 72–3, 152–3, 193, 220
    purple, red, or bronze leaves 74–5, 154–5, 221
    variegated leaves 66–7, 148–9, 191, 218
Forsythia 12
    F. x *intermedia* 'Lynwood' 127, 136
    F. suspensa 100
Forsythia, Weeping 100
Fothergilla gardenii 125, 157
    F. major 156

Foxglove 22, 24
    Fairy 55
Foxtail Lily 16
fragrant plants, see scented plants
Francoa sonchifolia 63
Fraser's Magnolia 204
Fraxinus americana 197
    F. angustifolia 212
    F. angustifolia 'Raywood' 223
    F. excelsior 'Allgold' 227
    F. excelsior 'Westhof's Glorie' 215
    F. mariessi 201, 206
    F. ornus 198, 207
    F. velutina 209
Fremontodendron 'California Glory' 99, 130
Fringe Cups 43
    Purple-leaved 75
Fringe Tree 110
Fritillaria imperialis 40, 79
    F. meleagris 61
    F. pallidiflora 59, 79
    F. pyrenaicum 79
Fritillary 79
    Snake's Head 61
fruit
    roses 112
    shrubs 161
    trees 224–5
Fuchsia 'Celia Smedley' 144
    F. 'Gennii' 150
    F. 'Golden Marinka' 151
    F. magellanica 138
    F. magellanica 'Riccortonii' 141
    F. magellanica 'Sharpitor' 148
    F. 'Mrs Popple' 117
    F. 'Riccortonii', see *F. magellanica* 'Riccortonii' 141
    F. 'Thalia' 145
    F. 'Tom Thumb' 170
Full Moon Maple, Golden 219

G

Galanthus 'Atkinsii' ▢ 84
  G. caucasicus 61
  G. elwesii 60, 84
  G. ikariae 84
  G. nivalis 'Flore Pleno' 41, 60, ▢ 84
  G. plicatus 41, 60
  G. plicatus subsp. *byzantinus* 84
  G. reginae-olgae 83
Galax aphylla 75
  G. urceolata 34, 43
Galega orientalis ▢ 20
Galium odoratum ▢ 30
Gallica Rose ▢ 112, ▢ 120
Galtonia candicans ▢ 81
  G. viridiflora 81
Garrya elliptica ▢ 100
  G. elliptica 'James Roof' 166
  G. x *issaquahensis*
    'Glasnevin Wine' 101
Gaultheria mucronata
    'Bell's Seedling' 163
  G. mucronata
    'Mulberry Wine' ▢ 170
  G. mucronata 'Pink Pearl' 163
  G. mucronata 'Wintertime' ▢ 161
  G. procumbens ▢ 108, 118, 160
  G. shallon 147, 163
Gean, Double ▢ 199
Genista aetnensis 110, 209
  G. lydia ▢ 142
  G. sagittalis 143
  G. tenera 'Golden Shower' 128, 158
Gentian ▢ 34
  Willow ▢ 46
  Yellow ▢ 87
Gentiana asclepiadea ▢ 46
  G. lutea 20, ▢ 87
  G. x *macaulayi*
    'Edinburgh' 34

G. x *macaulayi* 'Wellsii', see *Gentiana*
  x *macaulayi* 'Well's Variety' ▢ 34
G. x *macaulayi* 'Well's Variety' ▢ 34
G. sino-ornata 34
G. verna ▢ 56
Geranium cinereum 'Ballerina' 57
  G. cinereum var. *subcaulescens* ▢ 56
  G. endressii 43
  G. endressii 'Wargrave Pink' ▢ 28
  G. grandiflorum,
    see *G. himalayense* ▢ 48
  G. himalayense ▢ 48
  G. 'Johnson's Blue' ▢ 25
  G. macrorrhizum ▢ 42, 48
  G. macrorrhizum 'Album' 42
  G. macrorrhizum
    'Ingwersen's Variety' 31, 32
  G. x *monacense* 'Muldoon' 42
  G. nodosum ▢ 42
  G. palmatum 67
  G. phaeum 42
  G. pratense 'Plenum Violaceum' ▢ 36
  G. psilostemon ▢ 20
  G. sanguineum ▢ 91
  G. sanguineum var. *striatum* ▢ 28
Geum 'Borisii' ▢ 48
Ghent Azalea ▢ 125
Giant Bellflower ▢ 52
Giant Himalayan Lily ▢ 85
Giant Oat ▢ 19
Gillenia trifoliata 21
Ginger Lily ▢ 19
Ginkgo 172
  G. biloba ▢ 174, 183
Gladiolus byzantinus, see *G. communis*
  subsp. *byzantinus* 40, ▢ 61, 81
  G. communis subsp. *byzantinus*
    40, ▢ 61, 81
  G. papilio ▢ 83
  G. purpureoauratus, see *G. papilio* ▢ 83
Gladwin ▢ 43
Glaucidium palmatum 44
  G. palmatum var. *leucanthum* 44
Glechoma hederacea 'Variegata' ▢ 29
Gleditsia triacanthos 'Sunburst' ▢ 208
Globe Thistle ▢ 16, ▢ 39
Globeflower ▢ 47, ▢ 91
Globularia cordifolia 28
Glory Flower, Chilean ▢ 106
Glory Tree ▢ 110
Goat's Beard ▢ 16
Gold Dust ▢ 54
Gold Lonicera, Baggesen's ▢ 151
Golden Acacia ▢ 219
Golden Bell Forsythia ▢ 136
Golden Elder ▢ 171
Golden Flowering Currant ▢ 151
golden foliage
  conifers 192
  perennials 68–9
  shrubs 150–1
  trees 219
Golden Full Moon Maple ▢ 219
Golden Guelder Rose ▢ 151
Golden Hop ▢ 92, ▢ 97

Golden Hop Tree ▢ 219
Golden Indian-bean Tree ▢ 219
Golden Ivy ▢ 104
Golden Japanese Sedge Grass ▢ 70
Golden-leaved Dogwood ▢ 150
Golden Lemon Balm ▢ 70
Golden Male Fern ▢ 53
Golden Marguerite ▢ 38
Golden Marjoram ▢ 71
Golden Meadow Sweet ▢ 70
Golden Mock Orange ▢ 151
Golden Moneywort ▢ 70
Golden Mossy Saxifrage ▢ 71
Golden Oat ▢ 19
Golden Pfitzer Juniper ▢ 176
Golden Privet, Vicary Gibbs ▢ 151
Golden-rain Tree ▢ 207
Golden-rayed Lily ▢ 81
Golden Red Oak ▢ 219
Golden Rod ▢ 33, ▢ 49
Golden Scots Pine ▢ 192
Golden-twigged Dogwood ▢ 168
Golden Weeping Willow ▢ 210
Golden Yew ▢ 183
Granny's Bonnet ▢ 52
Grape Hyacinth ▢ 59
Grass
  Chinese Silver ▢ 85
  Dwarf Pampass ▢ 85
  Golden Japanese Sedge ▢ 70
  Pampas ▢ 18
  Squirrel-tail ▢ 39
grasses, tall 17
Greater Celandine ▢ 52
Greek Mallow ▢ 21
Greek Windflower ▢ 58, ▢ 78
Green Alkanet ▢ 53
Grevillea 'Canberra Gem' ▢ 129, 130
  G. juniperina f. *sulphurea* 125, 130
Grey Alder ▢ 202
grey foliage
  conifers 193
  perennials 70–1
  shrubs 152–3
  trees 220
Grindelia chiloensis ▢ 131
Griselinia littoralis ▢ 141
ground cover plants
  conifers 190
  perennials 28–9, 30–1
  shrubs 118–9, 121, 147
Ground Cover Rose ▢ 121
Ground Elder, Variegated ▢ 30
Ground Ivy, Variegated ▢ 29
Guava, Pineapple ▢ 99
Guelder Rose ▢ 135, ▢ 163
  Golden ▢ 151
Gum
  Mountain ▢ 208
  Snow ▢ 201, ▢ 227
  Spinning ▢ 220
  Sweet ▢ 223
Gum Cistus ▢ 160
Gunnera manicata ▢ 19, 47
  G. tinctoria 64

Gypsophila cerastioides 57
   G. elegans □ 26
   G. paniculata 'Bristol Fairy' □ 39
   G. paniculata 'Rosenschleier' 37
   G. repens 28

H

Hakonechloa macra 'Aureola' 69, 70
   H. macra 'Alboaurea' 25
x *Halimiocistus sahucii* □ 118
Halimodendron halimifolium 138
   H. halodendron 128
Halimum ocymoides 'Susan' 117
Hamamelis x *intermedia* 'Copper Beauty',
   see *H.* x *intermedia* 'Jelena' □ 166
   H. x *intermedia* 'Jelena' □ 166
   H. mollis 'Pallida' 166
   H. vernalis 134
   H. vernalis 'Sandra' □ 157
Handsworth Box □ 140
Haquetia epipactis 44
hardy autumn bulbs 83
Hardy Cyclamen □ 41, □ 60, □ 83, □ 84
hardy perennials for containers 62–5
Hardy Plumbago □ 116
Hare's-ear, Shrubby □ 138
Hart's Tongue Fern □ 44
Hawthorn □ 162
Hazel, Corkscrew □ 168
Headache Tree □ 209
Heath
   St. Dabeoc's □ 124
   Tree □ 150, □ 159
   Winter □ 166, □ 164
Heather □ 124, □ 150, □ 152, □ 164
   Bell □ 125
heathers □ 172
heavy soils, see clay soils
Hebe albicans □ 164
   H. 'Amy' □ 155
   H. cupressoides 'Boughton Dome' □ 142
   H. x *franciscana* 'Blue Gem' □ 139, 140
   H. pimeleoides 'Quicksilver' □ 152
   H. recurva □ 117
Hedera canariensis
   'Gloire de Marengo' 104, 107
   H. colchica □ 102, 107
   H. colchica 'Dentata Variegata'
     □ 92, □ 96
   H. colchica 'Paddy's Pride',
     see *H. colchica* 'Sulphur Heart'
     □ 96, 104, 107
   H. colchica 'Sulphur heart'
     □ 96, 104, 107
   H. helix 'Arborescens' 163, □ 164
   H. helix 'Buttercup' □ 104
   H. helix 'Cavendishii' 107
   H. helix 'Eva' □ 97
   H. helix 'Glacier' □ 119
   H. helix 'Goldheart' □ 107
   H. helix 'Green Ripple' □ 97
   H. helix 'Ivalace' □ 119
   H. helix 'Minigreen',
     see *H. helix* 'Ivalace' □ 119

   H. helix 'Poetica Arborea' 117
   H. helix 'Pedata' 107
   H. nepalensis 107
   H. pastuchovii 97
hedge bottoms, perennials for 52–3
Hedgehog Holly, Silver □ 149
hedges 140–1, 186–7
Hedychium densiflorum □ 19
   H. gardnerianum 62
Helenium 'Moerheim Beauty' □ 33
Helianthemum apenninum 'Roseum' 143
   H. 'Fire Dragon' □ 143
   H. 'Wisley Pink' □ 29
   H. 'Wisley Primrose' □ 39
Helianthus annuus □ 89
   H. annuus 'Taiyo' 22
   H. x *multiflorus* □ 17
   H. x *multiflorus* 'Loddon Gold' □ 17
Helichrysum italicum □ 153, 160
   H. 'Schweffellicht' □ 25
   H. selago 142
   H. 'Sulphur Light',
     see *H.* 'Schweffellicht' □ 25
Heliopsis 'Ballet Dancer' □ 33
   H. 'Light of Loddon' □ 21
Hellebore
   Corsican □ 66
   Stinking □ 66
Helleborus argutifolius 24, □ 66
   H. foetidus 43, □ 66
   H. lividus subsp. *corsicus*,
     see *H. argutifolius* 24, □ 66
   H. orientalis □ 44, □ 91
   H. viridis 44
Hemerocallis flava,
   see *H. lilio-asphodelus* □ 76
   H. fulva 'Kwanzo Variegata' 68
   H. 'Golden Chimes' □ 21
   H. lilio-asphodelus □ 76
Hemlock
   Eastern □ 181
   Western □ 183
Herbaceous Clematis □ 76
herbaceous plants 10–1, 14
herbs 86–9
Hermodactylus tuberosus 40
Hesperis matronalis □ 77
Heuchera micrantha
   'Palace Purple' 25, □ 74
Hiba, Variegated □ 191
Hibiscus manihot 'Cream Cup' 22
   H. syriacus 'Blue Bird' □ 131
   H. syriacus 'Red Heart' □ 126
   H. syriacus 'Woodbridge' □ 129
Hick's Yew □ 187
Hickory, Shagbark □ 222
Highclere Holly □ 218, □ 224
Hill Cherry □ 199
Himalayan Honeysuckle □ 162
Himalayan Jasmine □ 101
Himalayan Lily, Giant □ 85
Himalayan May Apple □ 35
Himalayan Whitebeam □ 220
Hinoki Cypress □ 180
Hippocrepis comosa 28

Hippophae rhamnoides 152, □ 214
Hoheria lyallii 159
Holboellia coriacea 104
   H. latifolia 97, 104
Holly
   Blue □ 161
   Highclere □ 218, □ 224
   New Zealand □ 146
   Silver Hedgehog □ 149
   Silver-margined □ 141
   Van Tol's □ 162
   Variegated Silver □ 149
Hollyhock □ 22
Honesty
   Perennial □ 43
   Variegated □ 23
Honey Locust □ 208
Honeysuckle □ 92, □ 94
   Fly □ 163
   Himalayan □ 162
   Japanese □ 97
   Late Dutch □ 105
   Shrubby □ 133
   Winter □ 167
Hoop-petticoat Daffodil □ 84
Hop Tree, Golden □ 219
Hop, Golden □ 92, □ 96
Hordeum jubatum □ 39
Horse Chestnut
   Double □ 202
   Sunrise □ 198
Hosta 'Blue Angel' 72
   H. fortunei 'Aurea' 70
   H. fortunei 'Aureomarginata' □ 68
   H. fortunei 'Yellow Edge', see
     H. fortunei 'Auromarginata' □ 68
   H. 'Frances Williams' □ 46
   H. 'Golden Prayers' 70
   H. 'Gold Standard' 64, 69
   H. 'Hapsden Blue' □ 72
   H. 'Invincible' 76
   H. lancifolia 25
   H. 'Midas Touch' 70
   H. 'Piedmont Gold' 70
   H. plantaginea 'Grandiflora' □ 77
   H. plantaginea var. *japonica*,
     see *H. plantaginea* 'Grandiflora'
     □ 77
   H. 'Shade Fanfare' □ 30, 68

Hosta sieboldiana var. *elegans* 47, □ 65
 H. sieboldiana 'Frances Williams',
  see *H.* 'Frances Williams' □ 46
 H. sieboldiana 'Golden Sunburst' 70
 H. 'Sum and Substance' 64, 70
 H. 'Sun Power' 70
 H. 'Tall Boy' 20
 H. undulata var. *univittata* □ 68
 H. 'Wide Brim' 64
 H. 'Wogon Gold' 70
 H. 'Zounds' □ 70
Houseleeks 29
Houttuynia cordata 'Chamaeleon' 64
 H. cordata 'Flore Pleno' 32
Humulus lupulus 'Aureus' □ 97
Hungarian Oak □ 197
Hupeh Crab □ 199
Hyacinth
 Grape □ 59
 Summer □ 81
Hyacinthoides hispanica □ 41, 60
Hyacinthus orientalis 'Delft Blue' 78
 H. orientalis 'L'Innocence' 78
 H. orientalis 'Pink Pearl' 78
Hybrid Musk Rose □ 120
Hybrid Tea Rose □ 112
Hybrid Wingnut □ 197
Hydrangea anomala 107
 H. anomala subsp. *petiolaris* 96, □ 107
 H. arborescens 'Grandiflora' □ 122
 H. aspera □ 114
 H. involucrata 'Hortensis' 116
 H. macrophylla □ 108
 H. macrophylla 'Ayesha' 138
 H. macrophylla 'Generale Vicontessa
  de Vibraye' 132
 H. macrophylla 'Joseph Banks' 141
 H. macrophylla 'Lanarth White' □ 139
 H. macrophylla 'Lilacina' □ 114
 H. macrophylla 'Munster' 145
 H. macrophylla 'Veitchii' □ 132
 H. paniculata 127
 H. paniculata 'Pink Diamond' 110
 H. petiolaris, see *H. anomala*
  subsp. *petiolaris* 96, □ 107
 H. plicatum 'Mariesii' 110
 H. quercifolia □ 111
  H. sargentiana 111
  H. seemannii 107

H. serrata 'Bluebird' □ 133
 H. serratifolia 107
Hypericum androsaemum 132
 H. calycinum □ 119, 147
 H. empetrifolium var. *oliganthum* 143
 H. forrestii 171
 H. 'Hidcote' □ 136
 H. kouytchense □ 170
 H. lancasteri □ 8
 H. x *moserianum* 'Tricolor' 148
 H. olympicum 'Citrinum' 142
 H. penduliflorum,
  see *H. kouytchense* □ 170
Hypolepsis millfolium 45
Hyssop □ 87
Hyssopus officinalis □ 87

I

Iberis amara □ 26
Ice Plant □ 85
Idesia polycarpa 224
Ilex x *altaclarensis* 'Belgica Aurea' □ 212
 I. x *altaclarensis*
  'Camelliifolia Variegata' □ 218
 I. x *altaclarensis* 'Lawsoniana' □ 224
 I. x *altaclerensis* 'Silver Sentinel',
  see *I.* x *altaclarensis*
  'Belgica Aurea' □ 212
 I. x *altaclerensis* 'Wilsonii' 224
 I. aquifolium 140, 204
 I. aquifolium
  'Argentea Marginata' □ 141
 I. aquifolium 'Bacciflava' 224
 I. aquifolium
  'Ferox Argentea' □ 149
 I. aquifolium 'J.C. van Tol' □ 162
 I. aquifolium 'Pendulum' 211
 I. x *attenuata* 'Sunny Foster' 151
 I. cornuta 'Burfordii' 140
 I. crenana 'Convexa' 140
 I. crenata 'Golden Gem' 151
 I. x *koehneana* 203
 I. latifolia 216
 I. x *meserveae* 'Blue Princess' □ 161
Illicium anisatum □ 100, 160
Immortelle □ 27
Impatiens balsamina 22
Imperata cylindrica 'Rubra' 75
Incarvillea delavayi 24
Incense Cedar □ 191
Indian Bean Tree □ 202
 Golden □ 219
Indian Shot □ 62
Indigo, False □ 20
Indigofera ambylantha 128
 I. gerardiana, see *I. heterantha* □ 126
 I. heterantha 98, □ 126
Inula helenium 86
 I. hookeri 33, □ 77
 I. magnifica □ 19, 17
Ipheion uniflorum 'Froyle Mill' □ 79
 I. uniflorum 'Wisley Blue' 79
Ipomoea alba 106
 I. 'Heavenly Blue' □ 106

Iris 'Bold Print' □ 91
 I. 'Early Light' □ 77
 I. ensata 47
 I. foetidissima □ 43, 85
 I. graminea 76
 I. histrioides 'Major' 59
 I. innominata
  Pacific Coast Hybrids □ 34
 I. pallida 'Argentea Variegata' 68
 I. pallida var. *dalmatica* 72
 I. pallida 'Variegata' 69
 I. reticulata 'J.S. Dijt' □ 58
 I. sibirica 47, 90
 I. unguicularis 37, 76
 I. xiphium 'Dutch Iris' 81
Iris, Bearded □ 77, □ 91
Irish Juniper □ 179
Ironwood, Persian □ 223
Isatis tinctoria □ 89
Italian Alder □ 215
Italian Cypress □ 178
Itea ilicifolia □ 99, 126, 159
 I. virginica 'Henry's Garnet' 155
Ivy □ 97, □ 119
 Golden □ 104
 Persian □ 96
 Tree □ 164
 Variegated Ground □ 29
Ivy-leaved Pelargonium □ 63
Ixiolirion tataricum 40

J

Jacob's Ladder, Variegated □ 69
Japan Pepper □ 169
Japanese Anemone □ 52
 tolerant of air pollution 49
Japanese
 Barberry □ 156
 Big-leaf Magnolia □ 217
 Black Pine □ 183
 Camellia □ 124
 Cherry □ 229
 Crab □ 207
 Honeysuckle □ 97
 Laurel □ 146
 Maple □ 142, □ 154, □ 156,
  □ 200, □ 222
 Red Cedar □ 174
 Rowan □ 225
 Sedge Grass, Golden □ 70
 Snowbell □ 199
 Spurge □ 133
 Stewartia □ 205
 Wisteria, White □ 94
 Yew □ 185
Jasmine
 Confederate □ 104
 Himalayan □ 101
 Star □ 104
 Winter □ 101
Jasminum humile □ 101, 126
 J. humile 'Revolutum' 101
 J. nudiflorum □ 101
 J. officinale 'Affine' 95

J. officinale 'Argenteovariegatum' □ 105

J x *stephanense* 105

Jeffersonia diphylla 44

    J. dubia □ 44

Jeffrey Pine □ 175

Jerusalem Sage □ 33, □ 131

Joe Pye Weed □ 16

Judas Tree □ 206

Juglans microcarpa 209

    J. nigra 197, 217

Juniper □ 172, □ 176, □ 177, □ 179, □ 190

    Chinese □ 178

    Creeping □ 190

    Dwarf □ 189

    Golden Pfitzer □ 176

    Irish □ 179

    Syrian □ 184

    Temple □ 184

Juniperus chinensis 185

    J. chinensis 'Aurea' 178, 180, 185, 192

    J. chinensis 'Kaizuka' 177

    J. chinensis 'Kaizuka Variegata' □ 191

    J. chinensis 'Keteleeri' □ 178

    J. communis 'Compressa' 189

    J. communis 'Gold Cone' 192

    J. communis 'Green Carpet' □ 190

    J. communis 'Hibernica' □ 179

    J. communis 'Sentinel' 189

    J. davurica 'Expansa Variegata' □ 176

    J. deppeana 185

    J. drupacea □ 184

    J. horizontalis 'Blue Chip' 190

    J. horizontalis 'Jade River' 190

    J. horizontalis 'Plumosa' □ 190

    J. horizontalis 'Turquoise Spreader' 190

    J. x *media* 'Blaauw' 177

    J. x *media* 'Blue Cloud' □ 176

    J. x *media* 'Gold Coast' 177

    J. x *media* 'Old Gold' 177

    J. x *media* 'Pfitzeriana' 177

    J. x *media* 'Pfitzeriana Aurea' □ 176

    J. x *media* 'Pfitzeriana Compacta' 177

    J. x *media* 'Pfitzeriana Glauca' □ 176

    J. x *media* 'Plumosa Aurea' □ 176

    J. x *media* 'Sulphur Spray' 177

    J. oxycedrus 185

    J. procumbens 'Nana' □ 190

    J. rigida □ 184

    J. sabina 'Blue Danube' □ 193

    J. sabina var. *tamariscifolia* □ 177

    J. scopulorum 'Skyrocket' □ 179

    J. squamata 'Blue Carpet' □ 177

    J. squamata 'Blue Star' □ 189

    J. virginiana 'Blue Cloud' 177

    J. virginiana 'Canaertii' 174, 185

    J. virginiana 'Frosty Morn' 177

    J. virginiana 'Glauca' 178

    J. virginiana 'Grey Owl' □ 177

    J. virginiana 'Skyrocket', see *J. scopulorum* 'Skyrocket' □ 179

K

Kaffir Lily □ 25

Kalmia angustifolia f. *rubra* □ 170

    K. latifolia □ 125

    K. latifolia 'Ostbo Red' 125

Kalopanax pictus □ 217

Kansas Gay-feather □ 49

Karo, Variegated □ 209

Kashmir Cypress □ 180

Kashmir Rowan □ 225

Katsura □ 222

Kerria japonica 132

    K. japonica 'Pleniflora' □ 101, 122, 168

Kilmarnock Willow □ 211

Kirengeshoma koreana 34

    K. palmata □ 33, 34

Knaphill Azalea □ 145

Knautia macedonica 21

Kniphofia caulescens 50, 67

    K. northiae 67

    K. 'Percy's Pride' □ 21

    K. 'Prince Igor' 18

    K. rooperi 18

    K. 'Royal Standard' □ 51

    K. triangularis 91

Koelreuteria paniculata 198, □ 207, 209

Kohuhu □ 216

Kolkwitzia □ 12

    K. amabilis 'Pink Cloud' □ 126

Korean Arbor-vitae □ 183

Korean Chrysanthemum □ 20

Korean Fir □ 180

L

Lablab purpureus 106

+ *Laburnocytisus adamii* □ 203

Laburnum

    Adam's □ 203

    Evergreen □ 101

    Scotch □ 207

    Voss's □ 213

Laburnum alpinum □ 207

    L. waterei 'Vossii' □ 213

Lace-cap Hydrangea □ 114, □ 132, □ 133

Lady's Eardrops □ 138

Lagerstroemia indica 98

Lamb's Tongue □ 71, □ 73

Lamium galeobdolon 'Florentinum' □ 31

    L. galeobdolon 'Variegatum', see *L. galeobdolon* 'Florentinum' □ 31

    L. maculatum □ 43

    L. maculatum 'Album' 48

    L. maculatum 'Beacon Silver' 30

    L. maculatum 'Cannon's Gold' 71

    L. maculatum 'White Nancy' □ 91

Lantana camara □ 145

Lantern Tree □ 132

Lapageria rosea □ 97, 104

larch □ 172

Lardizabala biternata 97

Larix decidua 175, 183, 187

    L. x *eurolepis* 175

    L. kaempferi 175, 183, 187

    L. kaempferi 'Blue Rabbit' 175

    L. kaempferi 'Pendula' 177

    L. x *pendula* 175

Larkspur □ 22

Late Dutch Honeysuckle □ 105

Lathyrus latifolius □ 51

    L. odoratus 'Annabelle' 106

    L. odoratus 'Anniversary' 106

    L. odoratus 'Painted lady' 106

    L. odoratus 'White Supreme' 106

    L. odoratus 'World's Children' 106

    L. vernus 24

Laurel

    Cherry □ 133, □ 141, □ 147

    Dog □ 170

    Japanese □ 146

    Portugal □ 141, □ 147

    Sheep □ 170

    Spotted □ 148

    Spurge □ 132

    Variegated Cherry □ 163

Laurustinus □ 167

    Variegated □ 149

Lavandula angustifolia 'Hidcote' 140, □ 164

    L. 'Hidcote Giant' 160

    L. stoechas 165

Lavatera 'Barnsley' 114, □ 129

    L. cachemiriana □ 17

    L. cachemirica, see *L. cachemiriana* □ 17

    L. maritima 98

    L. olbia 'Rosea', see *L.* 'Rosea' □ 114

    L. 'Rosea' □ 114

Lavender □ 164

    Cotton □ 153

Lawson Cypress □ 178, □ 186

leaves, see foliage

Lemon Balm, Golden □ 70

Lemon Verbena □ 144

Lenten Rose □ 44, □ 91

Leontopodium alpinum □ 56

Leonurus sibiricus 22

INDEX

Leptospermum anigerum □ 153
 L. humifusum, see *L. rupestre* □ 119
 L. rupestre □ 119
 L. scoparium 'Red Damask' 125
Lespedeza thunbergii □ 129
Lesser Periwinkle □ 119
Leucanthemella serotina 17
Leucanthemum x *superbum* 'Esther Read' 48
Leucojum aestivum 41, 60
 L. autumnale 59, □ 83
Leucothoe 'Scarletta' 155
Levisticum officinale □ 87
Lewisia Cotyledon Hybrids □ 34
 L. 'George Henly' □ 55
Leycesteria formosa □ 162, 168
Leyland Cypress □ 186
 Variegated □ 191
Liatris spicata □ 49
 L. spicata 'Kobold' 24
Libocedrus chilensis,
 see *Austrocedrus chilensis* □ 178
Ligularia dentata 'Othello' 47, 75
 L. przewalskii □ 47
 L. stenocephala 'The Rocket' 33
Ligustrum lucidum 206, 209, 216
 L. lucidum 'Excelsum Superbum' 128
 L. ovalifolium 'Aureum' 151
 L. quihoui □ 165
 L. sinense □ 110, 165
 L. sinense 'Variegatum' 148
 L. 'Vicaryi' □ 151
Lilac □ 115, □ 137, □ 159, □ 165
 Persian □ 127
Lilium auratum var. *platyphyllum* □ 81
 L. candidum □ 40
 L. 'Enchantment' □ 81
 L. giganteum,
  see *Cardiocrinum giganteum* □ 85
 L. hansonii 61'
 L. martagon □ 61, 81
 L. pyrenaicum 60
 L. regale □ 9, 63, □ 81
 L. x *testaceum* 40

Lily □ 81
 African □ 50
 Belladonna □ 40
 Cape □ 80
 Day □ 21, □ 76
 Foxtail □ 16
 Giant Himalayan □ 85
 Ginger □ 19
 Golden-rayed □ 81
 Kaffir □ 25
 Madonna □ 40
 Martagon □ 61
 of the Valley □ 42
 Plantain □ 30, □ 46, □ 65, □ 68,
  □ 70, □ 72, □ 77
 Regal □ 81
 St. Bernard's □ 36
 Toad □ 45
 Trout □ 41
lime-free (acid) soils 10, 12
 perennials 34–5
 shrubs 124–5
 trees 204–5
limy soils, see alkaline soils
Linaria purpurea 'Canon J. Went' 21
Lindera benzoin □ 134
Ling □ 124, □ 150, □ 152, □ 164
Linnaea borealis 34
Linseed □ 89
Linum arboreum □ 143
 L. flavum 'Compactum' □ 39
 L. narbonense 37
 L. usitatissimum □ 89
Lippia citriodora,
 see *Aloysia triphylla* □ 144
Liquidambar styraciflua 205
 L. styraciflua 'Lane Roberts' □ 223
Liriodendron tulipfera □ 196
 L. tulipfera 'Aureomarginatum' □ 218
 L. tulipfera 'Fastigiatum'
  □ 194, 229
 Liriope muscari □ 43, 63
Lithodora diffusa 'Grace Ward' 34
 L. diffusa 'Heavenly Blue' □ 34
Lobelia 'Queen Victoria' □ 75
 L. siphilitica 47
Locust
 Black □ 213
 Honey □ 208
Lomatia myricoides 159
London Plane □ 213
Lonicera x *americana* □ 94
 L. caprifolium 105
 L. japonica 104
 L. japonica 'Halliana' □ 97
 L. ledebourii 137
 L. nitida 'Baggesen's Gold' □ 151
 L. nitida 'Red Tips' 155
 L. nitida 'Silver Beauty' 148
 L. periclymenum
  'Graham Thomas' 95, □ 103
 L. periclymenum 'Serotina' □ 105
 L. pileata □ 133
 L. x *purpusii* 'Winter Beauty' 101, □ 167
 L. xylosteum □ 163

Lonicera, Baggesen's Gold □ 151
Loosestrife □ 91
 Spotted □ 53
Loquat □ 111
Lotus berthelotii □ 62
 L. hirsutus,
  see *Dorycnium hirsutum* □ 128, 152
Lovage □ 87
Love-in-a-mist □ 27
Love-lies-bleeding □ 22
Luma □ 216
Lunaria annua var. *alba* 23
 L. annua 'Variegata' □ 23
 L. rediviva □ 43
Lupin □ 21
 Russell □ 49
Lupinus arboreus □ 139
 L. 'Inverewe Red' □ 21
 L. 'The Chatelaine' □ 49
Luzula nivea □ 35
 L. sylvatica 'Marginata' 30
Lychnis chalcedonica □ 49
 L. coronaria 90
 L. flos-jovis □ 72
Lycium babarum 138
Lyonothamnus floribundus
 subsp. *aspleniifolius* 205
Lysichiton americanum 47
Lysimachia clethroides 47, □ 91
 L. ephemerum 72
 L. nummularia 'Aurea' □ 70
 L. punctata □ 53
Lythrum salicaria 'The Beacon' 47
 L. virgatum 'The Rocket' □ 21

M

Maackia amurensis □ 209
Macedonian Pine □ 182
Macleaya cordata 'Flamingo' 72
 M. microcarpa
  'Kelway's Coral Plume' □ 17
Madonna Lily □ 40
Madrone □ 226
Magnolia acuminata 197
 M. delavayi 111
 M. fraseri □ 204
 M. grandiflora 216, 228
 M. 'Heaven Scent' 205
 M. hypoleuca 217
 M. liliiflora 'Nigra' □ 110
 M. x *loebneri* 'Leonard Messel' □ 198
 M. x *loebneri* 'Merrill' 198
 M. x *soulangeana* □ 203, 212
 M. stellata 'Waterlily' □ 123
 M. 'Susan' 122
 M. 'Wada's Memory' □ 198, 201
Mahonia aquifolium □ 163
 M. aquifolium 'Apollo' 145
 M. aquifolium 'Smaragd' □ 136
 M. lomariifolia 111
 M. x *media* 'Buckland'
  126, 146, □ 167, 171
 M. x *media* 'Lionel Fortescue' 110
 M. nervosa □ 133, 147, 157, 163

Maianthemum canadense 34
Maidenhair Fern, Northern ▣ 34
Maidenhair Tree ▣ 174
Maiten ▣ 216
Male Fern, Golden ▣ 53
Mallow,
    Greek ▣ 21
    Marsh ▣ 86
    Musk ▣ 49
    Tree ▣ 114, ▣ 129
Malope trifida 22
Maltese Cross ▣ 49
Malus 194
    M. baccata var. *mandschurica* 212, ▣ 228
    M. floribunda ▣ 207
    M. hupehensis ▣ 199, 203
    M. 'John Downie' ▣ 224
    M. 'Lizet' 221
    M. 'Professor Sprenger' ▣ 224
    M. 'Profusion' 212
    M. 'Red Sentinel'
        ▣ 194, 201, 206, ▣ 224
    M. x *robusta*, see *Malus*
        'Red Sentinel' ▣ 224
    M. sargentii 110
    M. transitoria 228
    M. tschonoskii 223
    M. x *zumi* 228
Malva moschata ▣ 49
Manchurian Bird Cherry ▣ 227
Manchurian Crab ▣ 228
Mandevilla laxa 105
    M. suaveolens 95
Manna Ash ▣ 207
Maple
    Chinese Paperbark ▣ 226
    Coral-bark ▣ 226
    Golden Full Moon ▣ 219
    Japanese ▣ 142, ▣ 154, ▣ 156,
        ▣ 200, ▣ 222
    Norway ▣ 215, ▣ 221
    Red ▣ 222, ▣ 229
    Rough-barked ▣ 200
    Sugar ▣ 229
    Silver ▣ 196
    Snake-bark ▣ 228
Marguerite ▣ 62
    Golden ▣ 38
Marjoram, Golden ▣ 71
Marsh Mallow ▣ 86
Martagon Lily ▣ 61
Masterwort ▣ 32, ▣ 48
Matilija ▣ 129
Matteuccia struthiopteris 85
Matthiola 'Giant Excelsior' 23
May Apple, Himalayan ▣ 35
Maytenus boaria ▣ 216
Meadow Sweet, Golden ▣ 70
Meconopsis betonicifolia ▣ 35
    M. cambrica ▣ 43
    M. chelidoniifolia 35, 44
    M. grandis 35
    M. x *sarsonii* 35
    M. x *sheldonii* 35
    M. villosa 35

medium-height plants 20–3, 114–15, 180–1
Meehania urticifolia 76
Melia azedarach 224
Melianthus major 65
Melica altissima 'Atropurpurea' 75
Meliosma veitchiorum 199, 217
Melissa officinalis 'All Gold' 70, 86
    M. officinalis 'Aurea' ▣ 70
Melittis melissophyllum ▣ 87
Mentha x *gentilis* 'Variegata' 32
    M. x *suaveolens* 'Variegata' ▣ 68, 86
Menziesia ciliicalyx 125
Merendera bulbocodium,
    see *M. montana* ▣ 83
    M. montana ▣ 83
Merry Bells ▣ 45
Mertensia pulmonarioides,
    see *M. virginica* ▣ 44
    M. virginica ▣ 44
Mespilus germanica 'Nottingham' 201
Mespilus, Snowy ▣ 222
Metasequoia glyptostroboides ▣ 172,
    174, ▣ 182
Meum athamanticum ▣ 87
Mexican Orange-blossom ▣ 150, ▣ 158
Mexican Pinyon ▣ 184
Michaelmas Daisy ▣ 32, ▣ 90
Microbiota decussata ▣ 190
Milium effusum 'Aureum' 70
Milk Thistle ▣ 89
Mimosa ▣ 158
Mimulus aurantiacus ▣ 145
    M. luteus ▣ 47
Miniature Daffodil ▣ 59
Miniature Iris ▣ 58
Miniature Roses 121
Mint Bush ▣ 160
    Round-leaved ▣ 145
Mint, Variegated Apple ▣ 68
Miscanthus sinensis 'Grosse Fontäne' 17
    M. sinensis 'Kleine Fontäne' ▣ 85
    M. sinensis 'Morning Light' 17
    M. sinensis 'Silberfeder' 17
    M. sinensis 'Variegata' 68
    M. sinensis 'Zebrinus' 17
Miss Willmott's Ghost ▣ 23
Mock Orange ▣ 115, ▣ 117, ▣ 123,
    ▣ 127, ▣ 137
    Golden ▣ 151
Modern Pink ▣ 76
Monarda 'Beauty of Cobham' 86
    M. 'Cambridge Scarlet' ▣ 33
    M. 'Croftway Pink' ▣ 77
    M. fistulosa ▣ 87
Moneywort, Golden ▣ 70
Monkey Puzzle ▣ 174
Monkshood ▣ 20
Montbretia ▣ 52, ▣ 80
Monterey Cypress ▣ 176, ▣ 184, ▣ 192
Monterey Pine ▣ 187
Mop-headed Hydrangea ▣ 108
Morning Glory ▣ 106
Moroccan Broom ▣ 98
Morus alba 'Pendula' 211
    M. nigra 206

Moss Rose
    Common ▣ 120
    Crested ▣ 120
Mossy Saxifrage, Golden ▣ 71
Mountain Ash 194, ▣ 214
Mountain Avens ▣ 55
Mountain Flax ▣ 65, ▣ 66
Mountain Gum ▣ 208
Mountain Pine ▣ 182
Mouse-tail Plant ▣ 44
Mrs Robb's Bonnet ▣ 53
Mullein ▣ 37, ▣ 73
multi-purpose trees 228
Musa acuminata 'Dwarf Cavendish' 65
    M. basjoo 65
Muscari armeniacum 40, 78
    M. aucheri ▣ 59
    M. latifolium 59
Musk Mallow ▣ 49
Musk Rose, Hybrid ▣ 120
Mustisia ilicifolia 95
Myrica cerifera 134
    M. gale ▣ 134, 160
Myrrhis odorata ▣ 53, 86
Myrtle, Bog ▣ 134
Myrtus communis 159, 160
    M. communis var. *tarentina* 140
    M. luma ▣ 216, 227

N

Nandina domestica 'Firepower' 157
    N. domestica 'Nana Purpurea' 155
Narcissus bulbocodium 59, 61
    N. bulbocodium subsp. *romieuxii*,
        see *N. romieuxii* ▣ 84
    N. cyclamineus 59, 84
    N. 'February Gold' ▣ 79, 84
    N. 'Kingscourt' ▣ 79
    N. 'Mount Hood' 78
    N. 'Peeping Tom' 61
    N. pseudonarcissus 60
    N. pseudonarcissus
        subsp. *obvallaris* ▣ 61
    N. romieuxii ▣ 84
    N. 'Spellbinder' 61, 78
Narrow-leaved Ash ▣ 212
Nasturtium ▣ 27
Nectaroscordum siculum
    subsp. *bulgaricum* ▣ 61
Neillia thibetica 114, ▣ 123, 134

Nemophila maculata ☐ 27
Nepeta x faassenii ☐ 91
    N. hederacea 'Variegata',
        see Glechoma hederacea
        'Variegata' ☐ 29
Nerine bowdenii ☐ 83
    N. bowdenii 'Pink Triumph' 83
Nerium oleander 144
Nettle Tree, Southern ☐ 208
New Zealand Daisy ☐ 34, ☐ 66
New Zealand Flax ☐ 85
New Zealand Holly ☐ 146
Nicotiana langsdorfii ☐ 23
    N. sylvestris ☐ 77
Nierembergia repens 57
Nigella damascena 'Persian Jewels' ☐ 27
    N. sativa 88
Nine-bark ☐ 134
Nootka Cypress, Variegated ☐ 191
Northern Maidenhair Fern ☐ 34
Norway Maple ☐ 215, ☐ 221
Norway Spruce ☐ 175, ☐ 190
Nothofagus dombeyi 205
    N. obliqua ☐ 197
    N. procera ☐ 204
Nutmeg, California ☐ 185
Nyssa sinensis ☐ 223
    N. sylvatica 205

O

Oak ☐ 13
    Algerian ☐ 209
    Cypress ☐ 229
    English ☐ 203
    Golden Red ☐ 219
    Hungarian ☐ 197
    Pin ☐ 197
    Red ☐ 205
    Variegated Turkey ☐ 218
Oak-leaved Hydrangea ☐ 111
Oat, Giant or Golden ☐ 19

Obedient Plant ☐ 51
Ocimum basilicum 'Purple Ruffles' 88
Oenothera biennis 88
    O. glaber 75
    O. odorata 50
    O. speciosa 'Rosea' ☐ 14, ☐ 39
Old-fashioned Pink ☐ 36
Olearia x haastii ☐ 137
    O. macrodonta 126, 140, ☐ 146
    O. x mollis 152
    O. nummulariifolia ☐ 139
    O. x scilloniensis,
        see O. x stellulata ☐ 131
    O. solandri 159
    O. stellulata ☐ 131
Oleaster ☐ 220
Omphalodes cappadocica
    'Cherry Ingram' ☐ 25
    O. linifolia 27
Onion, Ornamental ☐ 40, ☐ 58, ☐ 80
Onopordum acanthium 23, ☐ 73
    O. arabicum 23
Ophiopogon planiscapus
    'Nigrescens' ☐ 75
Opium Poppy ☐ 23
Orange Ball Tree ☐ 138
Orange-blossom, Mexican
    ☐ 150, ☐ 158
Oregon Grape ☐ 136, ☐ 163
Oriental Thorn ☐ 206
Origanum 'Kent Beauty' ☐ 57
    O. laevigatum ☐ 37
    O. majorana 88
    O. vulgare 'Aureum' ☐ 71
Ornamental Crab Apple ☐ 194
Ornamental Onion ☐ 40, ☐ 58, ☐ 80
Ornamental Pear ☐ 213
Ornamental Quince ☐ 100, ☐ 122
Ornamental Rhubarb ☐ 19
Ornamental Tobacco ☐ 23, ☐ 77
Ornithogalum balansae 59
    O. narbonense ☐ 81
    O. nutans ☐ 41, 60
    O. umbellatum 40
Osmanthus x burkwoodii
    123, 126, ☐ 159
    O. delavayi 127, 158
    O. heterophyllus 133
    O. heterophyllus 'Variegatus' ☐ 149
    O. x osmarea burkwoodii, see
        O. x burkwoodii 123, 126, ☐ 159
Osmunda regalis 18, 47
Osteospermum 'Buttermilk' ☐ 63
    O. jucundum ☐ 51
    O. 'Pink Whirls' 62
    O. 'Silver Sparkler' 62
Othonna cherifolia 28, ☐ 51
Othonopsis cheirifolia,
    see Othonna cheirifolia 28, ☐ 51
Ourisia macrophylla ☐ 45
Oxalis adenophylla ☐ 37, 57
Ox-eye, Yellow ☐ 24
Oxydendrum arboreum 198, ☐ 205, 224
Ozark Witch Hazel ☐ 157
Ozothamnus rosmarinifolius ☐ 147

P

Pachyphragma macrophyllum ☐ 43
Pachysandra terminalis ☐ 133
Pacific Dogwood ☐ 204
Paeonia 'Bowl of Beauty' ☐ 21, 90
    P. delavayi ☐ 115
    P. delavayi var. ludlowii ☐ 111, 114
    P. emodi 76
    P. lutea var. ludlowii, see
        P. delavayi var. ludlowii ☐ 111, 114
    P. mlokosewitschii 63
    P. officinalis 'Rubra Plena' 91
Pagoda Dogwood, Variegated ☐ 200
Pagoda Tree ☐ 209
Palm
    Chusan ☐ 217
    Windmill ☐ 217
Pampas Grass ☐ 18
    Dwarf ☐ 85
Pancratium illyricum 81
Papaver rhoeas Shirley Series ☐ 27
    P. somniferum ☐ 23
    P. somniferum
        Peony-flowered Series ☐ 23
Paperbark Maple, Chinese ☐ 228
Parahebe catarractae ☐ 143
Paris Daisy ☐ 62
Parrotia persica 199, ☐ 223
Parthenocissus henrayana 96, ☐ 107
    P. thomsonii 96
    P. tricuspidata 'Lowii' 95, 96, 107
    P. tricuspidata 'Robusta' 96
    P. tricuspidata 'Veitchii' ☐ 107
Partridge-berry ☐ 108
Pasque Flower ☐ 37
Passiflora caerulea ☐ 94
Passion Flower, Blue ☐ 94
Patagonian Cypress ☐ 180
patios, small shrubs for 116–7
Paul's Scarlet Thorn ☐ 212
Paulownia tomentosa 206
paving, perennials in 54–5
Pea, Perennial ☐ 51
Pear,
    Ornamental ☐ 213
    Weeping Willow-leaved ☐ 220
Pearly Everlasting ☐ 48
Pelargonium 'Bredon' ☐ 63
    P. 'Dolly Varden' ☐ 65
    P. 'Morwenna' 62
    P. 'Red Cascade' ☐ 63
    P. 'Royal Oak' ☐ 65
    P. tomentosum ☐ 65
Peltiphyllum peltatum ☐ 47, 64
    P. peltatum 'Namum' 32
Pennisetum villosum ☐ 37
Penstemon 'Apple Blossom' 24
    P. digitalis 'Husker's Red' ☐ 75
    P. 'Garnet' ☐ 21
    P. pinifolius 142
    P. serrulatus ☐ 143
Pentaglottis sempervirens ☐ 53
Peony ☐ 21
    Tree ☐ 111

Pepper Bush, Sweet ▣ 134
Pepper, Japan ▣ 169
Peppermint Geranium ▣ 65
Perennial Cornflower ▣ 48
Perennial Honesty ▣ 43
Perennial Pea ▣ 51
Perennial Phlox ▣ 68, ▣ 77
perennial plants10–1, 14
    air pollution tolerant 48–9
    alkaline soils 36–7
    bog gardens 46–7
    coastal exposure 50–1
    containers 62–5
    cool moist soils in shade 44–5
    decorative seed heads 85
    deer-proof 90
    evergreen leaves 64–5, 75
    golden or yellow leaves 68–71
    ground cover 28–31
    heavy clay soils 32–3
    hedge bottoms 52–3
    herbs 86–7
    lime-free soils 34–5
    medium height 20–1
    purple, red, or bronze leaves 74–5
    rabbit proof 90–1
    retaining walls and paving 54–5
    rock gardens and screes 56–7
    scented flowers 76–7
    shady areas 42–3
    silver or blue-grey leaves 72–3
    small 24–5
    specimen plants 18–9
    sunny areas 38–9
    tall 16–7
    variegated leaves 68–9
Perennial Sunflower ▣ 17
Perennial Wallflower ▣ 24, ▣ 76
Periwinkle
    Lesser ▣ 119
    Variegated Large ▣ 133
Pernettya 161, ▣ 170
Perovskia atriplicifolia 'Blue Spire' ▣ 153
Persian Ironwood ▣ 223
Persian Ivy ▣ 96
Persian Lilac ▣ 127
Persian Stone Cress ▣ 56
Persicaria affinis ▣ 29
    P. affinis 'Superba' 63
    P. amplexicaulis 'Firetail' 47
    P. bistorta 'Superba' 32, ▣ 47, 48
    P. campanulata 20, 47
    P. vacciniifolia 28, ▣ 55
    P. virginiana 25
Petasites fragrans 42, 76
Pfitzer Juniper, Golden ▣ 176
pH 10, see also alkaline and lime-free soils
Phacelia tanacetifolia 88
Phellodendron amurense 212
Philadelphus 'Beauclerk' ▣ 137
    P. 'Boule d'Argent' ▣ 127
    P. coronarius 'Aureus' ▣ 151
    P. coronarius 'Variegatus' ▣ 115
    P. 'Manteau d'Hermine' ▣ 117
    P. 'Virginal' ▣ 123

Philadelphus 'Belle Etoile' 114, 158
    P. 'Sybille' 158
Phillyrea latifolia 209, ▣ 214, 216
Phlomis fruticosa ▣ 131
    P. italica 117, ▣ 131
    P. russeliana 20, 37, 67, 85
Phlox adsurgens 'Red Buttes' 34
    P. adsurgens 'Wagon Wheel' ▣ 35
    P. bifida 57
    P. douglasii
        'Boothman's Variety' 28, ▣ 57
    P. 'Emerald Cushion' 54
    P. maculata 'Alpha' 76
    P. maculata 'Omega' 21, ▣ 77
    P. paniculata 'Harlequin' 20
    P. paniculata 'Norah Leigh' ▣ 68
    P. x *procumbens* 'Millstream' 34
    P. stolonifera 'Ariane' ▣ 35
    P. stolonifera 'Blue Ridge' 34
    P. subulata 'Marjory' 38
Phormium 'Bronze Baby' 75
    P. cookianum 50
    P. cookianum 'Cream Delight' ▣ 65
    P. cookianum 'Tricolor' 67
    P. cookianum 'Yellow Wave' ▣ 65
    P. 'Sundowner' ▣ 65
    P. tenax ▣ 85
    P. tenax 'Purpureum' 18, 7
    P. tenax 'Yellow Wave' 65, ▣ 66
Photinia davidiana ▣ 225
    P. x *fraseri* 'Red Robin' 110
    P. villosa 134, ▣ 228
Phuopsis stylosa ▣ 29
Phygelius x *rectus* 'Moonraker' ▣ 117
Phyllitis scolopendrium,
    see *Asplenium scolopendrium* 43, ▣ 44
Phyllostachys nigra 19
    P. nigra var. *henonis* ▣ 66
    P. viridiglaucescens ▣ 67
Physocarpus opulifolius
    'Dart's Gold' ▣ 134, 151
Physostegia virginiana subsp. *speciosa*
    'Variegata' 68
    P. virginiana 'Vivid' ▣ 51
Picea abies ▣ 175
    P. abies 'Cupressina' 174
    P. abies 'Gregoryana' 188
    P. abies 'Reflexa' ▣ 190
    P. abies 'Remontii' 189
    P. abies 'Repens' 190
    P. abies 'Tabuliformis' 177
    P. asperata ▣ 186
    P. bicolor 'Howell's Dwarf' 177
    P. breweriana ▣ 180
    P. engelmannii 'Glauca' 193
    P. glauca var. *albertiana* 'Conica' ▣ 189
    P. glauca var. *albertiana* 'Laurin' 189
    P. glauca 'Coerulea' ▣ 193
    P. likiangensis 182, 185
    P. omorika ▣ 179
    P. orientalis 'Skylands' 192
    P. pungens 'Fat Albert' 193
    P. pungens 'Koster' ▣ 193
    P. pungens 'Montgomery' ▣ 189
    P. pungens 'Procumbens' 190

    P. purpurea 182, 185
    P. sitchensis 175, 187
Pick-a-back Plant ▣ 31
Picrasma quassioides 205
Pieris 'Forest Flame' ▣ 125
    P. formosa var. *forresti*
        'Wakehurst' ▣ 110
    P. japonica ▣ 115
    P. japonica 'Little Heath'
        117, ▣ 145, 149
Pileostegia viburnoides 97, ▣ 104, 107
Pin Oak ▣ 197
Pine
    Aleppo ▣ 184
    Austrian ▣ 187
    Bishop ▣ 185
    Bosnian ▣ 182
    Bristlecone ▣ 181
    Chile ▣ 174
    Dwarf ▣ 189
    Golden Scots ▣ 192
    Japanese Black ▣ 183
    Jeffrey ▣ 175
    Macedonian ▣ 182
    Monterey ▣ 187
    Mountain ▣ 182
    Scots ▣ 179
    Scrub ▣ 185
    Stone ▣ 185
    Umbrella ▣ 185
    Virginia ▣ 185
    Weymouth ▣ 182
Pineapple Flower ▣ 40
Pineapple Guava ▣ 99
Pink Siris ▣ 206
Pink
    Alpine ▣ 56
    fragrant border 76
    Modern ▣ 76
    Old-fashioned ▣ 36
Pinus aristata ▣ 181, 182, 184
    P. armandii 184
    P. ayacahuite 175
    P. brutia 184
    P. bungeana 184
    P. cembra 187
    P. cembroides ▣ 184
    P. contorta 184, 187
    P. contorta 'Frisian Gold' 192
    P. contorta var. *latifolia* 187
    P. coulteri 182, 184

Pinus edulis 184
   P. halepensis □ 184
   P. x *holfordiana* 175
   P. jeffreyi 175
   P. leucodermis 182, 187
   P. leucodermis 'Schmidtii' □ 189
   P. mugo 'Mops' □ 182
   P. mugo 'Ophir' 188
   P. mugo 'Pal Maleter' 191
   P. muricata □ 185
   P. nigra 175, □ 187
   P. nigra subsp. *nigra*,
      see *P. nigra* 175, □ 187
   P. omorika □ 179
   P. parviflora 180
   P. parviflora 'Negishi' 189
   P. peuce □ 182
   P. pinaster 184
   P. pinea □ 185
   P. ponderosa 182
   P. pumila 'Glauca' 193
   P. radiata 175, □ 187
   P. x *schwerinii* 175
   P. strobus □ 182
   P. strobus 'Fastigiata' 174
   P. strobus 'Minima' 188
   P. strobus 'Prostrata' 177
   P. sylvestris 175, 184, 187
   P. sylvestris 'Aurea' 180, □ 192
   P. sylvestris 'Beuvronensis' 188
   P. sylvestris 'Bonna' 193
   P. sylvestris 'Fastigiata' □ 179
   P. sylvestris 'Moseri' 192
   P. thunbergii 183, 187
   P. virginiana □ 185
   P. wallichiana 175
   P. wallichiana 'Nana' 193
   P. wallichiana 'Umbraculifera' 188
   P. yunnanensis 184
Pinyon, Mexican □ 184
Piptanthus nepalensis □ 101
Pittosporum colensoi 140

P. crassifolium 140
P. crassifolium 'Variegatum' □ 209
P. 'Garnettii' 149
P. tenuifolium □ 216
P. tenuifolium 'Irene Paterson' 147
P. tenuifolium 'Tom Thumb' □ 155
P. tobira 159
Plane, London □ 213
Plantago major 'Rubrifolia' 75
Plantain Lily □ 30, □ 46, □ 65, □ 68,
   □ 70, □ 72
   Fragrant □ 77
Platanus acerifolia 197, 203, □ 213
   P. hispanica,
      see *P. acerifolia* 197, 203, □ 213
   P. orientalis 197
Platycodon grandiflorus 24, □ 37
Playstemon californicus 27
Pleioblastus auricomus 69, □ 71
   P. variegatus □ 69
   P. viridistriatus,
      see *P. auricomus* 69, □ 71
Plum, Purple-leaved □ 155, □ 221
Plumbago, Hardy □ 116
Podocarpus salignis □ 181
Podophyllum emodi, see *P. hexandrum* □ 35
   P. hexandrum □ 35
Polemonium caeruleum
   'Brise D'Anjou' □ 69
   P. reptans 'Lambrook Mauve' □ 33
polluted (air) areas
   perennials 48–9
   shrubs 136–7
   trees 212–13
Polygonatum multiflorum 42
Polygonum acrostichoides 45
   P. affine 'Donald Lowndes',
      see *Persicaria affinis*
      'Donald Lowndes' □ 29
   P. baldschuanicum □ 103
   P. bistorta 'Superbum', see
      Persicaria bistorta 'Superba'
      32, □ 47, 48
   P. vacciniifolium,
      see *Persicaria vacciniifolia* 28, □
Polystichum munitum 43, □ 45, 67
   P. setiferum 53
   P. setiferum 'Divisilobum' 45, □ 67
Pomegranate, Dwarf □ 143
   Pond Cypress □ 181
   Poplar □ 203
      Tulip □ 196
      White □ 214
Poppy
   Blue □ 35
   California □ 26, □ 129
   Opium □ 23
   Shirley □ 27
   Welsh □ 43
Populus alba 204, □ 214, 220
   P. alba 'Raket' 220, 229
   P. alba 'Richardii' 210
   P. x *canadensis* 'Robusta' 214
   P. x *candicans* 'Aurora' 218
   P. canescens 204

P. maximowiczii □ 203, 210
P. nigra 'Italica' 215
P. 'Robusta' 212, 215
Portugal Laurel □ 141, □ 147
Potentilla □ 12
   P. 'Abbotswood' □ 117
   P. alba 28
   P. 'Elizabeth' □ 123, 128
   P. fruticosa var. *mandshurica*
      'Manchu' □ 129
   P. 'Gibson's Scarlet' 48
Prickly Castor Oil Tree □ 217
Pride of India □ 207
Primula florindae 47
   P. 'Garryarde Guinevere' 75
   P. pulverulenta □ 47
   P. veris □ 77
Privet □ 165
   Chinese □ 110
   Vicary Gibbs Golden □ 151
Prostanthera cuneata 117, □ 160
   P. rotundifolia □ 145
Provence Rose □ 113
Prunella grandiflora □ 25, 28
   P. grandiflora 'Loveliness' 33
Prunus 'Amanogawa' □ 229
   P. amygdalus 'Roseaplena',
      see *P. dulcis* 'Roseaplena' □ 213
   P. avium 'Plena' □ 199
   P. cerasifera 'Hessei' □ 155
   P. cerasifera 'Nigra' □ 221
   P. 'Cheal's Weeping' □ 211
   P. x *cistena* □ 155
   P. dulcis 'Roseaplena' □ 213
   P. glandulosa 'Alba Plena' 116, 122
   P. jamasakura □ 199
   P. 'Kursar' 201
   P. laurocerasus 162
   P. laurocerasus 'Magnoliifolia' 111
   P. laurocerasus 'Marbled White'
      149, □ 163
   P. laurocerasus 'Otto Luyken'
      □ 133, 145, 171
   P. laurocerasus 'Rotundifolia' □ 141
   P. laurocerasus 'Zabeliana' □ 147
   P. lusitanica □ 141, 216
   P. lusitanica subsp. *azorica* □ 147
   P. maackii 226
   P. 'Mount Fuji' 206
   P. mume 'Alphandii' 98
   P. mume 'Beni-shidore' 98
   P. padus 'Watereri' 198, 203
   P. pendula 'Pendula Rubra' □ 211
   P. 'Pink Perfection' 212
   P. 'Pink Shell' 201
   P. pumila var. *depressa* 119
   P. sargentii 223, 228
   P. serotina □ 215
   P. serrula □ 226
   P. serrulata spontanea,
      see *P. jamasakura* □ 199
   P. 'Shogetsu' 206
   P. spinosa 141
   P. spinosa 'Purpurea' □ 155
   P. subhirtella 'Pendula Rubra', see

P. pendula 'Pendula Rubra'  211
P. tenella 127
P. tomentosa 168
P. 'Ukon' 206
P. virginiana 'Schubert' 221
P. x *yedoensis* 207
Pseudocydonia sinensis 228
Pseudolarix amabilis 180
Pseudotsuga menziesii 175
Ptelea trifoliata 'Aurea' 151, 219
Pterocarya fraxinifolia 210
P. x *rehderiana* 197
Pterostyrax hispida 198, 224
Pulmonaria officinalis 86
P. saccharata 33, 86, 91
P. saccharata 'Argentea' 25, 33
P. saccharata 'Leopard' 68
Pulsatilla vulgaris 37
Punica granatum var. *nana* 143
P. granatum 'Flore Pleno' 98
Purple Beech 221
Purple-bell Vine 106
purple foliage
perennials 74–5
shrubs 154–5
trees 221
Purple-leaf Elder 155
Purple-leaf Filbert 154
Purple-leaf Sand Cherry 155
Purple-leaf Sloe 155
Purple-leaved Bugle 74
Purple-leaved Clover 29
Purple-leaved Cow Parsley 74
Purple-leaved Fennel 74
Purple-leaved Fringe Cups 75
Purple-leaved Heuchera 74
Purple-leaved Plum 155, 221
Purple-leaved Sweet Spurge 74
Purple-leaved Wood Spurge 74
Purple Sage 75
Purple Vine 92
Purslane, Tree 138
Puschkinia scilloides 'Alba' 59
Pyracantha 'Mohave' 169
P. 'Orange Glow' 101, 123, 169
P. rogersiana 101
P. 'Watereri' 165
P. x *watereri*, see *P.* 'Watereri' 165
Pyrus calleryana 'Chanticleer' 213
P. nivalis 220
P. salicifolia 'Pendula' 211, 220
P. ussuriensis 198

Q

Quercus agrifolia 209
Q. canariensis 197, 209
Q. cerris 197, 204
Q. cerris 'Variegata' 199, 218
Q. frainetto 197
Q. ilex 212, 214, 216
Q. palustris 197, 203
Q. petraea 197
Q. petraea 'Columna' 229
Q. robur 197, 203, 204, 215

Q. robur f. *fastigiata* 229
Q. rubra 205
Q. rubra 'Aurea' 219
Q. suber 20
Quince, Ornamental 100, 122

R

rabbit-proof plants 90–1, 170–1
raised beds 58–9, 142–3
Ramanas Rose 141
Ramonda myconi 55
R. pyrenaica, see *R. myconi* 55
Ranunculus aconitifolius 24
Rauli 204
Red Alder 210
Red Cedar
Dwarf 189
Japanese 174
Western 187, 192
Red Chokeberry 134
red foliage, see purple foliage
Red-hot Poker 51
Red Maple 222, 229
Red Oak 205
Golden 219
Red Orache 88
Red Valerian 50
Redbud 221
Redwood 175
Dawn 182
Regal Lily 81
Regal Pelargonium 63
Reineckiea carnea 43
Reseda odorata 27
Reticulate Willow 143
Rhamnus alaternus 'Argenteovariegata' 149
R. imeritina 111
Rheum palmatum 'Atropurpureum' 75
R. palmatum 'Atrosanguineum' 19, 47
Rhodochyton atrosanguineum 106
R. volubile, see *R. atrosanguineum* 106
Rhododendron arboreum 216
R. barbatum 168
R. bureaui 146
R. campanulatum subsp. *aeruginosum* 152
R. cinnabarinum 160
R cinnabarinum Concatenans Group 152
R. 'Corneille' 156
R. dauricum 'Midwinter' 166
R. 'Dora Amarteis' 147
R. 'Exquisitum' 158, 171
R. 'Hinomayo' 125
R. 'Homebush' 125, 145
R. 'Hotspur' 125
R. 'Hydon Dawn' 145
R. 'Lady Alice Fitzwilliam' 159
R. luteum 159
R. 'May Day' 125
R. 'Mrs. G.W. Leak' 123

R. 'Narcissiflorum' 125
R. occidentale 122, 134
R. 'P.J. Mezitt' 125
R. schlippenbachii 125
R. 'Strawberry Ice' 170
R. 'Susan' 137
R. thomsonii 168
R. 'Vuyk's Scarlet' 145
R. yakushimanum 12, 117, 125
Rhodohypoxis baurii 'Margaret Rose' 57
Rhodotypos kerrioides, see *R. scandens* 135
R. scandens 132, 135
Rhubarb, Ornamental 19
Rhus glaba 111
R. x *pulvinata* 'Red Burgundy Lace' 111
R. trichocarpa 201
R. typhina 'Dissecta' 223
R. typhina 'Laciniata', see *R. typhina* 'Dissecta' 223
Ribes alpinum 'Aureum' 151
R. aureum, see *R. odoratum* 157, 158
R. laurifolium 101
R. odoratum 157, 158
R. sanguineum 'Brocklebankii' 151
R. sanguineum 'Pulborough Scarlet' 137
R. sanguineum 'White Icicle' 122
R. speciosum 98
Ricinus communis 'Impala' 65
River Birch 210
Roast-beef Plant 43
Robinia hispida 99
R. hispida 'Macrophylla' 128
R. pseudoacacia 213
R. pseudoacacia 'Frisia' 194, 199, 219
R. x *slavinii* 'Hillieri' 206
Roblé Beech 197
rock gardens 56–7, 58–9, 142–3, 188–9
Rock Rose 29, 39, 143
Rocket 89
Sweet 77
Rodgersia aesculifolia 19
R. pinnata 'Superba' 18, 20
R. podophylla 33, 47, 64

Romneya coulteri ▣ 129, 152, 171
Rosa 'Alba Maxima' 113
　R. 'Alba Semiplena' 113
　R. 'Albertine' ▣ 103
　R. 'Alexander' ▣ 112
　R. 'Anytime' 121
　R. 'Baby Gold Star' 121
　R. *banksiae* 'Lutea' 95
　R. 'Blanc Double de Coubert' 113
　R. *bracteata* 104
　R. 'Buff Beauty' ▣ 120
　R. 'Canary Bird',
　　see *R. xanthina* 'Canary Bird' ▣ 113
　R. *carolina* 120
　R. 'Cecile Brunner' 120
　R. x *centifolia* 'Cristata' ▣ 120
　R. x *centifolia* 'Muscosa' ▣ 120
　R. 'Chapeau de Napoleon', see
　　R. x *centifolia* 'Cristata' ▣ 120
　R. 'Chelsea Pensioner' 121
　R. 'Chianti' 120
　R. *chinensis* 'Mutabilis', see
　　R. x *odorata* 'Mutabilis' ▣ 99
　R. 'Complicata' ▣ 112
　R. 'Comte de Chambord' 120
　R. *damascena* 'Versicolor' 120
　R. *davidii* 112
　R. 'Dublin Bay' ▣ 91
　R. 'Dupontii' 113
　R. *eglantiera* 113, ▣ 169
　R. *fedtschenkoana* 152
　R. *filipes* 'Kiftsgate' ▣ 103
　R. 'Frühlingsgold' 112
　R. *gallica* var. *officinalis* ▣ 120
　R. *gallica* 'Versicolor' ▣ 120
　R. *glauca* 113, ▣ 153
　R. 'Grouse' ▣ 121
　R. 'Hillieri' 112
　R. 'Hokey Pokey' 121
　R. 'Iceberg' ▣ 112
　R. x *jacksonii* 'Max Graf', see
　　R. 'Max Graf' ▣ 121
　R. 'Jaques Cartier' 120
　R. 'Little Sir Echo' 121
　R. 'Little White Pet' 120
　R. 'Lutea Maxima' 120
　R. *macrantha* 121
　R. *macrophylla* 112
　R. *macrophylla* 'Master Hugh' 112
　R. 'Madame Hardy' 113
　R. 'Maigold' ▣ 92

R. 'Marguerite Hilling' ▣ 112
R. 'Max Graf' ▣ 121
R. 'Mme Gregoire Staechelin' ▣ 92
R. 'Mme Isaac Pereire' ▣ 112
R. *moyesii* 112
R. *moyesii* 'Geranium' ▣ 113
R. 'Nevada' ▣ 113
R. *nitida* 121
R. 'Nozomi' ▣ 121
R. x *odorata* 'Mutabilis' ▣ 99
R. 'Partridge' ▣ 121
R. 'Paulii' 121
R. 'Perle d'Or' 120
R. 'Petit Four' 121
R. 'Pheasant' 121
R. 'Pink Groptendorst' ▣ 113
R. 'Pink Wave' 121
R. x *polliniana* 121
R. *polyantha grandiflora* 105
R. 'Popcorn' 121
R. *prattii* 112
R. 'Robin Redbreast' 121
R. 'Rose de Rescht' 120
R. 'Roseraie de l'Hay' ▣ 113
R. 'Rosy Cushion' ▣ 171
R. 'Roulettii' 121
R. *roxburghii* 112
R. *rubifolia*, see *R. glauca* 113, ▣ 153
R. *rubiginosa*,
　see *R. eglantiera* 113, ▣ 169
R. *rugosa* ▣ 141
R. *rugosa* 'Scabrosa' 112
R. 'Sea Foam' 121
R. 'Seagull' ▣ 121
R. *sericea* f. *pteracantha* 168
R. *setipoda* 112
R. 'Snow Fairy' 121
R. 'Snowball' 121
R. *soulieana* ▣ 113
R. 'Stacey Sue' 121
R. *sweginzowii* ▣ 112
R. 'The Fairy' 120, 121
R. 'Tour de Malakoff' ▣ 113
R. *virginiana* 121
R. 'Wedding Day' ▣ 105
R. 'White Grootendorst' 113
R. 'William Baffin' 121
R. *willmottiae* 113
R. 'Wintonensis' 112
R. *xanthina* 'Canary Bird' ▣ 113
Rosa Mundi ▣ 120
Rose
　Apothecary's ▣ 120
　Bourbon ▣ 112
　China ▣ 99
　Climbing 94, ▣ 95, ▣ 121
　Common Moss ▣ 120
　Crested Moss ▣ 120
　Floribunda ▣ 112
　Gallica ▣ 112
　Ground Cover ▣ 121
　Hybrid Musk ▣ 120
　Hybrid Tea ▣ 112
　Provence ▣ 113
　Shrub ▣ 112–3

　　Species ▣ 113
　　Rugosa ▣ 113
Rose Acacia ▣ 99
Rose of Sharon ▣ 119
Rosemary ▣ 160, ▣ 171
roses
　ground cover 119, 121
　low growing 121
　miniature 121
　restricted spaces 118
　small shrubs 120
　specimen shrubs 112–3
Rosmarinus lavandulaceus ,
　see *R. officinalis* 'Prostratus' ▣ 160
　　R. officinalis ▣ 171
　　R. officinalis 'Prostratus' ▣ 160
Rough-barked Maple ▣ 200
Round-leaved Mint Bush ▣ 145
Rowan ▣ 214, ▣ 225
　Chinese ▣ 201
　Japanese ▣ 225
　Kashmir ▣ 225
Royal Horticultural Society 11
Rubus 'Benenden' 127, ▣ 165
　R. *biflorus* 168
　R. *cockburnianus* 165, 169
　R. *cockburnianus* 'Golden Vale' 151
　R. *henryi* 104
　R. *illecebrosus* 163
　R. *odoratus* 111, 132
　R. *parviflorus* 'Sunshine Spreader' 151
　R. *spectabilis* 162
　R. *spectabilis* 'Olympic Double' 132
　R. *thibetanus* 152, 168, ▣ 169
　R. *tricolor* 118, 133, 147
　R. *ulmifolius* 169
Rudbeckia fulgida
　　'Goldsturm' ▣ 33, 48, 90
　R. 'Herbstsonne' 17
　R. *laciniata* 'Goldquelle' ▣ 17
Rue ▣ 73
Rugosa Hybrid ▣ 121
Rugosa Rose ▣ 113
Rum Cherry ▣ 215
Rumex alpinus 'Ruber' 86
　　R. *scutatus* 'Silver Shield' 86
Ruscus aculeatus ▣ 171
　R. *hypoglossum* 133
Russian Almond, Dwarf ▣ 127
Russian Comfrey, Variegated ▣ 69
Russian Sage ▣ 153
Ruta graveolens 'Jackman's Blue' ▣ 73

S

Safflower ▣ 89
Sage ▣ 160
　Common ▣ 165
　Jerusalem ▣ 33
　Purple ▣ 75
　Russian ▣ 153
　White ▣ 72
St. Bernard's Lily ▣ 36
St. Dabeoc's Heath ▣ 124
Saint Patrick's Cabbage ▣ 31

Salix acutifolia 135
   S. alba ▣ 214
   S. alba f. *argentea* 220
   S. alba var. *vitellina* 210, 227
   S. babylonica 'Tortuosa', see
      S. matsudana 'Tortuosa' 210, ▣ 227
   S. caprea 'Kilmarnock' ▣ 211
   S. caprea 'Pendula',
     see *S. caprea* 'Kilmarnock' ▣ 211
   S. 'Chrysocoma', see *S.* x
     sepulcralis 'Chrysocoma' 210, 228
   S. daphnoides ▣ 135, 210
   S. discolor 135
   S. elaeagnos 135, 152
   S. exigua 135, ▣ 153, 220
   S. gracilistyla 'Melanostachys' 135
   S. hastata 'Wehrhahnii' ▣ 117
   S. irrorata 135
   S. japonica 135
   S. lanata 152
   S. matsudana 'Tortuosa' 210, ▣ 227
   S. nakamurana var. *yezoalpina* 119
   S. pentandra 203, 210
   S. pupurea 'Nana' 135
   S. reticulata ▣ 143
   S. x *sepulcralis* 'Chrysocoma' ▣ 210
   S. x *seringeana* 220
   S. triandra 135
   S. udensis 'Sekka' 135
   S. uva-ursi 119
Salvia lavandulifolia 165
   S. microphylla var. *neurepia* ▣ 160
   S. nemorosa 'May Night' 21
   S. officinalis ▣ 165
   S. officinalis 'Purpurascens' ▣ 75
   S. officinalis 'Purpurea' ▣ 75, 86
   S. sclarea var. *turkestanica* 23
   S. x *superba* 37
Sambucus canadensis 'Maxima' 111, 162
   S. nigra ▣ 163
   S. nigra 'Aurea' 151, ▣ 171
   S. nigra 'Guincho Purple' 137, ▣ 155
   S. nigra 'Pulverulenta' 148
   S. racemosa 162
   S. racemosa 'Plumosa Aurea' 151
   S. racemosa
     'Sutherland Gold' 122, ▣ 151
Sand Cherry, Purple-leaf ▣ 155
Sandwort ▣ 54, ▣ 56
sandy soils 12
   shrubs 128–9
Sanguinaria canadensis 44
   S. canadensis 'Plena' 44
Santolina chamaecyparissus 128, ▣ 153, 160
   S. pinnata subsp. *neapolitana*
     'Sulphurea' ▣ 127
Saponaria 'Bressingham' 63
   S. ocymoides ▣ 29
   S. officinalis 32
   S. x *olivana* 57
Sarcococca confuasa 117, 133, 158
   S. hookeriana var. *digyna*
     126, 136, ▣ 167
   S. hookeriana var. *humilis* 147
Sasa albomarginata, see *Sasa veitchii* ▣ 67

   S. veitchii ▣ 67
Sassafras albidum ▣ 205, 228
   S. officinale, see *S. albidum* ▣ 205, 228
Savin ▣ 193
Sawara Cypress ▣ 192
Saxegothaea conspicua 182
Saxifraga x *apiculata* 57
   S. fortunei 'Rubrifolia' 63
   S. x *geum* 30
   S. 'Gregor Mendel' ▣ 57
   S. moschata 'Cloth of Gold' ▣ 71
   S. 'Southside Seedling' 54
   S. spathularis ▣ 31
   S. x *urbium* 30
   S. 'Wada' 75
Saxifrage, Golden Mossy ▣ 71
Scabiosa atropurpurea Cockade Series 22
Scented-leaved Pelargonium ▣ 65
scented plants 76–7, 105, 158–9, 160
Schizanthus pinnatus 22
Schizophragma hydrangeoides 96, 107
   S. hydrangeoides 'Roseum' 96, 107
   S. integrifolium ▣ 97, 107
Schizostylis coccinea 'Major' 83
   S. coccinea 'Mrs Hegarty' 83
   S. coccinea 'Sunrise' 25, 83
Sciadopitys verticillata 180
Scilla hispanica,
   see *Hyacinthoides hispanica* ▣ 41, 60
   S. peruviana 40
   S. scilloides 83
   S. siberica 'Atrocoerulea' ▣ 59
Scopolia carniolica ▣ 45
Scotch Laburnum ▣ 207
Scotch Thistle ▣ 73
Scots Pine ▣ 179
   Golden ▣ 192
screens 140–1, 186–7, 215
screes 56–7, 58–9, 142–3, 188–9
Scrophularia aquatica 'Variegata',
   see *S. auriculata* 'Variegata' ▣ 69
   S. auriculata 'Variegata' ▣ 69
Scrub Pine ▣ 185
Sea Buckthorn ▣ 214
Seaside Aster ▣ 50
seaside gardens
   perennials 50–1
   shrubs 138–9
   trees 214
Sedge ▣ 64
   Grass, Golden Japanese ▣ 70
Sedum acre 'Aureum' 29
   S. album 'Coral Carpet' 29
   S. kamtschaticum 29
   S. obtusatum 29
   S. spathulifolium
     'Cape Blanco' 54, ▣ 73
   S. spathulifolium 'Purpureum' 29
   S. spectabile ▣ 85
   S. spectabile 'Brilliant' 24
   S. spurium 'Schorbuser Blut' 29
   S. telephium subsp. *maximum*
     'Atropurpureum' ▣ 75, 91
   S. 'Vera Jameson' 37
seed heads, decorative 85

self-clinging climbers 95, 107
Self Heal ▣ 25
Semiarundinaria fastuosa 19
Sempervivum arachniodeum 29
   S. ciliosum 29
   S. 'Commander Hay' 29
   S. 'Othello' 29
   S. tectorum 29, 54
Senecio monroi,
   see *Brachyglottis monroi* ▣ 128
   S. 'Sunshine', see *Brachyglottis*
     'Sunshine' 128, ▣ 136, 139, 152
   S. tanguticus 52
Senecio, Shrubby ▣ 128, ▣ 136
Senna, Bladder ▣ 138
Sentinel, Silver ▣ 212
Sequoia sempervirens ▣ 175
   S. sempervirens 'Adpressa' 191
Sequoiadendron giganteum ▣ 175, 187
   S. giganteum 'Glaucum' 178
Serbian Spruce ▣ 179
Serviceberry, Allegheny ▣ 212
Setcreasea purpurea 'Purple Heart',
   see *Tradescantia pallida*
     'Purple Heart' ▣ 65
shady areas 13
   climbers 96–7, 100–1
   perennials 30–1, 41, 42–5, 60
   shrubs 132–3
Shagbark Hickory ▣ 222
Sheep Laurel ▣ 170
Shibataea kumasasa ▣ 67
Shirley Poppy ▣ 27
shoots, ornamental 226–7
Shortia galacifolia 34
Shrub Rose ▣ 112, ▣ 113, ▣ 171
Shrubby Euphorbia ▣ 130
Shrubby Hare's-ear ▣ 138
Shrubby Honeysuckle ▣ 133
Shrubby Hypericum ▣ 136, ▣ 170
Shrubby Mimulus ▣ 145
Shrubby Potentilla ▣ 117, ▣ 123
Shrubby Senecio ▣ 128, ▣ 136
shrubby willows for damp sites 135
shrubs 11, 108
   air pollution tolerant 136–7
   alkaline soils 126–7
   aromatic leaves 160
   autumn colours 156–7
   berries 162–3
   bold foliage 111
   butterflies 164–5

shrubs *continued*
  carpeting 143
  climbers for 102–3
  coastal exposure 138–9
  containers 144–5
  damp sites 134–5
  dry sunny sites 130–1
  fragrant flowers 158–9
  golden or yellow leaves 150–1
  ground cover 118–9
  heavy clay soils 122–3
  hedges and screens 140–1
  lime-free 124–5
  medium-sized 114–15
  ornamental fruits 161
  ornamental twigs 168
  purple, reddish, or bronze leaves 154–5
  rabbit proof 170
  rock gardens, and screes 142–3
  roses 112–13, 118–19
  sandy soils 128–9
  shady areas 100–1, 132–3
  silver or blue-grey leaves 152–3
  small areas 116–18
  specimen plants 110, 112
  spiny or thorny branches 169
  sunny sites 98–99, 130–1
  variegated leaves 148–9
  winter-flowering 166–7
Sidalcea 'Sussex Beauty' 37
  S. 'William Smith' 21
Silene schatfa 28
Silk-tassel Bush 100
Silk Tree 206
Silver Grass, Chinese 85
Silver Hedgehog Holly 149
Silver Maple 196
Silver-margined Holly 141
silver or blue-grey leaves
  conifers 193
  perennials 72–3
  shrubs 152–3
  trees 220

Silver Queen Euonymus 100
Silver Sentinel 212
Silver Variegated Dogwood 148
Silver Wattle 158
Silybum marianum 23, 89
Siris Pink 206
Sisyrinchium striatum 90
  S. striatum 'Aunt May' 69
Skimmia x *confusa* 'Kew Green' 123, 137, 145, 146
  S. japonica 171
  S. japonica 'Fragrans' 158
  S. japonica 'Fructo-albo' 133
Sloe, Purple-leaf 155
slow-growing or dwarf conifers 188–9
small plants 24–7, 116–17, 118, 200–1
Smilacina racemosa 35
Smoke Bush 156
Smoke Tree 154, 223
Smooth Sumach 111
Smyrnium olusatrum 88
  S. perfoliatum 23
Snake's Head Fritillary 61
Snake-bark Maple 228
Snow Glory 58, 78
Snow Gum 201, 227
Snow-in-summer 28
Snowbell, Japanese 199
Snowdrop 61, 84
  Double 84
Snowy Mespilus 222
Snowy Woodrush 35
Soft Sheild Fern 67
soils 12
  alkaline 36, 126, 206
  clay 32, 122, 182, 202
  lime-free 34, 124, 204
  sandy 128
Solanum crispum 'Autumnale',
    see *S. crispum* 'Glasnevin' 99
  S. crispum 'Glasnevin' 99
  S. jasminoides 95
  S. jasminoides 'Album' 95
Solidago 'Goldenmosa' 33
  S. 'Laurin' 49
Sollya herterophylla 95
Sophora davidii 131
  S. japonica 'Pendula' 211
  S. japonica 'Violacea' 206, 209
  S. viciifolia, see *S. davidii* 131
Sorbaria aitchisonii 134, 137
Sorbus 194
  S. alnifolia 198, 203
  S. aria 'Lutescens' 207, 220
  S. aria 'Majestica' 212
  S. aucuparia 214
  S. cashmiriana 225
  S. commixta 225
  S. commixta 'Embley' 223
  S. cuspidata 199
  S. forrestii 201, 225
  S. hupehensis 'Pink Pagoda' 224
  S. x *hybrida* 204
  S. intermedia 203, 204, 206
  S. 'Joseph Rock' 225

  S. 'Mitchellii', see *S. thibetica*
      'John Mitchell' 220
  S. poteriifolia 142
  S. reducta 163
  S. scalaris 225
  S. thibetica 'John Mitchell' 220
  S. vilmorinii 201
Sorrel Tree 205
Southern Nettle Tree 208
Spanish Bluebell 41
Spanish Broom 139
Spanish Chestnut 196
Spanish Dagger 67
Spartium junceum 137, 139
Species Rose 113, 153
specimen plants 18–9, 110, 112, 196–7
Speedwell, Caucasian 29
Speirantha convallarioides 43
Spice Bush 134
Spider Flower 22
Spiderwort 91
Spignel 87
Spikenard, False 35
Spindle, Winged 157
Spinning Gum 220
spiny branches, shrubs 169
Spiraea canescens 127
  S. japonica 116
  S. japonica
      'Anthony Waterer' 123, 171
  S. japonica 'Candle Light' 151
  S. japonica 'Goldflame' 151
  S. nipponica 'Snowmound' 123, 171
  S. x *vanhouttei* 114, 122, 135
Spotted Deadnettle 43, 91
Spotted Laurel 148
Spotted Loosestrife 53
Spray Chrysanthemum 62
Spring Cherry, Weeping 211
Spring Gentian 56
spring flowering bulbs, 78–9
Spruce
  Blue 193
  Brewer 181
  Chinese 186
  Colorado 193
  Dwarf 189
  Norway 175, 190
  Serbian 179
  White 193
Spurge Laurel 132
Spurge, Japanese 133
Squirrel-tail Grass 39
Stachys byzantina 73
  S. byzantina 'Silver Carpet' 25
  S. byzantina 'Primrose Heron' 71
  S. lanata, see *Stachys byzantina* 73
  S. macrantha 'Superba' 25
  S. olympica, see *S. byzantina* 73
Stachyurus chinensis 'Magpie' 148
Stag's-horn Sumach 223
Star Jasmine 104
Star Magnolia 123
stems, shrubs with coloured 168
Sternbergia lutea 59, 83

Stewartia monodelpha ▨ 228
   S. pseudocamellia 198, ▨ 205
   S. sinensis 227
Stinking Hellebore ▨ 66
Stipa gigantea ▨ 19, 17, 37
Stone Cress, Persian ▨ 56
Stone Pine ▨ 185
Stonecrop 29, ▨ 73
Stransvaesia davidiana, see *Photinia*
   davidiana ▨ 225
Stranvaesia ▨ 225
Strelitzia reginae ▨ 63
Stuartia monodelpha,
   see *Stewartia monodelpha* ▨ 228
   S. pseudocamellia, see
      Stewartia pseudocamellia 198, ▨ 205
Styrax japonica ▨ 199
Sugar Maple ▨ 229
Sumach
   Smooth ▨ 111
   Stag's-horn ▨ 223
summer-flowering bulbs, 80–1
Summer Hyacinth ▨ 81
Sun Rose ▨ 116, ▨ 118, ▨ 128,
   ▨ 130, ▨ 152
Sunflower ▨ 89
   Perennial ▨ 17
sunny areas 13
   climbers 94–9
   conifers 184–5
   perennials 28–9, 38–9, 40, 60
   shrubs 98–9, 130–1
   trees 208–9
Sunrise Horse Chestnut ▨ 198
Swamp Blueberry ▨ 135
Swamp Cypress ▨ 183
Swan River Daisy ▨ 26
Sweet Box ▨ 167
Sweet Briar ▨ 169
Sweet Chestnut ▨ 196
Sweet Cicely ▨ 53
Sweet Gale ▨ 134
Sweet Gum ▨ 223
Sweet Mignonette ▨ 27
Sweet Peas 106
Sweet Pepper Bush ▨ 134
Sweet Rocket ▨ 77
Sweet Spurge, Purple-leaved ▨ 74
Sweet Woodruff ▨ 30
Sword Fern ▨ 45
Sycopsis sinensis ▨ 167
Symphoricarpos x *chenaultii* 'Hancock' 132
   S. 'White Hedge' 141
Symphytum caucasicum ▨ 53
   S. 'Gold in Spring' 70
   S. 'Goldsmith' 69
   S. grandiflorum ▨ 31
   S. 'Hidcote Pink' 31, 42
   S. ibericum 'All Gold' 70
   S. orientale 52
   S. x *uplandicum* 52
   S. x *uplandicum* 'Variegatum'
      ▨ 47, ▨ 69
Syrian Juniper ▨ 184
Syringa x *hyacinthiflora* 'Esther Staley' ▨ 165

S. x *josiflexa* 'Bellicent' 110
S. 'Mme Antoine Buchner' ▨ 159
S. microphylla 165
S. microphylla 'Superba' ▨ 115
S. x *persica* 114, ▨ 127, ▨ 139
S. villosa 158
S. vulgaris 'Charles Joly' 122
S. vulgaris 'Mme Lemoine' ▨ 137

T

Tamarisk ▨ 137, ▨ 139
Tamarix pentandra,
   see *T. ramosissima* ▨ 139
   T. ramosissima ▨ 139
   T. ramosissima 'Rubra' 138
   T. tetrandra ▨ 137, 138
Tanacetum argenteum 57, ▨ 73
   T. balsamita var. *tomentosum* 86
   T. parthenifolium 'Aureum' ▨ 71
   T. parthenium 'Aureum' 70
   T. vulgare 52
   T. vulgare 'Isla Gold' 70
Taxodium ascendens
   'Nutans' 175, ▨ 181, 183
   T. distichum ▨ 183
   T. distichum 'Pendens' 174
Taxus baccata ▨ 187
   T. baccata 'Aurea' ▨ 183
   T. baccata 'Cavendishii' 190
   T. baccata 'Dovastoniana' 177
   T. baccata 'Dovastonii Aurea' ▨ 177
   T. baccata 'Fastigiata Robusta' ▨ 179
   T. baccata 'Ingeborg Nellemen' 177
   T. baccata 'Repandens' 190
   T. baccata 'Repandens Aurea' ▨ 190
   T. baccata 'Repens Aurea', see *T.*
      baccata 'Repandens Aurea' ▨ 190
   T. baccata 'Standishii' 178
   T. baccata 'Summergold' 190
   T. cuspidata ▨ 185
   T. x *media* 'Hicksii' ▨ 187
   T. x *media* 'Sentinel' 178
Tellima grandiflora ▨ 43, 90
   T. grandiflora 'Purpurea' ▨ 75
Temple Juniper ▨ 184
Tenby Daffodil ▨ 61
Tetraclinis articulata 185
Teucrium fruticans 86, 152
   T. polium 142
   T. scorodonia 'Crispum' 86
Thalictrum speciosissimum 72
Thamnocalamus tessellatus 19
Thistle
   Cotton ▨ 73
   Globe ▨ 39
   Milk ▨ 89
   Scotch ▨ 73
Thorn ▨ 194
   Oriental ▨ 206
   Paul's Scarlet ▨ 212
thorny branches, shrubs with 169
Thuja koraiensis ▨ 183
   T. occidentalis 182
   T. occidentalis 'Europe Gold' 192

T. occidentalis 'Golden Globe' 192
T. occidentalis 'Holmstrup' 178
T. occidentalis 'Malonyana' 178
T. occidentalis 'Pyramidalis' 186
T. occidentalis 'Smaragd' ▨ 179
T. occidentalis 'Spiralis' 178, 180
T. occidentalis 'Sunkist' 187, 188
T. occidentalis 'Tiny Tim' 188
T. occidentalis 'Trompenburg' 192
T. orientalis 'Elegantissima' 189
T. orientalis 'Meldensis' 188
T. orientalis 'Rosedalis' 187
T. plicata ▨ 187
T. plicata 'Atrovirens' 186
T. plicata 'Collyers's Gold' ▨ 192
T. plicata 'Irish Gold' 192
T. plicata 'Rogersii' 189
T. plicata 'Stoneham Gold' 189, 192
T. plicata 'Zebrina' ▨ 191
Thujopsis dolabrata 'Nana' 188
   T. dolabrata 'Variegata' ▨ 191
Thunbergia alata ▨ 106
Thyme, Common ▨ 165
Thymus x *citriodorus* 'Silver Queen' 86
   T vulgaris 86, ▨ 165
Tiarella cordifolia ▨ 31
Tibetan Cherry ▨ 227
Tilia cordata 215
   T. cordata 'Rancho' 214
   T. 'Euchlora' 212
   T. mongolica 199, 203
   T 'Petiolaris' 197
   T. platyphyllos 'Rubra' 212
   T. tomentosa 197
   T. tomentosa 'Brabant' 206
Tithonia rotundifolia 'Torch' 22
Toad Lily ▨ 45
Toadshade ▨ 41
Tobacco, Ornamental ▨ 23, ▨ 77
Tolmiea menziesii 'Taff's Gold' ▨ 31
Toon ▨ 217
Toona sinensis ▨ 217
Torch Flower ▨ 21
Torreya californica ▨ 185
   T. californica 'Spreadeagle' 177
Trachelospermum asiaticum 95, ▨ 107
   T. jasminoides 95, ▨ 104, 105

Trachelospermum jasminoides
    'Variegatum' 95
Trachycarpus fortunei 216, ☐ 217
Trachystemon orientalis 31, 42
Tradescantia x *andersoniana*
    'Zwanenburg Blue' 24
    T. pallida 'Purple Heart' ☐ 65
    T. 'Purple Dome' ☐ 91
trailing perennials for containers 63
Tree Cotoneaster ☐ 161, ☐ 202
Tree Fern, Australian ☐ 64
Tree Flax ☐ 143
Tree Heath ☐ 150, ☐ 159
Tree Ivy ☐ 164
Tree Lupin ☐ 139
Tree Mallow ☐ 114, ☐ 129
Tree Peony ☐ 111, ☐ 115
Tree Purslane ☐ 138
Tree Rhododendron ☐ 216
trees 11, 194, 198–9
    air pollution tolerant 212–13
    alkaline soils 204, 206–7
    autumn colour 222–3
    bold foliage 217
    climbers for 102–3
    coastal exposure 214
    columnar 229
    conifers, see conifers
    dry sunny sites 208–9
    evergreen 216
    golden or yellow leaves 219
    heavy clay soils 202–3
    lime-free soils 204–5
    medium size 198–9
    multi-purpose 228
    ornamental bark and shoots 226–7
    ornamental fruit 224–5
    purple, reddish, or bronze leaves 221
    silver or blue-grey leaves 220
    small 200–1
    specimen plants 196–7
    variegated leaves 218
    watersides 210
    weeping 211
    windbreaks and screens 215
Tricuspidaria lanceolata, see *Crinodendron*
    hookerianum 101, 125 ☐ 132
Tricyrtis formosana ☐ 45
    T. stolonifera, see *T. formosana* ☐ 45
Trientalis borealis 44
Trifolium incarnatum 88

T. pratense 'Susan Smith' 69
    T. repens 'Purpurascens' ☐ 29
Trillium grandiflorum ☐ 45
    T. sessile ☐ 41, 44
    T. ovatum 44
Triteleia laxa ☐ 40, 81
Tritonia rubrolucens 81
Trollius x *cultorum* 'Alabaster' ☐ 47
    T. europaeus ☐ 91
Tropaeolum majus 'Alaska' ☐ 27
    T. peregrinum 106
    T. polyphyllum ☐ 57
    T. speciosum ☐ 103
Trout Lily ☐ 41
Tsuga canadensis ☐ 181
    T. canadensis 'Horstmann' 189
    T. canadensis 'Jeddeloh' 188
    T. heterophylla ☐ 172, 175, ☐ 183,
      185, 186
    T. mertensiana 180
Tuberous Begonia ☐ 62
Tulip ☐ 40, ☐ 59, ☐ 61, ☐ 79
Tulip Poplar 196
Tulip Tree ☐ 194, ☐ 196
    Variegated ☐ 218
Tulipa 'China Pink' 78
    T. clusiana 40, 79
    T. fosteriana 'Madame Lefebre' ☐ 79
    T. 'Garden Party' 78
    T. kaufmanniana 61
    T. 'Keizerskroon' 78
    T. praestans 40
    T. praestans 'Van Tubergen's Variety'
      ☐ 79
    T. saxatilis ☐ 40
    T. sprengeri 40
    T. sylvestris ☐ 61
    T. tarda ☐ 59
    T. 'White Dream' 78
Tumbling Ted ☐ 29
Tupelo, Chinese ☐ 223
Turkey Oak, Variegated ☐ 218

U

Ulex europaeus 'Flore Pleno' 169
    U. gallii 'Mizen' 118
Umbellularia californica ☐ 209
Umbrella Pine ☐ 185
Umbrella Plant ☐ 47
Uvularia grandiflora ☐ 45

V

Vaccaria hispanica 88
Vaccinium corymbosum 125, ☐ 135,
    156, 163
    V. glaucoalbum ☐ 147
    V. parviflorum 163
    V. vitis-idaea 147
    V. vitis-idaea 'Koralle' 163
Valerian ☐ 71
    Red ☐ 50
Valeriana phu 'Aurea' ☐ 71
Van Tol's Holly ☐ 162

Variegated Adam's Needle ☐ 69
Variegated Apple Mint ☐ 69
Variegated Archangel ☐ 31
Variegated Box ☐ 148
Variegated Buckthorn ☐ 149
Variegated Century Plant ☐ 64
Variegated Cherry Laurel ☐ 163
Variegated Cornelian Cherry ☐ 148
Variegated Cotoneaster ☐ 149
Variegated Dogwood, Silver ☐ 148
Variegated False Holly ☐ 149
variegated foliage
    conifers 191
    perennials 68–9
    shrubs 108 148–9
    trees 218
Variegated Ground Elder ☐ 30
Variegated Ground Ivy ☐ 29
Variegated Hiba ☐ 191
Variegated Honesty ☐ 23
Variegated Jacob's Ladder ☐ 69
Variegated Karo ☐ 209
Variegated Large Periwinkle ☐ 133
Variegated Laurustinus ☐ 149
Variegated Leyland Cypress ☐ 191
Variegated Nootka Cypress ☐ 191
Variegated Pagoda Dogwood ☐ 200
Variegated Russian Comfrey ☐ 69
Variegated Tulip Tree ☐ 218
Variegated Turkey Oak ☐ 218
Variegated Water Figwort ☐ 69
Variegated Weigela ☐ 149
vase-shaped conifers 176–7
Veratrum viride 90
Verbascum dumulosum 54
    V. 'Gainsborough' ☐ 37
    V. olympicum 20, ☐ 73
Verbena bonariensis ☐ 37
    V. patagonica ☐ 37
    V. rigida ☐ 77
    V. 'Silver Anne' 63
    V. 'Sissinghurst' ☐ 63
Verbena, Lemon ☐ 144
Veronica peduncularis
    'Georgia Blue' ☐ 29, 63, 75
    V. prostrata 'Kapitan' ☐ 57
    V. prostrata 'Trehan' ☐ 71
    V. spicata 'Romiley Purple' 21, ☐ 49
Viburnum x *bodnantense* 'Dawn' ☐ 167
    V. x *carlcephalum* ☐ 159
    V. davidii ☐ 119, 123, 133, 147
    V. lantana 'Aurea' 151
    V. lantanoides 134
    V. macrocephalum 'Sterile' 98
    V. odoratissimum 99
    V. opulus ☐ 135, 162
    V. opulus 'Aureum' ☐ 151
    V. opulus 'Compactum' ☐ 163
    V. opulus 'Notcutt's variety' 137, 156
    V. opulus 'Xanthocarpum' 134, 161
    V. plicatum 'Mariesii' ☐ 108
    V. plicatum 'Pink Beauty' ☐ 115
    V. 'Pragense' ☐ 147
    V. sargentii
      'Onondaga' ☐ 108, ☐ 115, 122, 171

V. sieboldii 134
V. tinus 140
V. tinus 'Eve Price' □ 167
V. tinus 'Variegatum' □ 149
V. wrightii 'Hessei' □ 161
Vicary Gibbs Golden Privet □ 151
Vinca major 91
V. major 'Elegantissima',
   see *V. major* 'Variegata'
   □ 133, 171
V. major subsp. *hirsuta* 52
V. major 'Variegata' □ 133, 171
V. minor □ 119, 171
V. minor 'Azurea Flore Pleno' 30
V. minor 'Gertrude Jekyll' 30
Vine, Claret □ 94
Vine, Cup and Saucer □ 106
Vine, Purple-bell □ 106
Vine, Purple □ 92
Viola cornuta 37
V. labradorica 'Purpurea' □ 43
V. odorata 86
V. odorata 'Wellsiana' 76
V. pedata 34
V. tricolor 'Bowles' Black' □ 57
Violet □ 43, □ 57
   Dame's □ 77
   Dog's Tooth □ 78
Violet Willow □ 135
Viper's Bugloss □ 89
Virginia Pine □ 185
Virginian Cowslip □ 44
Vitis coignetiae □ 103
V. vinifera 'Purpurea' □ 95
Voss's Laburnum □ 213

W

Wake-Robin □ 45
Waldsteinia ternata □ 31
Wallflower □ 26
   Perennial □ 24, □ 76
walls
   annuals and biennials 106–7
   climbers 96–7
   perennials 106
   retaining walls 54–5
   shrubs 98–101
Wand Flower □ 81
Warminster Broom □ 116
Water Figwort, Variegated □ 69
waterside areas
   conifers 176–7
   shrubs 134–5
   trees 210
Watsonia beatricis 81, 85
Wattle, Silver □ 158
Wedding-cake Tree □ 218
Weeping Birch □ 211
Weeping Cherry, Cheal's □ 211
Weeping Forsythia □ 100
weeping plants 177, 211
Weeping Spring Cherry □ 211
Weeping Willow, Golden □ 210
Weeping Willow-leaved Pear □ 220

Weigela coraeensis 137
W. 'Fiesta' 122
W. florida 'Foliis Purpureis' 155
W. florida 'Variegata' □ 149
W. 'Looymansii Aurea' □ 127 151
W. 'Mont Blanc' 114
W. praecox 'Variegata' 148
W. 'Rubidor' 151
W. 'Victoria' 171
Wellingtonia □ 175
Welsh Poppy □ 43
West Himalayan Birch □ 226
Western Abor-vitae □ 191
Western Catalpa □ 196
Western Hemlock □ 183
Western Red Cedar □ 187, □ 192
Westonbirt Dogwood □ 168
Weymouth Pine □ 182
White Fir, Colorado □ 193
White Japanese Wisteria □ 94
White Poplar □ 214
White Sage □ 72
White Spruce □ 193
White-Stemmed Bramble □ 169
White-Striped Bamboo, Dwarf □ 69
White Willow □ 214
Whitebeam □ 207
   Himalayan □ 220
wide-spreading conifers 176–7
Wild Aniseed □ 53
wild areas, bulbs for 60–1
Wild Bergamot □ 87
Wild Bleeding Heart □ 42
Willow □ 117
   Coyote □ 153
   Dragon's Claw □ 227
   Golden Weeping □ 210
   Kilmarnock □ 211
   Reticulate □ 143
   Violet □ 135
   White □ 214
Willow Gentian □ 46
willows, shrubby, for damp sites 135
windbreaks 186–7, 215
Windflower □ 60
   Greek □ 58, □ 78
Windmill Palm □ 217
Winged Spindle □ 157
Wingnut
   Caucasian □ 210
   Hybrid □ 197
Winter Aconite □ 60, □ 84
Winter Daphne □ 146
winter-flowering plants 84, 166–7
Winter-flowering Viburnum □ 167
Winter Heath □ 166
Winter Honeysuckle □ 167
winter interest 85, 168, 224–5, 226–7
Winter Jasmine □ 101
Wintersweet □ 166
Wisteria chinensis, see *W. sinensis* 95, □ 105
   W. floribunda 'Alba' □ 95
   W. foribunda 'Macrobotrys' □ 103
   W. sinensis 95, □ 105
Witch Hazel □ 166

Ozark □ 157
Woad □ 89
Wolfsbane □ 90
Wood Anemone □ 30
Wood Spurge, Purple-leaved □ 74
Woodruff, Sweet □ 30
Woodrush, Snowy □ 35
Woodwardia orientalis 45
   W. radicans 45

X

Xanthoceras sorbifolium 98, □ 127, 130
Xeranthemum annuum □ 27

Y

Yellow Asphodel □ 36
Yellow Azalea, Common □ 159
yellow foliage, see golden foliage
Yellow Gentian □ 87
Yellow Ox-eye □ 24
Yellow-wood □ 208
Yew □ 177, □ 179, □ 187
   Hick's □ 187
   Golden □ 183
   Japanese □ 185
Yoshino Cherry □ 207
Yucca flaccida 'Golden Sword' 69
   Y. glauca 152
   Y. gloriosa 18, □ 67, 152
   Y. gloriosa 'Variegata' □ 69
   Y. recurvifolia 18, 111

Z

Zantedeschia aethiopica 'Crowborough' 81
Zanthoxylum piperitum □ 169
Zauschneria californica 'Dublin' 130
Zea mays 'Gracilima Variegata' 22
Zelkova carpinifolia □ 197
Zenobia pulverulenta 125
Zephyranthes candida 83
Zonal Pelargonium □ 65

Acknowledgments

ROY LANCASTER'S CREDITS:
A number of people have either directly or indirectly influenced the preparation of this book, none more so than my wife, Sue, whose unfailing support, including the typing of my scribbled notes and lists, helped bring it to fruition.

Sarah Drew, Jacqueline Postill, Martin Puddle, and James Wickham all made helpful comments based on their considerable collective experience dealing with customers' problems and queries in plant centres.

Five years of travelling the length and breadth of Britain with Channel Four Television's *Garden Club* has taken me to a multitude of gardens large and small, while also introducing me to some helpful and resourceful gardeners. In acknowledging their contribution

I should also like to thank the present and former members of the *Garden Club* team, who have helped me in so many ways.

They include John Bennett, Matthew Biggs, Adrian Brennard, Karen Brown, Derek Clarke, Penny Cotter, Mary Foxall, Tony Griggs, Margaret Haworth, Elaine Hinderer, Sylvia Hines, Paddy McMullin, Ken Price, Rebecca Pow, Rebecca Ransome, Jo Redman, Sue Shepherd, Richard Stevens, and Steve Stunt.

Finally, I thank my publishers, especially Mary-Clare Jerram for asking me to compile this book, and Lesley Malkin and Colin Walton, my editor and designer respectively, whose enthusiasm and professionalism greatly impressed and encouraged me. I could not have asked for better.

DORLING KINDERSLEY would like to thank Lyn Saville and Ian Whitelaw for additional editorial assistance; Gloria Horsfall and Sue Caffyn for design assistance; Jane Parker for compiling the index; Ann Kay for proof reading; Dr. Alan Hemsley for his assistance in finding and identifying plants to photograph; and Julia Pashley for additional picture research. Thanks also to the A-Z team, particularly Ina Stradins, Helen Robson, and Susila Baybars, for their patience with our shared resources, and to Rebecca Davies for all her trips to the post office.

ARTWORK CREDITS

Aspect Illustration by
Karen Cockrane 13

Tree Illustrations by
Laura Andrew, Marion Appleton, David Ashby, Bob Bampton, Anne Child, Tim Hayward, Janos Marffy, David More, Sue Oldfield, Liz Pepperell, Michelle Ross, Gill Tomlin, Barbara Walker

PHOTOGRAPHY CREDITS

Key: t=top, b=bottom, c=centre, l=left, r=right

All photographs by
Clive Boursnell, Deni Bown, Jonathan Buckley, Andrew Butler, Eric Crichton, Andrew de Lory, Christine Douglas, John Fielding, Neil Fletcher, John Glover, Derek Hall, Jerry Harpur, Sunniva Harte, Neil Holmes, Andrew Lawson, Howard Rice, Robert Rundle, Juliette Wade, Colin Walton, Matthew Ward, and Steve Wooster, **except:**

Garden Picture Library:
Lynne Brotchie: 92 bl
Brian Carter: 93
Robert Estall: 194 br
John Glover: 13 tr, 14 bl, 108 br, 194 bl
M Lamontagne: 195
Marianne Majerus: 2
Gary Rogers: 13 br
Ron Sutherland: 4
Brigitte Thomas: 9 b, 172 bl, 173
Steven Wooster: 13 bl, 92 br

John Glover: 85 bc, 174 tc, 187 tc, 213 bl

Derek Gould: 165 bl

Andrew Lawson: 219 tr

Roy Lancaster:
8 bl, 8 br, 9 tr, 9 tc, 12 bl, 31 tl, 31 cl, 31 bl, 42 tr, 45 tl, 49 bl, 67 br, 69 br, 83 cr, 84 bl, 85 bl, 85 tc, 85 tr, 86 bc, 87 bc, 87 tr, 87 br, 96 tr, 102 bl, 104 bl, 104 bc, 105 bl, 105 tr, 106 tl, 106 bl, 107 tl, 107 tr, 107 cr, 111 tl, 113 cr, 117 cr, 128 bl, 128 tc, 129 tl, 129 tr, 133 cl, 135 bc, 138 tl, 140 tl, 141 tc, 151 cr, 156 tl, 156 bc, 156 tr, 157 tl, 157 br, 161 br, 162 bc, 163 tl, 163 bl, 164 tr, 169, tl, 169 bl, 172 tr, 172 br, 174 bl, 176 tl, 179 br, 181 tr, 184 tl, 185 cl, 187 tl, 190 bl, 190 bc, 191 tl, 191 br, 192 tc, 192 tr, 194 tr

Nature Photographers Ltd:
Brinsley Burbage: 187 tr

Clive Nichols:
Chenies Manor Garden, Buckinghamshire: 109
Dartington Hall Garden, Devon: 14 br
Longacre, Kent: 14 cl

Photos Horticultural:
77 cl, 83 bl, 141 cr, 165 bc, 177 tc, 178 tr, 186 cr, 187 br, 191 bc, 193 bc, 207 bl, 212 bl, 213 tr, 229 cr

Harry Smith Collection / Polunin:
210 cl, 215 br

40-637-2

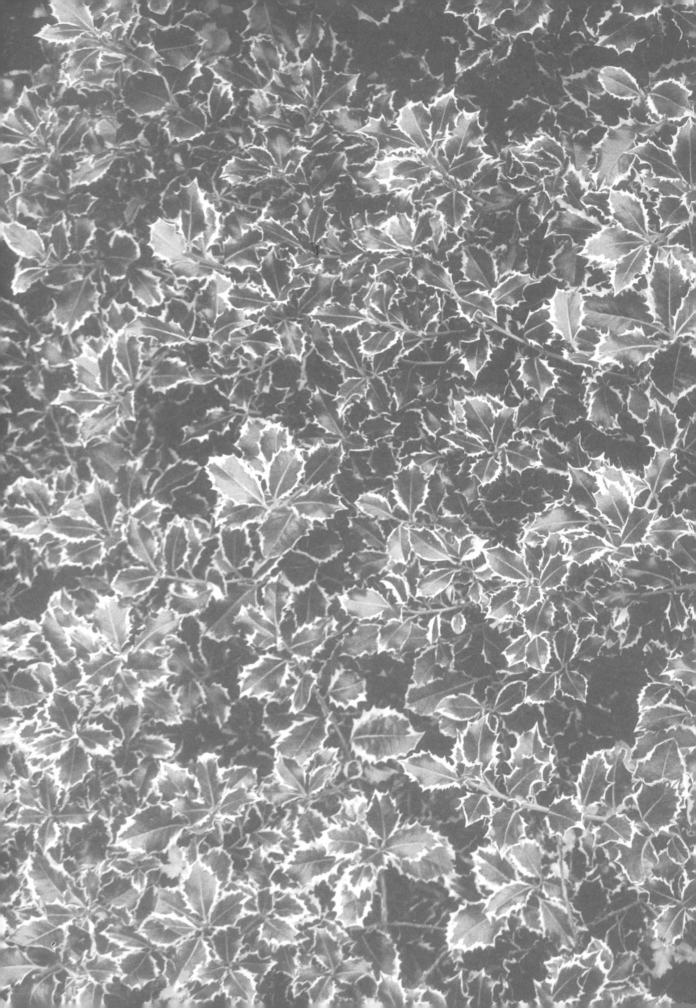